The Adams Papers

RICHARD ALAN RYERSON, EDITOR IN CHIEF

SERIES I

DIARIES

Diary of Charles Francis Adams

Diary of Charles Francis Adams

MARC FRIEDLAENDER,

ROBERT J. TAYLOR, CELESTE WALKER,
RICHARD ALAN RYERSON

EDITORS

————————————— ☆ —————————————

Volume 8 · *March 1838–February 1840*

Index

THE BELKNAP PRESS

OF HARVARD UNIVERSITY PRESS

CAMBRIDGE, MASSACHUSETTS,

AND LONDON, ENGLAND

1986

Printed in the United States of America

Funds for editing *The Adams Papers* were originally furnished by Time, Inc., on be-half of *Life*, to the Massachusetts Historical Society, under whose supervision the editorial work is being done. Further funds were provided by a grant from the Ford Foundation to the National Archives Trust Fund Board in support of this and four other major documentary publications. In common with these and many other enter-prises like them, *The Adams Papers* has continued to benefit from the guidance and cooperation of the National Historical Publications and Records Commission, chaired by the Archivist of the United States, which from 1975 to the present provided this enterprise with major financial support. Important additional funds were supplied by The Andrew W. Mellon Foundation and The J. Howard Pew Freedom Trust through the Founding Fathers Papers, Inc.

Library of Congress Cataloging in Publication Data

Adams, Charles Francis, 1807–1886.
    Diary.

    (The Adams papers. Series 1, Diaries)
    Vols. 3–6 Marc Friedlaender and L. H. Butterfield, editors.
    Vols. 7– edited by Marc Friedlaender et al.
    Includes bibliographies and indexes.
    Contents: v. 1. January 1820–June 1825—[etc.]—v. 7. June 1836–February 1838—v. 8. March 1838–February 1840.
    1. Adams, Charles Francis, 1807–1886. 2. Statesmen—United States—Biography. I. Donald, Aïda DiPace. II. Donald, David Herbert, 1920– . III. Fried-laender, Marc, 1905– . IV. Title V. Series.
E467.1.A2A33 1964   973.5′092′4 [B]   64-20588
ISBN 0-674-20399-2 (v. 1-2)
ISBN 0-674-20401-8 (v. 3-4)
ISBN 0-674-20402-6 (v. 5-6)
ISBN 0-674-20403-4 (v. 7-8)

Contents

Descriptive List of Illustrations

Storm's engraving, commissioned by James Barton Longacre and James Herring for inclusion in their *National Portrait Gallery of Distinguished Americans* (4 vols., Phila. and N.Y., 1834–1839, 4:252) is after the portrait in oil by Charles R. Leslie done in Sept. 1816, one of the pair of Louisa Catherine and John Quincy Adams that her brother Thomas Baker Johnson had commissioned (see Andrew Oliver, *Portraits of JQA and his Wife*, p. 57–64). The originals had been in the possession of Charles Francis Adams since 1836, and it was to his home in Boston that Storm, an English artist lately settled in Philadelphia, came to work upon the engraving of Louisa Catherine Adams (vol. 6:372–373, 386; entry for 2 June 1837).

The engraving, when published in Longacre and Herring, was accompanied (4:253–262) by the carefully wrought and sensitive biographical sketch of his mother that Adams had written (entries of 11 Nov. 1837 – 2 Feb. 1838 *passim*). In it he provides us with something of her state of being when she sat for Leslie during the family's residence in England, she then at the age of forty-one: "There were ties in Great Britain to Mrs. Adams, where her husband's new duty as the Minister from the United States called him. . . . These ties were her children, who had come out from America to join her, and whose arrival afforded her a joy, for the absence of which no brilliant scenes could compensate. In itself, a residence in England so immediately after a war between the two countries, which had terminated not quite to the satisfaction of her pride, was not calculated to be productive of much pleasure; yet it may fairly be questioned whether, in the bosom of her reunited family, and in the sweet but modest country-seat in the vicinity of London selected for their habitation, Mrs. Adams did not draw as much enjoyment from her domestic feelings, as she ever did from witnessing any of the more busy and exciting scenes in which she has been called to participate" (Longacre and Herring, 4:259–260).

After the death of John Quincy Adams and the installation of Louisa Catherine Adams in her Washington home, Charles Francis Adams in the summer of 1849 moved his family "as a matter of duty" into the newly renovated Old House from the house he had built twelve years earlier. The house he had constructed on a hillside an eighth of a mile from his parents' was on President's Lane, formerly called Stonyfield Hill, on an ample tract given to him by his father. The white clapboard two-story house "thirty-eight feet square without an ornament excepting a simple portico supported by four ionic columns on the first story" had been completely to his taste. "I built the house ... from a plan furnished by an architect in the city [William Sparrell], who did little more than reduce my directions to paper. . . . I do not know that if I were to build again with the same dimensions, I should make a single alteration in the internal arrangement." (CFA, Diary, 16 May 1849; CFA to A. J. Davis, 16 Aug. 1844, Adams Papers, Microfilms, Reel 158.)

The pleasure Adams took in his house persisted from the moment he occupied it to the day he gave it up, and in the years beyond: "My home repays me at every look for the quantity of labour which it has cost me"; "My house is a creation of my own. . . . I shall never occupy it again and it may be that none who come after will look upon it with the same interest"; "Went up to my house on the hill, which made me feel exceedingly sad as reminding me of the best hours of my life. I shall never again enjoy any thing as I enjoyed that." (Entries of 14 June 1838, below; Diary, 22 May 1849; 30 April 1850.)

The idea of building a house for his growing family had formed itself in his mind in early 1836. For some time he studied volumes on domestic architecture by John Charles Loudon, Sir John Soanes, and others, but was not satisfied by them. He then consulted the developer Cornelius Coolidge who directed him to numerous projects without profit. With his ideas already well defined, he chose William Sparrell to carry them out. When the architect, after several tries, met his client's wishes, Adams was ready to proceed on the site his father had deeded to him (vol. 6:358, 361, 372, 379, 401; entries for 14 June – 20 Oct. 1836 *passim*).

During the winter months of 1836–1837, he accumulated building supplies, had the lot prepared, the foundations forwarded. In April 1837, construction began. Adams participated physically in the building process at almost every stage, at the same time becoming increasingly aware that the expenses incurred almost always exceeded the anticipated costs. In November, as completion neared, he found that the house "will have cost me about $8,000 dollars or about double my estimate." But, "having done it with all the caution possible, having committed no extravagance," there was no regret then or during the years of occupancy. (Entries of 16 March, 31 May, 26, 31 Oct., 7 Nov. 1837, below.)

Satisfied as the Adamses were with their house, as the years passed they recognized two unmet needs. Increases in the size of the family brought them to feel "cramped for room." Further, the obligation to satisfy his father's long-held desire that a fireproof building of stone be constructed to house his library became a present need. Adams, seeking a response that would meet both needs, proposed the addition of two wings to the house. In 1844 he had the New York architect Alexander Jackson Davis draw a succession of plans; but when the difficulties of combining the several purposes appeared insurmountable, Adams, influenced by the proximity of the railroad to his property and by the feeling that he might find himself "in the center of town in a few years," abandoned the idea of adding to the house. Instead, he asked Davis to turn to plans for a home on Mt. Wollaston, a dream Adams had entertained from the beginning of his marriage.

Repeating his wishes for a simple edifice of stone that avoided "the modern fopperies of Grecian or Gothic," he expressed a preference for one "after the Italian manner of Palladio in rusticated work." But this too was not prosecuted. (CFA to A. J. Davis, 16 Aug., 22 Nov. 1844, reel 158; 17 June 1845, reel 159, Adams Papers Microfilms; vols. 3:268, 309–310; 4:362–363; 5:82–83, 362.)

After the house on the hill became vacant in 1849, it was rented to a Mr. and Mrs. Lyman. It became Adams-occupied again only in 1870, when Charles Francis Adams 2d was building his own house on the summit of the hill, and from 1871–1893 when he resided in that house and used the house that had been his father's as a place in which to carry on his literary work, calling it "The Annex." The house still stands, though much altered.

Courtesy of the U.S. Department of the Interior—National Park Service, Adams National Historic Site, Quincy, Massachusetts.

3. THE FIRST PAGE OF THE LECTURE "MATERIALS FOR HISTORY"   141

In Dec. 1837, when Charles Francis Adams was invited by I. P. Davis to deliver a lecture in the Masonic Temple before the Massachusetts Historical Society, he responded with a suggestion that he could "make something out of my grandmother's papers," subsequently attaching the condition, "if I can obtain the use of the papers in my possession . . . such . . . as would illustrate the female character of the age of the Revolution." In due course, John Quincy Adams authorized him to use "any papers I like" (entries of 14, 18, and 26 Dec. 1837, below).

Charles Francis Adams, though probably unaware of it, had been anticipated by John Adams in seeing Abigail Adams' letters as literarily and historically significant beyond their original intent. He had written to his friend Francis Adrian Van der Kemp in 1809 that "A Collection of her Letters for the forty-five Years that We have been married would be worth TEN times more than Madame Sevignés, though not so perfectly measured in Syllables and Letters; and would or at least ought to put to the blush Lady Mary Wortley Montague and her Admirers." But while conceding that two or three of her letters to Thomas Brand Hollis and one to John Quincy Adams had been printed [copies not located], he resisted Van der Kemp's plea to make her letters available. This had remained the family's position about correspondence relating solely or primarily to domestic matters. Numerous letters of John Quincy Adams had been put in print by him and by others in the intervening years, but they had been written with publication in mind. Mostly they dealt with political issues, although his two series written to Thomas Boylston Adams in 1800 and 1801 for publication in *The Port Folio* (Phila., 1801) on "various topics of foreign literature" and on "a Tour through Silesia" verged on the personal.

When Charles Francis Adams on 23 Jan. 1838 delivered a lecture that consisted almost entirely of letters exchanged in 1774 and 1775 between John and Abigail Adams to an audience of two hundred that listened in "silence and [with] profound attention," it was the first occasion on which any considerable number of letters from the Adams family archives were communicated publicly. Its success caused him to accept invitations to repeat the lecture for eight other audiences during the next two years. Favorable notices appeared in newspapers as far away as Baltimore. The response must be accorded an influence upon Adams' reversal in 1840 of his earlier decision that "there would be no publication." His edition of *Letters of Mrs. Adams, the Wife of John Adams*, appearing in September of that year, reached a fourth edition by 1848. Meanwhile, in 1841, it was joined by his edition of *Letters of John Adams, Addressed to His Wife* (entries of 23 Jan., 10 Feb. 1838, below; *Adams Family Correspondence*, 1:xxxii; Adams Papers Editorial Files).

The holograph text of the lecture is in the Adams Papers shelved as M/CFA/23.3, not microfilmed.

From the original in the Adams Papers.

4. *Beatrice*, BY WASHINGTON ALLSTON   232
The *Beatrice* by Washington Allston exhibited at the Harding Gallery in Boston in 1839 was completed in 1819. In 1816 in London, however, John Quincy Adams saw a different version of the subject or this picture in an earlier state and recorded in his diary that the "ideal Portrait of Dante's Beatrix is a beautiful face" (entry for 24 Sept. 1816). Although the artist in giving it the title he did, provided it with the literary association he sought in most of his paintings, the facial features seem clearly those of his first wife, Ann Channing, sister of William Ellery Channing. He recorded her face in a number of drawings before her death in 1815 and carried her image in his memory thereafter.

The other paintings in the 1839 exhibition grouped by Charles Francis Adams with *Beatrice* and said by him to represent with it a deterioration or a "frittering [of] his power into miserable unmeaning pictures" with a deplorable lack of "significance," however excellent their "manual execution," are *Lorenzo and Jessica*, 1832, *Young Troubadour*, 1833, and *Rosalie*, 1835 (entry for 9 May 1839). *Rosalie*, like *Beatrice*, is a single half-length female figure described by later historians as "listening to music at evening time 'that dreamy hour of the day.'" Again, *Young Troubadour* is "a dreamy figure playing his guitar beside a fountain and singing to his fair Isabel." In *Lorenzo and Jessica*, derived from act 5 of Shakespeare's *Merchant of Venice*, "a young woman and her male companion recline in a reverie in a moonlit landscape." Rather than the "degeneration" in manner that Adams finds in *Beatrice* and the companion pictures, all of them are judged to reflect an elegaic or poetic mood that marks them "as precursors of late nineteenth-century expressive figure paintings and more particularly of the images of reverie that populate late nineteenth-century American iconography." These, and most particularly *Beatrice*, were of the kind singled out by the romantically inclined reviewers of the exhibition such as Margaret Fuller, as among Allston's greatest works. Adams' view, however, is echoed by a later critic of note, James Jackson Jarves, who is quoted as finding *Beatrice* "weak and pale, a sentimental nothing."

The 1839 exhibition, arranged by Allston's nephew, the painter George Flagg, included much more than examples of Allston's recent work. It was, in fact, a comprehensive retrospective exhibition of 47 of his works drawn from his entire career. It was also "of significance . . . as a milestone in the history of American art exhibitions, displaying as it did the full range of the work of an eminent *living* artist" (William H. Gerdts and Theodore E.

Stebbins Jr., *"A Man of Genius," The Art of Washington Allston*, Boston, 1979, p. 13, 130, 131, 134, 135, 139, 141, 142, 229; the works referred to above are illustrated at p. 117, 198, 199, 227).
Courtesy of the Museum of Fine Arts, Boston.

The two daughters of the recently deceased John Adams 2d and of his wife Mary sat for their portraits to Asher Brown Durand in Quincy and Boston in June 1835. The portraits had their inception from the commission given to Durand several months earlier by Luman Read, New York merchant and art patron, for examples in duplicates of portraits of each of the first seven Presidents. When Durand in consequence came to request sittings of John Quincy Adams, he bore also Read's request for a likeness of little Georgeanna Frances, then aged four, which Read intended to present to her grandfather. Durand found Georgeanna Frances "a beautiful little girl" and John Quincy Adams a rewarding subject; Adams was so pleased with Durand's early efforts that he asked the painter to undertake additionally a portrait for him of Mary Louisa, aged six, that he wished to give to her mother. Durand's work so satisfied the Adams family and connections that before he moved to other subjects he had executed a commission for an additional likeness of John Quincy Adams from Charles Augustus Davis, partner of a brother of Abigail Brooks Adams, for presentation to her and a commission from Charles Francis Adams for a portrait of his father-in-law, Peter C. Brooks. The children's portraits remained in the possession of Mrs. John Adams 2d during her lifetime, descending in Mary Louisa's line to her granddaughter Mary Louisa Adams Clement, who presented them in 1950 to the Smithsonian Institution. (Oliver, *Portraits of JQA and His Wife*, p. 169, 174; vols. 2:ix – x, 6:vii – viii, 156, 160, 165.)

Georgeanna Frances' death in 1839 gives to her portrait a special poignancy. Named for her uncles George Washington Adams and Charles Francis Adams, she had a delicacy and beauty that made her a favorite within the family, especially of her grandmother Louisa Catherine Adams. A number of earlier illnesses preceded the final painful onset which lasted a month and which John Quincy Adams had pronounced "remediless" almost from the beginning. Both children had had somewhat more illnesses during their early years than were ordinarily experienced. Mary Louisa, shortly after the death of her sister, was seriously ill with symptoms that seemed disturbingly like Georgeanna's, but the fear for her proved unfounded and recovery followed. Mary Louisa's health grew better; she became vigorous and lively, socially attractive; in 1853 she married her third cousin William Clarkson Johnson of Utica, N.Y., bore three children, and died in 1859, predeceasing her mother. (Vol. 3:330; entries for 5, 21 Nov. 1839; 13 Jan. 1840, below; Adams Papers Editorial Files.)
Courtesy of the National Museum of American Art, Smithsonian Institution, Adams-Clement Collection, gift of Mary Louisa Adams Clement in memory of her mother, Louisa Catherine Adams Clement.

VOLUME 8

Diary 1838–1840

Diary of Charles Francis Adams

THURSDAY MARCH IST.

Morning cloudy with every appearance of preparation for a storm but it cleared afterwards. I suffered from a head ach which disabled me from doing much. At the Office. Wife growing better again. Talk principally relating to the ferocious duel at Washington, the details of which are shocking enough. Short walk owing to a lame foot and stop in to see Sayer about my furniture.

I did not read much of Sophocles, but as my head began to trouble me less in the afternoon, I worked upon the coins with some industry and in the evening instead of attending one or two places to which I was invited remained at home following up Eckhel's prolegomena respecting the coins. The mode of detecting counterfeits is laid down with some pretension but I fancy experience will be the only true guide.

FRIDAY. 2D.

A beautiful morning with some little admonition of the return of a more genial season. My Wife still continues much in the same condition, but mending. Office, where was Mr. Walsh on a begging errand of which I am tired and besides myself much straitened. Then Mr. Ladd to pay rent and finally Mr. S. O. Mead to announce his entire inability to do any thing about his Note. This was not unexpected to me though I confess very far from agreeable. How I shall get out of the scrape I know not but it is at present a pretty deep one. After talking it over a good deal without coming to any result we separated. Home. Sophocles.

Afternoon, Mr. Eddy[1] called to notify me of annual accounts on a committee of the Middlesex Canal from which I had once been liberated and now remonstrated against my serving. He asked me to go over and look at a house which is just finished in the Neighborhood which he was showing to Mr. Brooks. I did so and was not greatly pleased with it.

At five I started to go to Medford according to arrangement to de-

I

liver my Lecture to the Lyceum there. Stopped to take tea at Mr. Angier's. Found my Aunt much as usual. Delivered the Lecture to a numerous audience and was received as favourably as I could expect. Home by a few minutes past nine. What a matter of vanity this Lecture eloquence is, and what is fame but a shadow? Yet how men pursue it. Eckhel finished. Read Poggiana.[2]

[1] Caleb Eddy was superintendent and treasurer of the Middlesex Canal Co.; see vol. 5:224.
[2] Jacques Lenfant, *Poggiana; ou La vie ... et les bon mots de Pogge Florentin* [Poggio Bracciolini], 2 vols., Amsterdam, 1720.

SATURDAY. 3D.

My Wife was again not so well this morning having had a bad night. She seems rather disposed to magnify her own evils, and that almost without any exercise of will. I regret it but trust firmly in the providence of God. I went to the Office where I had some accounts to make up but otherwise did perhaps too little. I always regret my mornings. Home to read Sophocles. Afternoon engaged upon the coins which I pursued very assiduously, but there are many rather provoking ones. Evening quietly at home. Poggiana and Potter's Archaeology.

SUNDAY. 4TH.

Morning very fine. My Wife was more quiet and better today. I am in hopes she will be making progress now. Worked on my coins until time for divine service which I attended and heard Dr. Frothingham preach from John 9. 41. "If ye were blind, ye should have no sin: but now ye say, We see; therefore your sin remaineth." The discrimination between the ignorant and the wilful guilt is an ingenious one to draw and perhaps the most useful question of practical morals which can be agitated.

Afternoon Job 29. 2. "Oh that I were as in months past, as in the days when God preserved me." A very beautiful moral discourse upon regret for the past, showing that it is inconsistent with the desire for progress which should animate men and can never be supposed to have existed in Jesus Christ the great exemplar of our faith. But this is no parallel for the consciousness of trial made life to him a suffering experience whereas to man generally the pleasures balance the pains.

Walk with my boy John, and Mr. Walsh dined with me. Read a discourse of Buckminster's upon the epistle of Philemon, illustrating historically the character of Paul. Evening at home. Wrote a short letter to my Mother,[1] and read attentively the seventh book of Politics of Aristotle.

[1] Letter missing.

MONDAY. 5TH.

Fine day. Abby had a better night and is now I hope gaining. I went to the Office but did little or nothing. My constant and unavailing regret is for the loss of my mornings, the time when my mind is clearest and when success best repays exertion. But this is an evil incidental to my mode of life, and remediless.

Received a letter from General Jones respecting T. B. Adams' affairs,[1] which I no sooner got than I wrote to Mr. Harrod the necessary directions respecting the wishes of the family.[2] Home. Sophocles. Afternoon, coins as usual. A puzzling though not disagreeable occupation.

Evening, turned my thoughts to reflection upon government and determined to read in connexion part of the Defence which I did begin with the Commentary upon Nedham.[3]

[1] Letter missing.

[2] CFA to Charles Harrod, LbC, Adams Papers. Adjutant General Jones having authorized the appropriate commander in the field to fulfill the wishes of Lt. Adams' family as to the disposition of the lieutenant's body and his effects, the accomplishment of Mrs. Adams' wishes that the body and effects be returned to Quincy is here delegated to her brother in New Orleans.

[3] Vol. 3 of JA's *A Defence of the Constitutions ... of the United States* is devoted to commentary upon Marchamont Nedham (Needham), *The Excellencie of a Free State, or the Right Constitution of a Commonwealth*, first published in 1656 and reissued at the direction of Thomas Hollis, London, 1767. A presentation copy of this edition from Hollis' heir Thomas Brand Hollis to JA is among JA's books in MB.

TUESDAY. 6TH.

A very lovely day. Office. My Wife appears really a little better today. Nothing new. I was engaged in accounts. Home, Sophocles with which I make some progress but not so much as I ought. Afternoon coins. Evening, Mr. Brooks came in to tea after which I accompanied him down to his son Edward's where there was a family party.

Conversation with Edward about his course in the Legislature, with the results of which he seems to have better cause to be satisfied than I had expected.[1] He has at least the satisfaction of thinking he has done some good.

From thence I went at nine o'clock to a party at Miss Scollay's where I had been invited and an acquaintance formed. A small number but not unpleasant. Returned by eleven rather fatigued.

[1] Edward Brooks had been a leading figure in the legislature in preventing action by that body to minimize or annul statutory penalties against failed banks. JQA was among those who predicted that the legislature would take such action and further that CFA would approve of it. CFA, in reporting Brooks' efforts, took somewhat heated exception to JQA's assumption (JQA to CFA, 4 March; CFA to JQA, 12 March, LbC; both in Adams Papers).

WEDNESDAY. 7TH.

Day cloudy with rain and snow. I went to the Office where I was taken up with accounts and methodizing my papers which need it excessively. I have occasionally thought of making a thorough reform, but my courage fails when I think of the mass of papers to be undertaken. I used to be a very strictly methodical man and believe I must become so again.

Wrote to W. B. Lewis,[1] Second Auditor of the Treasury about T. B. Adams affairs and a note to Mr. Mead.[2] Home. Sophocles. My Wife begins to encourage me by her appearance. In the afternoon coins. Evening, T. K. Davis took tea and spent an hour. After which I sat with my Wife, and the rest of the evening, continued the examination of Nedham.

[1] LbC, Adams Papers.
[2] Missing.

THURSDAY 8TH.

Clouds and fog and snow. Abby continues better and is I hope now really on the mending hand. Office where I turned my attention to the pamphlets which have been multiplying on my table until it exceeds all proportion. Whether many of them are worth binding admits of question but as they are generally the gift of the author I keep them for that reason.

Home. Sophocles. Felt a little out of order today which reminds me that I have neglected exercise for some time. Afternoon, Coins in which I make less rapid progress as I get to the less legible ones.

Evening at home. Finished the examination of Nedham which terminates the Defence. There is a great deal of truth in it, and the only matter to regret is that the work had not been condensed and methodized.

FRIDAY. 9TH.

Morning mild and cloudy. I went to the Office and my time was taken up in Accounts and in arranging my pamphlets. Not any thing new. Read a little of Sismondi's second volume which is upon the subject of currency and contains many valuable thoughts. Political Economy is the strangest science in the world. It contains so many propositions true in themselves when made precisely to regard a certain combination of circumstances, which become untrue when those circumstances change.

Home. Sophocles. Afternoon coins. My Wife grows better slowly. Evening, read Swift's Pamphlet upon the Civil dissensions in Rome and Athens[1] and wrote for exercise a page or two of composition for possible future use.

[1] "Contests and dissensions between the nobles and commons in Athens and Rome" in vol. 3 of *Works of Jonathan Swift*, ed. Sir Walter Scott, 19 vols., Edinburgh, 1824.

SATURDAY 10TH.

Morning clear but it clouded, and the mild weather has flooded the streets. Office where I am endeavoring to reform my habits about papers. I destroy many but retain more. The only plan for me is to return to my old habit of filing, especially letters which crowd upon me. Pamphlets also I am attempting to bind up.

Home. Sophocles in which I make regular progress of about a hundred lines a day, although I find a difficulty in pursuing Greek in this manner from the number of collateral investigations which are necessary to a thorough understanding of the text.

Afternoon coins, and wrote a letter to my father.[1] The condition of my Wife is so little improving that the doctor has recommended her not nursing her child, and I went out to Mrs. Frothingham's to see about it.

[1] See note to entry of 6 March, above.

SUNDAY. 11TH.

Fine clear day. Morning passed upon coins excepting a portion spent with my Wife who appears now gradually on the recovery. Attended divine Service and heard N. Hall Jr. preach in the morning from Acts 3. 6. "Silver and gold have I none; but such as I have give I thee." A good sermon upon the cultivation of the kindly affections as

5

superior to the possession of wealth. Afternoon. 2 Peter 3. 18. "Grow in grace." Moral culture. Mr. Hall is evidently a sincere and an earnest preacher and thus he gives to his words additional force.[1]

Walk after both services with one or the other of my children. Read a Sermon of Buckminster's, John 6. 12. "Gather up the fragments that remain, that nothing be lost." A Sermon upon the profits of economy or frugality being a charity lecture written about at the time of the commercial restrictions here. Very good though not so remarkable as some of the others. Copied part of the letter to my father and went in the evening to see Mr. Brooks. Nobody there. Home at ten.

[1] On Rev. Nathaniel Hall Jr., a kinsman of ABA, see vol. 6:32.

MONDAY. I2TH.

Fine day. Our weather now begins to have a touch of spring, and the snow is disappearing pretty rapidly. I went to the Office. Nothing very new. Received from England advices of the arrival of some of my remittances but none of the power of Attorney respecting which I had written and indeed no letter at all from Mr. Johnson. Mr. Beebe called about it this day.[1] Home. Sophocles. Afternoon coins as usual. Evening wasted some time in drawing a sketch of an article for the Courier without success. Wife better but wet nurse fails.

[1] A power of attorney from T. B. Johnson was needed to complete the mortgage transaction which had been pending.

TUESDAY. I3TH.

A very fine morning, but the weather soon came round to the East-ward wind feeling which is the sign of our spring. I went to the Office. Received today a letter from Mr. T. B. Johnson inclosing a power of Attorney as I had desired. I immediately wrote to the various persons concerned to that effect.[1] Letter from Washington also,[2] but nothing new. My Wife is becoming better, but the first nurse will not do and we are to have another.

Sophocles and coins in the afternoon. Evening I went to a party at Mrs. Lawrence's, given to Lord Gosford[3] whose presence here seems to have turned the heads of half the Bostonians. This is a peculiarity of our national tastes singularly at variance with our professed principles. The number invited was large and the party very dull.

[1] Although the letter from T. B. Johnson and those written by CFA upon its receipt are missing, CFA, in a letter to LCA, 15 March (Adams Papers), gives

"the sum and substance of [Johnson's] remarkable letter": "He complains of the physicians upon whom he expends most of his substance in vain, and of his health. He says living in England and France is detestable, and he must come to America, but not to seek the crowded haunts of men. His wish is a retired spot in the vicinity of Washington or Baltimore, to which he desires his friends to direct their attention for him. He has tried to get Shepherd to do so without success, that he and his relations have tried to frighten him out of this plan by bug-a-boo terrors of the blacks, but that he is not convinced, inasmuch as he finds the whites in Europe to be not a whit more honest and a great deal more impudent. Finally he has conceived a violent dislike of the absurd vanities of rank &c. in the old countries and wishes to return home soon, for after all he concludes 'America is the only country, where man is seen to advantage.' ... I know what allowances are to be made for the unfortunate position he occupies in life and therefore I will not allow myself even a smile at the extraordinary revulsion of feeling here betrayed."

[2] LCA to CFA, 8 March, Adams Papers.

[3] Archibald Acheson, 2d earl of Gosford, lord lieutenant of Armagh and governor-general of Canada. His visit is the occasion of extended comment in the letter from CFA to LCA referred to in note 1, above.

WEDNESDAY. 14TH.

Our weather now is remarkably pleasant. Clear and cool but not too cold. My Wife now appears to be gaining strength pretty rapidly, and will I hope feel the benefit of her decision about the child.

I went to the Office and was occupied in matters of account. Mr. Beebe called in and begged off from the payment of the principal until better times. This was somewhat unexpected and hardly agreeable. I told him I would consult with Mr. Brooks. The state of affairs can hardly be worse now. I did talk with Mr. B. and found he agreed with me.

Home too late for Sophocles. Afternoon, coins. Evening, an hour with Abby who now sits up, after which I went to a party at Governor Everett's. A small number compared with yesterday and many members of the Legislature but on the whole pleasant.

THURSDAY 15TH.

Fine mild day. I went to the Office as usual and was occupied in Accounts &c. Received letters from Washington which made necessary the writing of some Notes &c. A long one from my father about the events of Washington, particularly the duel.[1] Home early as my Wife had fixed the dinner hour a little earlier to accommodate herself. I therefore read Sophocles in the afternoon, and began Adam Ferguson's Essay on Civil Society with which I was pleased.[2] I took a day of vacation from my coins today, and enjoyed it. Evening sat some time with Abby after which I wrote quite a long letter to my Mother.[3]

¹ The letter from JQA referred to is apparently that dated 27 Feb. (Adams Papers) but which, on internal evidence, was not completed and dispatched until 10 March; see also the note to the entry for 28 Feb., above.

² A copy of Adam Ferguson, *Essay on the History of Civil Society*, 8th edn., Phila., 1819, is in MQA.

³ Adams Papers. On the letter see the notes to the entry for 13 March, above.

FRIDAY. 16TH.

Fine weather. Nothing new at Washington. Mr. Webster has been making a speech which his puffers pronounce the very most superhuman thing possible.¹ Such is the way of manufacturing public opinion in this country! What profligacy in both of the parties. What utter disregard of the popular interest.

Office where I finished my reformation of the papers. Then call to see Mr. Brooks where I met Gorham who has just arrived from Baltimore. Home to dine at two so that I read Sophocles after dinner. A singular piece the Œdipus of Coloni, full of fine poetry and sentiment but with very little of action.

Gorham Brooks called in the afternoon and took tea, after which I accompanied him down to his father's where there was a small party of the family. These very rarely have much interest but were better tonight. Home at about ten or a little after. My Wife still grows better.

¹ On 31 Jan. and 12 March, Webster delivered speeches in the Senate, widely praised for their eloquence, opposing the sub-treasury bill.

SATURDAY 17TH.

Fine day although the easterly wind and gathering clouds portend a storm. I went to the Office where all my disposable time was taken up by Mr. Walsh and Deacon Spear who paid me visits. Nothing material with either.

I gained a walk today and finished the Œdipus Coloneus, being the second of the tragedies of Sophocles. It is a less active and impassioned piece than the former, but excels in lyric poetry and fine sentiment. The character of Antigone is superior to any female sketch I remember in Antiquity and that of Theseus is noble and well sustained. The death of Œdipus is a high poetical conception given in a masterly narrative. How this piece could have acted I do not know but as a dramatic poem it must have been the delight of the Athenians.

Mr. Walsh dined with me and spent much of the afternoon. He seems better content now he is fixed, although evidently wishing for something more. Evening at home, Ferguson, a very laboured style.

March 1838

A high Easterly gale all night followed by a pretty heavy fall of snow today. My Wife now gains steadily and the baby improves so that I feel grateful, deeply grateful to the divine being for having once more carried her through the dangers of her condition. Do I endeavour to make myself better for all the manifestation of blessings to me and mine? I trust I do but fear not.

Attended divine service and heard Mr. Ellis, a youngish man from Job, 26. 14. "Lo, these are parts of his ways: but how little a portion is heard of him? but the thunder of his power who can understand?" A very calm, well reasoned discourse upon the difficulty made by sceptics in regard to matters which they cannot satisfactorily explain. The inattention to the order of providence produces this by which for certain purposes we are left to a very imperfect consciousness of the existence of a Deity. Yet that it exists is little to be doubted, and that it's power is inestimable can hardly be questioned.

In the afternoon, discourse upon that passage in James 2. 10. "Whosoever shall keep the whole law, and yet offend in one point, he is guilty of all." An argument in support of works combined with faith against the notions of the Jews — an argument to prove that the neglect or violation of one rule must be followed by the same punishment morally speaking that in law falls upon the committer of a single crime. He is treated as if he had committed all.

A sermon of Buckminster upon faith from Hebrews 11. 1. "Now faith is the substance of things hoped for, the evidence of things not seen." After a definition he considers in this Sermon the objects of faith or enumerates the things not seen a conviction of which must be derived from faith alone. These may be past events which we believe have happened through the testimony of others, or may be future promises as yet not realized. But it seems to me this is not quite all, for faith may be the result of the simple operations of the mind, and I may be as thoroughly convinced of the existence of a beneficent Deity from the material world as from an account of a special revelation. The senses supply nothing but the facts, and reasoning supplies an ingenious argument, but neither of these yield certainty — faith must supply that. Evening at home. I sit now until nine with Abby, after which Ferguson.

The morning cloudy and moist but it cleared and the streets very soon presented great difficulties in walking. I went to the Office where

I spent my time rather idly. Read a little of Sismondi. I have come to that part of his book which is now most interesting, that which relates to money. And in this, many of his views strike me as sound. Call from a Mr. Stearns who is now Tenant of the House at the corner of the Common. Application to renew the Lease. Agreed to call tomorrow.

Home. Sophocles. Read Brumoy's account of the play of Antigone, with his occasional translations and references to a piece on the same subject by Rotrou long since obsolete. Afternoon coins. In the evening I now sit until nine with my Wife and try to amuse her with reading &c. Afterwards I read Potter's translation of the Œdipus Coloneus.[1]

[1] A copy of *The Tragedies of Sophocles*, transl. Robert Potter, Oxford, 1819, is in MQA.

TUESDAY. 20TH.

Market and so forth which makes a late morning. I felt today anxious about my little girl who had scratched her hand with a nail and appeared otherwise unwell. That affair of Fry last summer has made me excessively nervous in these matters.

Occupied at Office, drawing up the Account as it now stands between my father and myself, then a walk down to see the House in Tremont Street according to agreement. It needs much repairing indeed, and the Tenants do not seem of that class for whom repairing is of much use. They are careless and not over neat.

Home. Late for Sophocles but began Antigone and read a hundred lines. Afternoon, coins. I am now in the lower Empire when the designs become almost barbarous. In the evening, a ball at Mrs. S. Appleton's where I went. A splendid affair. The house is very showy, and gives one a better notion of entertainment than any I have seen.[1] I remained late although not in spirits and not amused.

[1] The Samuel Appleton residence at 36 Beacon Street.

WEDNESDAY 21ST.

Morning cloudy with flakes of snow. I went to the Office where I read Sismondi more attentively than usual. His chapter upon Banking is quite instructive. I took the book home with a view to translating it and sending to some Newspaper, but when I came to reflect upon the state of the press I was discouraged. If I print, I must pay for my printing, that is clear enough, for the expression of opinions which have no party bearings is coldly received by all sides.

Letter from Washington. My mother gives an account of a dinner at the President's at which Abraham Van Buren spoke of the ability of my Pamphlet.[1] Home. Sophocles. I find my text so erroneous in my own copy that I need another and as I have one volume of another from the Athenæum which contains Electra and not Antigone, I thought I would read that first. Afternoon continued the work upon coins which is becoming tedious in the lower Empire.

Evening, Mr. Brooks was here. Abby is improving slowly but has been made uneasy for some days by the ailing of our little girl who seemed quite heavy tonight. The baby grows.

[1] LCA to CFA, 18 March [in 18–21 March], Adams Papers. Abraham Van Buren was the eldest son of the President.

THURSDAY. 22D.

Cloudy, dull weather. I went to the Office and was occupied there for some time. Received letters from T. B. Johnson who is at New York just arrived from England[1] and A. H. Everett at Washington.[2] The former could not restrain himself from returning, even in the winter, notwithstanding his dread of suffering from the voyage. He now goes to Washington whither he desires me to transmit to him an account of his funds, and this I sat down to execute this morning.[3]

The other letter is a curious one. It's only object seems to be [to] repeat to me a request made by President Van Buren through him for two more of my Pamphlets. He says that he did not get those he understood I had sent to him. This conversation took place at the dinner mentioned in my letter from my Mother yesterday, at which Abraham the son mentioned my Pamphlet to I. Hull. This looks a little inconsistent, for first, how should the President have known of my sending to him before, secondly, where could Abraham have got his opinion. I infer the whole to be a contrivance to flatter me with the view of operating upon my father's course on the Subtreasury bill in the House, where he might save it or kill it. This is a little confirmed by what is given in the same letter of my father's opinions. I was much edified by this exposition of the case, and wrote in reply to Mr. Everett a very frank exposition of my own views,[4] my entire distrust of the doctrines of Mr. Webster and the Bank Whigs, my dissent from Mr. Van Buren, and the impossibility of my acting with any party satisfactorily to myself. If he shows this letter, it will not lead Mr. Van Buren very far into my father's opinions, and if he does not I shall be satisfied with having avoided the trap set for me.

I forwarded the Pamphlets as desired but without a letter. The copying these, took most of the afternoon. I read Sophocles however. Evening, sat with my Wife until nine and then Ferguson. Louisa still poorly.

¹ Missing.
² 18 March, Adams Papers.
³ CFA to T. B. Johnson, LbC, Adams Papers.
⁴ CFA to A. H. Everett, LbC, Adams Papers. The views there stated are: "I am still in favour of a new Bank to control [Biddle] as well as others in which the Government influence should be equal to that of the Stockholders and the President of it a Government officer removable by Stockholders. These of course are individual views, they square with those of no party."

FRIDAY 23D.

My uneasiness about Louisa much relieved although she still seemed poorly. My Wife better. I went to the Office and occupied myself with drawing my Account for the Quarter with my father in order to perceive its consistency. This took just about my usual time.

Kirk here from Quincy about the work to be done, came in on my horse and detained me a good while in talking of nothing. Walk to see horse who looks in good condition. The idea of going to renew the work at Quincy is a little burdensome this year. Particularly as there is some little preliminary fitting up. But variety is the spice of life. And after it is all done I hope we shall enjoy it.

Home. Sophocles. Electra. Afternoon, coins. My Wife had several of her family visiting her, and Gorham Brooks took tea and spent part of the evening. The remainder with my Wife after which I finished Ferguson.

SATURDAY 24TH.

This was one of my *dies non*.¹ I woke with a slight feeling of tightness rather than pain which developed itself through all the stages of head ach until it became one of my worst kinds. I managed to employ the morning, particularly as I had Deacon Spear, and Mr. Stearns the tenant making a call about the House which he takes at the raised rent. I then walked until dinner time to try to cure myself but without success. The air was pleasanter than any time hitherto this season. I have no afternoon nor evening to account for excepting in suffering.

¹ Italics supplied.

SUNDAY 25TH.

Fine day. I passed an hour upon the coins which go on slowly, then to attend divine Service. Heard Dr. Frothingham who preached from

1. Corinthians 15. 26. "The last enemy that shall be destroyed is death." Some fine reflections upon the moral preparation necessary to render death less painful ending with an eloquent application to the late instance of Dr. Bowditch.[1]

Walk with my daughter and call afterwards upon Dwight for the fifth or sixth time without success. Then met Davis and short walk with him. Abby came down to dinner today for the first time.

Afternoon, John 3. 6.7.8. "That which is born of the flesh is flesh; and that which is born of the Spirit is spirit. Marvel not that I said unto thee, Ye must be born again. The wind bloweth where it listeth and thou hearest the sound thereof, but canst not tell whence it cometh, and whither it goeth: so is every one that is born of the spirit." I confess I did not pay the attention to this discourse which I ought to have done.

Afterwards, one of Buckminster's Sermons upon the reasonableness of Faith in continuation of last Sunday's discourse. The text the same. He considers faith to be nothing more than belief in evidence of testimony. This does not quite satisfy me. Nobody has seen God at any time. Nobody knows the sun will rise tomorrow. The idea of a future state of rewards and punishments rests in most minds not altogether upon testimony. Yet faith attaches to each from reasoning independently of testimony. A strong argument in favor of Christianity from the spread of the gospel as a matter of faith at the close. In the evening my Wife sat down stairs. Conversation after which I wrote a letter to my Mother.[2]

[1] Nathaniel Bowditch, astronomer and mathematician, had died on 17 March (*DAB*).
[2] Adams Papers.

MONDAY 26TH.

Morning fine. I went to the Office. Letters from Washington. One from my father apparently historical giving an account of the late duel. This is a sequel to a former one on the same subject.[1] I read Sismondi, a Chapter upon Paper Money. The whole portion of the work which relates to Currency is exceedingly valuable and merits reading over very often. Home. Sophocles. I find the Lyric Poetry somewhat hard to manage but the dialogue quite easy. Afternoon, studied my coins which rather hang on now, and which ought to be finished. I must accellerate my pace about them.

Evening, T. K. Davis came in just as I had done tea. He seemed to have a desire to communicate the result of a conversation with Bancroft respecting the arrangements of party affairs here. Bancroft wishes to organize a more respectable one both in talent and character than has heretofore existed, and in pursuing that end is much harrassed and hampered by the materials which are provided for him. He has already more than half drawn in Davis who in his turn wishes to operate upon me. The object appears to be to make my father the "point d'appui"[2] and round him form a body of talent for the support of the party in the New England States. I read to him my father's letter to show the futility of that expectation and then my own to Mr. Everett to explain my feelings. I told him that I inclined to maintain my present position unless Mr. Van Buren was disposed to make sufficient concessions in principle to enable me conscientiously to support him. He was now standing upon such slippery ground that it would be no sinecure to any one to take a post in his defence. After a long discussion of whys and wherefores, Davis left with the understanding that he was to tell Bancroft we meant shortly to go to Washington and investigate matters for our own satisfaction. He stayed so long that I was unable to fulfil an engagement at W. G. Brooks'. Read Condillac's Commerce and Government.[3]

[1] The letter from JQA is that of 19 March (Adams Papers; printed in MHS, *Procs.*, 2d ser., 12 [1897–1899]:288–292). It provides a full account of the events occurring upon the day of the duel and afterward; the earlier letter (see entries for 28 Feb. and 15 March, above) dealt with the background of the duel.
[2] That is, fulcrum.
[3] The Abbé Etienne Bonnot de Condillac's "Le commerce et le gouvernement," 1776. Copies of the 3-vol., Paris, 1777, and of the 31-vol., Paris, 1803 edns. of the *Œuvres* are in MQA.

TUESDAY 27TH.

Morning clear but it afterwards was cloudy with a very raw wind from the Eastward. I went to market and from thence to the Office. Call in at a house in Otis place lately occupied by Mr. Bond and lost some time there. No furniture that I wanted. And the remainder of my morning was so dissipated in various ways that I have little account to give of it.

The news from Washington is of the defeat of Mr. Calhoun's specie section in the Treasury bill, which seems to put the Administration in greater peril than before. I do not clearly see how it can sustain itself.

Home after a walk. Exercise is becoming absolutely necessary to me as my Spring feelings come in to act upon me. Sophocles. Afternoon, reading Condillac's Commerce and Government. A tolerable summary of first principles. Evening. Went to a small party at Mrs. Parkman's —rather dull. Talk with R. G. Shaw about Mr. Biddle.

WEDNESDAY 28TH.

A cloudy, very raw day. I was detained a long while at home by S. Conant the Tenant of the Weston Farm with whom I had some sort of account to settle for leaving it to take care of itself. He seemed a little frightened which I rather intended. He paid one year's rent. I went to the Office where I was busy in accounts. Purchased a draft for E. C. Adams and remitted it with a letter to her.[1] This takes off of my mind one of the burthens which have long been on it. There appears to me to be a little glimmering of sunshine in matters of finance now perceptible. But it is yet not decisive enough to form a judgment upon it, as to the future. Walk, part of it with T. Dwight and talk of the Subtreasury bill in which I promulgate anti Whig doctrines. Home. Sophocles. Afternoon, continue Condillac and do a little upon coins. Evening Mr. Brooks took tea and spent an hour after whom, W. Dwight came in and finished the evening.

[1] LbC, Adams Papers.

THURSDAY 29TH.

Morning snow with a cold Easterly wind. Office. The news from Washington is of the passage of the amended Treasury bill by a majority of two in the Senate. I was a little curious to observe the tone adopted by the Globe. The leading article is very subdued, but endeavours to put the best face on the matter and intimates a hostility to credit which if thus kept up will certainly overturn the Administration.

At Office I found T. K. Davis who sat with me nearly all the morning. Conversation principally turned as it usually does with us upon political prospects and the difficulties in the way of useful and independent action. He made an allusion to my own particular position which gave me a turn into personal views which I do not often indulge and which are not frequently worthy of exposition. He left and Stanwood came in about his Mortgage. This consumed all my time so that I had little even for Sophocles.

Afternoon continue the coins which I must hasten if I propose to get through it this season. Evening at home. Read to my Wife part of Mrs. Inchbald's Simple Story.[1]

[1] A copy of Mrs. Elizabeth (Simpson) Inchbald's, *A Simple Story*, 4 vols., London, 1799, is in MQA.

FRIDAY. 30TH.

Morning cloudy but it cleared pleasantly, though the melting snow made the walking bad. I went to the Office where I drew up an Account between Mr. Johnson and myself preparatory to the reception of a letter from him. Received a pamphlet from my father containing an abstract of the Bank returns for the United States which I examined with some curiosity. Interrupted by Mr. Ayer who came for his money which I paid him, and was obliged to go up with him to the House in Tremont Street where I was ordering some repairs. This consumed my time for my exercise which I still too much neglect. Sophocles. Afternoon coins, in which I continue to make progress. Evening, to my Wife part of the Simple Story.

SATURDAY 31ST.

A fine clear day. I went to the Office where I was engaged in looking through Mr. Woodbury's Pamphlet about the Banks, a pretty useful though very unmethodical summary. Surprised by the appearance of John Q. Adams Junior who came with Elizabeth, his sister from Washington. They were hastened by the account of their Mother's sickness. She is now however better. Letters from W. B. Lewis respecting the Administration of T. B. Adams' effects, and from my father very brief,[1] but none yet from Mr. Johnson. Call upon T. K. Davis respecting our proposal of starting to go to Washington. Home. Sophocles. Afternoon coins, and evening read to my Wife from the Simple Story and afterwards Eckhel.

[1] The letter from W. B. Lewis is missing; that from JQA, 27 March, is in Adams Papers.

SUNDAY. APRIL 1ST.

A clear morning with a cold Northwest wind blowing pretty hard. My Wife went out notwithstanding to ride and I accompanied her, before service. Attended as usual and heard Dr. Frothingham preach from 2. Acts 42. "And they continued stedfastly in the apostles' doctrine and fellowship, and in breaking of bread and in prayers." A communion sermon to which I should have listened very attentively if my boy had not troubled me. Walk. Met Mr. Walsh who dined with me.

Afternoon, Mr. Muzzy of West Cambridge from Mark 9. 23. "If thou canst believe, all things are possible to him that believeth." Faith is a favourite topic with Unitarian preachers who as a class believe less than almost any Sect of Christians. They consider faith only in its more limited applications to credibility, or to the qualities of humanity. Mr. Muzzy seemed to complain of the want of it in the actions of men, the doubt of human virtue and disbelief in progress.

The discourse which I read today from Buckminster was the third of a series on the same subject, and particularly upon it's importance as well as a cause of fear as of consolation. There is one very eloquent passage in it, but on the whole the series has disappointed me. Evening at home. Read Eckhel, and Condillac.

MONDAY 2D.

Morning clear but quite cold. I went to the Office and became very soon engaged in my usual Quarterly accounts, which would have kept me had not J. Q. Adams come in, and mentioning his being about to go to Quincy alone, I determined to accompany him. In this way I may gain something in regard to my arrangements which must now be rapidly making. I found Kirk and got him to prepare for me my horse and chaise to return, then to the Painter's whom I could not find after all. This is always the way in the country. Notified him however to meet me on Wednesday and after stopping to look at my place I came back and thence home which I did not however reach until after my dinner hour. Afternoon coins. Evening, a game or two of backgammon with my Wife, and then, Menagiana.[1]

[1] A copy of Gilles Ménage, *Menagiana, ou Bons mots recontres agreables, pense'es judicieuses et observations curieuses*, Amsterdam, 1713, is in MQA.

TUESDAY. 3D.

Our weather begins to grow favourable. Today was pleasant enough. I went to the Office and was occupied very much in bringing up my Accounts which are as usual upon quarters a little troublesome. I was also engaged in going round upon my labour of finishing my work for my house. This is a little tedious to me as I had felt as if I had nearly finished, and my indolence has certainly very much increased within a year.

Home where I found a man from Weston lying in wait for me seeking the Farm. It took me until dinner time to get rid of that. Mrs. Angier dined with us. Afternoon I went on with my work upon coins which is tedious enough. There is not much to delight in when we are watching the progress of barbarism. Evening Mr. Brooks and T. K. Davis came and took tea, and passed the evening. Conversation amusing and instructive.

WEDNESDAY 4TH.

Fine day. I went to Market and from thence to Quincy where I had agreed to meet several workmen on matters connected with my house. Found it looking far more pleasant and cheerful than I had anticipated. The winter has on the whole left the work pretty fairly. I went over the house and opened it to receive the air. Made arrangements with the painter and grate maker. Decided upon a furnace. And then home. The South side of the house looked exceedingly warm and agreeable at this time in the year when I had expected it would be bleak. But the day was fine and the wind westerly, which makes a great difference. Home but rather late so that I had little time to do any thing. Afternoon, coins. Evening at home. H. G. Gorham here for an hour.

THURSDAY. 5TH.

A very fine day. The one fixed upon according to custom for the observation of a general fast but which has of late years been observed as a kind of quiet holiday. As such I like it. It is unique in it's character. None of the noise and bustle, the guns, drums, blunderbuss and thunder of our Jubilee days, and none of the stuffing of thanksgiving. If there is excess and I fear there is, it is at least not the prominent external feature.[1]

I spent an hour upon coins and then attended divine Service and heard Dr. Frothingham from Psalms 25. II. "For thy name's sake O Lord, pardon mine iniquity; for it is great." I am afraid I can give no account of this discourse of which I am a little ashamed. After service walk with my children, the day was lovely and the common was crowded with boys playing ball. Spent some time before dinner upon the collection of coins.

T. K. Davis dined and spent the afternoon during which we walked twice round the common. Pleasant enough. He left at eight after which we had a short evening. Being fatigued, I retired early.

[1] On spring fast-days in Massachusetts and on CFA's earlier attitude on their observance, see vols. 3:208–209; 4:23.

FRIDAY 6TH.

A very lovely day, such as we have here and there in the course of our Spring to relish more from its contrast with the others. I went to the Office first to meet an applicant for the farm from Weston. After talking with him I then went to Quincy where I found Sayer hard at work upon the bookshelves. This seems like setting the heavy machinery in motion. After measuring for the rest of the furniture which detained me until later than I intended, I returned to town not getting there until after two. Of course nothing material could be done. Home. Afternoon coins. Evening, Dr. and Mrs. Frothingham spent with us pleasantly. No news.

SATURDAY 7TH.

A clear day though a change of wind had taken off the very genial feeling which marked the air of yesterday. I was much occupied at the Office in attending to Accounts and collecting various Dividends. W. Spear came in from Quincy on the settlement of his annual Account which was effected as usual. Mr. Walsh also came in and sat some time. Also I had a call from Mr. Bryent the furnace maker. Thus the whole morning passed and I went home late.

Missed Sophocles. Indeed it becomes usual from the time my country visits begin to neglect my literary occupations, and as yet I have some burden of care in regard to the arrangement for occupying the house. Mr. Walsh dined with me and sat so long that I did not much upon the coins. Evening, reading to my Wife resumed, the sixth volume of Scott which has just come out. After which, Eckhel's Chapter upon votive coins.

SUNDAY 8TH.

A raw cold East wind, but clear until towards evening. I worked upon the coins pretty steadily until the time for divine service when I attended and heard Dr. Frothingham from Luke 24. 29. "Abide with us; for it is toward evening and the day is far spent." I failed in mastering the object of this discourse although I thought it applied generally to the employment of life and particularly to the close of an aged member of the Society during the past week, Mr. Homer.[1] Walk.

Afternoon, Mr. Austin preached a very uninteresting discourse from Matthew 28. 8. "Lo, I have told you." His text and his discourse upon virtue appeared to me to have no distinctly visible connexion. Afternoon a sermon of Buckminster's upon the character and writings of the Apostle Paul. 2. Peter 3. 15.16. "Even as our beloved brother Paul, also, according to the wisdom given unto him, hath written unto you, as also in all his Epistles, speaking in them of these things, in which are some things hard to be understood, which they that are unlearned

I. LOUISA CATHERINE ADAMS, ENGRAVED BY G. F. STORM, 1837
See page vii

and unstable wrest, as they do also the other Scriptures, unto their own destruction." An interesting and instructive discourse.

Evening after a short visit from Mr. Tucker and Mr. Brooks, quiet at home. Reading the sixth volume of Scott which is interesting from it's melancholy change. What a moral of life! Letter to my Mother.[2]

[1] Benjamin Homer, since 1805, had been a pew-holder in the First Church, hence a proprietor or member of what was variously designated as the Society of the First Church or the Old Brick Society, the entity through which the church acted on corporate as distinct from religious matters (*The Records of the First Church in Boston, 1630–1868*, ed. Richard D. Pierce, Col. Soc. Mass., *Pubns.*, 40 [1961]:610, 482–492, 573–594 *passim*).

[2] Adams Papers. Accompanying the letter was CFA's biographical sketch of LCA for her approval and transmission to the publisher.

MONDAY. 9TH.

A wet morning but it cleared afterwards. I was nevertheless discouraged from going to Quincy and therefore turned my attention to the arrangement of affairs here. Made purchase of part of my stock for the Quincy house which my Wife seems anxious to have done before our departure,[1] and busy upon accounts, writing letters and so forth.[2]

Home where I returned to the Electra of Sophocles, but my visits are very necessarily now but few. The finance matters are upon my mind as they must be upon every man's who has any thing at stake in the community. I am responsible for much which belongs to others, which now that things appear so bad, I think I will relieve myself of at the first opportunity. Afternoon at work upon the coins which I now anxiously desire to finish. Scott in the evening and Condillac.

[1] A trip to Washington for the benefit of ABA's health was being contemplated (CFA to LCA, 8 April, Adams Papers). A desire to test the political winds with T. K. Davis may have provided further motivation for the trip.

[2] One of the letters was to T. B. Johnson (LbC, Adams Papers).

TUESDAY 10TH.

Wet but it cleared. Went to Quincy where it looked full cheerless. The workmen were however all very busy in their occupations and I felt a little ray of prospect ahead of land. This house has been a burden upon me, undertaken in such disastrous times, but I am now upon the last of the heavy draughts. Home.

Much sensation created by a letter of Mr. Biddle's announcing his determination to decline specie payments whatever the New York banks may do. It has satisfied me of the impolicy of leaning much upon him.[1] I regret to be obliged to withdraw my confidence from him but I cannot help it. My disposition is to answer it, but where is the medium.

Afternoon continued work upon the coins. Evening T. K. Davis here. Conversation upon the general theory of our Institutions as usual. Not much gained from speculations of this kind.

[1] For a discussion of CFA's position on currency questions, including payments in specie, see Duberman, *CFA*, p. 58–59.

WEDNESDAY 11TH.

Morning rainy and continued so all day. I went out to make purchases for Quincy and was detained in this until late so that I had very little time after I reached the Office to do much work. Calls from various tenants but no letters from Washington. The New York Banks seem determined to begin the work of resumption notwithstanding the resistance of Mr. Biddle. On the other hand, there seem to be indications of breaking in the Administration party. Mr. Hamer of Ohio has made a step which may or may not lead to consequences. Both parties appear excessively embarrassed.[1] And in the mean time the country suffers. Home late. Afternoon coins. Evening at home reading that melancholy volume of Walter Scott.

[1] Thomas Lyon Hamer, U.S. representative from Ohio and a Democrat, had announced to the House that considering that "the business, commerce, circulation, and exchanges . . . are in a deranged and embarrassed condition; and considering, also, that a part of the Bank of the United States have expressed a desire to resume specie payments at an early period," he intended to introduce a resolution "That if the banks, or a portion of them, do thus resume it will be the duty of the General Government . . . to aid such banks . . . in regaining public confidence, and to sustain them in their laudable efforts to fulfil their obligations . . . to restore to the people a sound circulating medium." In the same issue, the Administration paper carried an editorial of "authorized" explanation that there was no intent on the part of the mover to indicate any change of position, nor any intent of the "party in power" to be hostile to such action if taken by banks or to throw "unnecessary obstacles in their way." Further explanations were offered, when the resolution was introduced, that there was no intent to attack Administration policy nor to embarrass it (Washington *Globe*, 7 April, p. 3, cols. 3, 5; 9 April, p. 2, col. 7 – p. 3, col. 1).

THURSDAY 12TH.

Morning clear but cold with Easterly wind. I was occupied much of my time in little details of various kinds which are consuming without being profitable. I fatigued myself too in my various walkings to and fro. Met T. W. Ward who spoke to me about my Pamphlet and who insinuated a wish that I should answer Mr. Biddle's last letter. But I have no time. I plead guilty to indolence, and I have no medium.

Met T. K. Davis and walked with him. Home to dinner, after which Davis again met me and we went to Quincy. Visit shortened by an accident which delayed me on the road, but I gave the necessary directions and then we returned. The weather quite raw and unpleasant for riding. After tea, too much fatigued to do much of any work, and retired early for me.

FRIDAY 13TH.

Morning mild and pleasant but it gradually clouded. I went to the Office and was busied as usual in and out in Accounts and the various commissions preparatory to going away. Procured a copy of Mr. Biddle's letter and read it with much attention. I think it of so much consequence that I shall endeavour to write an attempt at an answer. I do not know how I may succeed but my motive is good. Various interruptions.

Home, but I give up my Sophocles until I am established in Quincy. Afternoon, went with Mr. Brooks, Mrs. Frothingham and Abby to Medford. We to see Mrs. Adams and Elizabeth. The latter has been very ill since her return. These visits are necessarily melancholy. I would gladly help them if I could, but that kind of grief is remediless in this world. Home.

SATURDAY 14TH.

A cold day with snow and rain. Disappointed of my visit to Quincy to regulate matters there. To the Office where I was occupied with many visitors. Further reflections upon Mr. Biddle and resolved to spare time, much as I need it, to write a reply. Several letters but not of much interest. Home. Afternoon began to write and then followed it up with much vigour during the rest of the day and evening. Mr. Brooks came in and sat with us an hour in the evening. Returns of the New York City Elections.

SUNDAY 15TH.

Morning clear but cold with a sharp frost such as we do not often have so late. I spent an hour in coins and then attended divine service. Heard Dr. Frothingham preach from Hebrews 11. 35. "Women received their dead raised to life again: that they might obtain a better resurrection." This is Easter Sunday, and the discourse was upon the resurrection. I did not however gather so much from it as from a very clear narrative discourse of Mr. Greenwood's upon the same subject. His text from Matthew 28. 6. "Come, see the place where the Lord lay." He entered upon a description of the spot of the agony and burial, and then drew a rapid sketch of it's history down thereby meaning to adduce additional evidence of the truth of the gospel history of the Resurrection. There was a neatness and accuracy of delineation joined with a high tone of moral reflection which made this on the whole one of the most interesting discourses I ever heard from the pulpit.

Read a Sermon of Buckminster upon the formation of habits. Jeremiah 13. 23. "Can the Ethiopian change his skin, or the leopard his spots? then may ye also do good that are accustomed to do evil." Buckminster's mind was a nicely discriminating one and his felicity of style enabled him very forcibly to describe his meaning. He wanted only a few years of experience to set him at the head of all English Sermon writers.

Wrote pretty steadily upon my letters to Mr. Biddle and having finished the first one, inclosed it to Mr. Buckingham with a proposal to publish. Will he do it?[1] At Mr. Brooks' for an hour and a half. P. R. Dalton there. Banking the talk. P. C. B. Jr. has just returned from New York where the Bank Convention has been sitting. I should judge from his talk that the majority of the Banks were at their old game. Mr. Gallatin was not popular with them and Mr. Biddle was. So it is. The Slough of Despond seems increasing. Home and continued writing.

[1] CFA's doubt of his success in gaining acceptance of his article from Joseph T. Buckingham, editor of the *Boston Courier*, derived from Buckingham's earlier animosity to JQA (vols. 3:321, 342; 4:125–126) and from the paper's strong support of Webster (vol. 6:68, 165).

MONDAY 16TH.

Morning very cold for the season of the year. I felt obliged to go to Quincy but it was one of those cold blustering days when one would by far prefer to be at home.

The ride out was not bad, but the cold was such as to render it difficult to do much when there and to make the return in the face of the North wind uncomfortable enough. There seemed to be indications of progress however which encourage me. The masons were at work doing their last jobs at the fire places, but on the whole every thing was sufficiently discouraging. The Country is no place of attraction during our month of April. Glad to get home. The ground did not thaw in the sun today.

Afternoon, busy writing my papers. A thought struck me which appeared to me of much value. T. K. Davis came in to tea and I read to him what I had by me, which he appeared to like. After he went, I finished the second and third numbers.

TUESDAY. 17TH.

Mr. Buckingham has not only done what I proposed but he being himself sick, my letter occupies the editorial department.[1] Here is an answer to my question of Sunday. I have nothing to complain of very certainly in this regard. And now I will wait with not a little of curiosity to perceive the effect. It is an indication of some estimation acquired in the Community that such civility has been conceded to me at once. Another indication is in the earnestness of Dr. Palfrey to solicit a contribution to the North American Review.[2] This encouragement comes so late and after such hard labour that it will not, thank Heaven, upset my balance. I trust in a higher power to guard me through the mazes of life.

Office where I worked as usual and various small commissions which consumed much time. Afternoon, went on writing which I continued in the evening. Read Lockharts Life for an hour. Finished my answer. It is not as complete as I meant to make it but I am hurried.

[1] CFA's four letters to Nicholas Biddle, president of the Bank of the United States, appeared on successive days (17–20 April) in the *Boston Courier* at p. 2, col. 1. Each was signed "A Citizen." In them CFA undertook to explain his shift from support of Biddle's monetary policies to opposition. He charged that Biddle's stand against resumption of specie payments was the result of a deliberate descent into the arena of party politics and called for reconsideration.

[2] On Rev. John Gorham Palfrey's acquisition of the *North American Review*, see vol. 6:237.

WEDNESDAY 18TH.

The second of my letters appeared today and reads so well that I think it will not fail of an effect. I have got beyond the time for being smothered, I suspect. There appears however at the head of it a distinct announcement of the editor's disposition not to be responsible for them which looks as if he had been assaulted about them.[1]

I went to Quincy where I found things advancing. The interior of the house begins to look like a human habitation. I gave a multitude of directions which may be of service during my absence and found many things done as directed. Home. The soft Southerly wind made it feel a very different thing today from Monday, and my return particularly was pleasant. Home.

Afternoon resumed my coins which have suffered a few days interruption by my other work. Evening Mr. and Mrs. Frothingham came and passed an hour very pleasantly. They come without form and take a little something sociably and go early. I sent today my last letter to Mr. Biddle. These four letters have cost me no great labour to write and yet on the whole I like them as well as any thing I ever did.

[1] The disclaimer read: "The Publishers of the Courier wish it to be distinctly understood, that, until the editor announces, under his own hand, his ability to resume his duties, he must not be considered as concurring in, or responsible for, any opinion expressed in its columns" (18 April, p. 2, col. 1).

THURSDAY 19TH.

My third letter was printed today, that which I think the best. They evidently make some sensation as there was besides a feeble attempt to array a quotation from Mr. Webster's Speech against me, a very short editorial betraying the fact of private remonstrances against their publication on the ground of their being loco foco in the extreme.[1] Such are the perversions of principle prevailing at this time here. It is matter of great surprise that they were admitted at all.

I was at the Office engaged partly in affairs and partly in executing various commissions, a little in translating Sismondi although I have abandoned my project of publication. Call upon T. K. Davis and settle our intention of departure for Tuesday.

Rainy all day. Afternoon engaged in working up the remainder of the coinage. Evening, Mr. Brooks spent with us. After which I rather dawdled.

[1] Accompanying the publication of CFA's third letter to Biddle in the *Courier* were two items related to it. The first was a brief editorial comment on the letters, headed "Mr. Biddle and the Banks," saying, "We see no reason, loco foco or not, why the public should not have advantage of the writer's opinions.... why we should refuse hearing to a respectable correspondent." The second, immediately following the first, was a letter to the editor, unsigned, with the heading, "Specie Payments and Mr. Biddle," in which Webster's position on specie payments in his sub-treasury speech is quoted, summarized, and praised (p. 2, col. 5).

FRIDAY. 20TH.

My fourth and last letter came out today. It is not quite so well written as the rest and is also defaced by misprints, but on the whole terminates the thing well. That they make some impression is clear from the announcement of an answer to appear tomorrow. I see it also in men's faces who look constrained before me. The pieces are thought very radical. Perhaps they may be, but I shall think better hereafter of radicalism if they are.

I went to Quincy this morning and occupied as usual in directions and so forth. They have gone on swimmingly and now really make the House look cheerful. I begin to feel as if there was some probability of an end. It has been irksome to me from the fact of my having to do the whole. Home in a cold wind.

Did some business at the Office and then to dinner. Afternoon, at work on coins, and finishing up all odd things. Evening at home. Read Walter Scott's melancholy Diary. Alas, what clouds over the pleasantest landscape. Such is life, and happy for us in the end, it is so, for what would be man's feeling if this was Paradise when he was called to leave it.

SATURDAY 21ST.

This morning appears a long communication from Mr. Buckingham endeavouring to weaken the impression made by my articles,[1] but bearing the mark of mental weakness resulting from his confinement by sickness so long. He professes not to know who wrote them. Is this true? I suspect it is although my friends think otherwise. I believe him partially but think he equivocates. It is clear that he has been hard pressed and seeks to find an outlet, although resolved to execute his intention. The letters met with no delay, nor were put in a corner, as might have been done if it was wished to injure their effect. My opponent promised yesterday, also appears but is a very poor creature.[2] The other papers persevere in the usual course towards me of silence. It remains to see how they will do in other places.

I was very much occupied all the morning by Accounts and payments of various debts which I wished settled previous to departure. I think I now begin to see light after the heavy expenditure which has now been pressing upon me with much severity for more than eighteen months, of shortened resources. W. Spear in from Quincy and called for a settlement. Thus the morning passed until half past one when I met my Wife for the purpose of taking her to see Celestini's pictures. He was civil but evidently out of humour by the failure of all negotiation. And he had therefore lost much of the courtesy of manner which he had while he had an object.[3]

Afternoon, continued at work upon the coins which I must now soon give up. I have got very nearly through the assorting and now the catalogue making only remains. Evening Mr. Brooks was here, after which I was not active.

[1] The editorial, dated "Cambridge, April 19" and signed "J. T. B.," undertakes a detailed refutation of CFA's position and concludes, "Of Mr. Biddle we are not the apologist. We give him credit for great talent as a financier, and for patriotism, so long as it was for his interest to be patriotic and public-spirited. For some of his selfish atrocities within the last two years, he ought to have his ears nailed to the pillory; and we could look upon him in that position with undiminished complacency, if Gen. Jackson and Mr. Van Buren were permitted to enjoy the same dignified and elevated station on either side of him" (*Boston Courier*, 21 April, p. 2, col. 1).

[2] The letter, addressed to "A Citizen,"

attacks CFA's position as having "a most unpleasant smack of locofocoism; it looked too much like — *cant*." The writer professes no admiration for Biddle either. He identifies himself as being in the mercantile business "in a small way, some eight or nine years" and signs the letter "C." (same, p. 2, col. 3).

[3] Despite the indication that Count Celestini failed to sell his paintings in Boston, he did succeed in disposing of nine of them to the Boston Athenæum. The particular works that CFA had admired on his several visits to the Gallery were not among those purchased (Mabel M. Swan, *The Athenaeum Gallery, 1827–1873*, Boston, 1940, p. 128).

SUNDAY. 22D.

A lovely day. I attended divine service all day and my wife in the morning for the first time for many months for the which God be praised. Dr. Frothingham all day. Morning from Ephesians 3. 16. "the inner man." Afternoon 1. Corinthians 3. 19. "For the wisdom of this world is foolishness with God." Good discourses not improved as much by me as they should have been. Walk. Nature looked cheerful.

Afternoon, Mr. Walsh came in and sat a long while, then after tea T. K. Davis and Gardiner Gorham — the two former remaining until after eleven engaged in very good and very instructive conversation. They are both thinking men and Such animals are not found everywhere. T. K. Davis postpones until Wednesday, which is as well for me. He is likely to become the Editor of a paper here to be established upon the basis of the old Advocate. I hope and wish him success though not without fear.

After their departure read a Sermon of Buckminster's upon communion. Matthew 10. 32. "Whosoever shall confess me before men, him will I also confess before my father, which is in Heaven." The obstacles to taking the communion discussed. A sermon deserving of some serious reflection by me as I become older.

MONDAY 23D.

Morning clear but cold. I went to Quincy where I found things under way. My orders have been nearly all executed and now I know of nothing in this direction which should detain me. Called at the

Bank to obtain some New York money with only partial success, then to see the painter for some final directions, then back to superintend Kirks planting of the thorns. Time only can give beauty to my place from the vegetation which I can only set going. Home after a cold ride.

Dined with my Wife at Mr. Brooks'. Nobody else, and a tolerably pleasant time, then to the Athenæum where I arranged matters respecting the coins with the librarian. Looked into the New York papers, they take no notice of my articles. The spirit of party is too strong and smothers them as usual. Afternoon, coins but so much fatigued that I worked upon them very languidly. Some pages of Lockhart and Diary. Over tired tonight.

TUESDAY 24TH.

Morning passed in attention to affairs at the Office. Brought up my Accounts, arranged Mr. Johnson's Affairs, converted my money and so forth. It is one indication of the changes of life that I cannot move as I used to. So many things require my personal attention and care and so many depend upon me that it is like tearing a tree by the roots. Home to dinner, after which packing. The day before a journey is commonly a Wasted and bustling day. Disposed of the remainder of the coins and put them away. Evening, finished the sixth volume of Walter Scott and had Mr. and Mrs. Frothingham to spend two hours very agreeably. Then to bed well fatigued.

WEDNESDAY 25TH.

Day fine. Morning passed in final arrangements. Kirk in town to take with him my horse. Ketchum, the owner of another which matches him came up and I was foolish enough to buy him. This was imprudent just as I am going away. Final directions to workmen in various departments and then home.

Dine early and off at 3 o'clock to the cars for Providence.[1] Found T. K. Davis there all ready for the start. Also Mr. Webster and Mr. and Mrs. Chadwick. His recognition of us was rather formal and cold. As to myself, I do not wonder, but as regards Davis, I think this singular.

We went to Providence and thence by railway to Stonington where we at about a quarter past 8 o'clock took the Steamer Providence to New York. Our trip was without incident and in no wise disagreeable. Being somewhat tired, I went to bed.

[1] It appears that the Adams party, in addition to CFA and ABA, consisted of seven-year-old LCA2 and Mrs. JA2 and her daughter Mary Louisa.

29

New York

THURSDAY 26TH.

We had a quiet trip and found ourselves at day break fast nearing New York. The day was drizzly. And we rode up to the Astor House in the rain, to breakfast. Found Sidney Brooks and his Wife very well and passed the greater part of the day with them excepting when I was out making a few purchases. The City looked dull under the clouds and I think I felt more depressed than I know well how to account for. The society of Mrs. Brooks is to me always fatiguing from the want of natural impressions derived from it. She is a fine woman without the feelings which you prize more in one than all the acquirement. Davis and I had a sumptuous dinner given to us, and wine of which we drank quite enough. I felt so fatigued afterwards that I soon retired.

[Philadelphia]

FRIDAY. 27TH.

Up early this morning and off to Philadelphia in the boat. Travelling between the great cities is now such a matter of fact affair that it is needless to describe it. The disagreeable portions of it arise from the crowd and the roughness of the companions with which one is thrown. We crossed from Amboy to Bordentown and then came to the City in a boat, arriving there at about two o'clock to dine.

Went by mistake to the North American Hotel but the rooms were so good I thought it needless to move. After dinner, Mrs. Henry called with T. K. Davis who went to his uncle's. The day was perfectly lovely, and I went out to walk after which I took my Louisa to the Museum. An uncommonly good one. So much fatigued in the evening that I went to bed early.

[Baltimore]

SATURDAY 28TH.

The weather is certainly very superior to our's, being free from the admixture of chilly East winds. We started a little before 7 in the Steamer for Wilmington, which we reached at about 10 and from thence took the cars to Baltimore. Nobody of our acquaintance with us but Madame Caradori Allan and her husband. We reached Baltimore at about one and found Gorham Brooks waiting for us at the depot. With him we went to his house. His Wife looks thin and anxious which is traceable to the condition of their younger child, which suffers from an eruption on the skin. Dined and spent the afternoon with him. Evening, Mr. West called to see Mrs. B., a painter of some merit. I walked down to Barnum's to see T. K. Davis who came in with the Afternoon cars. Retire early quite fatigued.

SUNDAY. 29TH.

Day fine. After breakfast called upon T. K. Davis and walked with him to the Catholic College[1] where he wanted to see a youth, the son of Mrs. Henry, a fine looking boy enough. Thence back to Mrs. Brooks' with whom we went to Church.

The service was well performed and affected me as it always does. Dr. Wyatt, the Clergyman preached a Sermon upon the necessity of faith and illustrated it by a variety of positions which were tolerably ingenious. He alluded to the disorganizing tendencies of the country with an exhortation to the practice of the Christian principles as the only effective counteraction. The discourse was not such as we are accustomed to hear, but agreeable to the usual strain of this Church.[2] After the service, we accompanied Gorham Brooks to the Water works and reservoir at Jones' falls and enjoyed a pleasant walk. Dinner quite pleasant, after which another walk and home.

Baltimore is a neat looking place in the upper end and on this visit recommends itself more to my feelings, but you see the hand of slavery in it clearly enough. Indolence is the characteristic, and this indolence leads to negligence internally and externally. So fatigued that I was glad to retire early.

[1] St. Mary's College and Theological Seminary was located on Pennsylvania Avenue, just north of Franklin Street (*Matchett's Baltimore Director, 1835/6*, Baltimore, 1835).

[2] St. Paul's Church, of which Rev. William Wyatt was rector (J. Thomas Scharf, *The Chronicles of Baltimore*, Baltimore, 1874, p. 30).

[*Washington*]

MONDAY. 30TH.

Colder. I left Baltimore at nine, and my Wife who is to remain two days longer. I left it rather willingly because I thought I saw both upon the spirits of Gorham Brooks and of his Wife a burden in the condition of their child which made visitors a little fatiguing. The effort to be attentive and civil is rather perplexing and provoking in such cases, I know, and although no attention has in my case been spared, yet I was glad to escape from them.

Met Davis, and by noon we got to Washington. J. P. Kennedy, the newly elected Whig member from Baltimore was in the cars and was cheered on his departure. Politics now run very high.

Found the carriage waiting for me, so I immediately went to my fathers, where I found my mother and the family well. T. B. Johnson came in, who looks far from sick certainly. I started directly to find Davis who had gone to Gadsby's, but not being successful I walked on to the Capitol; found my father speaking upon the duelling question; the attention of the house very great but I could not stop. Back to Gadsby's and being more successful this time, we went together to call upon the French Minister who gives a ball tomorrow night, and to find better lodgings for him.

My father did not get home until very late so that we dined by candle light and after it, I had a long conversation with him about Mr. Biddle and the course of his bank. To bed, therefore very late.

TUESDAY. MAY I.

Warm. Davis came down according to agreement after breakfast and we went in the carriage with my father to the Capitol. But the debate being rather dull, we drove to the race ground to see the humours of that scene so novel to a New England man like him. The race itself was a failure, although run for very high stakes, but the characteristics of the people were to be perceived very easily. And what a marked contrast to the Yankee. Who that observes it can fail to see the causes of our National dissensions.

Home walking. Davis came to dinner, and Mr. Fry in afterwards.[1] Political conversation. The condition of the Administration, its duties and its errors.

Evening with my father to the ball at the French minister's, Mr. E. de Pontois. A very crowded affair, but ten years have changed the face of society here. I found very few whom I knew. And the general aspect of society was altered as I thought for the worse, but this may be only in my imagination. Home early before supper.

[1] Nathaniel Frye Jr. was LCA's brother-in-law; see vol. 1:4.

WEDNESDAY. 2D.

The morning was showery but mild. I went out in the carriage with my father, who on his way to the Capitol was kind enough to stop at the President's with me to make a call. We were admitted and found him alone in the room where my father used to have his study, at least upon our entrance the persons whom he had with him left him.

He is much altered from what he was, looks older and as he grows old his face takes a meaner expression. I was disposed to watch him with attention inasmuch as his character has been singularly represented to the world. Upon our first entry, I thought I perceived a slight flutter in his manner by no means indicative of the equability ascribed to him, and this did not wear off until my father himself led the conversation into English politics. He appeared here exceedingly well informed and skilful in the denouement of party tactics. He afterwards answered some questions made by my father upon home matters, but rather briefly and not with ease.

I left him glad of having had this opportunity of seeing him and we then went on to the Capitol, where having left my father I went on to the depot to wait for my Wife who arrived in the Cars and accompanied me home. Having left her, I then walked to the Capitol to listen to the debates.

In the House my father was speaking who was followed by Thomas of Maryland and then by Boon of Indiana who seemed excessively enraged by one of my father's sarcasms. This led to calls for yeas and nays and questions of amendment which destroyed the interest, and so we transferred ourselves to the Senate. We were quite fortunate here, as we came just as the debate was going on upon Mr. Clay's resolution to receive bills of specie paying banks. We heard Col. Benton, Mr. Clay, Mr. Preston, J. Davis, Mr. Calhoun and Mr. Niles in such a manner as to form a good idea of each. They all speak well but there is a great difference as well in the matter as the manner which is worthy of more study. On the whole we were glad of this opportunity of seeing the leaders in the Senate so favorably. Home rather fatigued. Evening short after dinner and I retired early.

THURSDAY. 3D.

Pleasant day. I rode early with my father to the Capitol and thence down to seventh Street where I stopped to call at Mrs. Latimer's for

Davis. Found him sitting with A. H. Everett and after a short talk we went down to call upon Mr. Clay. Found him alone and had quite an agreeable visit. He led the conversation to Mr. Webster in a way somewhat curious, and appeared to be sounding Davis' own opinions. We left him and went round to call upon Mr. Rives. I was induced to this by a very civil invitation of his when I met him yesterday as I was returning from the Capitol. He was not at home. I then parted from Davis and returned home, where I joined my Mother and Wife in making visits in the Carriage. We called upon Mrs. Madison, and my Aunts Mrs. Frye and Mrs. Smith whom we found at home, and left cards with Mrs. Forsyth and Mrs. Poinsett. Returned after a short ride and a little shopping. Dinner and evening at home.

FRIDAY. 4TH.

Rainy day. I passed a large part of last evening as I forgot to state at the Concert of Madame Caradori Allan. The music was ill selected and pleased me very little. But in witnessing the number of persons present I could not help being struck with a repetition of the same appearance of change in the face of Society. Here was an abundance of persons no one of whom hardly had figured upon this stage ten years ago, and those who had been here were now dissipated, they cannot be dead.

At home all day. Occupied in making a draft of a letter to the Editor of the Courier occasioned by the articles in his paper so anxiously disavowing any responsibility for my letters. I think to assume them to myself in a perfectly distinct manner, and to take the opportunity to restate my principle of action in an intelligible form.[1]

The day was such as to prevent my going out and to keep us all very quiet at home. Nothing of course transpired. Evening I sat up until rather late writing my final copy of my proposed letter.

[1] Contrary to CFA's impressions, his letters to Biddle in the *Courier* had, during his absence from Boston, been given considerable attention by the press. On 28 April the *Courier* reprinted (p. 2, col. 1) part of an article from the Washington *Globe* (23 April, p. 3, col. 4) praising the letters and the *Courier* for printing them. This was followed by excerpts from a *Boston Centinel* article attacking the *Courier* for them and by reference to a similar attack in the *Boston Post*. To these, Buckingham attached a further disclaimer that the views of "A Citizen" represented in any way the *Courier*'s position on the currency question. CFA, in his present letter to the editor, dated 3 May and which would appear in the *Courier* on the 11th (p. 2, cols. 1–2), made explicit, both in the text and in signing it "A Citizen," its identity of authorship with the "Letters to Biddle." Sole responsibility for the views expressed in those letters is taken, and the *Courier* is explicitly absolved of sharing those views. The author denies any loco-focoism or any desire to defend the administration, and indeed any party purposes. "I am, individually, not a Whig—but neither can I be reckoned among the

Tories.... It may have been noted down, locofoco, by men who would consider Adam Smith, Hamilton or Gallatin locofoco, if extracts from their writings should now be arrayed against them." His design was to counter the mistaken policies of Biddle and to support those banks which were disposed to resume specie payments. He had been convinced by the experience "that the expression of independent opinion, in the newspaper press of the day, is so difficult as to impose upon an editor, willing like yourself to allow it, a task he should not hastily be called to perform."

SATURDAY 5TH.

Weather doubtful, more than half the time showery. T. K. Davis called in the morning and sat talking until noon. We then accompanied my father to see the studio of a sculptor by name Pettrich who called here this morning and who is seeking for employment. He had a bust of Commodore Rodgers which was very good, two of a couple of Indian chiefs done with great spirit and some sketches in charcoal on his walls of the same which appeared to me well done. I think this man has much talent.[1]

From here we went into Pennsylvania Avenue and I parted from Davis with the object of making a call upon Mr. J. Pope. He is now a Representative from Kentucky.[2] I found him in a poor room enough, but enjoying it alone. The surprise to me is that men who live comfortably and even luxuriously at home can submit to spend half their time here in the Metropolis in such lodgings. Conversation mainly political. Pope is disposed to [be] non committal. He has no fondness for any man among the leaders, and opposes the Administration just enough to keep himself well at home. He appears to be shrewd in his judgment, but not great either by nature or education.

Home. Dine at the President's by invitation. Mr. Tallmadge and his daughter with his brother the Senator, Mr. Howard, his Wife, and daughter and Miss Swan of Baltimore, Mr. Rives, Mr. Legaré of S.C., T. K. Davis, my Wife and myself with two sons of the President made the company. A small dinner in what used to be called the yellow sitting room, next to the Circular room. The house looks in much better condition than it ever did before within my knowledge. The dinner was therefore very conservative in its character and for a democratic President sufficiently aristocratic. Mr. Van Buren is very well fitted for the ceremonials of Office but I cannot help mistrusting upon more important points a great deficiency within. Perhaps I may be in error. I sat between the sons of the President, two youths of little acquirement and less talent. The dinner was fatiguing and I was glad to get away at ten o'clock home.

Of all the gentlemen whom I have met with here Mr. Rives is the man whose personal address has pleased me most. On my return I found my father reading the Journal of Commerce sent to him containing the letters to Mr. Biddle all in one paper.[3] I had expected that press would from its slightly neutral position transfer them as it has done.

[1] Ferdinand Friedrich August Pettrich, a native of Dresden and a student of Thorwaldsen, had come to Washington in 1835. His most productive years would be spent in Rome (Emmanuel Bénézit, *Dictionnaire ... des peintres, sculpteurs*, 8 vols., Paris, 1960). JQA, in his account of the visit, provides a more detailed survey of the contents of the gallery (Diary, 5 May).

[2] On John Pope, U.S. representative from Ky. and another of LCA's brothers-in-law, see vol. 1:28. He had been territorial governor of Arkansas until 1835.

[3] The *New York Journal of Commerce* reprinted CFA's "Letters to Biddle" on 3 May, p. 1, cols. 1–5.

SUNDAY 6TH.

The weather is constantly showery and unpleasant. I went out early this morning to call upon T. K. Davis at Mrs. Latimer's. Found him sitting with the Prussian Chargé d'Affaires, the Baron de Roenne. Upon my entering, Davis said they had been talking of my pamphlets, and thereupon the Baron took occasion to speak with great politeness of them and said that he had procured them when at Northampton and forwarded them to his Government. This as the testimony of an impartial witness is the most gratifying thing I have yet met with. The Pamphlets have been smothered by party in this Country, but that they deserved a better fate I have hope in believing.

A. H. Everett spoke of my letters to Mr. Biddle, and of a notice in the Globe which I looked at. This is a trap. It alludes to my former pamphlet upon Executive patronage in such a manner as either to desire to draw me into the appearance of having taken a side or to get my father's name associated with this answer to Mr. Biddle.[1] I did not like the notice as well as that in the Journal of Commerce.

T. K. Davis accompanied me to see Mr. Fletcher, our representative whose position since his unfortunate affair has made me feel some sympathy for him.[2] He was quite civil and although manifestly soured towards the Whigs and their leader in our State seemed to be in tolerable spirits.

From here we went to Church at the Presbyterian church formerly Mr. Baker's.[3] A young man preached from Isaiah 55. 2. "Wherefore do ye spend money for that which is not bread, and your labour for that which satisfieth not?" A sermon marked by the characteristics of this

36

school, plain, dealing much in ordinary illustration, direct and delivered extemporaneously in a very animated manner, at the same time, very common place and a little minatory.

We returned home in a shower and then Davis and I called to see Mr. Woodbury. Found him at his door and was introduced into a room where was one of the Van Buren's flirting with the daughter. A short visit. Woodbury is a good looking man but with a half closed, sneaking eye, which I would never trust. Dine early and conversation.

Davis went at five, and I spent the rest of the day reading a discourse of Buckminster's. Luke 8. 18. "Take heed how ye hear." Upon the little effect of pulpit instruction, it's causes and remedies mainly on the part of hearers. I somewhat doubt whether it is not difficult to define the value of pulpit instruction. It runs into all the details of life with a current scarcely perceptible. We expect too much from it when we imagine it will rectify all the evil inclinations of man.

[1] The comment in the Washington *Globe* headed "Mr. Biddle's Letter" (5 May, p. 3, col. 3) read: "We have had occasion to allude ... to the able articles which appeared in the *Boston Courier* ... in reply to Mr. Biddle's notorious letter to Mr. [J. Q.] Adams. They are attributed to the same vigorous and discriminating hand which dissected so skilfully, two years ago, Mr. Webster's project for depriving the Executive of the appointing and removing power, in a series of papers which appeared originally in the Boston Advocate, and were republished at the time in The Globe. Mr. Buckingham ... is now laboring with might and main to shake off the responsibility for these articles."

[2] On Congressman Richard Fletcher's difficulties, see entry for 18 Dec. 1837, above.

[3] That is, the Second Presbyterian Church whose pulpit had been occupied by Rev. Daniel Baker; see vol. 1:77.

MONDAY. 7TH.

A continuation of our weather. I walked up to the Capitol after seeing Mr. Pope at home who called to visit my Wife. The debate upon the duel still continues. Mr. Bynum, Mr. Menifee and Mr. Duncan all let loose their feelings upon the subject,[1] they are each implicated in the transaction and the course of the debate has brought the burden heavily upon two of them. Bynum seemed most to feel the weight of my father's speech, and therefore directed his fury most against him. But the feeling of the majority seemed to run most decidedly against the course of the Administration party so far as it was possible to judge from the secondary questions decided today. Finally a motion to lay upon the table and print was made and decided as a test vote against the Administration by twenty majority. We left the House for a short time to go to the Senate where a brief discussion of the bill to sell the bonds of the U.S. Bank took place between Wright and Webster. Then home. After dinner, Davis came in, and two gentlemen, Messrs. Campbell and Smith came in with Hull, also Mr. Frye. We had some very good glee singing which finished the evening and we did not retire until late.

¹ Representatives Jesse A. Bynum of N.C., Richard H. Menefee of Ky., and Alexander Duncan of Ohio.

TUESDAY. 8TH.

Weather cold as usual. I was at home all the morning, particularly as my father returned from the House with the intelligence of the death of a member, Mr. Lawler of Alabama. Occupied the time in bringing up the Arrears of my Diary and in writing a letter to Mr. Brooks. My Wife received three from her friends in Boston last evening, one of which was from him and this I answered.¹

Our dinner rather earlier than usual for the sake of riding out to Woodley where my Uncle Mr. Johnson lives. This is a little secluded country place beyond Georgetown where he has retired consulting his taste for solitude. My mother and Mary, my Wife and myself. Found him there but quickly following us came Mr. Pope and Mrs. Hellen.² So the party being large we returned and took tea at Mrs. Smith's. Home by ten.

¹ The letter to Peter C. Brooks is missing; that from him to ABA, 4 May, is in the Adams Papers. It brought a full account of the good health of each of the three Adams boys.
² LCA's sister Adelaide was the second wife of Walter Hellen.

WEDNESDAY. 9TH.

Continued cold and raw weather. T. K. Davis came in and sat for an hour talking of his various conferences with individuals. I am satisfied that the whole party which goes under the name of conservative is waiting to see whether Mr. Van Buren will not be forced from his present position and obliged to take theirs. I advised Davis of the opinions held by my father, and stated very freely my own. As at present advised, I saw nothing to authorize me to vary from my preceding course.

We then walked to the Capitol, calling on the way to see Govr. Dickerson and Mr. Legaré. We found the latter at home and had a pleasant visit. He is a dashing talker, with many new ideas, but rather brilliant than solid.¹ Out of an allusion to slavery made by Davis there

grew a discussion between us which lasted until we reached the Capitol.

They were engaged in the ceremonial of the funeral of the member.[2] After it was over, we returned and I dropped in to see the Indian Gallery of Mr. Catlin. This is a collection of Portraits of various American Indians of different tribes, and pictures illustrative of their principal ceremonies as well as landscapes. There are also various articles of dress &c. which Catlin has collected in his personal travels. The whole is curious as a specimen of one great branch of man, but Indians after all are but Indians. They represent the first stages of civilization which are by no means, properly considered, the most interesting.[3]

Home to dinner. Evening, a small party by invitation of Mrs. Gilpin. Principally members of the Administration party and the Corps diplomatique. Very dull. Home, and to bed quite fatigued.

[1] Hugh Swinton Legaré, as well as representing South Carolina in the Congress, was a founder and editor of the *Southern Review* in Charleston (*DAB*).

[2] A broadside of the order of service for Representative Joab Lawler of Ala. is in the Adams Papers.

[3] After his visit to the "Wigwam," JQA wrote: "The Portraits have no merit as works of art. The War dances and Council fires are caricatures of disgusting nature. The views on the Missouri river from 1200 to 1900 miles above St. Louis are very indifferent landscapes, and the buffaloes hunted by wolves are not comparable to Snyder's Boar hunting. The collection is perhaps valuable as unique" (Diary, 4 May).

THURSDAY 10TH.

Cool morning. Mr. Frye came in and asked me to accompany him to see the Mill property of my father, so we walked there. A pretty spot situated upon a narrow creek, but the property wretchedly out of repair. The dam which had been carried away is now repairing in a thorough manner, but it would hardly seem worth while to attempt it. Complaints on the part of the Miller of encroachments, on all sides. My father is a wretched provider of his own affairs.[1]

I returned home and then went in the carriage with the ladies to the foot of the Capitol, on the way to the House of Representatives. The report upon the duel still the subject of debate. Mr. Underwood was making a speech as I went in, after whom Mr. Thomas repeated his proposal to lay on the table and print. This brought on a series of manœuvres on the part of either party, which came very near bringing a regular flare-up in which my father promised to make a prominent figure. But the Speaker was quite collected and decided so rapidly as to smother the fire. So after a series of Yeas and nays, Thomas carried his motion and thus terminates the subject.[2] T. K. Davis and Mr. Campbell in after dinner. But I was tired and went to bed.

[1] The Columbian Mills (flour and meal) in the District of Columbia, acquired by JQA in 1823, had from the beginning proved a severe drain upon his capital; CFA had repeatedly and without success urged its sale or abandonment. See vols. 3:104; 4:16–17, 91–92, 369–370; 5:355; and Bemis, *JQA*, 2:197–200.

[2] CFA is in error. The two-part motion of Francis Thomas of Md. to lay the majority and minority reports on duelling on the table but to print both reports lost when the vote on the first part was adverse. A motion to adjourn without action on the report prevailed (*Congressional Globe*, 25th Cong., 2d sess., p. 355–356).

FRIDAY. 11TH.

A cold but fine, clear day. Occupied in the morning in writing and then accompanied the ladies to the Capitol, where they were going to look at the two houses. In the Representatives hall, Mr. Cambreleng was making an opening upon the bill to authorize the issue of Treasury Notes. His tone was by no means conciliatory, and he took a sort of credit to the Administration for the present state of things which bordered a little upon the ludicrous. C. Cushing of Massachusetts made a brief reply during which we transferred ourselves to the Senate where a lazy debate was going on about the District Banks.

The ladies then left us and I returned to the House where Mr. Thompson of S. Carolina was then speaking—a premeditated Essay upon the general subject with a very occasional allusion to the matter in hand. Thompson has not gone with the rest of the Carolinians and Mr. Calhoun in their new policy, and being thus in a degree hazarded in his own State, he takes the present opportunity to make his justification.[1] Before he had finished the Committee rose[2] and I walked home. Mr. Frye here in the evening. Conversation general.

[1] Waddy Thompson Jr., taking issue with the Administration's bill to issue ten million dollars in Treasury Notes, sought to justify his position both on constitutional and theoretical grounds, proposing instead that the government seek direct loans (*Congressional Globe*, 25th Cong., 2d sess., p. 365).

[2] The House was sitting as a Committee of the Whole on the state of the Union (same, p. 363).

SATURDAY 12TH.

A lovely day. I walked up early to the Capitol, calling on my way at Mrs. Latimer's, to see Baron de Roenne, who had left a card for me some time ago. Much conversation with him upon the state of our political and financial affairs. Banking and Texas. On the latter subject he seemed unwilling to put much confidence in the professions of the

Administration. I am inclined to think this is true. The Government acts upon no public question fully up to it's professions.

Called for T. K. Davis but he was not at home. At the Capitol, Mr. Thompson, after a little preliminary business, continued his Speech. Then came Rhett of Carolina, a high flying disciple of the new school. Nothing more violent nor more absurd than his speech could well be conceived. Menifee and Southgate of Kentucky replied in the manner for which they are peculiar and with much point.[1] Then came an apparent struggle between the two parties to settle the question or delay it, and at seven o'clock I left them in the full expectation of a late Session. I could not help thinking all the time, of the fact that in the anxiety to play the game, the final object was perpetually going out of sight. Dinner late and short evening.

[1] JQA recorded that Menefee characterized Rhett's speech as a "volcanic eruption," and Southgate called it an "earthquake." JQA himself wrote of its "ranting" and its "emphatic inconsistency and absurdity." "In delivering this rhodomontade, he threw himself into convulsive attitudes reminding me of those by which Satan is said to have been discovered at the gate of Paradise in Milton's Poem" (Diary, 12 May). The substance of the speeches for and against the issuance of Treasury Notes, by R. Barnwell Rhett of S.C. and Richard H. Menefee and William W. Southgate of Ky., is reported in the *Congressional Globe*, 25th Cong., 2d sess., p. 369–370.

SUNDAY. 13TH.

My father did not get up from the House until nearly two o'clock this morning and yet the Administration party did not succeed in carrying their bill. The game continued, sharply contested by votes of only one, two or three majority. And after all, with what object, merely to embarrass Mr. Van Buren and Mr. Woodbury.[1] And for the sake of this, the Country pays it's thousands.

After breakfast, I filled up Arrears, and then attended divine service at the Presbyterian church with my father. A young man whose name I did not know preached from John 5. 40. "Ye will not come to me that ye might have life." The various reasons for irreligion, fear, shame, pleasure &c. discussed in an ordinary way, but I still think in manner better than the clergymen with us.

Read a Sermon of Buckminster which I think is one of the best I have yet read. Philip. 1. 9. "And this I pray, that your love may abound yet more and more." Upon the different effect of reason and of feeling in religion, the excess of coldness produced by one and of vehemence or fanaticism resulting from the other. The introduction of the affections in religion is one of the most difficult and yet the most necessary of operations. Indeed I would go further and apply my remark to life in general. Reason is a sure guide only when in conjunction with that moral feeling which is if not originated at least in its perfect state has been much cultivated by the action of the affections. There are passages in this discourse which run very much in my way of thinking.

At three we went by invitation to Woodley, Mr. Johnson's residence to dine with him. My father and I accompanied Governor J. Pope, and the ladies came with I. Hull. This place was once a pretty country seat of one of the Maryland planters but now partakes of their decay. It has fallen into the hands of one of the french purveyors of the Metropolis, who has made a little out of the foreign legations. Our dinner was a formal one consisting of every thing that could be given, and the wine was abundant. We returned home by eight. I found my letter to the Courier sent from here on the 5th was published in the paper of the 11th. To bed early.

[1] The opponents of the bill authorizing the Treasury to issue notes sought to show that the proposal was dictated by the Treasury's near insolvency (same, p. 370–372).

MONDAY. 14TH.

A fine day but very warm. T. K. Davis called and sat an hour, after which I walked with him to the Capitol. He gave me an account of his visit to Mr. Rives, from whence I infer that the Conservatives feel the vanity of their middle position very much. In politics as regulated by parties, there can be no influence that is not exerted in one direction or the other. So Mr. Rives who has already sacrificed much of his personal feeling to attain it by now stopping looks only weak.[1] The experiment of making no sacrifice is one which either has not yet been made or if it has been, has proved unsuccessful. And yet this is the very experiment towards which circumstances as well as my own temper are driving me. My experience of political life here is such as to make me very lukewarm in my exertions to embrace it. Davis seems to have become more anxious to do so since his arrival here but I confess I am not.[2]

At the Capitol, we were rather poorly entertained for two or three hours by opposition speakers against time. Then returned home to dine parting with Davis who positively goes tomorrow. I shall regret this a good deal, and indeed feel much inclined homeward by it.

Went to the Theatre with the ladies to hear the Somnambula, and Caradori as the prima donna. Brough as Rhodolpho. The piece was better performed than I expected, and although I think Mrs. Wood a more brilliant singer yet this lady is in excellent taste. The house crowded and fashionable.

¹ William Cabell Rives, senator from Va., failing in the attempt to reconcile his convictions with the political necessities in his state had resigned his seat in the Senate in 1835 rather than vote as instructed against Jackson's removal of the federal deposits from the Bank. Re-elected in 1837 as a supporter of Jackson's and Van Buren's fiscal policies, he again asserted his independence by opposing the specie circular and the sub-treasury system, by advocating the deposit of federal monies in the state banks, and

by leading in the formation of an independent group of "Conservatives" in Virginia (*DAB*). Apparently he now regarded the moves as having been made at the cost of his political effectiveness.
² The example of Rives' career and their own experiences in Washington seem to have brought CFA and T. K. Davis to a parting over whether it was then possible for a person of convictions to seek political office without sacrificing personal commitments to the demands of party.

TUESDAY 15TH.

The weather is waxing warmer. I went out early this morning and made a call upon Dr. Thomas returning a visit from him, and also one from A. H. Everett who is still up in his room, although nearly recovered. Much conversation with him upon the state of politics here and in Boston. I stated very frankly my difficulties as I always do and expressed my unwillingness to put confidence in an Administration which drew it's support from a sacrifice of the North to the sectional pride of Mr. Calhoun. He told me that Mr. Van Buren had written me a note acknowledging my Pamphlets which note I never received. Also that Mr. Foster wrote to him that the Advocate was to be abandoned, and complained of the doubtful course of the Government. What a turbid state.

My difficulties are of a peculiar character. I want confidence in every thing and every body, and feel almost as hostile to one party on principle as I do to the other from feeling. I trust in an overruling providence both for the country and for myself.

Went to the Capitol. Mr. R. Biddle was speaking and I very soon became interested in his argument. Indeed it is the only one which I have heard which is of a high character. He took up in turn each of the Administration party and certainly exposed them in a manner which could not be exceeded. There was an elegance of style and a facility of imagery which is uncommon where mere talent seems to be almost universal.

After he ceased Mr. Bell took up the debate and as I think little of him, I returned home. T. K. Davis really went this morning and I felt his absence. Mr. Everett says he [Davis] has been very well received and made a favorable impression. So far, so good.

After dinner, again to the play. Mrs. Smith taking the place of my Mother whose visit to the theatre last evening proved too much for her, and she has been unwell ever since. The Barber of Seville. Caradori as Rosina, Walton as Figaro, Pearson as Almaviva and Brough as Basil. The piece quite tolerably sustained. Pearson did well in parts but he spoilt the Quintette at the close of the second act. The trio "Zitti, zitti," very well indeed. Caradori also sung Una voce, very well. On the whole the Barber carried off the piece most effectively. Home late.

WEDNESDAY 16TH.

The heat of the Theatre last night made my head ach and I got up with it which made a bad prospect for me for the day. I of course tried to go out to get the benefit of the air. Called on the way to see Madame Caradori, found her not yet up but saw her husband, then left a card for Mr. Cushing and went on to the Capitol.

A speech from Mr. Hoffman, attacking the South Carolinians, then a plain, sensible address from Mr. Jones of Virginia on the Administration side, to which Mr. Wise made a reply. Hoffman is a mere declaimer, but I think Wise may become a great man if he tries to learn wisdom by experience. The interest in the debate appeared to flag a little and my head disabled me from relishing as much of it as I otherwise should.

At four I left Wise speaking to return home. The sun was scorching, and upon my reaching the house I felt much exhausted by the fatigue. My system has become so accustomed to the bracing cold of our Eastern Atmosphere that the enervating influence of this air is almost intolerable.

After dinner, the ladies went in the carriage and I accompanied them to Mr. Frye's where the members of the family were assembled, excepting my father who was detained until too late at the Capitol and my mother unwell. We had cards and then a pretty Supper and music from I. Hull and Campbell, after which we went home.

THURSDAY 17TH.

I felt so much fatigued that I almost determined upon remaining at home all day, but although warm the day was cloudy with drops of rain so as to make the walking less difficult. After writing up the arrears of my Diary, I went in the Carriage with the ladies calling at Mrs. Thornton's,[1] as far as Claggett's shop where I got out and walked from thence to the Capitol.

The question was upon the passage of the Treasury Note bill which had been squeezed through last night, but was arrested on a reconsideration this morning. It was clear that this was a close party test in a full house and as such excited great interest. The vote turned out 110 in the affirmative and 109 in the negative to which the Speaker added his vote thus producing a tie and defeating the reconsideration. Thus it appears pretty plain that allowing the Administration nearly all the Carolinians, they are still in a minority in the House.

After this was well over, the House went upon some matter connected with the question of Northwest boundary, and Mr. Cushing went upon it[2] in so dry a way that I transferred myself to the Senate where they were discussing as drily the District Bank charters.

So I returned and found my father up making an explanatory Speech respecting our boundary titles to the Westward in the course of which he went over much interesting matter as well relating to the history of the discovery, as to certain cabinet proceedings of which he gave a pleasing sketch, and of his own agency therein. It was amusing to observe how he collected his audience from a handful, for the excitement of the preceding days had exhausted the House, to a little collection around him. Shortly afterwards the House adjourned but I left beforehand. Quiet evening at home. A curious notice in the Boston Courier of my letters which is too flattering.[3]

[1] On Mrs. William Thornton, see vol. 1:36.

[2] While the Oregon boundary question as a national issue was still several years in the future, the numbers involved in the movement westward during the 1830s had already served to bring to general attention the land claims of Great Britain and the United States in that area that remained unresolved. Most recently, the President had addressed the matter of title in a message. When the message was taken up in the House, Caleb Cushing, representative from Mass., spoke, moving to instruct the committee considering the question "to inquire into the expediency of establishing a post on the Columbia river ... and the expediency of making further provision ... to prevent any intermeddling by any foreign power with the Indians there" (*Congressional Globe*, 25th Cong., 2d sess., p. 380).

[3] In the issue of 15 May, p. 2, col. 5, appeared a note with the heading, "A Second Junius": "We do not believe that our correspondent, 'A Citizen,' will thank us for giving him this title, knowing as we do that he has no desire to be called one of the first or best writers of his day, but we have been somewhat amused at the conjectures of many of our friends as to who he is.... We have invariably refused to say yes or no to the questions propounded on the subject. A contemporary has attributed the articles ... to a distinguished politician of the present day, while some others attribute them to two or three gentlemen who have retired from political life, or to young men who may be called, perhaps, unfledged politi-

cians. If our correspondent is to be a second Junius, we intend to be a second Woodfall." (Henry Sampson Woodfall, printer and publisher of the *Public Adver-* *tiser* in whose columns the Junius letters appeared, disclaimed agreement with their content and steadfastly refused to identify their author [*DNB*].)

FRIDAY 18TH.

We had showers in the morning which moderated the heat a little. Mr. Frye called after breakfast and I gave him the papers of Lt. Casey sent to settle T. B. A.'s affairs. I then accompanied my father in the carriage to the capitol, returning the visits of the Russian Minister[1] on the way.

But the House did not appear disposed to take any thing up so I walked home, calling upon Mr. Meredith who had left town[2] and upon Johnson Hellen.[3] The latter I found in his room complaining of his condition much. He does not look sick, but has the appearance of a heautontimorumenos.[4] I could not help pitying the condition to which a man can by his own art reduce himself. He reminds me much of the passage of years. After a slight conversation, the entrance of a client interrupted us and I promised to call again.

Home where I amused the rest of the day in reading the report upon the West India Emancipated Colonies, and the Bank Report made by Mr. Woodbury.[5] Quiet evening at home.

[1] Baron de Maltitz.
[2] Probably George Augustus Meredith, a Harvard classmate of CFA; see vol. 2:227.
[3] On Johnson Hellen, a nephew of LCA and brother of Mrs. JA2, see vol. 5:195.
[4] A self-tormentor, adapted from the title of a play by Terence (*Webster*, 2d edn.); and see vol. 5:265.

[5] An essay on the results of emancipation in the British colonies in the West Indies was in the current issue of the *Eclectic Review* of London (68:450, 532). The text of the Bank Report of Levi Woodbury as transmitted by the President to the Senate on 10 May appeared in the Washington *Globe*, 11 May, p. 2, col. 1.

SATURDAY. 19TH.

A very fine day. I spent it very quietly at home with the exception of a long walk. Read more of the Emancipation Report and of the Bank pamphlet of Mr. Woodbury. The first although manifestly ex parte yet carries with it a vast amount of evidence of the practicability of immediate abolition. I think it tends to confirm me in my preconceived notions upon that subject. My walk extended to the Potomac River and bridge, over ground frequently crossed by me as a boy, the recollections of which are pleasant enough, and yet slightly melancholy from the passage of time.

I am beginning to feel the want of my occupations, and to look with a slight impatience to the hour of return. This will, I hope not be delayed beyond the week after next. Nothing of interest in Congress. News from Philadelphia of the destruction by a mob of the hall lately erected for free discussion.[1] Such is the nature and extent of American liberty. A call from General Macomb.[2] Evening at home. Visits from Captain and Mrs. Williams and Mr. Campbell. After which I read part of Senator Wright's report.

[1] The news was contained in a letter from Benjamin Lundy to JQA with an accompanying broadside that sets out in detail the action of the anti-abolitionist mob in setting fire to and destroying the new Pennsylvania Hall during a meeting of the Female Anti-Slavery Society addressed by Angelina Grimké Weld on 17 May (Lundy to JQA, 18 May, Adams Papers; JQA, Diary, 19 May).

[2] Maj. Gen. Alexander Macomb, commander in chief of the Army.

SUNDAY. 20TH.

A fine day. Morning passed in writing Diary. Then to Church at St. John's. Service performed by Mr. Hawley[1] and Sermon by a Mr. Slaughter from Virginia. John 7. 17. "If any man will do his will, he shall know of the doctrine, whether it be of God, or whether I speak of myself." An extremely common place Sermon as I thought it upon the evidences of Christianity and the duties it imposes, predicated upon a mistaken view of it's character. But his manner was effective and I found afterwards he had made some impression. The difference between us and the South seems to be in matters of Oratory, that their manner is better than their matter, and our matter is better than our manner. The audience was quite fashionable.

Home. T. J. Frye[2] and Miss Johnson dined with us. Afternoon, read a Sermon of Buckminster's. Proverbs. 25. 28. "He that hath no rule over his own spirit, is like a City that is broken down, and without walls." Upon the government of the mind through the thoughts, the tongue, the appetites, and passions. An excellent discourse and very just.

Evening, a ride, and thence to see Mr. and Mrs. Gilpin with our ladies. Met there Mr. Ingersoll of Philadelphia, Mr. Prime of New York, and Mr. O'Sullivan. Conversation not material. Mr. Gilpin showed me his library which is a fine one, and we had some talk of the classics.[3] Home at ten and retired early.

[1] Rev. William Hawley, rector of St. John's Episcopal Church; see vol. 2:7.

[2] Thomas Baker Johnson Frye, the son of Nathaniel Frye; see vol. 1:63.

[3] Henry Dilworth Gilpin of Penna. was solicitor of the Treasury and later attorney general. His library and scholarly tastes were noteworthy (*DAB*).

MONDAY 21ST.

Warm, cloudy morning. After writing my Diary, I went up to the House of Representatives, calling on my way at Judge Cranch's.[1] There being nothing of interest in that body, I went to the Senate where upon the presentation of petitions Mr. Clay took occasion to bring forward his views of a National Bank.

He read them from a paper, an unusual course with him and showing the meditation with which it had been concerted. The points were important and well calculated as I thought for his object. Buchanan in reply attempted to turn his flank by assuming that the place was New York for the sake of rallying Pennsylvania jealousy, but he did not succeed. After a lively conversation, the matter dropped and I returned home.

Early dinner for the sake of going with the ladies to a regatta held at the Navy yard. Great numbers of persons there including almost all the official personages. We did not leave the Carriage, but procured a situation very favorable for seeing. There were five or six boats entered, five of which started, and moved to a flag boat stationed at a distant point round which they went and returned. The rounding was the act of trial and in that a white boat succeeded in gaining the advantage. After it was over, we concluded not to remain for the festivities but returned home. Evening at home. Retired early.

[1] William Cranch, judge of the federal Circuit Court of the District of Columbia, was a nephew of AA and a Harvard classmate of JQA; see vol. 5:107.

TUESDAY 22D.

A very hot, windy morning. I felt so much fatigued as to be very unwilling to undertake any long walk in the sun, so that I decided upon remaining in the house. This detention is in this place quite disagreeable as all the places of resort are at a distance from each other, and thus make motion to them laborious and fatiguing. I begin to be very impatient and wish to return. My own occupations on the whole cannot be long supplied by any dissipation.

Wrote Diary, and a letter to Boston,[1] also reading the Bank Reports of the State of Alabama. Made a call upon Mrs. Smith and sat an hour conversing in a very easy way. She would have been well calculated for a much higher situation in society.

Evening, accompanied the ladies to a party at Miss Tayloe's given to the bride, Mrs. Kane. The party was small and composed entirely of strangers. Washington is certainly much changed from what it was.

There is an absence of the haut ton which it used to have, and a prevalence of half gentcel which makes the difference. This is no doubt owing to the bachelor style of the late President and the absence of any presiding female character in the higher departments of Office. We returned at twelve. A thunder shower and rain following.

[1] No letter of this date has been located; it was probably written to Peter C. Brooks in reply to his second report on the Adams children (to CFA, 14 May, Adams Papers).

WEDNESDAY 23D.

Very heavy rain with occasional gusts of wind throughout the day, which prevented my going out until evening. But as I thought it scarcely advisable to waste so much time, I finished the Bank Report, and then read the whole of the original debate upon the first charter of the United States Bank. This is a very interesting exposition of the views originally entertained of this much vexed question, and I am not aware that much more could have been said. The argument of Mr. Madison against the Bank is very able and would be convincing if experience had not shown even to his own satisfaction that it was fallacious. A national mode of some kind of regulating the currency is indispensable to every country. Mr. Ames is not so strong upon the general position as I should have expected, and the argument drawn from the particular clauses weakens itself by its multiplication.[1]

After dinner, in the evening, my Wife and I went to see the President. Introduced into his sitting room formerly called the green room, where were numbers of persons, of whom I found out the names only of Mr. Wright of N.Y., Mr. Hubbard of N.H., Senators and a Mr. Kelly from Peru, Illinois. They all left and then Govr. Dickerson came in.[2] On the whole, the visit was very well, but I was much struck with the air ennueyé of the President and distrait too. He certainly manifests the cares of Office very much.

During our stay Mr. Hubbard mentioned his having received the intelligence of Mr. Woodbury's nomination to be Chief Justice in New Hampshire, which seemed to spread a momentary gleam of satisfaction over his features. Yet the rumor is that Kendall is to succeed. A man in his way likely to be even more troublesome. Returned home reflecting upon the moral of ambition in ordinary men — and extraordinary ones too where the difference is only in the gloss which ability throws over the picture.

[1] The debate on the "bill to incorporate the subscribers to the Bank of the United States" in the House of Representatives, 1–7 Feb. 1791, is recorded in M.

49

St. Clair Clarke and D. A. Hall, comps., *Legislative and Documentary History of the Bank of the United States*, Washington, 1832, p. 37–85. A copy is at MQA.
² Although the brothers Mahlon and

Philemon Dickerson had each been governor of New Jersey, neither was presently so. Mahlon Dickerson was currently secretary of the navy (*DAB*).

THURSDAY. 24TH.

Morning fine, but much cooler than it has been. After devoting some time to making up Diary, &ca. I accompanied the ladies to the Capitol. In the House of Representatives, we found the discussion upon the Appropriation for the Cherokee Treaty which is about being executed. It seems the President has lately manifested some inclination to concede something to the public opinion of the fraudulent origin of the Treaty. The announcement of this in a message two days ago came like a clap of thunder upon the Representatives of the States interested. And they are now upon this bill uttering their complaints. We heard first Genl. Glascock and then Mr. Downing, a delegate from Florida, the latter violent and savage.[1]

A strong proof of the debased moral principle of the House may be found in the fact that such a speech as this could be listened to with even tolerable patience. It is Slavery that is at the bottom of this. I am more satisfied of the fact every day I live. And nothing can save this country from entire perversion morally and politically but the predominance of the Abolition principle. Whether this will ever take place is very doubtful. I have not much hope.[2]

Mr. Graham of North Carolina followed,[3] but we left him to go to the Senate where was a short debate upon the Naval expedition.[4] Nothing of interest so we returned home. Mr. Campbell dined here. Evening at home.

Conversation with my father who seems puzzled to explain the difficulties into which our public affairs are becoming involved. He says, Mr. Calhoun is sanguine of becoming the next candidate for the Presidency on the Antibank principle, opposed to Clay as a bank candidate. How this is to be done over the head of Van Buren and the Southern Union party, as well as against the Whig interest remains a fearful mystery.

[1] On 21 May, the President had sent a message to the Senate asking that the Congress adopt measures supportive of Secretary of War Poinsett's undertaking to secure for the Cherokees compensation for their removal in excess of the terms specified in the disputed Treaty of 1835.

Debate in the House on the issues raised began on the 23d and was continued on the 24th (*Congressional Globe*, 25th Cong., 2d sess., p. 401–402, 405–406, 408). Thomas Glascock, representative from Ga., had been a brigadier general in the Seminole war (*Biog. Dir. Cong.*).

² CFA's present position on these matters should be compared with his earlier view, and JQA's, cited in note 3 to the entry for 29 Jan., above.

³ JQA thought he spoke "ingeniously and impressively," that his "judgment and feelings like those of Fillmore, fair, just and humane in all cases which touch not the immediate interests and passions of their Constituents, are unseated when Cherokee or Seneca Indians are parties concerned in the question" (Diary, 24 May).

⁴ A South Sea Exploring Expedition (*Congressional Globe*, 25th Cong., 2d sess., p. 409).

FRIDAY 25TH.

Morning cloudy with rain and severely cold for the advanced season. I remained at home working up my Diary as usual, until noon and then walked up to the Capitol.

Nothing doing in the House but matters of private claim; I went into the Senate where Mr. Clay was speaking upon his resolution for the reception of State Bank paper. He re-stated the circumstances under which the Treasury Circular had been sustained and the reasons why it should not be adhered to. He was answered by Col. T. H. Benton in his usual style and tone. There is however an appearance of heavy pressure upon the Administration party throughout all of it's movements. And a vacillation of purpose which has the effect to dishearten the friends and encourage the enemies. Benton himself, boaster as he is, boasts in a subdued manner, as under correction from a majority. Home to dinner.

Evening, all the family but my Mother who is still quite unwell went to Mrs. Smith's to a small party of the family, Mr. and Mrs. Randall and Genl. and Mrs. Macomb. Cards and a Supper. More company than room and very cold indeed, but there was every effort to do the "possible" and on the whole we retired before midnight handsomely entertained.

SATURDAY 26TH.

Clear and cool. On the whole, a very fine day. After breakfast, I called to see Dr. Huntt who is now confined to his house.¹ He is a mere skeleton, and the most wretched looking one I ever saw, but he keeps up his spirits and talks as rapidly as ever. Indeed far more so than he used to do. He takes great interest in politics, curses the present dynasty and looks to a revolution which he is not likely to witness. While he is under no sense of religion to prepare him for his change, I feel friendly to Huntt for his attention to myself as well as to my Mother and am sorry to think I see him for the last time.

Home. Diary. At noon, we that is the ladies and Hull with myself went by agreement to see some curiosities of Major Hook's arranged in his bachelor establishment.[2] They consist mainly of Indian relics and pictures representing their habits. The ornaments of Oseola were perhaps the most interesting. But there is much sameness in Indian dresses when unassociated with persons. From thence to the Capitol where the Senate was sitting in debate upon the resolution of Mr. Clay. Mr. Sevier of Arkansaw spoke mainly against that part of the Report of the Finance Committee which touches the Specie Circular. He was followed briefly by Mr. Clay, Mr. Calhoun, Mr. Niles, Mr. Rives and Mr. Wright. The debate was interesting, particularly Mr. Rives' examination of the Report. He was strong in attack but feeble in explaining his own position, which is not tenable. Home to dinner. Evening passed quietly. My father dined out at Mr. Pontois to meet the Prince de Joinville, a youth of 18, the son of Louis Philippe of France who is travelling for his pleasure. He was in the Senate. An olive complexioned young man with marked features, but not handsome, nor distinguished in any way. He excited much curiosity. Mr. and Mrs. Smith here for an hour.

[1] Dr. Henry Huntt had, for many years, been the Adams family physician in Washington (vol. 2, index).

[2] Maj. James Harvey Hook of Maryland (Heitman, *Register U.S. Army*, vol. 1).

SUNDAY 27TH.

The weather is very certainly far from favorable. Wind and cold and heat each in undue proportion. Attended divine service at St. John's Church, where Mr. Hawley preached from Hebrews 8. 13. "In that he saith, a new covenant, he hath made the first old." My attention was not fixed and Mr. Hawley is not interesting. The Church was not so full as last Sunday.[1]

Visits from Govr. Dickerson, Mrs. Frye and others. Read a sermon of Buckminster's. 1. Corinthians 11. 31. "If we would judge ourselves, we should not be judged." A singular text for a discourse upon self knowledge, the difficulties and the advantages of it. Mr. Campbell dined with us. Evening, the ladies with my father and I went to Mrs. Frye's where we spent a couple of hours. Nothing of interest.

On this day, my little boy, Charles is three years old. May heaven preserve him for utility and honor. I feel the burden of absence from my children increasing.

MONDAY 28TH.

The weather continues cold, but pleasant to walk about. I felt slightly unwell with symptoms of an impending head ach. Went with the ladies to make some return visits prior to leaving and then to the Capitol where I was not however well rewarded for my walk; for in the Senate, Mr. Morris of Ohio was making an extreme Speech in the Radical way marked by little but its vehemence, and in the Senate,[1] the debate on the Cherokee treaty was dragging slowly along. On the whole, the prospect seemed best in the Senate for the future, but after Mr. Morris finished, the question was taken first upon the motion made by him to repeal the act of 1816,[2] which was lost by a large vote, and then upon the third reading of the amended Resolution of Mr. Clay which was carried. Home.

After dinner the ladies went to Mrs. Turnbull's.[3] Conversation with Mr. Gilpin who was there with his Wife and members [i.e. numbers] of others. Some political hints to him, but nothing of interest. He is a politician of the democratic school much too mild for his business. And I judge his character is that of almost all the present managers of the Government. They are small men who look to the present, and to themselves. We had singing from Mr. Campbell and I. Hull and did not return until twelve.

[1] An inadvertence for "House."
[2] That is, the act establishing the Second Bank of the United States.
[3] Mrs. Turnbull was the wife of Capt. William Turnbull, a topographical engineer (JQA, Diary, 28 May; Heitman, *Register U.S. Army*, vol. 1).

TUESDAY. 29TH.

Morning at home, the weather cool and showery. I finished the arrangements of our departure and packed up the trunks, somewhat to the regret of my Wife, who seems to have taken a fancy to this place. A little before noon, accompanied the two ladies and Mrs. Turnbull for whom we called, to the Arsenal at Greenleaf's Point where we had been invited by the commanding Officer, Capt. George Ramsay the brother of Mrs. Turnbull.

The site is a beautiful one, just at the fork of the Potomac and commands a fine view down to Alexandria. Here are manufactured by steam power gun carriages both of wood and iron and various mountings. It is also the receptacle of arms from Harper's Ferry, which are again distributed from here to the places where they are wanted. At this moment a schooner was loading at the wharf with arms for the Cherokee country, the scene of present cruelty. Capt. Ramsay is a courteous gentleman and did every thing in his power to amuse us, so that we spent more time than I could well spare, and I thus lost the opportunity to make the remaining calls I had designed.

Dinner a little later than usual, my father not returned from the Capitol. Mr. Campbell dined with us and we had a song or two afterwards. Then came in the various members of the family to take leave. Mr. and Mrs. Frye and Miss Johnson, Mr. and Mrs. Smith.

Much talk of an insurrection of the blacks supposed to be about to break out at 11 o'clock this night and instigated by an Abolitionist from New York or elsewhere. The alarms of the whites sufficiently show the horrors of the slavery system without the need of exaggeration. Their fears magnify their own danger, and this produces all the violence they dread. I imagine the whole story grows out of a very small affair, but such is the character of the whites that it may not improbably lead to bad consequences. My mother and the family are always apprehensive at such times of the possible direction of the public feeling against my father for having taken so much part in the matter. I hope she has no cause.[1] The family retired early and so did we, being early to be called. My father detained at the house.

[1] JQA noted, "There is a panic rumour abroad, artificially gotten up; of Slave insurgency, amounting to nothing" (Diary, 30 May).

Philadelphia

WEDNESDAY 30TH.

The morning was clear and beautiful as we rose with the sun to prepare for our Journey. After a rapid breakfast we started from the house for the Railway depot, taking leave of my father, I. Hull, and those of the household who were up. It is now just a month since I reached this place, a month of much enjoyment to my Wife and myself, as a relaxation from the cares of life.

My reception at the Metropolis has been better than I had any reason to expect. My personal vanity has been flattered as much by the attentions bestowed by many here, as by the absence of them from others; but my gratification has arisen from a better motive, the improved health of my Wife.

The spectacle of politics has not made me more in love with the trade as it is here carried on, and I am a little fearful that my way of viewing them will never become popular enough to be practicable. Be this as it may. My motto remains the same, and will do so, I hope, through all the vicissitudes of life. I am grateful to the divine being for my present position, and will remain content however he may regulate my line of usefulness.

We reached Baltimore by eight o'clock, and after an hour and a half of delay during which I walked into the town with Louisa, we started again for Philadelphia. The trip was favourable and the day could not have been finer. But towards the last of it there was delay. We went through in the cars as far as the road is finished and were then transferred to omnibuses, which completed the three miles very slowly and heavily.

Accidentally a small spark from the engine adhered to the ball of my eye which gave me acute suffering until I was able to extract it in the city but not until after the inflammation had become quite considerable. At last after five o'clock we reached the Marshall House where we stopped, and after dinner and a brief stroll down Chesnut Street, I returned with so violent a head ach and so much fatigued that I was glad to go early to bed, but the noise of the house was incessant until after midnight.

THURSDAY 31ST.

I passed a very disturbed and heavy night but yet felt relieved from pain when called up at five to prepare to go in the boat for New York. The day was charming, but we found the steamer overloaded with passengers. In my opinion this forms much the worst part of the route from the overloading which perpetually takes place, and the consequent crowding and personal inconvenience. We found on board several Boston acquaintances with whom we had passing conversation until we reached New York which happened uncommonly early.

I immediately transferred myself and family and baggage to the Steamer for Providence which lies at the next wharf, after which we drove to the Astor house for the purpose of seeing Sidney Brooks and his Wife and dining there. The latter part of it only we accomplished, as Sidney had left for Boston last week. I spent part of the time in a walk after toys and the remainder in a very luxurious dinner, upon rising from which it became time to return to the boat.

The same Steamer that brought us from Stonington, the Providence was now bound for Providence and I was glad to perceive had no great number of passengers. The evening was delightful and we had a very favourable run until the close of daylight reminded me of the fatigue I had endured, and that my eye which still suffered from the inconvenience of yesterday needed rest.

Boston

FRIDAY JUNE 1ST.

I slept better than I usually do but yet was up shortly after the sun. Our course had been very favorable and we were off Point Judith with little to mark the circumstance. We reached Newport at seven and Providence at nine where we took the cars and found ourselves at home by twelve, thus having accomplished in fifty four hours the whole distance without any considerable fatigue. What a difference in travelling since I can remember it, when I went over the whole ground by land at great cost of personal strength in five days and nights.

It was so soon before dinner that I dressed only and did not go out. After dinner, time taken up in putting away things and dawdling as people do before they can get settled down to any active occupation. Evening at home. Sidney Brooks called in.

SATURDAY. 2D.

Morning cloudy but it cleared away warm. In resuming my usual routine of domestic occupations I feel a repugnance which I can myself hardly account for. These intervals of amusement ought not to strike me with so much preference over the habits of home. The secret must lie in a slavery to money to which my mind ought not to be subjected, but the thing cannot be avoided.

Almost all my time was taken up this morning in attendance upon an auction sale to buy a carriage or gig for my mother or myself. Accomplished the first but failed in the other. By this time one of my head achs began to set in with severity and my afternoon was of course sacrificed to languid indolence. Sidney and his Wife came in for a short time, and I was barely able to sit up until they left the House.

June 1838

Fine day. I was relieved of my headach and turned my attention to my catalogue of coins, but made not much progress before it was time to attend divine service at the Meeting house in Chauncy Place.[1] Dr. Frothingham preached from Genesis 11. 1. "And the whole earth was of one language and of one speech." His view of the confusion of tongues at the building of Babel was new to me. He regards it not so much as any manifestation of the divine anger as one of the instruments in his hands for the dispersion of man over the world, in execution of a part of the ends of creation.

Afternoon, Mr. Lothrop. Romans 2. 11. "For there is no respect of persons with God." A discourse I did not find very interesting. After service read a discourse of Buckminster upon grace. Ephesians 2. 5. "By grace ye are saved." He considers the sense in which the word grace has been used, in connection with election, or with works or with mediation and then gives his own which appears to resolve itself into works simply.

Evening quiet. My mind has been slightly depressed almost without my being able to analyze the cause since my return. The visit to Washington has been a pleasant and a flattering one to me, but it should not have the effect of rendering me dissatisfied here where I am not treated quite as favorably as others. This is my native land upon which my fathers have stood their ground since the country was peopled and I will not desert it or even think a wish to be elsewhere. No other ground is like this for me however the case might be were I not precisely in the situation that I am.

[1] On the First Church or "Meeting house in Chauncy Place," see vols. 3:xi, 14; 4:xiv.

Fine day, the usual attendant upon Artillery Election.[1] I went down to the Office and was occupied very soon in Accounts. Mr. Kirk from Quincy came in with the horses and I then had to work very briskly to get every thing in order for him to return in good season. I had also to finish the orders for the remainder of the furniture and bedding, and for this purpose met my Wife at the Asylum for the blind,[2] to select it. Thus the time passed so rapidly that I found the hour for dinner had arrived and I returned home weary enough.

The afternoons in these cases ought at least to be allowed me, and yet I feel ashamed not to improve it more than in reading the wishy washy collections of the English Society for entertaining knowledge.[3] Mr. and Mrs. Frothingham and children here during part of the Afternoon. And the noise of guns and of people quite intolerable.

Evening, T. K. Davis came in, the first time that I have seen him. He appeared lively enough but had little that was new. His Washington journey has enlarged his views if it has not resulted in fixing his party principles.

[1] On the day of Artillery Election, see vol. 3:255.
[2] Probably the Perkins Institution for the Blind; see vol. 5:79.
[3] For the *Library of Entertaining Knowledge*, see vol. 3:51.

TUESDAY 5TH.

Heavy rain in the morning, but it cleared before night. I went to the Office and was occupied in preparing the Accounts for the case of Mr. Johnson who wishes to know his position. I prepared them all very fully and despatched them before night.[1] I then went in quest of some kind of vehicle for my summer use, my gig having given out rather unexpectedly to me. The matter having been expedited, I next turned my attention to the remainder of the orders, most of which I got through with. Thus again went the day.

Home to dinner, weary and somewhat discouraged by this heavy load of small cares. I sometimes feel as if I had done wrong to assume so many of them, and incline to adopt rather a strict system of reduction until I get back. Afternoon packing up books and reading Hindoo manners.[2] Perhaps this information may stand me in good stead some time or other. Evening, called upon Sidney Brooks and his Wife and from thence to Edward Brooks' where were Mr. and Mrs. Frothingham and Mr. W. Boott.[3] After an hour's talk, home.

[1] CFA to T. B. Johnson, 5 June, LbC, Adams Papers.
[2] Vol. 4 of William Ward's *Account of the Writings, Religion, and Manners of the Hindoos*, 4 vols., Serampore, 1811, contains "The domestic manners and customs of the Hindoos." Ward's work was also published from 1817 onward with the title, *A View of the History, Literature, and Mythology of the Hindoos*.
[3] Probably, William Boott, brother of Mrs. Edward Brooks.

WEDNESDAY 6TH.

Morning pleasant with flying clouds. I went to the Office and from thence walking to accomplish commissions. Met Kirk who had come in with one of the horses and expected me to go out so that I might return with the other. Accordingly I started in my new Conveyance which I liked very well, and reached the house about eleven.

Every thing looked very much improved from what it was when I started and yet I could not help feeling how rough it all was and how much attention it would require before I could make any thing comely out of it. I was led into a more extensive undertaking than I have either disposition or means to keep up. My grounds are yet but poorly clothed with green and that at a time when the country has it's richest coat.

After giving such directions as I could, I returned home, just in time for dinner. Afternoon at home quietly reading of the Hindoos. Unable to assume more active or useful work from the proximity of my removal. Evening writing Diary, which I brought up.

THURSDAY 7TH.

Fine day. I was occupied much of my morning in various duties appertaining to the great object of removal to Quincy and in a few connected with the Tenants. Then to the Office where I tried to put some order in my papers. Called to see Davis for a few moments and exchange a word upon politics. There is little now of interest since the rumors of cabinet changes have died away, and nothing happens but a brawl or two in the House. Davis is still talking with others about his project of contributing to a press but as I suspect with very little prospect of success. Thus went the morning.

Home. My Wife had to dinner, Mr. and Mrs. Frothingham, and Sidney and Mrs. Brooks. Pleasant enough, excepting that it is so long since I have had any company it appears new. They spent the afternoon and took tea. T. K. Davis dropped in to tell me that he considered his project a failure. He had seen the men and was satisfied.

FRIDAY 8TH.

Warm but pleasant day. My morning was passed in the usual way. A great variety of little things very tedious to me to execute but absolutely essential. My exercise has been pretty well kept up since my return and it may have been fortunate for me that it was so, inasmuch as my spirits might otherwise have flagged.

At the Office engaged in Accounts, then home early to dine. Immediately afterwards, I started for Quincy. Found progress making slowly. A new house requires so much thought, and care and attention. And strange to say, I have ceased to feel the interest I did in it. At present it weighs as a burden.

Home before sunset and then to a small party at Mr. B. Gorham's given to Commodore and Mrs. Hull.[1] Only members of his and her family, pleasant enough. Home very tired.

[1] On Como. Isaac Hull, see vol. 4:76.

SATURDAY 9TH.

Fine day. After walking up to the house at the corner of Tremont Street[1] to see that the painter was at his work, I returned to the usual duties at the Office and various commissions. But I had several hours in which I could work more steadily than usual at accounts and thus made preparation for the annual balance which I am accustomed to make for July. This is a vexatious affair, for trifles frequently give one very great inconvenience. I was quite uninterrupted until the time for me to return home.

After dinner, went to Quincy. One great load of things gone out hardly relieves the weight of things to be sent but it at least appears like removal. Arranged as many books as I had and gave other directions, until sunset when I drove to Mrs. Adams', to see her. Found Elizabeth looking better and Mr. and Mrs. Angier there, but I stayed only a few minutes before going home. Evening quiet and short.

[1] That is, the rental property at the corner of Tremont and Boylston streets, then numbered 105.

SUNDAY 10TH.

This was a specimen of Summer heat; there not having been last year any day when the Thermometer rose higher. I spent some time in the work of making a catalogue of coins and then attended divine service and heard Mr. Stetson of Medford preach from John 4. 29. "Come, see a man, which told me all things that ever I did": the revealing of religion through the Saviour by discovery of self. Perhaps I do not express the thought strongly, for there is a thought in it. The awakening of the moral sense to a state of things until then unknown. Mr. Stetson is not a pleasing preacher but has talent.[1] Afternoon. James 4. 7. "Resist the devil and he will flee from you." Upon the performance of duty as a guard against sin. Mr. Stetson is not interesting and yet he thinks, so that after all mere thought is not sufficient to make an attractive speaker.

Sermon of Buckminster's Luke 18. 10 "Two men went up into the temple to pray; the one a pharisee and the other a publican." Humility as exemplified in the text and parable connected with it. A very good discourse. Evening, we walked up and down the mall with T. K. Davis to witness the resort of people. Quite a lively scene. Home—heat intense.

¹ Earlier comments on Rev. Caleb Stetson are in vol. 3:76, 117.

MONDAY 11TH.

The heat very great. I went down to see how the work in Tremont Street went on, and from thence upon various commissions as usual most of which I finished. Then to the Office resuming the labour upon my Accounts but without entire success. Thus went the time until my return to dinner. Afterwards, I went to Quincy.

Found my house so much cooler than it was in town that I deeply regretted not having got it ready. They were busy in various matters appertaining to preparation. I arranged books and gave directions. But my spirits keep falling as I approach the end of my undertaking very singularly, not that I wish it continued for I have had care enough, but that I see no very immediate termination to it. Went to Mrs. Adams' to tea and returning brought Elizabeth with me. Found Gardiner Gorham who made a short visit.

TUESDAY 12TH.

A continuation of this heat which is believed to be almost without example at this season of the year. I went to the Office and spent time in Accounts much as usual. Mr. Beebe called with a view to settlement of his affair, but the papers were not drawn, so it was postponed until tomorrow. As usual many different commissions, home early with the design of taking my Wife to Medford, and my boy John to dine with Mr. Brooks.

Found the family as usual but with the addition of Gorham and Ellen to dine. All pleasant enough but the heat. After dinner, we went up to see the improved residence of the latter and were there caught in a shower which detained us until sunset. Gorham has fitted up an old house comfortably and will probably enjoy it for the good reason that he is not afraid of it. Perhaps the anxiety for a new house is the worst part of it. Home late. Mr. and Mrs. Frothingham came in and spent an hour pleasantly. But I was dull.

WEDNESDAY 13TH.

Continuation of the heat, notwithstanding the thunder shower of last evening. I went to the Office after a laborious piece of work attending to the packing up of the things designed to go to Quincy. Every thing at this time is fatiguing. Yet my anxiety to get out is the greater for the very reason of the heat. Usual work in accounts. Mr. Beebe came but was not ready so we had to postpone again, until Friday. Home early for the sake of putting away my clothes.

After dinner, I took Catherine with me and the two elder boys John and Charles in my little conveyance and brought them to my new residence in Quincy. We got there just previous to a heavy thunder shower which was followed by a magnificent display of the landscape. My first impressions were those of enjoyment, but the disarrangement of every thing and the severe care and labour depressed me. I read some of a book upon political Economy written by one Poulett Scrope, in which are some views of banking which confirm my impression of the correctness of my theory.[1]

[1] George Poulette Scrope, *Principles of Political Economy*, London, 1833.

THURSDAY 14TH.

The light of the sun roused me at an unwonted hour and I could not help opening the window to see the scene. There is a charm, a freshness about the Country which no town life can ever entirely replace. At least this is the feeling to me who have always lived in open scenes.

This which I have chosen for my own home repays me at every look for the quantity of labour which it has cost me. I could hardly enjoy it enough today although I spent much of my time in doing so. But I had the two children to take care of and this was no small trouble. The heat was as great as ever until noon when the wind came to the eastward, and we had a succession of storms of rain, thunder and lightning which produced a sublime effect here where they are so visible, not unmingled with awe.

My Wife and the rest of the family came out towards evening and thus completed the removal of this year. But we were of course in some confusion and I was fairly fatigued out so as to be very glad to get to bed pretty early.

2. CHARLES FRANCIS ADAMS' SUMMER HOUSE IN QUINCY, 1838–1849

See pages vii–ix

FRIDAY 15TH.

Another warm day. Shortly after breakfast I went to town and finding it difficult to make much exertion I concluded to remain at the Office and work over my Accounts. My principal occupation was to attend to the remaining arrangements for our comfort this summer which I concluded more satisfactorily to myself than I had expected. The difficulties of country life arise from want of provisions which the city must afford, but the transportation is the main thing. I hope I have now got the thing in order.

Returned to dinner and could not help feeling the delight of a free air and a cool room. My situation when I look at it compensates me for all my trouble, great as it has been. Afternoon, reading and arranging my books inside and my grounds about the house. Evening, Mr. and Mrs. Lunt called for an hour. And I retired earlier than I commonly do in town.

SATURDAY 16TH.

Morning warm. I remained at home quietly to enjoy the breeze at the house instead of rambling about the City. Walked down to the old house where I selected more books to bring out here and looked over the garden. The season is a remarkable one for vegetation. Every thing assumes a green tinge which makes the scenery unusually rich. I returned home and sat down to write a letter to my father which I made a long one, and which took the remainder of the morning.[1]

In the afternoon, I began the letters of Pliny the younger which I propose to read as my usual relaxation in the classics this Summer.[2] And I continued Scrope. Writers on political economy make their books very uninteresting because they stuff them full of theories of their own without much reference to the inductive process which is the only philosophy. Evening at home.

[1] The letter (Adams Papers) consists almost wholly of reflections on his Washington observations and further thoughts on the current banking and currency situation.

[2] At MQA are two copies of the *Epistolæ et panegyricus* of Plinius Secundus, one published at Leipzig, 1739, the other at London, 1821. Also there, are translations in English and French.

SUNDAY 17TH.

Fine day and warm with a thunder shower and light rain before sunset. I occupied myself in reading, a luxury which is rather new to me of late, until the time for divine service when I attended and heard

Mr. Angier preach from Mark 12. 30.[1] "Thou shalt love the Lord thy God with all thy strength," but I gathered little from the discourse as it was in the mystical, spiritual style which now prevails so much among us. Afternoon, Mr. Lunt preached, but as I did not gain my usual nap, I was not as attentive as I ought to have been. The congregation was uneasy from a different cause, the approaching storm.

I read a Sermon of Buckminster's upon the character of Peter, marked by the usual merits of his style. Matthew 26. 35. "Peter said unto him, though I should die with thee yet will I not deny thee." Also Luke 22. 61.62. "And the Lord turned, and looked upon Peter. And Peter remembered the word of the Lord, how he had said unto him, before the cock crow, thou shalt deny me thrice. And Peter went out and wept bitterly." The point of the discourse seemed to be to raise a new evidence of the truth of the Christian Religion from the very denial of Peter. Ingenious but not so striking as the sketch of the man himself. Evening at home. Mr. Price Greenleaf came in and passed some time, as also Mr. Beale and his two daughters. The first Quincy visitors excepting the Lunts that we have had.

[1] On Rev. Joseph Angier, see vol. 5:107–108.

MONDAY 18TH.

The morning brought with it a great change in the weather, and a brisk wind from the Eastward which made it very cold. I remained quietly at home reading with the exception of a visit to the house and up in town. I am looking over works of political Economy which give no new ideas and the study of which is like wasting time. As a relaxation in the afternoon, I take up Pliny's letters with which I am much pleased. They describe life and manners perhaps not so vividly as Cicero but still strongly. Evening, read a chapter of Tucker's light of Nature.[1] My studies are thus desultory enough, but this may well be as yet when I am still in the enjoyment of a fresh return to books.

[1] In MQA is Abraham Tucker's *Light of Nature Pursued*, 7 vols., London, 1805.

TUESDAY 19TH.

A cold easterly wind but very clear. I. Hull breakfasted with me and accompanied Mrs. Adams and myself to Boston where we went to get sundry things. At the house, we were surprised by a visit from Miss Harriet Welsh accompanied by Mr. and Mrs. Downing, the newly married couple from Fishkill.[1] This was not apropos but we got through it as well as we might. My principal difficulty was in the delay it occasioned me through which I lost [a] great part of the time I intended to have spent in objects for which I came to town.

Letter from Mr. Johnson which required attention, and an immediate answer.[2] Call from Mr. Beebe not yet quite ready to make a final conveyance but fixed tomorrow so that I come in again. Call from I. H. Adams too with whom I called to see Judge Leland and refer the matter of the will. He seemed to favor it's validity,[3] and gave me a blank to get ready. Then home to Quincy much fatigued. I. H. dined with us. Afternoon, Pliny. Evening quietly at home but fatigued enough to be glad to retire early.

[1] Two weeks earlier, Caroline Elizabeth de Windt, a daughter of the John Peter de Windts, had married Andrew Jackson Downing, who would later have a distinguished career as landscape gardener and architect (*DAB*).

[2] CFA's letter is in the Adams Papers (LbC); T. B. Johnson's is missing.

[3] That is, Lt. T. B. Adams' will.

WEDNESDAY 20TH.

I went to town again this morning to execute the business which I had failed in getting through with yesterday. I was tolerably successful with it and completed the long talked of arrangement with Mr. James M. Beebe and the Mortgage. I also paid off a number of the heaviest bills for the balance of my furniture purchased since my return. Thus the time vanished until my return which I made by the way of the new road lately opened in competition with Neponset. It is a nice road enough but rather laborious for a horse coming this way.

After dinner amused myself with reading Pliny. A great deal of good feeling, honesty beyond the age, a little vanity and some artifice are the characteristics of his style. The letters are rather curiously jumbled but still very interesting. The Roman Empire even in it's corruption still retained much of the noble appearance of it's antique form. Evening, Mrs. Adams and I to Mrs. E. Miller's to see Mr. and Mrs. Downing who were here for the day. Nobody but the Adams family.

THURSDAY 21ST.

Morning clear with a cold Easterly wind. I spent more time than I had intended running over the books in the library down at the house and selecting such as I wished. Out of my fathers whole collection there are comparatively few that come within the range of my present wishes. I propose to devote the summer to increasing my acquaintance with American history and my general knowledge of the geography of the world. This is a branch of science I always had a fancy for, and my father's library is pretty well provided with ancient works. The modern ones are more numerous but not so valuable. Afternoon Pliny in whose letters I take much pleasure. Evening, called with Mrs. Adams at Mr. Beale's and sat an hour.

FRIDAY 22D.

It was warm today until a thunder shower came and cooled the air. I went to town and was employed every minute of my time in something or other. Among the rest, I was obliged to go to Cambridge for the purpose of returning some books to the library, it being near the moment for the annual examination. This I effected by taking the omnibus in and out, although not without heat and fatigue. Of course I was abridged of my time here.

Glad as I always am to get out of the dust and bustle of the city and enjoy the fresh breeze from the sea. Afternoon, Pliny. Took up Grahame's history and bethought myself of the possibility of making it conducive to my studies and to the satisfaction of a request of Dr. Palfrey's for a review for the much fallen North American.[1] Evening passed in looking over the work.

[1] For CFA's long interest in James Grahame's *History of the United States*, both on the appearance of the original edition and of the revised and extended edition of 1836, see above, entry for 3 Nov. 1836, and vol. 6:394.

SATURDAY 23D.

Day pleasant but cool. I remained at home and enjoyed my occupation much. Having gone down to the house, I there procured the papers relating to my grandfather and commenced an examination of them with a view to a more direct comprehension of the record of the early part of his life, as well as a methodical arrangement. This kept me fully engaged the whole morning, and I felt great satisfaction in it too.

After dinner, I indulged in reading Pliny, and resumed Grahame comparing him with Hutchinson and finding a slight notice of the incidents at the commencement of the 18th century was tempted to examine more minutely. I am only deterred from writing by the probable labour of investigation. Evening Mrs. Adams took tea at my Aunt's, and I joined her where we spent the evening, and returned at or before ten.

SUNDAY 24TH.

Warm, cloudy day. I passed my morning very quietly, occupied as usual in papers. I take great interest in this new business of the journals because I feel as if it may lead me to something useful. And they are in themselves so interesting that they ought to be published, for safety's sake if for nothing else.

Attended divine Service and heard Mr. Young preach from Proverbs 20. 27. "The spirit of man is the candle of the Lord." An ingenious view of the operation of the principle of religious faith in the human mind developing itself in moral results beneficial to the world. Afternoon Luke 10. 27. "And he answering said, Thou shalt love thy neighbour as thyself." An essay upon the spirit of the Christian Religion influencing man's relations to his fellows. The term neighbour implying all men with whom we may through the force of circumstances be drawn into intercourse.

Afterwards Mr. Buckminster upon Religious education. Ephesians 6. 4. "Fathers, provoke not your children to wrath; but bring them up in the nurture and admonition of the Lord." Very excellent instruction respecting the moral education of children which I feel much and hope to profit by. I will resume my lessons with my daughter which circumstances had broken off. Wrote a letter to my Mother[1] and in the evening after a conversation with my Wife read Graham, &c.

[1] Adams Papers.

MONDAY 25TH.

A sea fog from the Eastward covered every thing up and prevented my being able to go to town as I intended. The greater part of my morning was therefore devoted to the comparisons of the copy of the old journals with the original which I pursued steadily and executed a great deal of. This is necessary as a first step. I find much that is interesting and much that is only amusing in the examinations. But it cannot be done with much rapidity.

Afternoon, a succession of thunder showers with at times very heavy rain, and sharp lightning. This is a position from which there is a great opportunity of witnessing all these results, and they are at times fearfully sublime. Mrs. Adams who was riding came home in the shower, bringing with her E. C. Adams who remained to drink tea and I returned with her in the evening. Read Pliny and Grahame. Quiet evening at home.

June 1838

TUESDAY 26TH.

The day was remarkably fine and clear. I was up early and started to Boston in the carriage with the view of returning with Mrs. Frothingham who with two of her children is to pay us a visit. My time was taken up in Accounts, and in various little commissions appertaining to my affairs and those of others. At one o'clock I returned and we all got home safe before half past two.

Afternoon, reading Pliny and afterwards examining Grahame. I do this in a very verveless manner, hardly prognosticating much result. My ambition certainly cannot be a very strong passion when it takes such frequent naps. Evening quietly at home. The news from Congress is of an adjournment on the 9th of July whence we may expect some of the family before long.

WEDNESDAY 27TH.

I was up this morning to see the sun rise, a very beautiful sight from this spot as a sublime one indeed from any. The sky was clear but a vapour in the east made the luminary appear in a blaze of red light. With the exception of a brief walk to the Bank and Post Office I was occupied all the morning in collating the copies of the small diaries with the originals. It is much to be regretted that these are not more complete because they relate to times of interest and are unique in their way.

I. Hull Adams called to let me know of his appointment to the survey of a Railroad in Maryland and he leaves on Friday. I talked with him about the execution of the trust of his brother's will which I am now anxious to hasten. But the settlement lags at Washington.

Afternoon Pliny. I walked to Mount Wollaston, a beautiful spot as ever but the orchard from the failure of most of the trees looked dreary to me. Home by the new road which will shorten the way somewhat when done. In the evening quiet. Read Grahame.

THURSDAY 28TH.

Cloudy with showers which continued with increasing force until sunset. I remained at home and occupied myself in copying a portion of the Fragmentary Journal which appears to have been omitted in the former experiment. The hand writing is so close that I make no very rapid way with even so small leaves. There is not much however of the omitted portion. An entry of the 26 February 1770 four or five days before the massacre giving an Account of the funeral of the child killed by Richardson,[1] but none on the day. Wrote a letter to Mr. Johnson,[2] and in the afternoon read Pliny and Grahame. Thus passed a day very quietly, more remarkable for the amount of my own occupation, than for incident.

[1] What CFA calls the "fragmentary journal" must be "Paper book No. 15"; see JA, *Diary and Autobiography*, 1:338; the copy which CFA undertook to make of the entries in the paper book is missing. For the entry of 26 Feb. 1770, see same, 1:349–350.

[2] To T. B. Johnson, 27 June, LbC, Adams Papers.

FRIDAY 29TH.

Morning fine. I went to town. Engaged all day in Accounts at the Office so that I remained steadily occupied at the Office and in one duty. As usual at the end of the year I am balancing my books and as usual there is a slight error of a few cents which embarrasses me. This keeping of Accounts by double entry is a vexatious affair.

Home to dinner. Afternoon reading Pliny. Much fine sentiment in his letters but a little too stiff and apprêté for epistolary style. Grahame. Evening at home. Very quiet. The town today all agog with the news from Washington of the defeat of the subtreasury bill. It seems the Administration party broke down by a most decisive vote, for which I for one cannot say I am sorry.

SATURDAY 30TH.

Cool day with an easterly breeze and fog clouds. I remained at home with the exception of a call at the old house to select more books, and was steadily occupied in copying the little Fragment of a Diary. In these little paper books it appears to have been my Grandfather's practice to insert almost any thing in his way at the time. Hence copies of several Newspaper articles for the time, also of a letter to Mrs. McCauley about his dissertation on the canon and feudal law,[1] good material.

Afternoon, Pliny and Grahame. J. H. Adams dined with us and I spent half an hour in digging my ground, a piece of pretty hard labour. Evening at home but I did very little. My plan is to retire early for the sake of early rising. Mr. Beale and youngest daughter here in the evening.

[1] The letter to Mrs. Catharine (Sawbridge) Macaulay, 9 Aug. 1770, is printed in JA, *Diary and Autobiography*, 1:360–361.

SUNDAY. JULY 1ST.

A cloudy foggy day with much vapour rising from the sea. I passed much time in copying and finished one of the omitted paper books,[1] then attended divine Service and heard Mr. Whitney preach from Psalms. "I am fearfully and wonderfully made." He was not interesting. Afternoon, Mr. Lunt Ephesians 3. 17. "That Christ may dwell in your hearts by faith." The meaning of the indwelling of Christ and the force of faith. This was a discourse I had heard before.

Read a sermon of Buckminster's upon the occasion of a thanksgiving, Deuteronomy 33. 29. "Happy are thou, O, Israel; who is like unto thee." An enumeration of our advantages as a people, and our duties growing out of them. We had afterwards sundry visitors — Mr. and Mrs. D. Greenleaf, and Mr. Price [Greenleaf], Joseph H. and Elizabeth C. Adams, they all left us by eight o'clock and then a quiet evening.

[1] For an account of the manuscript scraps and fragments from which JA's Diary has had to be constructed, see JA, *Diary and Autobiography*, 1:xli–xlii. CFA's word "omitted" may mean omitted from the booklet which in the preceding entry he called "the little Fragment of a Diary." Doubtless, these are some of the "paper books" he numbered serially 1–31.

MONDAY 2D.

Foggy morning with a heavy shower but it afterwards cleared and became very warm. I accompanied Mrs. Frothingham into town who terminated her visit with us today. My own time taken up as it always is in a variety of little commissions and in the transaction of money affairs, then to the House to procure some things which I wanted and from thence I returned home in the carriage, rather earlier than usual.

Afternoon reading Pliny. Letters about his Uncle's death interesting but Pliny as a letter writer does not gain on you as you advance. He has much which commands your respect, but is artificial to a degree which makes you cease to like him. Continued Grahame. In the evening, for the first time it was pleasant outside the house. Letters from Washington announcing the speedy return of the family.[1]

[1] Letters of 26th and 29th June from LCA (Adams Papers) forecast their arrival in Quincy on 11 July, or earlier. However, a later note from her (8 July, Adams Papers) made the date of their arrival problematical owing to JQA's exhausted state as the Congress moved to adjournment.

TUESDAY. 3D.

Morning, a promise of a very hot day which it was. I accompanied the children to school, and from thence to Mrs. Adams' for the purpose of settling the quarterly accounts with her and Elizabeth as usual. This took up an hour after which I returned and devoted the remainder of the time until dinner to my copying process, which goes on slowly notwithstanding. I wish to fill up this lacuna or I would not undertake so much of this drudgery.

Afternoon rode to Squantum to attend the annual meeting of the Proprietors of Neponset Bridge. Present, the usual company with the addition of Mr. J. H. Foster, and the exception of Mr. Whitney. I sat between Dr. Frothingham and Mr. Foster. The day was very lovely and Squantum appeared to great advantage. The dinner was much as usual and I returned at six very well pleased with my day.

Evening for the first time warm enough to sit upon the Portico in front of the House. The scene has been remarkably lovely today. Indeed as much like enchantment as possible. As I look upon it, I can describe to no one my feelings nor ask sympathy, for the effect is upon my whole mind, lighting it with sunny rays.

WEDNESDAY 4TH.

A very hot day. This is a Summer such as we have not had for several seasons. I went down to the old Mansion for the sake of trying a horse offered for sale, and of making some selections of books. This took up time I had proposed to devote to copying.

Home where I had hardly become seated before the bell rung and I concluded to go to the Meeting House to hear Mr. Lunt deliver the Address to the schools. This is an interesting mode of celebrating the National Anniversary. The schools of both sexes made a handsome display and the citizens of the town, probably most of the parents occupied the remainder of the House.

Mr. Lunt opened by an eloquent exordium alluding to the propriety of learning the true principles of liberty here in the very spot where two of the men of that day who signed the first great declaration of them, were baptized.[1] He then went into a discussion of the moral in connection with the political system, and the introduction of this now for the first time into the decision of political questions. He glanced at the present dangers of our system for the purpose of insisting upon the necessity of moral education, concluding with a brief allegory addressed to the children. The Address was not all of equal merit, passages of it were eloquent, and others well thought out but others were feeble and inconclusive. On the whole however, it deserved a better audience than it had and was delivered with a degree of animation uncommon for him. After some other brief ceremonies the parties retired as they came.

I went home and found there T. K. Davis come to spend the day. Talk of many things, but he has taken of late to ultra opinions which I admire very little and his manners are less pleasing every hour. I regret this much on his account as it does him injury with others, but experience must teach him as it does us all even like it as we may.

Before he left Col. Quincy and his Wife and sister Anna came, who were followed by Mr. Beale and his daughters, Mr. Angier and his Wife, E. C. Adams and Mr. Price Greenleaf. The evening was warm and we sat until late watching the fireworks in Boston many of which were distinctly visible, and very handsome. To bed but not to sleep for the musquitoes.

[1] JA and John Hancock.

THURSDAY 5TH.

Very warm indeed, perhaps the hottest day yet of this hot season. I rode to Boston however taking Kirk in with me for the sake of riding the horse back and allowing me to drive a new one for trial. My time much taken up in Accounts and with interruptions. Saw Mr. Angier, Mr. A. H. Everett and Mr. Brooks, and two or three others. Nothing very new.

At one I started to return with the new horse, but owing to a misunderstanding I was allowed to take him without a pulley bridle to which he had been used. The consequence came near being fatal to me, for my hold was entirely unequal to restraining him for any length of time, so after two effectual attempts, I gave way on the third and he ran away with me. Luckily his former master had been in the habit of stopping to water him at a pump by Glover's store, and to this he directed his course so I by a last effort brought him up there. But my strength was so entirely gone that I had to hire a young man to accompany me the rest of the way and by doubling the reins back, he obtained the necessary control of the horse to make him go gently. Thus was I saved from an imminent peril, for which I felt duly grateful to that being who in all cases tries us for our good. The horse was also saved from injury as a further run on this hot day would have ruined him.

I was so fatigued as not much to enjoy my Afternoon. But I read Pliny, and Grahame. E. C. Adams spent the day here and Mrs. Stebbins took tea in the evening. We had a thunder shower but not a severe one. I retired to bed in a tone of mind which I hope may benefit me.

FRIDAY 6TH.

The air was perfectly clear this morning and cool enough to be very agreeable. I went to town accompanied by my man John, and drove in the horse I brought yesterday. He was by the aid of the contrivance of yesterday entirely under control and seemed to be docile and tractable, without tricks.

I was much occupied at the house and in various ways today. Accounts more especially. A call from Dr. King the electrician who had much to say of his experiments, and of my house.[1] Home by half after twelve taking with me another horse for trial. And if I had so much work yesterday to stop the one, I had nearly as much to get the other on. He was slow and awkward.

Afternoon reading Pliny and feeling somewhat stiff from my yesterday's effort, to remove which I resorted to the spade and rake. Short evening and retire early.

[1] The *Boston Directory*, 1838, lists a "William King, electrician," whose place of business was at 54 Cornhill and home at 1 Lyman Place. The likelihood is that the conference related to the installation of lightning rods on the new residence.

SATURDAY 7TH.

Morning clear and cool, growing warmer however as the day advanced. My Wife wished to go to Boston, so I accompanied her with the Nurse and baby. At the Office where I finished the very profitless inquisition in rectifying my Account and without success which is worse.

A short call from Alex. H. Everett, who does not appear to me to be in very good spirits. The news from Washington is not at all of a character to favour the continued domination of the Administration party, but it seems willing to set it's all upon the cast and the Autumn elections will probably decide the hazard of the die. I wish the Government had made for itself a better cause.

Dined with Mr. Frothingham and had a pleasant talk about the University and the modes of study best adapted to the forms of our country. Afterwards, returned to Quincy. Glad to get there and wish during the hot weather that I was not so often called to leave it. Drive to Braintree with Miss Sampson after my return and sat an hour on the porch. Quite a luxury.

July 1838

SUNDAY 8TH.

A very warm day having however at noon a Slight easterly breeze which checked the excessive heat. Occupied some time in copying which I still endeavour to continue.

Dr. Frothingham came out shortly before service and I attended him to the building. He preached in the morning from Psalms 22. 29. "And none can keep alive his own soul." A sermon upon the duty of prudence and selfpreservation occasioned by the late disasters at sea and the drowning of a little boy in his parish.[1] The merit of his discourses to me is in the nice moral discrimination which he endeavours, a merit he rarely can get much credit for, as the tendencies of men are ever to general conclusion. Afternoon from 2 Kings 5. 25. "And Elisha said unto him, whence comest thou, Gehasi? And he said, Thy servant went no whither." The prevailing tendency to conceal the truth by covering it with a shield of obscurity. A great deal of ingenious thought here, but I lost my nap by being obliged to attend him after dinner and was drowsy.

He returned and took tea before his departure for town with two of his boys who accompanied him. Evening my Wife and I went down to see Col. and Mrs. Quincy, who were not at home, but one of his sisters and T. K. Davis' grandmother were there as was Price Greenleaf a visitor. We returned shortly after nine, I walking—a most glorious evening.

Read a sermon of Mr. Buckminster's. Philippians 4. 3. "I entreat thee—help those women, which laboured with me in the gospel, whose names are in the book of life." This appears to have been a discourse delivered before a society of females and is a review of the historical record of the benevolent of the sex. I do not think it in the author's best manner, for it betrays the confined extent of his observation, but yet it has some of his merits too.

[1] On one of the disasters, see the entry for 15 July, below.

MONDAY 9TH.

I was up and dressed early this morning for the sake of going to Cambridge through Boston, in time for the commencement of the examination of the Junior class in Homer's Iliad. Found there were present four other members of the Committee, J. C. Gray, Judge Merrill, Mr. Hillard, and Mr. Forbes, a new member.[1]

The general appearance of the class was creditable, and that of some members, very good. But of the whole, there was but one thorough recitation. A young man, Eliot, who bears a high character here as a scholar. I recollected him last year.[2] At dinner, the usual persons with a Mr. Couthouy, attached to the expedition which is to go out in time.[3] Conversation not so lively as usual.

I returned home through town by four o'clock, with my horse who ran away with me, and which I have purchased. The heat of the day very great indeed. I amused myself with Pliny. Evening quiet on the portico watching the beauty of the scene and luxuriating in the freshness of the breeze.

[1] There was no one then living who bore the Forbes name and had attended Harvard College before 1838 (*Harvard Quinquennial Cat.*). Perhaps John Murray Forbes (1813–1898), not a Harvard man, is meant (*DAB*).

[2] Samuel Eliot, class of 1839, later professor of history and president of Trinity College, Hartford, and a Harvard overseer (*Harvard Quinquennial Cat.*).

[3] J. P. Couthouy, a sea captain, was associated with the Wilkes Exploring Expedition which sailed from Norfolk, Va., in 1838 for the Antarctic (MH-Ar).

TUESDAY 10TH.

The morning threatened great heat but the rising of the east wind furnished us a great luxury and reduced the temperature. I went to town for the morning. Time in that fatiguing business of accounts which is disgusting from its tedium. I have now verified the accuracy of all the entries and still there is an error. Home to dinner. Afternoon, Pliny and some labour in my ground. But the heat increased towards night. I. H. Adams, Mr. C. Miller and Mr. Smith passed half an hour. I felt much fatigued.

WEDNESDAY 11TH.

There was a fine wind today, but the heat of the sun was excessive. I walked down with my children to their schools and although moving slowly and stopping often, found it very hot. Most of the morning was spent at home writing copy of the Journal,[1] but at noon I had one of the horses and after bringing my Louisa home, went with my boy John, and my man down to Mount Wollaston beach where I bathed with the former. Perhaps the wisdom of this in the heat of so intense a day was not apparent, but we came home safe.

Afternoon, a short thunder shower after which the atmosphere became hotter than ever. We rarely have a more intense day. I read Pliny however, but did little else. Evening, on the portico seeking a little air, and I found some relief. Hot as this day has been, it has proved the capacity of my house for when perfectly quiet in it I felt no inconvenience, and the night which must have been intolerable elsewhere was cool enough to sleep. My father today 71.

[1] The editors have found no evidence that CFA applied the term "autobiography" to JA's manuscript that we now know by that name but that does not bear the title on its face. It seems likely that CFA is here referring to it as "the Journal," possibly from JA's excerpting extensively in its first part from the *Journals* of the Continental Congress (JA, *Diary and Autobiography*, 1:xliv–xlvi).

THURSDAY 12TH.

Up early enough to watch the sunrise, although it was in a cloud. The scene was notwithstanding very beautiful and the choral song of the birds made it sublime. I started after an early breakfast for Cambridge, having omitted attendance yesterday. It was the day fixed for the examination of the Sophomore Class in Homer's Odyssey. Present of the Committee, Messrs. Gray, Merrill, T. K. Davis and myself. The examination was on the whole not a very favorable one. It seemed to me that the young men had gone backward since last year both in their roots and general information, but still it is an intelligent class. I think Felton is not the man to carry them far. He looks to me sleepy.[1] At dinner, we had the Latin class examiners, Mr. Young, Mr. Andrews and G. B. Emerson. Professor Channing and Dr. Beck not so amusing as usual.[2] Home by four, thus finishing the labours of another year. Read Pliny and worked upon the ground. Evening at home.

[1] An iteration of the view expressed a year earlier (above, entry for 12 July 1837).
[2] Edward Tyrrel Channing, Boylston Professor of Rhetoric and Oratory, on whom see vol. 3:383; Charles Beck, University Professor of Latin (*Harvard Quinquennial Cat.*).

FRIDAY 13TH.

The morning was cloudy with an Easterly wind and rain. I felt unwilling to risk a day in Boston in a Storm so declined going; after my decision upon which, it cleared. I nevertheless spent a very useful morning and almost finished the paper book which I am copying. A curious account of a Journey to Stafford Springs, then a watering place of some repute but now eclipsed by Saratoga.[1]

Afternoon, spent some time in reading Pliny whose uniform egotism becomes tedious, and also in working upon the grounds. This has taken an hour of almost every day. I also rode with my Wife and the children to Milton in quest of some flowers, but we did not succeed in procuring any. Evening at home. Writing Diary and reading.

[1] JA's journey to Stafford Springs, Conn., and vicinity, 3–12 June 1771, is recounted in JA, *Diary and Autobiography*, 2:21–33.

SATURDAY 14TH.

Pleasant day. I went to town. Occupied as is usual with me in Accounts and in doing commissions. Office where I concluded to sum up my Annual settlement and leave the error which I cannot explain. This is vexatious but I cannot help it.

Returned to Quincy accompanied by Joseph H. Adams who dined with us. Afternoon I read Pliny and dawdled away some time. Evening Mr. Beale and his daughters and Mr. and Mrs. Wales Jr. paid a visit. E. C. Adams returned with my Wife and also passed the evening, I accompanying her home.

As the time passes, I am more and more impressed with the insignificance of my use of time. Speaking of this, A. H. Everett came in only for a moment and proposed to me to write more about Mr. Biddle, but I declined having no wish to aid the Administration in its projects which appear to me to run so much against the best interests of the people.

SUNDAY. 15TH.

A warm day and cloudy but cleared before sunset. I occupied myself in copying the remainder of the MS Journal which I wished to execute but did not quite finish it. Attended divine service and heard Mr. Briggs[1] preach from Ecclesiastes 9. 2. "All things come alike to all." Rather a peculiar view of this text as applied to the moral discriminations of life, the inequalities of character resulting from the inequalities of condition, all which vanish whenever the artificial necessities of life cease to control. He illustrated by the case of the late Steamer Pulaski in a striking and quite eloquent manner.[2] Though not generally animated he had passages of great power. Afternoon, Matthew 18. 2.3. "And Jesus called a little child unto him, and set him in the midst of them and said, Verily I say unto you, Except ye be converted and become as little children, ye shall not enter into the kingdom of Heaven."

Afternoon, read a sermon of Buckminster's being the 24th and last of the volume. 2 Peter 1. 5.7. "And to your faith, virtue; and to virtue, knowledge; and to knowledge, temperance and to temperance patience and to patience godliness; and to godliness brotherly kindness and to brotherly kindness, charity." The meaning of these terms and the combination required of knowledge with godliness and charity. Perhaps little can be said beyond the text itself. Evening at home. Thomas, my mother's man came today with the luggage and informed us he had left the family at Providence detained by Louisa's sickness.[3]

[1] On Rev. George Ware Briggs, see vol. 5:385–386.

[2] The steam packet *Pulaski* from Savannah, after calling at Charleston, on 14 June sailed with 153 passengers bound for Baltimore. On the same night off Wilmington, N.C., its boilers exploded. It sank rapidly; there were only 17 survivors (*Daily Advertiser*, 23, 25, 29 June, p. 2, col. 4; p. 2, cols. 1–2; p. 1, cols. 5–6 respectively).

[3] That is, Mary Louisa Adams; see above, entry for 21 Aug. 1836.

MONDAY 16TH.

A pleasant day. I was occupied most of my morning in finishing the copy of the Fragmentary Journal and in correcting what was already copied. I have now supplied the interval which was not copied and propose to turn my attention to a collateral branch of investigation in reviewing Grahame's two last volumes.

I have formed a somewhat extensive plan but doubt my energy in execution. The little success corresponding to all my exertion has the effect of damping my ardor in undertaking. I go about a plan with a sense of the pressure of a resisting medium.

The Carriage went in for the family and brought them out before noon, the remainder of the morning spent with them. My father remains behind a few days, to correct and publish his last Speech. My Mother looks better but fatigued. Afternoon, divided between Pliny and the superintendence of my ground, which requires constant care to look well. Evening at my Mother's.

TUESDAY 17TH.

Weather fair. I went to town this morning and passed my time in the variety of avocations usual with me. These Accounts are very tedious things but it is better to be rid of them punctually or they grow to be most annoying. Home at one, bringing out with me Miss Smith, who is to spend the summer with my Mother.

Afternoon passed in reading Pliny whose ninth book I finished. This finishes the miscellaneous letters. They are thrown together without any order or attempt to settle the dates, which might be partially done. On the whole they give a pretty good view of Pliny's character. His main spring seems to have been his vanity, but it impelled him into actions not often the result of this cause. He was fond of the praise for doing noble things. Yet we must remember we have his own Account only. Evening down to see my Mother. Nothing of interest.

WEDNESDAY 18TH.

A beautiful day. I remained at home and occupied myself pretty steadily with the exception of a walk with the children to school and down to the house to see my Mother. I commenced this day my attempt at a Review. It is remarkable what difficulty I find in this. My practice in the Newspapers if it had no other effect gave me great facility and this I find I lose by occasional neglect. There is another difficulty in the distraction of thought occasioned by external circumstances. The air, the heat, the vegetation and every thing of nature. Still it is something to say that I commenced. Two hours I devoted to correcting the copy made of MS. Afternoon, Pliny, and engaged as usual a little in working upon my grounds. Evening, with my Wife at the Mansion.

THURSDAY 19TH.

Fine day. I remained at home all the morning with the exception of a walk down to the Mansion. I made some progress in my undertaking although I feel very much the want of more precise information. This must be procured at some rate or other, or I cannot go on. Continued my labour upon the MSS copy which grows more and more interesting and important.

Afternoon, Pliny's Letters to Trajan and the replies. They give one a very favorable opinion of that Emperor. Short, and direct, they contrast favorably with the more effeminate style of Pliny.

Intelligence was brought that my father had arrived so I went down to see him and converse with him. He seems better than I expected but complains of exhaustion. No wonder. Returned home to tea and then down in the evening. W. Lee there.[1] After a conversation until nearly ten, home.

[1] William Lee was an old friend of JQA's, from their years in diplomacy; see vol. 3:355.

FRIDAY 20TH.

Fine day although the easterly wind made it rather cool, and we had a little rain towards night. I went into town accompanied by my man John who went in to inquire for some persons for my mother's family. My time much taken up in commissions of various sorts, and in regulating accounts. It was one of the days in which I did much of what I intended and yet left something. Home rather late. Afternoon reading Pliny, but interrupted by a visit from Mrs. Bigelow and Miss Scollay, who staid a short time. I also worked a little while upon the ground. Evening down at the Mansion notwithstanding the rain.

SATURDAY 21ST.

Morning clear and cool. I went to the Bank, taking the children with me to school. Also a visit to the House where I got so engaged with Mr. N. Curtis and with copying that I feared I should lose my morning, but nevertheless, I made some progress in my review which I begin to hope may turn out something. Nobody ever commenced with less expectation or continued more languidly. I devoted an hour also to correcting MS copy. After dinner, Pliny, interrupted however by a visit from Mr. and Mrs. Edward Brooks and their children as also one from my father after they had gone. Evening at the Mansion as usual. Nothing new.

SUNDAY 22D.

An agreeable, cool day. I devoted some time to writing on my project which I fear I shall not satisfactorily execute. Then attended divine service and heard Dr. Parkman of Boston preach from   , the extract too long to quote. And my attention was not well fixed so that I can not give much account of it. Afternoon. 1. Timothy 2. [2] "That we may lead a quiet and peaceable life in all godliness and honesty." A good practical discourse upon the duty of religion and good faith in the details of life, together with a direct application to economical habits which would have suited the meridian of Boston on Tuesday next at the dinner to Mr. Webster to a charm.

Afternoon, having finished the volume of Sermons of Mr. Buckminster I began in continuation of my practice, the first volume of a Collection called the English Preacher,[1] with a Sermon by Bishop Tillotson. Philippians 3. 8. "I count all things but loss for the excellency of the knowledge of Christ Jesus my Lord." The excellence of the Christian Religion as a law for the regulation of our lives to secure happiness both here and hereafter. A good sensible but as it appeared to me not a very powerful discourse. In the evening at the house where were assembled many of the society of the town.

[1] JQA's copy of *The English Preacher*, 9 vols., London, 1773, is in MQA.

MONDAY 23D.

A very fine day. I passed it for the most part at home, engaged in writing upon my projected Review and in correcting MS. I believe I have in my mind a better thing than I am likely to execute. My energy does not seem equal to the investigation which I meditate. Joseph H. Adams here a little while, who tells us of his mother's illness. Apparently a grievous case of suffering from the death of poor Thomas, her son. I can feel for her where I regret her sensibility.

Afternoon, my father accompanied me in a ride round Milton, my favourite resort. He seemed to enjoy it much. Home in time to finish the letters of Pliny. These as relics of a particular age are interesting. Those to Tacitus are interesting as well as the correspondence with Trajan which is perhaps the only one extant of the kind. But after all Pliny was not a mind of the first class. Evening at the house. Conversation as usual.

TUESDAY 24TH.

Morning I went to town and was actively occupied in various commissions as usual until eleven o'clock, when I went to the Office. Calls from P. C. Brooks Jr. with a Note from his father,[1] P. P. F. Degrand and S. E. Greene who has at last sold Mr. Johnson's Exchange. Then home.

This was the day fixed upon for the great dinner to Mr. Webster, the manifestation of the feeling of the citizens of Boston against the Administration and in his favour. I do not attend, first because I dislike all of these sorts of display. Secondly, because I dislike the public character of the hero.

Afternoon read Pliny. Panegyric upon Trajan in the extreme of the adulatory spirit though regarded in that age as moderation. Evening at the Mansion.

[1] Note missing.

WEDNESDAY. 25TH.

The morning looked very threatening with rain but there was only a little and it cleared away. My time much taken up in my work a sketch of which I finally accomplished this day. But it is a mere skeleton of skin and bones which requires all of the filling up, and somehow or other my energy seems to be laid asleep. A great many books to consult and some to read more attentively than I am likely to do. Corrected some portion of text also.

I expected Mr. Brooks today to dine with me, but he did not come. My father whom I had asked to join him came and spent an hour, after which I went to ride accompanied by him. We went to Braintree, thence through Weymouth over the bridge to Quincy Point and home. I read a little of Pliny and but little. Evening my father, Mother and family at my house until nine.

THURSDAY. 25TH [i.e. 26TH].

Quite a thunder shower during the night but it was beautifully clear this morning. I did not effect much. Strolled down to the other house and there got caught in reading desultorily for a couple of hours. My review must now wait for a pamphlet which has been promised me or rather a lecture of Mr. Felt's to extend my information as to facts.[1] Hutchinson is in these respects the fullest authority I have.

Corrected MS until dinner time, when Mr. Brooks came. This was not entirely expected but nevertheless he was welcome, and after dinner, he went with me in my vehicle to Mount Wollaston and Germantown, a pleasant ride, thence home by the new lane. We then walked over to the quarries on the farm and across the hill home. The family from the other house took tea with us and passed the evening and Mr. Brooks spent the night here.

[1] Rev. Joseph Barlow Felt had earlier delivered a lecture at the Massachusetts Historical Society (see entry for 19 Dec. 1837, above) on the "old Currency of Massachusetts," which he would expand and publish as *A Historical Account of* *Massachusetts Currency*, Boston, 1839. Whether the MS of the lecture said in the succeeding entry, below, to be available to CFA at the State House was as originally delivered or as it would be published is not clear.

FRIDAY. 27TH.

Morning clear and very pleasant. I went to town where I was occupied as usual. Accounts and various little commissions. Call from I. P. Davis about Felt's Lecture which he does not get but promises if I go and get it, at the State House. Spoke of the dinner and then of his son Thomas whose course he seems to regret, and partly charges upon me. I told him that I leaned that way but did not sustain the Administration in its course of imbecility and error. I am myself sorry that Davis gives this uneasiness to his father, but like all sanguine temperaments he must be allowed to work his own way out of the evil. Home. Afternoon, Pliny's Panegyric upon Trajan and evening down at the Mansion.

SATURDAY 28TH.

A turn towards greater heat again today. I remained very quietly at home with the exception of a short visit at the house. Time devoted to reading, particularly Hamilton's Report upon funding the State debts. He certainly puts into the back ground all the modern politicians of the modern school who know little of the value of Office but in it's perquisites. Hamilton was certainly a great man if not in all respects a judicious one.

Afternoon Pliny's long Panegyric. In the midst of tedious and fulsome adulation, there are passages relating to the time of Domitian which are of value as showing the character of his reign. An address of this kind to a reigning prince, delivered before a crowded auditory could not have treated of such matters if they were not generally known to be true. And what a picture they give, in connection with the details of the historians. Evening as Mrs. Adams has gone to town I took tea and spent the rest of it at the Mansion.

SUNDAY 29TH.

This was a morning of as great heat as any we have had, but we had a tremendous shower at noon which refreshed the herbage if it did not greatly cool the air. I began today Dr. [William] Paley's Horæ Paulinæ[1] being a system of evidences made up of casual coincidences in the various writings of Paul.

Attended divine service and heard Mr. Lunt from Hebrews 3. 2. "Be not forgetful to entertain strangers: for thereby some have entertained angels unawares." A very neat discourse upon hospitality full of allusion to ancient manners and of good doctrine upon this subject. Perhaps I have something in this matter to charge against myself. J. H. Adams dined with me. Afternoon Sermon from 2. Colossians 3. 14. "Above all these things put on charity, which is the bond of perfectness." Charity is among the most pleasing of the Christian virtues. It expands the heart and exercises the affections. Mr. Lunt's view was a sensible one but I was not attentive.

Read a Sermon by Bishop Tillotson in the English Preacher. Psalm 119. 165. "Great peace have they that love thy law and nothing shall offend them." Upon the effect of Religion to tranquillize the mind. After working my usual exercises through, I began a sort of review of the Address of the Republican Members.[2] Evening at the Mansion. The air cooler.

[1] A copy (London, 1790) is in MQA.

[2] On the "Address" and CFA's review of it, see entry of 3 Aug., below. On the equivalence of "republican" and "demo-cratic" during this period, see Hans Sperber and Travis Trittschuh, *Dictionary of American Political Terms*, N.Y., 1964, p. 368.

MONDAY 30TH.

A very warm day, but the heat was tempered with us by a high wind blowing with violence, which though warm was better than calm. I rose early and went to Mr. Greenleaf's Wharf and took a bath, alone. Then home where I sat most of my time occupied upon the Review I undertook yesterday. Of this I finished three numbers which I inclosed in a Note to the Editor of the Courier. This is a new step that I have taken and has not been done without reflection. My feelings would have led me to continue neutral between the parties but my principles would not. The Address is a step into the jaws of Nullification which I can never follow, and if I mean to acquire any influence at all which I must resist. For the letters to Mr. Biddle have leaned the balance the wrong way for me. Afternoon I read a little of Pliny's Panegyric, and a few of Bayle's letters.[1] Evening at the Mansion to tea. The air growing cooler until it became much changed.

[1] Pierre Bayle's *Lettres* (3 vols., Amsterdam, 1729) is in MQA.

TUESDAY 31ST.

A cool morning. I accompanied my father to Mr. Greenleaf's Wharf where we took a bath. The water many degrees cooler than yesterday. After breakfast went to town. Time taken up in commissions. Called to see Mr. Felt and procured the Lecture of which I was in quest. He showed me the State Records and his work in compiling them and ar-ranging their order for binding. A very valuable labour which does as much credit to him as to the State that authorized it.[1]

Then to my own house to get from there some specie about which I had become uneasy and therefore proposed to change it into Treasury Notes. This done with various other commissions, I returned home better satisfied with my day's work than I commonly am.

Sent my papers to the Courier. They will furnish another experi-ment upon the popular feeling. The letters to Biddle are the first of my efforts which ever broke the walls of party. It remains to be seen if these will do the same. Afternoon, Pliny, and Bayle. My father came up in the evening with his glass which we found and amused ourselves looking at the Islands of the bay.

[1] Joseph Barlow Felt had in process the arrangement of the state records of Massachusetts in categories and, ultimately, their binding in 326 volumes. They remain in the State Archives as "The Felt Collection."

WEDNESDAY AUGUST 1ST.

Quite cool. I nevertheless accompanied my father to the bath which was pleasant. Morning passed for the greater part at home in reading Mr. Felt's Lecture which after all contains very little that I did not know before, and in making up a sketch of my last and most difficult number of my review. I did not succeed in this to my satisfaction.

Dined with all my family at my fathers but was obliged to devote a great deal of my time both morning and afternoon to overseeing some men who are putting another coat of gravel upon my roads. Read a little of Pliny but on the whole I passed a pretty unsatisfactory day. Evening, Tea and two hours at the Mansion in general conversation.

THURSDAY 2D.

Up early and breakfasted below with my father whom I accompanied to Hingham on a fishing party by invitation of the gentlemen of that town. We reached Mr. Loring's house shortly after seven, and there my father got out to proceed to Cohasset in Mr. L's conveyance, and Mr. C. Brooks took his place in mine. Having arrived at the house we found about as many persons as we saw last year and most of the same.[1] We divided into parties, some going to fish on the rocks, others taking to the boats. I went with Mr. Brooks, Capt. Ford, Mr. Baker and a Mr. Bovee, and we had tolerably good success. Our return was hastened by the qualmishness of one of our number.

The dinner was of fish as usual but much better than last year. After it was over we harnessed again and returned to Hingham where the ladies proposed to have a little party in a wood called Tranquillity Grove, at which they expected to see the President and return him thanks for his efforts in their behalf, at the last Session of Congress. The number of persons assembled was large for the place, and tables of refreshment, tea, coffee &c. were spread for them all. Mr. Loring made an Address to which my father briefly replied.[2] And after sunset we all started on our return home. The night was very fine and we reached my father's just before nine, pretty well fatigued, though satis-

86

fied with the day. Such parties as these are growing and are a great improvement upon former guzzling festivals.

[1] The earlier visit to Hingham is recounted in the entry for 3 Aug. 1837, above.

[2] The gathering in Tranquillity Grove, organized by the ladies of Hingham to pay "their respects to the eloquent defender of their rights in congress," was attended by some five hundred persons. It was given detailed coverage in the *Hingham Patriot* on 4 Aug. (a handwritten copy is in the Adams Papers). As there reported, Thomas Loring, in introducing JQA on behalf of the ladies, said their wish was "to express their heart-felt gratitude for the eminent services which [he] had rendered to the cause of humanity and justice, in defending the sacred right of petition, and for the bold and independent stand which he had taken ... against the practice of rejecting petitions unread, unheard, and unexamined." JQA's response included his thanks for being "thus welcomed by his constituents, for ... 'I consider the Ladies of this Congressional District as much my constituents as their relatives by whose votes I was elected. I know ... that it is asserted that women have no political rights. Their petitions had been treated ... as if they had none. But all history refuted this position.' They had political rights but he would not say it was their duty to exercise them except in cases of great, pressing, public emergency.... Their rights he was determined ever to defend, and he trusted they would be maintained in Massachusetts, if no where else." The ode, composed for the occasion and sung to conclude the exercises, began:

"Thrice welcome, hoary sage,
To this our Tranquil Wood;
New England's daughters raise the song,
'Gainst whom was aimed the burning wrong,
Which Adams has withstood."

FRIDAY 3D.

I arose this morning with the kind of warning which precedes a head ach. Nevertheless I went to town and busied myself in the usual range of commissions.

I find my first and second numbers of the Review have been published exactly in the manner of the former numbers but without comment.[1] And none of the other papers of either party notice them. At any rate I cannot now complain of the want of distinction given to them by the mode of publication. On the other hand my publisher's Account came today[2] for my last pamphlet and shows me conclusively that it is not expedient to try that mode again with all the press determined to be silent.

Home but I omitted dinner and have no great account to give of the rest of my day, nor did I get free from pain until late into the night.

[1] CFA's four papers, entitled "The Democratic Address" and signed "A Conservative," appeared in the *Courier* on 2, 3, 4, and 8 Aug., each at p. 2, cols. 1–2. They undertake a review of the "Address to the People of the United States" by a Committee of Administration supporters in the Congress. To that document's confession that "political elements of the country never were in greater confusion," he asks, "How came they so?" and holds the administration's poli-

cies responsible. If the Bank was such a failure, why have pecuniary affairs run into such great difficulties two years after its demise? A national banking authority is essential, he asserts, simply to promote a uniform currency, "to check the State institutions in their tendency to saturate the circulation with paper," but it must be subjected to severe public oversight. However it has been impossible for the Administration to devise any nationally directed scheme because it has been crippled by adherence to a strict constructionism enforced by its Southern, pro-slavery adherents. Finally, he alleges that the threat of nullification is invoked in the Address to stifle national initiative on the currency and to prevent legislation on slavery in the District.

² Missing.

SATURDAY 4TH.

We have had dry and hot weather for so long that the country begins to show signs of suffering. I was visited by my father to enquire of my condition, and to talk of my papers of which he penetrated the authorship.

My time was principally consumed in drawing out the last number which embraces the vexed question of Slavery, which I finished before dinner although it does not quite satisfy me. The difficulty of the subject and of the audience to address it to is such that I hurry matters which ought to be dwelt upon.

Afternoon, Pliny's Panegyric which goes over every thing in the world that would furnish material, and Bayle's Letters which are rather amusing. Evening at the other house spent in conversation. Remarkably beautiful night.

SUNDAY 5TH.

Warm though hazy and ending in clouds. I read some of Dr. Paley's Horæ Paulinæ. Attended divine service and heard Mr. Lunt preach from a text in 1 Corinthians 10. 16. "The cup of blessing which we bless, is it not the communion of the blood of Christ." A communion sermon turning very much into the cast of thought of his 4th of July Address, the progress of Religion in ameliorating the social feeling of the world, and hence extending the effect of benevolence in dissipating the great evils of life. Afternoon. Revelations 11. 17. "We give thee thanks, O Lord God Almighty which are, and wast, and art to come;" The consideration of the Deity in these three relations, very ingeniously managed but rather pretty only.

At home I read a discourse from the English Preacher by Dr. Smalridge. Luke 8. 18. "Take heed therefore how ye hear." The duty of preparation for instruction, that is by listening with attention and with meekness for the purpose of improvement. A good discourse. Evening Mr. E. Price Greenleaf came in, and accompanied us to the Mansion. It rained slightly.

MONDAY 6TH.

Morning warm but at noon the wind changed and brought with it a very cool and refreshing shower. I had just seated myself to pursue my morning avocations when Deacon Spear came up to inquire if I would accompany my father to see the course of a new road through his land, as laid out by the Commissioners. This passion for new Roads is one of the fancies of the times, occasionally doing good but more often wasting money. I think this is the case here.

We returned at twelve, and I passed the remainder of the time before dinner in correcting MS and filling up an omission. After dinner, I finished the Panegyric of Trajan and with it the works of Pliny. As a book it has interest from it's date, but the gratification from reading it is not the same derived from the works of Cicero or any of the classical writers. His mind is artificial and his style rhetorical. His letters are compositions as much as his oration. Nothing further of interest. Evening at the Mansion.

TUESDAY 7TH.

Pleasant day. I went to town and was occupied mostly at the Office after going through the usual routine of my affairs. Nothing new but the arrival for the third time of the Great Western. This seems to be making the question of Steam Navigation across the Atlantic almost a matter of certainty.[1]

The Courier of today contains an acknowledgment of my fourth number but not the number itself. No notice whatever of the series, in any press of either side and I begin to think they are of no value and that I have made a blunder. Home.

Afternoon, began Titus Lucretius, de Rerum Natura,[2] and consumed some time idly in reading a French book picked up the other day about the rules of entertaining. Evening at the Mansion. Conversation. No finer night could be imagined.

[1] The steam packet *Great Western* from Bristol arrived at New York on the 5th after a voyage of 14½ days. It brought London papers of 20 July (*Boston Courier*, 8 Aug., p. 2, col. 3).

[2] At MQA are four copies of Lucretius' *De rerum natura*, two having belonged to CFA (Glasgow, 1813; London, 1821), two to JQA (Birmingham, 1772; Zweibrücken, 1782).

WEDNESDAY 8TH.

I spent my day at home very quietly, devoting a good deal of the morning to a new draught of my projected review of Grahame. I continue to write although I must know beforehand that my views do not suit the popular taste. To bend to the passions of the day appears to be the road to reputation in our country and generation, and I have studied to form myself upon a different model, the investigation of truth. Yet it is my duty to make the best use I can of my talents, if I have any, and to try to be of service in some manner.

Two hours devoted to the reading of the MS which I corrected almost to the end of the paper books.[1] These make a valuable collection of which there is now a complete copy. Dined at my father's with the family.

Afternoon, a ride accompanied by my father round Mount Wollaston to the end of the road, thence to Germantown, from there by Quincy Point round to the Weymouth Road. Evening conversation at the house, T. K. Davis and Edmund Quincy, and opinions respecting them.

[1] See entry of 1 July, above.

THURSDAY 9TH.

Fine day but it gradually clouded up. I was occupied in the morning pretty industriously upon my proposed review which is going on slowly and not very satisfactorily. I incline to distrust of myself.

At the Mansion house where I read the Newspapers. Found my fourth number inserted but very badly printed. This is one of the vexations incident to the American Newspaper Press. Well, they are printed and will find nobody to approve of them. All parties will vote them disagreeable because they run in lines with none. Why should I trouble my head with composition when I can follow my humour so much more luxuriously in study.

Passed some time in examining old MS. Mrs. E. Everett and Mrs. Frothingham with her son Thomas came out to dine and spend two or three hours. Of course I could do little during the remainder of the day, but a few lines of the first book of Lucretius. Evening in consequence of the setting in of rain in slight showers we did not go down as usual, but I sat and read Bayle.

FRIDAY. 10TH.

The day cloudy but without rain. I went to town and my time was taken up in Accounts and in a call at my house to superintend the receipt of my chair from Washington. This is the way in which time goes. Made some other calls and passed a little time in Accounts at the Office. Then return.

Nothing new in town to start the wits of the public. I see in some distant papers extracts from my numbers with moderate praise, but so shockingly printed that I wonder they were not censured. In town no notice has been taken of them whatsoever. Home.

Afternoon at home. Read Lucretius whose text appears to have suffered somewhat by corruption and to be rather antique. Also, Bayle. Literary letters but not very interesting. Evening at the Mansion.

SATURDAY 11TH.

Cloudy but no rain. I sat down to work upon my Review of Grahame. But on the whole I find I can do little with it. My inclination is to give it up as a bad job. The vis does not seem to be in me to make a good thing of it, and if I could summon it, the result would be to unfit it for appearance before the public.

My father came in just then and I followed him down to his house soon after where I wasted some time over the papers. This settled the matter for the day, so on my return I went to work upon the MS and read a large part of J. A's answer to Hamilton ⟨*already*⟩ never published.[1] This is the work to which I must and will turn my attention — The arranging all these papers and reading the material ones. Afternoon, Lucretius and Bayle. Evening to tea at the Mansion and an hour afterwards. But returned early home.

[1] JA's published answer to the *Letter from Alexander Hamilton Concerning the Public Conduct and Character of John Adams, Esq., President of the United States*, N.Y., 1800, first appeared in the form of 18 letters to the *Boston Patriot*, 15 April – 24 June 1809. It was reprinted in part as *Correspondence of the Late President Adams, Originally Published in the Boston Patriot. In a Series of Letters*, Boston, 1809.

CFA's word "already," over which he wrote "never," would suggest that at the time he first wrote the journal entry, he believed that the MS he had found among his grandfather's papers had provided the text for the published reply. At a later date, but before he came to prepare the papers for publication in JA's *Works*, 1850–1856, he became aware that the versions already printed did not derive from the 90-page MS draft, probably written in 1801 (Adams Papers, Microfilms, Reel No. 399). For the *Works* CFA chose to use as his text the letters in the *Patriot*, deleting some passages but supplementing that text with footnote additions of paragraph length taken from the draft; see *Works*, 9:240.

In a note in his hand attached to the 1801 MS, CFA wrote that the "Draught ... [is] unsuited for publication." That view seems to derive from the tone of vindictiveness and bitterness in it. His editorial practice generally was to excise passages from the papers where JA had indulged his emotions about Hamilton; see JA, *Diary and Autobiography*, 1:lii;

3:386–388, 434–435. His action seems partly dictated by sensitivity to the "belligerent measures in which we have for two generations been involved" and partly by an admiration for Hamilton which a younger Adams could admit to after an interval of nearly fifty years; see vol. 6:358–359, and entry for 28 July 1838, above.

SUNDAY 12TH.

A clear fine day in which the beauty of the landscape again shone out with the greater effect from the previous days of mist. I read a little of the Horæ Paulinæ in the morning and found the MS Paper book which had been omitted during my revisal of the copy, so I corrected it in part.

Attended divine service and heard Mr. N. Hall of Dorchester preach from James. 4. 14. "What is your life?" Afternoon Psalms. "God hath set the solitary in families." Both these discourses bear the stamp of Mr. Hall's mind, a meditative, rather poetical spirit, cast in the mould of the dreamer rather than the observer of life as it is. I am so little in this way myself that I fear I cannot do justice to those who are. Mr. Hall dined with us.

After service I read a discourse by Dr. Clark from the English Preacher. Proverbs 14. 9. "Fools make a mock at sin." The definition of courage as distinct from audacity or insolence which disregards religion, and hence the unreasonable nature of their behaviour. A sensible sermon but not great — the characteristic by the way of most of those from the British Church. Read a little of Lockhart's last volume, which has a very interesting piece of Diary, and Bayle. Evening at the Mansion. Spirits a little affected.

MONDAY 13TH.

The air was clear and it was warm today but not oppressive. I went to town instead of my regular day, tomorrow, because the Probate Court proposes to meet at Quincy tomorrow and I wish to attend to poor Thomas Adams's affairs. My time was taken up in a variety of Commissions which kept me going pretty steadily from the moment of arrival until that of departure. This was somewhat fatiguing as it involved the walk over a pretty large space of ground. Home.

Afternoon, Lucretius who writes vigorously upon a subject too crabbed for Poetry. Bayle, and the last volume of Lockhart which is interesting from it's melancholy tone. The great charm of Scott is to be found in that of Terence's line, "Homo sum; nihil humani alienum a me puto."[1] Evening, lady visitors but we spent an hour notwithstanding at the Mansion. Louisa seven years old this day. Heaven be praised.

[1] That is, "I am a man, and nothing that is human is uninteresting to me." The passage, slightly altered by CFA, is from Terence's play *Heautontimoroumenos*, I, I, 25. CFA, along with his brothers, had studied this and Terence's five other comedies at school in England in 1816 and, at the same time, been the benefi-ciary of extensive notes on them in letters from JA. In 1834, on rereading the plays, he entered JA's comments and translations of selected passages, including the present one as translated above, in his own copy of the London, 1825, edn. now in MQA. See vol. 5:xviii, 265–269.

TUESDAY 14TH.

Morning cold with an Easterly wind. I remained at home almost all day. Attended the probate Court held at the Hotel and presented my papers for the order of notice, but was stopped for want of the presence of the other executor. I must now write to Isaac Hull to know what his determination is.[1]

Much time taken up in correcting MS. Finished the missing paper book which I since found, and read the continuation which is not copied. Also at the other house the MS fragment written by my father which makes me regret it was not completed. But it is brief and somewhat over compressed.[2]

Afternoon after dining at the Mansion, read Lucretius and Scott. A very fascinating production. I have had Mr. Rowley a picture cleaner out here all day to attend to my frames, and the younger ladies went to town. I must improve my time better.

[1] LbC of CFA's letter to Isaac Hull Adams, 15 Aug., is in the Adams Papers.
[2] On the "Memorial of the Life of John Adams" that JQA had undertaken in 1829 and on which he had worked spasmodically until 1831, but which remained a fragment, see vols. 3:257; 4:84, 126–127, 175–176, 352.

WEDNESDAY 15TH.

Cool day. After breakfast, walked down to the House to see how Mr. Rowley got along. Found him at work still.

Received by mail from Boston, a copy of the Washington Globe of last Saturday the 11th, containing some strictures upon my papers together with a transfer to it's columns of the second number.[1] This is singular enough. But as the Editor of the Courier probably marked this paper as an invitation to me to notice it, I took it home and devoted the remainder of the morning to writing a reply. Curious is the fate of my productions. The Globe makes them a charge against Mr. Webster, and the Whigs shun them as they would pestilence. They nevertheless attract a little attention, and perhaps may be the means of insuring to me respectability in the world.

After dinner which I took at my father's as usual on this day, he accompanied me in a ride to Squantum which consumed the afternoon. Evening, called with the family upon Mr. Lunt. Found F. A. Whitney and his sister there. Nothing material. Home by ten.

[1] To its reprint of the second of CFA's four letters to the *Boston Courier* signed "A Conservative," *The Globe* added the argument and conclusion of the fourth letter, that of 8 August. The letters were offered (mistakenly) as examples of the Webster effort to effect an alliance between the abolition party and the National Bank party "upon the broad platform of national consolidation" (11 Aug., p. 3, cols. 2–4).

THURSDAY 16TH.

Cloudy day with occasional showers. I remained at home and occupied myself steadily in reading over the MS papers of J. A., the old journals and controversial papers which seem to be numerous in our family.

I also for the sake of refreshing my German resumed Lessing's Laocoon which I had partially read last year.[1] I began it over again and was still more pleased than ever with the critical acumen it displays. There is something exceedingly agreeable in turning from the tempestuous sea of politics to which I have been bred, to the calm and sunny repose of art.

Afternoon, read Lucretius finishing the first book and reviewing a part of it in the annotated edition of Gilbert Wakefield. A scholar, but a bold conjectural critic of the Bentley school.[2] Continued Lockhart also. Evening at the Mansion and home in rain.

[1] Above, entry for 23 July 1837.
[2] Of the four copies of *De rerum natura* at MQA (above, entry of 7 Aug.), that in 4 vols., Glasgow, 1813, contained the commentary of Gilbert Wakefield. On him, see *DNB*.

FRIDAY. 17TH.

A fine, clear day. I went to town where I was occupied much as usual. Looked into the National Office[1] and found that the Courier had published my communication,[2] but as usual without a remark. It reads tolerably well, but will I suppose be received like the rest and the Globe finding it can make no political use of the article will fall into the general silence.

August 1838

My various duties carried me to different parts of the town but I still had a leisure hour at the Office. Home. Afternoon, Lucretius. A nervous writer with occasionally beautiful passages. Also Scott whose last days are like the gray clouds of evening closing over a setting sun.

My father came up after tea to look for Mercury whose greatest elongation from the sun permits him to be now visible with the naked eye. We saw him for half an hour as he rapidly descended towards the horizon. Mr. E. P. Greenleaf came and passed an hour, also.

[1] The National Insurance Co. offices at 66 State Street.

[2] The letter to the editor, signed "A Conservative," is a reply to the Washington *Globe*, which had on 11 Aug. reprinted a part of CFA's review of the "Democratic Address" along with an attack upon the review's author as a follower of Webster, a whig, and an abolitionist. While denying the rest of the charge, he directs his answer principally to a definition of his differences with the abolitionists: "Their views are not my views. They look to the single question of slavery as a question of abstract right.

I look to it as operating upon every interest in our country. They regard the Southern citizens as subjects to make proselytes of. I regard them as responsible politicians. They move heaven and earth to accelerate the abolition of slavery. I stand by waiting its downfall by ... irresistible destiny ... and only resist attempts whencesoever they may come to harness my fellow-citizens and myself into the criminal work of pulling down the constitution to make the materials with which to struggle to the last against that destiny" (*Boston Courier*, 17 Aug., p. 2, cols. 1–2).

SATURDAY 18TH.

On this day I count myself thirty one years old. The change into middle life is now complete and I bid adieu to it's spring time. Well, I have had more than a common share of enjoyment and feel grateful to God that I have reached this day with health unimpaired, and with more of the blessings of this world than fall to an ordinary lot. I have striven to deserve them with not so much success as I had hoped. Indeed my remembrance of my own errors is always keen, and though it has not always the effect to correct them, very much moderates my propensity to ambition of worldly distinction. The desire to be useful is one thing, the anxiety to be prominent is another, and perhaps the task of a conscientious man is greatest when he strives to draw the line which divides the duty consequent from the first from the selfish variety prompting the last.

My time was quietly passed in reading in the morning, MS, and Lessing. Afternoon, Lucretius and Scott. Evening, took Tea at the Mansion. Mrs. Frothingham's two sons, Octavius and Edward are with us.

My plans for improving my Diary have all failed, yet I am mortified by its present insipidity, and propose to try another from today, of this kind, first in memorandum form to notice the weather, then my general employment of the day. Visitors if any of interest, and upon the plan of Gibbon a statement of my reading, and remarks if I have any to make. Perhaps I may fail in this new scheme, but any thing is better than this monotony of trifles.

SUNDAY 19TH.

Day clear and cool. Divine Service both parts, and a walk to the Quarries to show the Frothinghams the way of getting stone, the evening at Mrs. Adams's to see her daughter Mrs. Angier. Walter Hellen[1] here with his Sister. He looks much improved since he was here before, and is to make a visit.

Mr. F. A. Whitney, a son of our minister preached. Texts. Matthew 20. 26. "Whosoever will be great among you let him be your minister." The morning discourse was rather ambitiously written and divided. He took up the origin of the idea of greatness. Supposed it first to have attached to physical power, then to wealth and lastly to moral power as displayed in Christianity. But he passed over the most uniform rule of human judgment respecting greatness which worships intellectual power in all it's manifestations, whether as controlling the sources of wealth, or those of beauty or of strength. Hercules would have been ridiculous if represented as an idiot. A miser never secures influence over his fellows. It is the guiding and directing mind which occasions the power, the rest are merely means. Christ did not introduce a new element in morals, he merely sanctioned and perfected what was dimly understood before. All this may be true but if so, it upsets Mr. Whitney's Sermon which was well for a young beginner, notwithstanding the introduction of personal compliments somewhat out of place, to the memorable names in the town.

Read Paley. Horæ Paulinæ p. 208–284. He is rather unequal in his argument, occasionally making a good point but appearing to labour too much for the sake of multiplying them. Sermon of Dr. Clark. Isaiah 5. 20. "Wo unto them that call evil good, and good evil; that put darkness for light and light for darkness; that put bitter for sweet, and sweet for bitter." The original difference between good and evil insisted upon as the natural and safe guide for the regulation of life.

Finished Lockhart's Life of Scott. He has thrown all his strength into the last Chapter which is a good one. There is more of moral in Scott's history than one is able at first satisfactorily to unravel. A great mixture of good and evil example, of the strength and the weakness of the human mind. On the whole Mr. Lockharts volumes are very interesting and will make a standard work of biography as Boswell has done.

¹ On Walter Hellen Jr., LCA's nephew, see vol. 5:355, 395.

MONDAY 20TH.

Clear and cold east wind. At home in study all day. My mother and the rest of the family took tea and passed the evening. Some time lost in the morning from an immethodical examination of MS letters at the old house, so discouraging I hardly know where to begin with them.

Read Lessing's Laocoon 104–172. Some books weaken the effect they first produce as we go along. This seems the case here. Lessing is an acute critic and often right, but not in those cases most clearly which he labours the most. Lucretius in review. Book I. l 185–450, much more distinct in this reading. Bayle's Letters. Vol. 2, p. 456–508, numbered as one volume.

TUESDAY 21ST.

Warm and clear. Morning to town. Afternoon taken up by company. Mr. and Mrs. Sidney Brooks to dine and spend the day. My father and Mary to meet them. My mother came in the evening. Of course my day not very productive. Read nothing.

One difficulty which I experience here this year is the revival of the desire for study which makes me feel as time wasted that which I cannot devote to it. I have therefore not attended so much to external exercise as I ought, and find in myself an increasing propensity to give up to indolence of motion. This will not do. The winter is the season for study, and the summer for that kind of relaxation which best prepares it.

WEDNESDAY. 22D.

Clear and warm. Two hours devoted to my article, one to a play of Marlowe, The Jew of Malta, and two to Lessing's Laocoon. Dinner as usual at the other house. Afternoon, reading and watering plants. Evening again at the Mansion.

The article goes very heavily indeed. I have no zeal and therefore it cannot be good. With respect to Marlow I took him up to see if I could find any Jewels in him, but quickly satisfied myself he was but a botcher of pewter. Lessing 172–208. continues interesting and in many respects just. Lucretius l. 450–578.

Such my reading for one day interrupted only by social meals. This is rather a poor account to give of valuable time. Joseph H. Adams and Elizabeth dined at the house, and the latter passed the evening.

THURSDAY 23D.

A very warm day. An hour upon my article which I finally conclude to give up as a bad job. Then fell into desultory reading which ended in the examination of Dr. Franklin before the House of Commons.[1] Lessing which was however cut short by a visit to Mount Wollaston with my two elder boys to take a bath. Afternoon reading and a ride towards sunset. Evening, to return Mr. Whitney's visit and home.

I never could entirely satisfy my mind respecting the distinctions set up about the power of Parliament over the Colonies. Dr. Franklin does not clear the matter. The fact is the connexion was not a fair nor just one and was therefore properly terminated. Lessing 208–222. Lucretius 578–735. Nothing of interest from Mr. Whitney nor in the Newspapers.

[1] *Examination . . . relating to the repeal of the stamp act, in 1766*, n.p., 1767.

FRIDAY 24TH.

Clear and very warm. Morning in town. Afternoon spent in reading and attending to my trees affected by the dry weather. Evening, a call at Mr. Daniel Greenleaf's for a short time and at the Mansion but hurried home from both by the threat of a thunder shower which however passed south.

Did little in town, having no business. The Afternoon was also much taken up by the process of refreshing my trees, made somewhat fatiguing by the hot weather. Lucretius 735–783. A pretty obscure part of the text. The author is vigorous but not clear. Our visit, (my Wife, and Mary with me) to Mr. Greenleafs was cut short by a dark cloud. It is one of the return visits in the neighborhood which I have neglected too long. After our return home I read a few of Bayle's letters which fail in interest.

SATURDAY 25TH.

A very warm morning which ended in a thunder storm shortly after dinner of unusual violence. Morning passed in reading at home till noon, and then a ride to Mount Wollaston for a bath with my boys. Afternoon and evening at home.

Locke on Education in the 8th volume of his works,[1] from page 1 to 106. I wonder that I never read this very sensible Treatise before, which points out to me a few errors in my own action upon my children and confirms my belief in some points to which I had already been brought without knowing his work. After all education is a great problem not often solved correctly by any general rule.

Of Lessing today in consequence of my bath only from 222 to 235. And Lucretius, 785–920. As we remained at home in the evening in consequence of the continued rain, I also accomplished some of Bayle's Letters.

[1] The London, 1794, edn. in 9 vols. is in MQA.

SUNDAY. 26TH.

Morning clear but with a cold high wind, a very great change since yesterday. Read an hour before service and attended as usual. Afternoon spent in reading and evening at the Mansion as customary.

Finished Dr. Paley's Horæ Paulinæ this morning. Much of the characteristic clearness in the style of the author and the same ingenuity that marks his other work on the Evidences of Christianity. But it is not equal to it either in depth or force. The coincidences are curious, often striking but not in themselves conclusive. The book is notwithstanding quite a valuable one.

Mr. Newell of Cambridge preached from Psalms 139. 7. "Whither shall I go from thy spirit? or whither shall I flee from thy presence?" Upon the omnipresence of God, but rather original by pushing old ideas into extravagance than by any variation of them. Afternoon, Matthew 10. 5.7.8. "These twelve Jesus sent forth and commanded them, saying, "As ye go, preach, saying, the kingdom of Heaven is at hand. Heal the sick, cleanse the lepers, raise the dead, cast out devils: freely ye have received; freely give."

Upon my return home, I read a discourse in the English Preacher by Dr. Waterland. 2. Timothy 3. 2. "Men shall be loved of their own selves." Upon Self love, defining how far it may be understood as prompting to virtue, and where it leads to vice. His foundation is upon the maxim Honesty is the best policy. A good practical foundation of morals or religion but not that which shines best in theory.

I read in leisure moments occasionally the letters of Bayle and today began Grimm. Met Mr. Degrand at my father's and Mrs. Smith who arrived yesterday.

MONDAY. 27TH.

Morning clear but it clouded afterwards and rained steadily in the evening. Day divided into study and supervision of the work upon my ground.

Finished Locke's Tract upon Education. A strong, sensibly written Essay full of truth of a practical kind. I think he underrates the value of the exercise of the memory as well as of the study of the Classics. In all other respects I think him correct, and feel glad I have read him. Also Lessing in continuation p. 235–275. A person who should devote himself to criticism would find great advantage in studying him. I think I could succeed in the business if I was to try, but my studies have not laid that way.

Afternoon Lucretius finishing the first book. The text must be much injured as well by conjectural emendation as I think, as by time. I also read a few letters of Bayle, one of the earliest of the modern school of critics, and Grimm who is acute as any of them. Germany seems to produce this article in perfection. At the Mansion in the evening. My Wife was quite unwell all day.

TUESDAY 28TH.

Morning clear and warm. In town. Afternoon devoted to reading and evening at the Mansion where the De Wint family had been dining.

I have no very good account to give of my morning time, wasted between the house and Office. Afternoon Lucretius 2d book, 150 lines, and a little of Bayle whose letters gain in interest as they come to relate to the compilation of his great dictionary. Mr. and Mrs. DeWint, their daughter Julia, and several others were at my father's in the evening. No news.

WEDNESDAY 29TH.

Clear and cool. I work about an hour upon my trees for the sake of exercise during the cool weather, then read until dinner time. Afternoon reading also until tea and Evening at the other house. P. C. Brooks Jr. here in the evening and spent the night.

Began to read Locke's Essay on the Human Understanding to p. 40. A book I know more of by what I have seen in others than in itself. The first proposition that there are no innate principles is the pulling away to make room for the edifice. I assent to the force of the reasoning with doubt and mistrust, and desire to examine more fully.

Continued Lessing 275–336. Also Lucretius 151 to 303rd line of 2d book. A very difficult portion of the text. But great poetical energy. Mrs. DeWint and her family called in the afternoon and we saw them again in the evening.

THURSDAY 30TH.

Rather warm with a heavy shower in the Afternoon. One hour passed in work, the remainder of the morning excepting that portion taken up by P. C. Brooks Jr. before his departure. Afternoon work and study also. Evening spent at the Mansion.

I continued Locke's Argument against innate ideas p. 40–76 and finished it. I am not satisfied with it and nevertheless should be troubled to answer the reasoning. Perhaps I should complain of a want of method in not defining what ideas are first and then proving that they are not innate. Then what is an innate idea? Do we get them all from mere sensation? I cannot believe this. The reasoning faculty seems to be above the senses. But we shall see. Continued Lessing p. 336–374. Also Lucretius 303 to 425 l, B. 2. A poetical account of the doctrine of atoms.

My father went to Cambridge to attend the exercises of the Φ B K and did not return until late. Nothing new.

FRIDAY. 31ST.

Morning clear and cold. Town accompanied by Miss Julia DeWint. Afternoon taken up with company. Evening at the Mansion. Not a profitable day.

My business in town was principally of the smaller sort. Commissions and Agency duties. But I called to see Mr. Brooks and there met Dr. Frothingham with whom I had a pleasant talk. He informed me of a fact which more pleased than grieved me. He had proposed me at the annual meeting of the Φ B K yesterday without success. This had vexed him and my friend T. K. Davis much, but I felt fully the causes which operated to my exclusion and which have always and will ever do so, and hence was neither surprised nor hurt at the result, whilst I was highly gratified as well by the opinion as by the zeal of my friends.[1] For the object itself I cannot say I feel in any degree anxious. The lesson is a good one to humble my arrogance as it respects enemies open or secret, and to stimulate me in deserving the estimation unduly put upon me by my friends.

Home. Mr. Lunt dined with me very pleasantly, and we had a visit from Mr. and Mrs. Joseph Angier afterwards by which much of the Afternoon was taken up. So that instead of reading I consumed what was left in a ramble to the quarries in the pasture and then round to measure the ground I am tempted to inclose in front of my house. Evening passed as usual.

Conversation upon Coins in connection with the very unexpected recovery of a set of ancient ones in silver purchased long since by my father and missing until now.[2] They make a very valuable acquisition to my collection. I looked over many of them and only doubted their genuineness because some are so rare. There can be no doubt however of the greater part of them.

[1] In 1840, when CFA was again proposed for membership, he was elected (CFA, Diary, 29 Aug. 1840). Although JQA was in Cambridge in 1838 for the Φ B K ceremonies, his journal contains no indication that he attended the meeting of the chapter at which membership was considered.

[2] On the earlier disappearance of that part of JQA's collection consisting of ancient coins, see vol. 6:279–280. The present entry renders the note there incorrect. JQA's account adds no details: "Found and gave to Charles my old Roman coins" (Diary, 31 Aug., Adams Papers).

SATURDAY. SEPTEMBER 1.

Sultry all day with occasional showers and thunder and lightning throughout. Morning passed in reading, and afternoon also. In the evening the family came and took tea. Charles was quite unwell.

Continued Mr. Locke's Essay p. 76–121. His division strikes me as so little new that I could almost fancy I had read the book before. I admire his clearness of ⟨thinking⟩ expression which evidently proceeds too rather from his natural constitution of mind than from study or precision in language. Finished also the first part of Lessing's Laocoon containing at the close some strictures upon Winkelman's History of Art, which book I happened to find and brought with me from the Mansion.[1]

Lucretius book 2, l. 425–623. Curious how he dovetails in poetical passages where his theory comes on dry. A short time spent in reading Bayle's Letters. O! the literature which these letters describe as crowding from the press and which now is naught.

[1] Winckelmann's *History of Ancient Art*, in the original or in translation, is not in MQA at the present time.

SUNDAY 2D.

Day clear and cool. Passed as usual. Attendance upon divine service and reading. Evening spent at the Mansion.

Read today my father's speech upon the question of Texas. It displays great acuteness and comprehensiveness of mind with less of declamation than has been usual with him. The tone is also more goodnatured and adapted to the temper of the house. It's defect is that of Repetition consequent upon the fragmentary mode of it's delivery and of a rather too desultory and immethodical manner. On the whole, it will form one of the most important of all the acts of his life, and will have a great influence upon the future condition of the country, either fortunate or otherwise.[1]

Heard Mr. Robbins of Boston preach from 2. Peter. 3. 11.12. and 13. The text too long to insert but the substance is the promise of a future state. He discussed this with spirit and explained his own views which leaned to a resurrection of the body. But this is too great a mystery for mortal brain. Afternoon Luke 8. 17. "For nothing is secret that shall not be made manifest; neither any thing hid, that shall not be known and come abroad."

Read a discourse by Dr. Batty in the English Preacher. Proverbs 1. 9. "They shall be an ornament of grace unto thy head, and chains about thy neck." The effect of Religion upon human nature through its action upon honour, good nature and civility. The views very sensible but common. Read also Grimm. Mr. and Mrs. T. Greenleaf called in the evening for a short time and we went down as usual to the Mansion.

[1] *Speech of John Quincy Adams, of Massachusetts, upon the right of the people, men and women, to petition; on the freedom of speech and of debate in the House of representatives of the United States; on the resolutions of seven state legislatures, and the petitions of more than one hundred thousand petitioners, relating to the annexation of Texas to this Union. Delivered in the House of representatives of the United States, in fragments of the morning hour, from the 16th of June to the 7th of July, 1838, inclusive,* Washington, 1838.

MONDAY 3D.

Cold and clear. Morning spent almost entirely in working at the garden with Kirk, superintending the various little improvements I wished to be made. This is after all the only way of gaining satisfaction with us. For directions are rarely executed in full.

But an hour of reading Afterwards. Afternoon devoted to riding, accompanied by my boy John. Evening Tea at my Mother's and walk to Mrs. T. B. Adams' to see her and the family. Thus I have no very material account of progress in study to give.

My reading of Lessing was interrupted as I found that the second part of the Laocoon was never completed and what remains of it is in small fragments, hardly to be retained in the memory if read. The ride was cold and so was the evening. Mrs. Angier and Mr. E. P. Greenleaf were at Mrs. Adams' besides the two families.

TUESDAY 4TH.

Cold East wind in the morning but warmer afterwards. Morning in town, the rest of the day devoted to the festivity gotten up for the occasion. I went to town with an incipient head ach and had so much to do that it did not improve it. Commissions of various kinds besides going to my house and from thence to the painter's in Tremont Street. Three or four persons to see me also. Mr. Boies, about a well, Sidney Brooks, Mr. Stanwood about the Mortgage &ca.

Home, dine at my Mother's and proceed soon after with the ladies to the Hancock lot where the Quincy people had prepared a sort of entertainment, which is now called a Pic nic. The general plan is for the females of the place to make contributions in money and in edibles, and then for all classes and conditions of persons to meet and amuse themselves either in speeches, or singing or dancing. This like the one at Hingham was given to my father who was addressed by Mr. Whitney and who made a handsome reply. The tables were handsomely decorated and the behaviour was orderly throughout.[1]

In the evening there was a ball at the Hancock house to which we returned after tea, which was also very quietly and properly conducted. I was much surprised to perceive how slight the difference was between the behaviour of a hundred and fifty mechanics and farmers and their families, and that of our Boston exquisites. A little more exactness in dancing and a slight roughness in motion were perhaps the most perceptible variations.

My head ach prevented me from acting the part which I should otherwise have done, but as it was I got through as well as I could without giving way. It is difficult to avoid giving some offence from misconstructions which spoil the best intended efforts. But it is wiser to try than to wrap one's self up in a mantle of pharisaical conceit and thus announce yourself to be better than your neighbours. In America there can be but one interest for all the members of the Community, but if you make artificial distinctions and divisions by which self is set up to the prejudice of others, those others having the majority will make you feel your folly in the end.

[1] An account of the event appeared in the *Quincy Patriot*, 8 Sept., p. 2, col. 5. JQA included in his journal entry a somewhat lengthy summary of his remarks together with a comment on Mr. Whitney's brief welcome: "Much to my relief he said no more, for more according to the custom which has lately crept in among us from England of beplastering a man with flattery to his face, more would necessarily have been fulsome and unmeaning adulation in the shape of praise" (Diary, 4 Sept.).

WEDNESDAY. 5TH.

Clear and warm. Morning work for an hour, then study. Dined at the Mansion and took a drive with my father in the Afternoon. Evening a visit to T. Greenleaf also with him.

Read Locke. p. 121 – 162. The various modes of thought subsidiary to the main division. Mr. Locke is a remarkably clear thinker and deserves to be studied for that quite as much as for his philosophy. With him, metaphysical science is not the impenetrable jungle it is often reputed by the unskilfulness of many to be. Read part of Lessing's Essay upon the Mode in which the Ancients represented death. Ingenious at least.

I rode to the edge of the town of Randolph and thence home by Weymouth where we stopped to see Col. Minot Thayer. A very ingenious politician who likes the strong side in his neighborhood.[1] He has a drop of flattery for all, and my share came today. He intimated that the people in Quincy had a great desire to send me to the Legislature this Autumn to which I answered very simply that just the same objection which existed last year existed this. I feel much pleased with the idea which this man's act thus holds out of the good will of my neighbors, but have schooled my mind to entire moderation in my political aspirations which I hope I may never lose. There is no reasonable prospect of greater happiness for me in public life than I now enjoy in private life, so that on my own account I cannot desire the change.

[1] Minott Thayer of Weymouth was a whig who maintained good relations with both JQA and Daniel Webster; see Edmund Soper Hunt, *Reminiscences: Weymouth Ways and Weymouth People*, Boston, 1907, p. 53, 67.

[*Medford*]

THURSDAY 6TH.

Morning fine. To town with my Wife. To Medford to dine, with Mr. Frothingham who took my Wife's place in my vehicle. Family dinner and Afternoon wasted.

I have no account of occupation to give beyond the ordinary dull routine of small commissions. The dinner embraced all the members of Mr. Brooks' family with the exception of the youngest who is (poor fellow) gone to destruction beyond recovery.[1] It is not often they all come together. It was pleasant and the party separated early.

I took a stroll after dinner with Dr. Frothingham and we got into conversation upon the motives of action in life and the anxiety for popular applause which influence us all more or less. In the course of it by a somewhat abrupt movement he intimated the possibility of my being solicited to go into public life and into Congress. What does this mean? I asked no questions, passed it off as a thing entirely improbable from my position, and not to be desired by me on my own account at all. This is one of his friendly feelings for which I have to be grateful. Many think better of me than I deserve and some worse. This is the way of the world. I wonder only in this case how the idea, considering my position to parties, could have originated. Evening quiet. Nothing of interest.

[1] That is, Horatio Brooks; see entry for 1 Sept. 1837, above, and references there.

FRIDAY 7TH.

Day fine. To town with Mr. Brooks and return. Dine at Gorham Brooks' and afternoon generally wasted in company.

My day has little of remark as I was entirely drawn away from books, and conversed unprofitably. I went to my house in consequence of the stories of housebreaking which have been generally circulated, and removed my coins and such silver as was most valuable, to Mrs. Frothingham's.

Nobody but Mr. Brooks and ourselves dined with Gorham but he lives very pleasantly and very genteelly, perhaps rather too luxuriously for this country. He is labouring at improving his place at much expense. This is for amusement and occupation, yet I see the kernel of discontent at bottom which will spoil the whole. He will be pleased only while he is pursuing.

Allyne Otis came out in the afternoon on a visit. He is really as empty a puppy of thirty as I can well conceive.[1] Evening Mrs. Angier called, and for want of other things I tried to extract from P. C. B. Jr. some commercial information which he gave fluently and intelligently.

[1] On Allyne Otis, CFA's Harvard classmate and a son of Harrison Gray Otis, see vol. 2, index, and Morison, *H. G. Otis*, 1969, p. 487–490.

Quincy

SATURDAY. 8TH.

The day cold. Morning to town. Return to Quincy to dinner and Afternoon spent in reading without progress. Evening at the Mansion.

I left Medford immediately after breakfast without regret, for I cannot spend time so idly with any satisfaction. The acquisition of knowledge in some shape or other being my principal pleasure, I feel not at home where I do not pursue it. My present mode of life has done much to fasten upon me attachments which the interruption of former summers tended to weaken.

My occupation in town was to read General Gaines's plan for the defence of the Western frontier, a document having some bearing upon the Texas schemes and remarkable for exhibiting the foibles of its author.[1]

Upon my return to reading Lucretius I found how much my mind had been dissipated and gave it up. So I read a little of the desultory criticism of Grimm. Dr. Palfrey and his daughter made us a visit. In the evening a discussion with my father upon the influence of College educations.

[1] The report of Gen. Edmund Pendleton Gaines submitted to the War Department on the defense of the western frontier proposed floating batteries for harbor defense and the construction of a network of railroads in the interior (*DAB*).

SUNDAY 9TH.

Fine day. An hour before service devoted to arrears of my Diary. Then attendance upon divine service and reading. Evening a walk with my father to see Mr. and Mrs. Quincy. Mr. W. Lee called to see us.[1]

Mr. Lunt preached two Sermons from the text John 17. 21. "Behold, the kingdom of God is within you." Full of excellent reflection upon the tendencies of the present age to error either by excess or deficiency with allusions to the doctrines in philosophy which are at present somewhat in vogue among us. Mr. Lunt dissented from the views of John Locke as tending to establish materialism which I agree with him in. At the same time he did not clearly explain the reply which I wish to obtain.

Read a sermon in the English Preacher by Bishop Hutton. 2. Corinthians 8. 21. "Providing for honest things, not only in the sight of the Lord, but also in the sight of men." Upon cultivating with proper attention the good opinion of the world. An unnecessary exhortation.

Mr. Lee was dull and out of spirits. At Mrs. Quincy's, a dissertation upon the Bible history and upon some disputed points of doctrine which cannot interest me much although Mrs. Q.'s mind seems much exercised by them.

[1] William Lee, a resident of Washington for most of his adult life, was a friend of JQA's both during their youth and in their foreign service years. See vols. 1:51; 3:355, 375.

MONDAY 10TH.

Warm and hazy. Morning to town. Afternoon devoted to reading and evening at the Mansion.

My duties were all of the drudging kind today connected with the management of my father's real estate and my own. I was very glad to get out of town and only felt worried at the amount of this kind of occupation which seems to be preparing for me during this Autumn.

The ride was dusty and unpleasant so that I enjoyed the more my sitting down after the lapse of a week to Lucretius 2d book. l. 623–825. A few of Bayle's letters afterwards.

My father appeared seriously unwell. He sinks from want of intellectual stimulus. Such is the formation of unnatural habits.

TUESDAY 11TH.

Warm and cloudy. Morning to town. Afternoon reading and evening at the Mansion.

I went to the City to perform the duties in which I failed yesterday and at last set in proper train the work for one of my houses. These visits are fatiguing and dispiriting. On my return I read Lucretius l. 825–930, and some of Bayle's letters. Deacon Spear interrupted me by a call on business.

My pleasure is mainly in the hours of literary occupation, varied in a degree by domestic and social relations. Evening is generally devoted to this at the other house. The political accounts from Maine this morning are rather favorable to the Administration.[1] Such are the fluctuations of popular opinion.

[1] In Maine, the Van Buren party succeeded in electing its candidate for governor, in gaining control of both branches of the legislature, and in winning all but two of the congressional seats (*Boston Courier*, 13 Sept., p. 2, cols. 1–2).

WEDNESDAY 12TH.

Heavy rain with a N. E. Wind which came on to blow very heavily at night. I remained at home all day reading.

Continued Locke's Essay p. 162–220. The ideas of duration, expansion and number all resulting from the repetitions of a simple idea. Mr. Locke certainly explains himself clearly. His theory does not come half fledged. I also continued Lessing enquiry into the modes in which death was represented by the ancients. p. 198 of volume 10 of his works. There is a sharp controversial tone which takes off in my mind from the merit of this work. A theory especially requires moderation to sustain it, particularly one in a study admitted to be very uncertain. Lucretius to the end of the second book. A few letters of Bayle, a portion of Grimm and a tale of Hamilton finished the evening.

THURSDAY 13TH.

Rain fell heavily but calm in the morning but it cleared at noon. At home all day, reading and working. Dined at the Mansion.

Continued Locke's Essay, Chapter on power. p. 220–252. A difficult topic not very satisfactorily developed. The famous question of liberty and necessity rather evaded than met. The title itself, power does not appear to me to express any very distinct idea.

Finished Lessing's Essay. Very ingenious and in portions almost convincing. Death as a skeleton certainly is in it's analogy more Gothic than Grecian. Yet it is a natural idea and was unquestionably adopted in some shape by Lessing's admission. Lucretius Book 3. 1–136. The work on my ground took some time. Evening passed at the Mansion.

FRIDAY. 14TH.

Fine day. Morning in town. Afternoon reading and work. Evening, a visit at Mrs. T. B. Adams's.

After reaching town I thought I would call at the State house for the purpose of returning to Mr. Felt the lecture I had borrowed, and look into my own house. Upon opening my inner entry door I found the parlour door which I had left locked was open, and was not long in convincing myself afterwards that the house had been forcibly entered. My precautions respecting the plate and the jewels of my Wife had not proved useless for I found the doors of the chambers forced like those of the parlour, and my Wifes draws[1] in which they were kept thoroughly ransacked. But the plunderers did not seem in quest of silver for they had left some pieces which I did not think to take with me. In my study they examined two or three draws and left the remainder untouched. My Cabinet they did not touch nor the sideboard. They appear to have entered in the cellar although I could not ascertain precisely where. On the whole, from the very cursory examination which I could make, I felt tolerably well satisfied with the result and my first sensations degenerated into mere surprise. I called at Mrs. Frothingham's to tell her and thence to the Office in Accounts.

Mrs. Smith and Mary dined with us, who with my Wife were startled by the information. Lucretius. b. 3, l. 136–258, and some time at work on my trees. Mr. and Mrs. Miller and Mr. Beale were at Mrs. Adams's.

[1] This shortened form had wide currency in America but never in England (*Dict. of Americanisms*). CFA's preference for the form, which he used with fair consistency, may have had its origin in his early years when his father corrected CFA's employment of the longer form in a letter: "You tell me that Priestley looked into Duncan's *Drawers* and found some Play-things and a flute—did he indeed? Well, Drawers are strange places to find a flute in! But was it not Duncan's *Draws*, where Priestley found the flute?" (JQA to CFA, 31 May 1814, Adams Papers).

SATURDAY 15TH.

Clear day. Morning to town. Afternoon reading and evening at the Mansion as usual.

My Mother, Mary, my Wife and I went to the City in order to take an account of the amount and nature of the losses. Upon examination, we could find nothing but a gold watch gone which I bought some years since at Washington. The object of this conduct seems difficult to divine.

The remainder of the morning was passed in hunting up workmen to repair damages, which all things considered are not great. And I feel on the whole very glad that as every thing was at the mercy of the plunderer, he took or spoiled so little.

Afternoon Lucretius l. 258–425. He makes a curious system of his metaphysical science. Finished the letters of Bayle.

SUNDAY 16TH.

Clear but cold with an Easterly wind. Day passed in the usual duties and evening at the Mansion. There has been a very bright Aurora borealis for four successive nights.

Attended divine service and heard Dr. Henry Ware Jr. preach in the morning from Proverbs 4. 23. "Keep thy heart with all diligence; for out of it are the issues of life." A very good discourse explanatory of Pope's verse "An honest man's the noblest work of God" which he considers as designed only to embrace that sort of honesty which is of the world and not the higher duty of faithfulness to God. Afternoon Matthew 16. 26. "For what is a man profited, if he shall gain the whole world and lose his own soul? or what shall a man give in exchange for his soul?" He first considered the probable meaning of the word in this text as it was used in other places indiscriminately for life or spirit, but whichever it might mean he regarded it as emphatically expressing the value of another life and the vanity of attaching the affections to the things of this.

Read a discourse of Bishop Atterbury's in the English Preacher upon the duty of praise and thanksgiving. Psalm 50. 14. "Offer unto God thanksgiving." I take much pleasure also in reading the criticism of Grimm, which though prejudiced is still excellent. He possessed a great deal of discriminating talent which is the sine qua non for the critic.

MONDAY 17TH.

Clouds and drizzle from the Eastward. At home all day reading and evening at the Mansion.

Continued and finished Mr. Locke's Chapter on power. p. 252–282. This does not satisfy me because it resorts to a distinction between liberty and the will which begs the question. The discussion itself seems to be hardly in place. Yet Mr. Locke is still a strong thinker even when he grapples with subjects too tough for him. Read Lessing's Criticism upon Voltaires Semiramis and Hamlet, and began Winkelman's History of Art, rather dry I think. Lucretius b. 3, l. 425–633. Grimm.

An evening visit at the other house had not much to interest us, and upon my return I sat down to write a little squib for the Newspaper about my late adventure at my house. It is remarkable how difficult writing becomes to me now, so as in fact to discourage me from often attempting it.

TUESDAY 18TH.

A thick heavy drizzle. I went to town notwithstanding and was occupied as usual in the performance of commissions and in a visit to the Athenæum. Home bringing to Mrs. T. B. Adams' Miss Julia DeWint. Afternoon, reading. Evening at home.

I called at the Athenæum for the purpose of procuring for my father Mr. Cousin's Report upon public Instruction in Prussia.[1] Saw Mr. Brimmer's late present to the Athenæum of expensive works of engravings.[2] Read the Newspapers which are now full of the result of the late election in Maine and the consequent abandonment of Mr. Webster by the Atlas in Boston.[3] Strange things take place in politics.

Read of Lucretius book 3. 633–800. And observed for some time an eclipse of the sun, through a cloud which was sufficiently thin to make it perceptible without obscuring it too much. How much one of these events brings to the mind the grandeur of the Universe. These orbs revolving in space all in their order without interference and no more permitted to us to know than they do so. Mr. Price Greenleaf spent an hour with us in the evening.

[1] The stimulation of JQA's interest in the *Report* by Victor Cousin may derive from an occasion noted in the entry for 25 Sept. 1836, above.

[2] During 1838, George Watson Brimmer gave to the Athenæum his extensive collection of books on art; it formed the nucleus of the institution's fine arts library (Mabel M. Swan, *The Athenæum Gallery*, Boston, 1940, p. 128).

[3] The *Atlas*, following the poor showing of the Webster-aligned whigs in Maine, announced its preference for William Henry Harrison (17 Sept., p. 2, col. 1).

WEDNESDAY 19TH.

Weather clear and warm. Morning spent in personal superintendence upon some improvement I wished in the road. Afternoon in reading. Evening at the Mansion where the family dined.

The necessity of personal direction prevented my attending to much study. A few pages of Locke 282–300 and Lucretius l. 800–915 comprised all of my reading. The days have now become so materially shorter that my afternoons cease to be profitable, and the evening is given to the family.

I perceive in the Morning Post of today an article which I presume to be from T. K. Davis, raising up Mr. Calhoun as the great man of the Country.[1] Davis is not yet fledged as a politician and appears to me consequently to run into error by taking shadows for substance. But he takes a fair start and if things undergo a change as now appears likely he will gain credit for it. I wish I could have taken the same, but the thing was utterly impossible. The junction[2] of Mr. Calhoun the very thing which fixes him entirely drove me off.

[1] "John C. Calhoun and the Credit System—A Final Appeal to all Real Merchants" (unsigned) was laudatory of Calhoun's position on the credit and banking systems; *Boston Morning Post*, 19 Sept., p. 1, col. 6 – p. 2, col. 1.

[2] "Association, coalition" (*OED*, 1b).

THURSDAY 20TH.

Morning fine. Ride to town. Afternoon, ride also. Evening passed at the Mansion.

I went to the City accompanied by my father, but not with my own horse, he having been fretted too much before he started. As a consequence I was however obliged to take him out in the Afternoon, and to exercise him. I went round through Braintree to the edge of Randolph and thence through Weymouth home. My Wife was with me. I thus have little or no progress to mark in study. My City hours are wasted in small profitless commissions so as to make me very unwilling to multiply them. Lucretius 915–1005. A very poetical portion of the work.

I find T. K. Davis out in continuation in this morning's paper.[1] There is only one remark which keeps perpetually returning to me in reading which is that he wants bottom. For the rest, the quarrel about Mr. Webster keeps on thickening, and may ruin the Whig party.

[1] The continuation of the article of the preceding day is headed "To the Mechanics of Boston," *Boston Morning Post*, 20 Sept., p. 2, cols. 1–2.

FRIDAY. 21ST.

Clouds and warm rain. At home all day in study. Evening at the Mansion.

Continued Locke's Essay 300–352. Chapter of Identity and Diversity. The line between things comprehensible and things not so is so thin that it is very difficult to keep exactly within the former. All identity springs from consciousness, says Mr. Locke, but then of what are we conscious? for all ordinary purposes we have clearer evidence than consciousness in the fact of existence in a shape readily cognizable by the senses, and for extraordinary ones what do we gain by changing the word.

Lucretius, finished the third book and read 100 lines in the fourth. On the whole the conclusion of the third book is most of all to my taste. Had Lucretius grappled with a subject more susceptible of the introduction of the graces, he would have scarcely been exceeded by his borrower Virgil. But philosophical abstractions are a potion the bitterness of which to most readers no honey of poesy can make palatable.

Finished the first Chapter of Winkelman's History of Art, which did not interest me. Also one or two Chapters in Bayle's Réponse aux questions d'un provincial, which led me to examine in the Causes Célèbres the curious case of Martin Guerre.[1] Nothing new from the conversation of the evening.

[1] This return to a reading of F. Gayot de Pitavel's *Causes célèbres et interessantes*, which had interested CFA in 1831 and 1832 (vol. 4:174 and index), was directed to the case of Martin Guerre who, in the 16th century, was the victim of an extraordinary imposture perpetrated by Arnaud du Tilh (Hoefer, *Nouv. biog. générale*).

SATURDAY. 22D.

Cloudy and warm. Morning spent in study. Afternoon in riding. My boy John five years old this day. Evening at the Mansion.

Continued Mr. Locke p. 353–393. His idea of the moral relations and of the force of law is very surely degrading to the notion of human virtue. If it is the mere consequence of arbitrary distinctions of right and wrong then are we poor creatures enough. I think the original theory is shaken through the bad deduction thus made from it.

Mr. Brooks came from Boston to pay us a visit. And my father and he dined with us. After dinner I took him a long ride to Braintree and Weymouth. Evening at the other house. Lucretius also, Book 4. 100–302.

My boy John was a little unwell on this his fifth birth day. I repeat the feelings with grateful adoration which prompted my entry of last year.

SUNDAY 23D.

Day cloudy with occasional heavy showers. Attendance on divine service. Reading. Dinner at the Mansion. Evening at home.

At the Morning service, my third son was held up by me to Mr. Lunt for baptism under the name of Henry Brooks. This is at once returning to the source of the family in this hemisphere and remembering a valued son of Mr. Brooks now no more. Mr. Brooks had to this end come from Medford as he has always appeared to take a great interest in the child. May he live to be fruitful in good works.[1]

Mr. Lunt preached a sermon from Hebrews'[2] and one from Mark 7. 11.12. "But ye say, If a man shall say to his father or mother, It is Corban, that is to say, a gift, by whatsoever thou mightest be profited by me: he shall be free. And ye suffer him no more to do ought for his father or his mother." The first of these discourses was an ingenious attempt to prove that sin was productive of as much ruin to the mind as to the moral of man. In short that sin was folly. I say this was ingenious but not convincing. The government of the world is conducted by laws beyond our knowledge or comprehension and the vicious man often makes a great use of the gifts of a fine intellect for purposes the most base and morally degraded. Mind is not Moral. If it was, the world would be a less difficult place to live correctly in. The second discourse was upon charity and the connexion between the practice of religious rites and the performance of religious duties. Very good.

It rained hard all the afternoon. I read a discourse in the English Preacher by Dr. Denne. Matthew 7. 12. "All things whatsoever ye would that men should do to you, do ye even so to them." I am struck with only one thing in reading this choice of English sermons and that is the mediocrity of style and thought which runs through them. Began today Mr. Milman's History of the Jews with which I was pleased.[3] Spent the evening in conversation with Mr. Brooks.

[1] The present account of the baptism differs both as to locale and participants from Henry Adams' own widely noted account with which *The Education of Henry Adams* begins.

[2] JQA, in his journal, identifies the text as from Hebrews 12. 14.

[3] Henry Hart Milman, *The History of the Jews*, 3 vols., N.Y., 1831, is in MQA.

MONDAY 24TH.

Clear and cold. Morning passed in study. Afternoon in a ride. Evening passed partly at the Mansion, partly at Mrs. T. B. Adams's. Mr. Brooks left us this morning.

Read Locke p. 393 – 427. Upon adequate ideas, and upon the association of ideas. Curious portions of the operation of thinking. This book of Mr. Locke's is like opening a new vein of knowledge to my mind which no preceding study of the subject had ever touched. What was the value of my College studies in this department, in which nevertheless my nominal scholarship stood better than in others. The vanity of college education. All I have done in study has been since twenty. Before that I only read and gathered.

Lucretius b. 4. 302 – 530. I took a long ride almost to the blue hills this evening with my father admiring the green surface of the country which the late rains have brought out.

TUESDAY 25TH.

Fine day. I went to town accompanied by my father. Afternoon at home. Evening at Mr. Miller's.

My morning was much given up to business. Various persons calling, to see me. A. H. Everett to notify me of his departure from my Office, a circumstance which I by no means regret.[1] Mr. Higgins to procure a job in deepening my well, and two or three applicants for my house in Acorn Street. Thus the time was very fully consumed excepting an hour spent in waiting for my father who after all did not come and join me, and I returned home without him.

Lucretius. b. 4. 530–709. Rather more corrupted in text and less interesting in substance. The evening at Mr. Miller's was very dull. Only a few of the neighbours and they seemed to have nothing to say.

[1] A. H. Everett had rented an office since 1830 in the 23 Court Street building managed by CFA (vol. 3:372).

WEDNESDAY 26TH.

Cloudy day with mist and rain. Morning to town. Dinner and afternoon at the Mansion.

My morning was almost entirely taken up by the various duties incident to the preparation of my house in Acorn Street for rent. So that I have not much to record. We dined as usual at my fathers, and it being rainy I did not return home until night. But spent some time in examining Col. Stone's Life of Brant the Indian.

Dr. Palfrey has sent me a letter requesting a Review of this book,[1] and in order to give an answer I looked into it. He takes nineteen pages to discuss who his hero's father was and that is enough for me. If Dr. Palfrey wishes an article he must select something less tedious.

[1] John G. Palfrey to CFA, 20 Sept. 1838; CFA dispatched a reply on the 27th; both in Adams Papers. A presentation copy to JQA of William L. Stone's *Life of Joseph Brant*, 2 vols., N.Y., 1838, is in MQA.

THURSDAY 27TH.

Drizzly morning. Study. Afternoon, spent an hour at the Wharf of Mr. Greenleaf, attempting to catch smelts. A Concert in the Evening.

Continued Locke's Essay p. 427–462. Upon Words and language. A fruitful subject and worthy of profound reflection, but it may reasonably be doubted if the ablest writers are among the greatest students of words. They come to attach too much importance to them and thus invest them with a meaning which not being exactly the popular or common one does not go home to the minds of the many. Lucretius 709–914. What is his theory good for, and yet his verses will remain for many of them are not excelled in Latin literature.

I took in the Afternoon an hour's recreation in catching or rather trying for smelts without success. On my return a few pages of Grimm. Both families attended a Concert at Mr. French's hotel given by Mrs. Valentine a woman who has instructed some of the girls here in singing. There was much bad and some good, showing however in general much progress in cultivation among our townspeople.

FRIDAY 28TH.

Cloudy, damp day. Morning to town. Afternoon at home in reading. Evening at the Mansion.

My father accompanied me to town. Time taken up in giving final orders about the repairs in Acorn Street, and in visiting it to see the progress. Mr. Apthorp finally agreed for it to take possession whenever I notify him. Lucretius b. 4. 914–1130, and Grimm.

My father today in conversation suggested to me the expediency of following up the examination of the South Carolina policy. I have had some idea of this myself, but there is to me little satisfaction in producing for others what they will not approve, or hardly read, and when even admission to a press appears to be rather tacitly granted as a favour than considered desirable. Nothing but a strong sense of duty to myself induces me to persevere in a system productive of such discouragements.[1] Evening with the family.

[1] The idea that CFA should prepare a piece on the subject here discussed eventuated in the publication of his "Political Speculations Upon the Carolina Policy"; see entry for 15 Nov., below.

SATURDAY 29TH.

Cloudy day with heavy rain at times. Morning divided between study and a search after papers at my father's. Afternoon study, evening at the Mansion.

Locke, finished the first volume of the Works which closes with the meaning of words. My mind has certainly been invigorated by the study of this Analytical Treatise. Much of my time was however wasted in trying to find materials for a composition which I now design. Whether I shall have either the ability or the perseverance to bring out what I propose I do not know but the attempt is at least an amusement. I did not succeed at any rate today and must therefore put it off until I go to Boston.

Lucretius through the fourth book and ninety lines of the 5th. The former is hardly philosophical and certainly very coarse. Read also some of Grimm who is amusing in spite of his ridiculous prejudices.

My boy John continues unwell and in consequence of the sickness prevailing we feel uneasy about him. Evening at the Mansion.

SUNDAY 30TH.

Morning study. Attendance upon divine service all day. Reading in the Afternoon and evening at the Mansion.

I read today several chapters of Milman's History of the Jews with which I am much pleased. He gives a clear abridged view of the Exodus of the Israelites which I never before perfectly understood.

Mr. Lunt preached today from Matthew 28. 19. "Go ye therefore, and teach all nations, baptizing them in the name of the Father, and of the son and of the Holy Ghost." A discourse upon baptism apparently occasioned by the incident of last Sunday, with an attempt to explain the text of the three persons—the Father, God the son, the mediator and the holy Ghost the spirit universally present and active upon man. I did not feel satisfied with this explanation, nor with any I have ever seen.

2. Peter 1. 7. "To godliness, brotherly kindness; and to brotherly kindness, charity." This was a fine continuation of the last Sunday afternoon's discourse, with a view of the improvement of the general principles of action in man, the increase of benevolence notwithstanding the dangerous radical tendencies of the day.

Read a sermon in the English Preacher by the Revd. Jas. Foster, Romans 5. 7. "Scarcely for a righteous man will one die, yet, peradventure, for a good man some would even dare to die." This is a better sermon than the generality of these. It marks the broad line between mere justice which is so much a duty as to be hardly a virtue and that extended goodness which seeks out the opportunities for the exercise of benevolent disposition. But even in this, there is room for the employment of great judgment and discrimination. The evening was passed in conversation and on our return we could not but be struck with the beautiful clearness of the sky.

MONDAY. OCTOBER 1.

A lovely day, more like June than this month. Morning in part in study and part out. Afternoon a ride. Evening at home.

Locke's Essay Volume 2, p. 1–42. On the abuse of words, a fruitful subject, if it could be followed up in all it's conclusions. Justness of thought depends exceedingly upon the right use of words because they often help to define what might otherwise lie cloudy.

Walked to Mrs. Adams' to arrange her Quarterly Sums and heard on the road of the increasing sickness which prevails. This makes me anxious about the children who are nevertheless tolerably well excepting John who has been drooping, but appears better this afternoon.

Lucretius 5 book, 90 – 300. The prophecy of the world's destruction does not appear very new and yet we see no symptom of it at this late day. My father rode with me round the beautiful town of Milton, my favourite and it never looked better than now.

Mr. Price Greenleaf called in the evening and I accompanied him to a meeting of citizens to prevent stealing of fruit. He sat with us an hour afterwards. Miss Julia DeWint here.

TUESDAY. 2D.

Fine day. Morning with my father to town. Afternoon, study and in the evening, company at home.

My time was very much taken up today, by the occupations incident to the commencing Quarter. Also in various walks to and fro to execute orders of different descriptions. It seems little to walk into so many different parts of Boston at any one time, but the sum total of distance is far from trifling.

Lucretius 5th book, 300 – 503. Amusing to follow his explanations of the system of the Universe, accommodating them to his theory. A small number of persons at tea tonight. Mr. and Mrs. Lunt, Mr. and Mrs. Miller, Miss Hedge, E. C. Adams, Mr. Beale and his daughters. Miss Harriet Welsh here to pass the night.

WEDNESDAY 3D.

Day threatening but after a brief shower it cleared. To town with my father and Wife in the carriage, returning in the evening.

We went to town for the sake of attending the christening of Gorham Brooks' younger child which took place at Mr. Frothingham's house a little before dinner time. The morning devoted to the Office and Accounts. The members of the family and my father dined with Mr. F. afterwards and we did not return until sunset. I was so much fatigued I could hardly keep awake.

Mr. Price Greenleaf called afterwards respecting a paper he was to draw up offering a reward for the discovery of robbers of fruit. Miss Welsh and Miss DeWint were also here tonight.

This day gives but an unprofitable Account of time, and entertainments are all productive of little to me but vanity and vexation of spirit.

THURSDAY 4TH.

Fine day. At home, an hour spent in fishing. Afternoon ride and evening at the Mansion.

Locke, 2 vol. p. 42–84. A valuable Chapter upon the remedy to abuse of words. In that which treats of the extent of knowledge he supposes it possible for the Deity to make matter think. His defence of this position is not marked with his usual strength. The ultimate deduction must necessarily be materialism as the presence of spirit as an independent power is thus dispensed with. Lucretius, 503–713, groping about in the dark for some explanation of the appearances of the natural world.

I lost some time in attempting to catch fish at Greenleaf's Wharf without success. My father rode with me round Mount Wollaston. Dined with him and spent the evening at cards. The men were blasting rocks all day below my house.

FRIDAY. 5TH.

Day very fine. Morning in town. Afternoon at home and evening at the Mansion.

My time was engrossed in town much as usual, but in a manner not at all interesting to record. I only note that I found the things which had been stolen from my house at the police Office, including a few I had never missed.

Lucretius, 713–920. Every now and then he blazes up with a fine poetical burst, like the march of the seasons today. The days are however getting so short as materially to diminish study.

Evening, Mr. Price Greenleaf was at my father's and general conversation. The men were blasting again today with good success.

SATURDAY. 6TH.

Warm, windy day. Morning passed out of doors. Afternoon at home. Evening at the Mansion.

I felt a little inclining to head ach today which however passed off as I was actively engaged in the field below my house in superintending the process of drawing out the masses of rock which the powder had split. Had Mr. Carr and Deacon Spear's son with four oxen and they did well. I should become very fond of farming improvement if I knew how to carry it on without imprudence.

Lucretius, 920–1150. The whole passage of the origin of civilization highly poetical in its character. The gems remain while the setting has ceased to be attractive. Grimm also who is Diderot mad, his critical opinions are good when they do not involve his prejudices.

SUNDAY 7TH.

Heavy rain, clearing away cold. Divine service as usual all day with reading and evening at the Mansion.

I continued Milman's History of the Jews which I keep for my Sunday reading. His account of the period of the Judges is brief and yet embraces as I suppose all that can be said upon it.

Mr. Whitney preached in the morning from Revelation 2. 10. "Be thou faithful unto death, and I will give thee a crown of life." Mr. Whitney considers the crown of life to mean a future state in which our sensation is to be far extended beyond its present limits. His sermons are however too much blanks to my mind. Mr. Angier of Milton preached in the afternoon from Luke   "One thing is needful." The great necessity of religion, illustrated and explained with warmth and emphasis.

Read a discourse from the English Preacher taken from Job 34. 22. "There is no darkness, nor shadow of death, where the workers of iniquity may hide themselves." By the Revd. John Holland. An extremely ordinary exposition of the omniscience of the deity with quotations from the Scriptures which make the only good portion of the production. Read also much of Mr. S. Hovey's book upon Slavery in the West Indies, a far more natural and agreeable work than that of Thome and Kimball while it in substance confirms the truth of all their statements.[1]

In the evening at the Mansion. Mr. Jos. Angier was there and we fell into conversation about Mr. Emerson's late productions. Much criticism elicited of an interesting kind.[2]

[1] The two works are Sylvester Hovey, *Letters from the West Indies*, and James A. Thome and J. Horace Kimball, *Emancipation in the West Indies*, both published at N.Y. in 1838; a presentation copy of the latter given by Sarah Grimké to JQA and LCA is in MQA.

[2] JQA identified the Emerson works being discussed as the "crazy Address and oration" (Diary, 7 Oct.), by which, presumably, he was referring to the 1838 Divinity School Address and the 1837 ΦBK Oration, "The American Scholar."

MONDAY 8TH.

A cold morning with the wind from the Eastward. Day spent in town. Evening at the Mansion.

My day was not a very profitable one and yet my duties in town required that it should be so spent. I was enabled to finish much of the matter regarding tenants which has embarrassed me of late, and to execute a great number of commissions.

Dined at Dr. Frothingham's and from thence went to attend a Meeting of the South Cove Corporation. The object was to consider a plan submitted by the Directors for releasing the Company from the great burden of debt which presses upon it. J. Quincy Jr. opened the project which in fact consists of dividing to the Stockholders a sufficient portion of the land to induce them to take up individually their share of the debt. The remainder would then be free from difficulty and divisible or convertible at the first favorable opportunity. The meeting was full and there was much discussion pro and con, but inasmuch as no easy alternative presented itself and the case was pressing the proposed plan was unanimously adopted.

This business is a vexatious one to me because I fell into it against my consent and am now becoming doubly responsible almost against my will. I must change my investments to meet this new aspect of things. The ultimate success of the property I hardly permit myself to doubt, but not through the contracting of double engagements. My anxiety of mind upon pecuniary subjects is such that I dislike the appearance of extended liabilities in any form. And yet to some extent I shall feel obliged to do so. I trust in this as in all other matters to a divine providence which will not desert those who seek to regulate their course with prudence and self distrust.

Home not until after sunset. Nothing material for the evening. Workmen blowing rocks again today.

TUESDAY 9TH.

Cold, chilly day. Morning to town. Afternoon at home and also evening.

My father accompanied me to town. I devoted the greater part of the morning to Accounts, particularly as my father called for those which are now back. Finished two, when the time arrived for return.

Afternoon spent partly in overseeing the men dragging out the stone, and in Lucretius, b. 5, 1150–1300, with whom I am more pleased as I go on. We remained at home this evening instead of visiting the Mansion as there was company there.

WEDNESDAY 10TH.

Stormy day. Time passed at home.

My head was not in order today so that the prosecution of my work languished. Continued Locke vol. 2, p. 84–126, but with rather flagging attention. I admire however the vigor of his reasoning and only wish that I could adopt it in the arrangement of my thoughts.

Lucretius, finished book 5 and 100 lines in 6th. The ingenious mind of man makes causes where it does not find them. Compare the natural history of Lucretius with that of the present day.

Afternoon a little of Winkelman and Grimm. My only excursion today was to the houses at the foot of Penn's hill[1] with Deacon Spear. My head soon prompted my retirement.

[1] The JA and JQA birthplaces.

THURSDAY 11TH.

Fine, clear, windy day. Morning passed in study. Afternoon and evening at the Mansion.

Continued Locke, b. 2, p. 126–⟨3⟩185. Upon Maxims, identical propositions &ca. Very clear yet after all he admits a kind of intuition which hardly consists with the origin from sensation and reflection, which he ascribes to all our ideas. Lucretius 6th book, 100–326. He proceeds to account for thunder and other extraordinary natural appearances, which he does pretty ingeniously.

Dined at the Mansion, Mr. Page, the artist who is taking my father being there.[1] Idled away an hour or two in desultory examination of the books in my grandfather's library and on my return found A. H. Everett and William Foster who were taking tea at my father's prior to the former's delivering a Lecture before the Lyceum. I remained at the Mansion having heard it.

[1] On the portrait of JQA by William Page and the circumstances surrounding the undertaking, see Oliver, *Portraits of JQA and His Wife*, p. 196–201, and below, entry for 16 November.

FRIDAY. 12TH.

Clouds and rain in the latter part of the day. Morning to town. Afternoon spent in fishing. Evening at home.

My father accompanied me to town, and I was engaged the greater part of my time in the usual occupations. The news of the result of the late general election in Pennsylvania came in today and is hardly favorable to the Whigs. There seems to have been a revival of confidence in the democratic party since the resumption of specie payments which will perhaps extend this struggle for an indefinite period. For myself, I feel great indifference as to the matter, both parties being in my opinion wrongheaded and unprincipled. I have endeavoured to form my political judgments on what appeared to me solid foundations without reference to individual interests or predilections.

After dinner I made an attempt to catch some smelts successfully but was driven away by rain.

SATURDAY 13TH.

Day clear and windy, passed at home in occupation of various kinds. I arose this morning an hour before daylight for the sake of catching the tide to fish. The moon was shining bright and every thing was perfectly still. I was there a little too soon and therefore had an opportunity to observe the scene, a new one in some respects to me. The most remarkable portion of it was the opportunity of seeing Venus and Mercury before sunrise, and so near together as they appear. I was tolerably successful and returned to breakfast, having now done what I never did before, fished by a solitary shore by moonlight.

My morning was devoted to superintending the workmen who are still at work upon the rocks in front of the house, and in beginning the work of transplanting trees. I moved today two of my father's Pennsylvania maples and put them where two English oaks have failed. Also an oak and a buttonwood in the Avenue. Then Lucretius b. 6, 326–533.

In the afternoon Mr. Price Greenleaf made me a short visit and I drove my gig to Braintree to take Miss Sampson home who has been at work this week for the fourth generation of the family.[1] Evening at the Mansion but so much fatigued, I was glad to get home.

[1] Possibly the same Miss Sampson who had been used by the Adams family as a seamstress in earlier years (see vol. 1:222, 224) and was now sewing for CFA's children.

SUNDAY 14TH.

Mild, clear day. Time divided in the usual manner on this day. Attended divine service all day. Mr. Lunt preached in the morning from 1 Corinthians 10. 31. "Whether therefore ye eat or drink, or whatsoever ye do, do all to the glory of God." A discourse which made no great impression upon me. Mr. Whitney had no better effect in the afternoon from John 15. 22. "If I had not come and spoken unto them, they had not had sin: but now they have no cloke for their sin." I remarked only in it that it appears to have been written long ago as a qualification of opinions thought to incline over much to Universalism.

Read a Sermon of Revd. John Abernethy upon the causes and danger of self deceit. Matthew 6. 22.23. "The light of the body is the eye, if therefore thine eye be single, thy whole body is full of light; but if thine eye be evil, thy whole body shall be full of darkness. If therefore the light, that is in thee be darkness, how great is that darkness." A respectable essay upon the operation of conscience and the common modes of soothing or neglecting or evading it's reproaches.

Finished the first volume of Milman's History of the Jews, which ends with the captivity. I am much pleased with this book so far. Also read a little of Grimm. Evening at the Mansion.

MONDAY. 15TH.

Rain and fog. Day at home writing and reading. Evening at the Mansion.

Read Locke, p. 185–240. Upon the general character of proof, certainty, probability &ca. and the degrees of assent. Lucretius 533–780. I think this sixth book appears put in to fill up.

I devoted much time to writing an essay upon the present state of political affairs. Whether it will come to any thing remains pretty doubtful. But I was satisfied with my work after I had finished it, which rarely happens to me. The returns of elections appear very much against the Whigs, more so than I think they in reality are. The people appear to have turned a somerset to the Administration moved by the popular impulses that party know so well how to use. Yet the opposition is more concentrated and effective and better able to take advantage of every bad accident which must involve the Government through it's own stupidity. The Administration now runs for luck purely.

TUESDAY 16TH.

Clear day. Morning to town. Afternoon reading, evening at the Mansion.

My time in the City so much taken up by tenants and commissions of various sorts that I have had only opportunity to draw up the Accounts of my father's affairs without copying them off. Four tenants called to see me and all require repairs. This multiplies my work very much, and at this season of the year I commonly have enough.

Afternoon, out attending to the setting of two cherry trees and one oak within my inclosure, and an elm tree in the road. Mr. E. P. Greenleaf called with a present of some bushes and then accompanied me to the house below. It is a pity, he has not some occupation to cure him of his foibles.

WEDNESDAY 17TH.

Fine day. Morning study excepting an hour in fishing. Afternoon, work on my ground. Evening, Lecture at the townhouse.

Locke, p. 240–282. Reason, Faith and Enthusiasm. He thinks of the syllogistic style of reasoning rather less than it appears to me to deserve. One proof of which to my mind is that men often reason so when they have never heard one defined in the schools. The mind of Locke appears to have been strictly philosophical and hence perhaps slightly rigid in it's judgments.

Lucretius, 780–1084. I have rather hurried over this part of the book containing the account of the natural appearances and their causes very discreditable to the general theory as from the point of view we now regard it. The remainder of my day taken up in work.

Dined at the Mansion. The Lecture at the Lyceum hall was very fully attended. My father read a paper prepared by him as a biography of his father for Mr. Herring's Portrait Gallery.[1] Very good but rather long.

[1] That is, Longacre and Herring, *National Portrait Gallery of Distinguished Americans*; see entry for 24 Dec. 1836, above. The lecture was reviewed favorably in the *Quincy Patriot*, 20 Oct., p. 3, col. 1.

THURSDAY 18TH.

Fine day. Morning partly in study and partly out. Afternoon short. Evening at the Mansion.

Finished Locke's Essay on the Human Understanding, a work from the study of which I think I have gained something. It has opened my mind to the whole field of mental philosophy, and exercised my faculties even where I have been slow to assent. Finished also Lucretius today, a poem full of knotty points but which has also a fine poetical vein running through it. Thus my Summer's occupations are over, they do not include much, but what has been done has been better done than in any preceding Summer.

Besides completing the revision of the Copy of Journal of J. A. I have read Locke on Education and on the Understanding, Lessing's Laocoon, Pliny and Lucretius besides some fruitless investigations for a project of an article since abandoned. To be sure the question occasionally arises cui bono? but I strive to think that this is impertinent, as my happiness is much advanced without considering what I cannot help. I attempt continually and even now work upon a series of papers upon the Carolina policy.

The rest of the day was devoted to superintending work upon trees and grounds. Evening at Mrs. Adams where the ladies had gone to tea.

FRIDAY 19TH.

Clouds and heavy rain. To town in the morning and rather late return. Afternoon and evening at home.

My trip to town was made in the expectation that it would clear up instead of which it rained harder and I got wet. My time however was at my own disposal and I kept at work steadily until I had finished the three Accounts due to my father. These with various commissions consumed my time so that it was later than usual when I returned home facing a Southerly rain.

I occupied myself the remainder of my day and evening in writing upon the series of papers which I have commenced now in earnest. John was quite unwell all day.

SATURDAY 20TH.

Clear fine day. Passed at home writing and in study. Evening at the Mansion.

I felt somewhat unwell this morning, the result of my exposure yesterday, so I deemed it prudent to remain in the house. My time much devoted to the continuation of my papers upon the Carolina policy the first draft of which I completed. My endeavour will be to make these papers as good as I know how, in order to test the strength of the public prejudice. My course is the most difficult ever undertaken by a young man and can only command success by ascribing to myself a degree of ability I fear I do not possess. At any rate my duty is to try. I began a fair copy directly after finishing it. Writing is to me a far more difficult process than it used to be because I feel my defects more. A single sentence often stops me some time.

Evening, at the Mansion. The family already talk of their probable removal.

SUNDAY 21ST.

Clear day. Attended divine service as usual and the remainder of the day passed in writing and reading. Evening at the Mansion.

I was unable to find the other volumes of Milman's History so that I could not go on. What time was not devoted to the usual exercises of the day was spent in continuing to copy my papers.

Attended as usual at Meeting and heard Mr. Muzzy of Cambridge, from Matthew 24. 35. "Heaven and earth shall pass away but my words shall not pass away." The permanency of the Christian faith from which neither the attacks of avowed infidelity nor the divisions of its disciples can detract aught of it's durable principle. Sensible enough. Mark 9. 23. "Jesus said unto him, If thou canst believe, all things are possible to him that believeth." Upon faith as the engine of power in the mind itself.

Read a Sermon of Mr. John Balguy from Job. 37. 14. "Stand still and consider the wondrous works of God." The creation is a never ending source of reflection and moral exhortation and is not treated in this discourse with remarkably new or striking thought. Mr. Beale and his daughter paid a short visit in the evening and we then accompanied them to the Mansion.

MONDAY 22D.

Fine day. Kept much at home by the effect of a severe cold. Evening at a meeting of the Society to prevent stealing.

I did not deem it prudent to hazard myself so much out as I have done, so I was industrious upon my papers, finishing two. The composition of these is pleasant enough and varies my occupations in a suitable manner.

Mr. Price Greenleaf called in the evening and I accompanied him to the adjourned meeting of the Society for the suppression of theft of gardens &ca. where about thirty persons spent the whole evening in adopting the Constitution and choosing Officers.

TUESDAY 23D.

Fine day. Morning spent in town. Afternoon busy planting trees. Evening at the Mansion where I dined.

My cold was extremely troublesome all day. I went to the Office where I tried to make a fire in my new Office and found it smoke so badly as to drive me away. Something has happened to the flue. My time very much thrown away in consequence of this vexation. Visit from S. Conant about the Weston farm. Home late.

We dined at my Mother's who talks of starting for Washington on Thursday. And spent the evening, partly in a game of whist. I was busy in setting trees all the afternoon with Kirk. The workmen removed my fence today to the new boundaries.

WEDNESDAY 24TH.

Heavy rain all day. Confined to the house where I worked on my papers.

I passed a bad night and arose in the morning so much indisposed as to see without regret good cause in the rain for keeping me at home. My papers kept me well employed, and in the course of the day I completed the fourth. At present they appear to me the most calm, the most statesmanlike production I have yet made, but it is impossible for me under the heat of composition ever to form such an estimate as comes near to correctness. And then what can I hope for even my best productions in opposition to the stubborn prejudices of the great mass of the people? My course is a hard and a doubtful one with nothing to sustain me but my belief of it's truth. These papers will be laid on the shelf with all the others, yet they have not been without use in amusing and instructing me. Such occupations by ennobling the mind bring their own reward with them.

THURSDAY 25TH.

Fine day. Morning to town. After dinner, superintending trees and evening at the Mansion.

I went to town out of course today for the sake of seeing to the opening of the house for our approaching return. This is usually a melancholy process with me as I leave a place with which I have many sympathies to go to one where the world seems to move without reference to me. But the change is perhaps beneficial to me by making me value my present agreeable residence more.

I was engaged in giving directions, making purchases &ca. all day. Home to dinner. Afternoon, placed a few walnut trees in the room of some which have failed. The removal of the fence is a great improvement. Mr. Price Greenleaf here this afternoon. Evening at the Mansion.

FRIDAY 26TH.

A very fine Autumn day. Occupied by writing and company. Afternoon dinner. Evening at the Mansion, and Mrs. Adams'.

My time was much distracted this day. I wrote and finished the fifth of my papers and there was obliged to leave them to superintend the planting of some trees. I had hardly done when some visitors drove up, Mr. Fletcher and Mr. Tarbell[1] and Mrs. Miller and her daughter. The object of the former appeared to be to invite me to dinner, he having been at my father's to ask him. He seems quite enlivened by his renomination to Congress.[2]

My father and Mr. Lunt dined with me and remained in conversation until after sundown. The ladies went up to see Mrs. T. B. Adams in the evening and I accompanied them.

[1] On Thomas Tarbell's connections with the Adamses, see vol. 3:59.

[2] CFA is in error. Richard Fletcher was currently serving as a Mass. representative in the 25th Congress, but perhaps because of the controversy that marked his term (see entry for 18 Dec. 1837, above) was not a candidate for renomination in 1838 (*Biog. Dir. Cong.*).

SATURDAY 27TH.

Morning promised well but it clouded and finally rained hard with a sharp thunder storm. To Boston. Afternoon, reading. Evening at the Mansion.

I went to Boston this morning and passed my time in various little duties incident to the preparation of the house, but finding the rain threaten seriously I hastened home arriving at my door exactly as the first clap of thunder rolled over our heads. This is the second time within a few days that we have had lightning, and the rain poured in torrents. Mrs. Adams returned half an hour later who had been to the City in the Carriage and it was drenched by it.

I do not ever recollect a thunder shower so late in the Season before, for it cleared up afterwards and became a clear moonlight evening. The afternoons are now so short as to prevent any thing like occupation. I found the family at the Mansion whither I went dull for the weather is discouraging to their departure.

SUNDAY 28TH.

The morning bright but it changed to rain and snow. Attended the services as usual and evening at the Mansion.

The near approach of the period of our migration and the completion of my course of study render my attention a little unsettled. I heard at Meeting today Mr. Briggs from Matthew 6. 9. "Our father, which art in Heaven." A very fluent and pretty discourse upon the relation in which the Deity is placed by the text toward us. Also from [Matthew 15. 6][1] upon the mere mechanical performance of the duties of religion rendering them valueless. Mr. Briggs is a fair Representative of a class of young men who have a kind of eloquence of style with which they clothe common thought and over-refined sentiment. What is wanted is nerve and manliness.

Read a discourse being the 15th and last in the first volume of the English Preacher. It is by the Revd. Jeremiah Tidcomb and taken from Hosea 6. 4. "O Ephraim! what shall I do unto thee? O Judah! what shall I do unto thee? For your goodness is as a morning cloud, and as the early dew it goeth away." Upon vacillation in religious principle either through unsteadiness or vice. No more striking sermon than the rest.

Read a little of Charlevoix History of Paraguay to form an idea of the Jesuit Missions.[2] Evening at the Mansion, the last family meeting of the season.

[1] Supplied from the entry of the day in JQA's Diary.
[2] Pierre François Xavier de Charlevoix, *Histoire du Paraguay*, 6 vols., Paris, 1757. JQA's copy is in MQA.

MONDAY 29TH.

Clear and windy. Morning wasted. Afternoon to Boston and return. Evening at the Mansion.

We found upon rising this morning the ground covered with a coating of snow thus presenting quite a winterish appearance. The landscape from this hill is pretty even so. My time was wasted in running forward and backward between this and the other house.

The family were making their preparations to move to Washington, accordingly after taking a short dinner I accompanied them in a Stage to the Depot of the Providence train at [i.e. to] Stonington and having seen them safely arranged in a Car I took my leave and after a short call at my house returned home in the conveyance I came in.

Found my Wife keeping company with my father who is left alone. And I spent the evening there. Mr. Price Greenleaf was there and talked as usual.

TUESDAY 30TH.

Clear and colder. Morning to town where I was all day not returning until evening.

I drove in the pair of horses this morning, with my father, Wife and son John to spend the day. My own occupations were of the usual kind, all having some relation to the approaching move to town. As the season advances and the family at the other house disappear from the scene I become reconciled to the change to winter quarters. But it is a cheerless process.

At the Office I could not raise a fire so had no temptation to stay. At my house it was not much better, so my father and I waited at Dr. Frothingham's until the hour for dining with Mr. Fletcher arrived.

It was curious to observe how little ten years had altered the old location,[1] and yet there were changes as well in others as in myself which carried their moral with them. The company consisted of Judge Story, Governor Everett, Judge Davis, Professor Greenleaf, Mr. Hale, Mr. Worcester, Mr. Gannett, Mr. Tarbell and ourselves. The first took the lion's share of the talk and harped upon his favourite strings. On the whole a handsome and a pleasant dinner. I drove home by moonlight.

[1] The dinner given by Richard Fletcher was held at Thomas Tarbell's home on Avon Place (JQA, Diary), where CFA had had a room in 1828 and 1829 (vols. 2:306; 3:59).

WEDNESDAY. 31ST.

Clouds and snow. At home all day busy packing up. Dine at the Mansion and spend the evening there.

I felt this morning a little inclined to head ach but it went off before dinner. Time not much improved as the preparations were going on for final removal. I wrote a little upon my series of papers but not vigorously.

I forgot to state that I consulted my father about their publication and he advised the offer of them at least to the Courier, in pursuance of which recommendation there were three sent to that paper, on Monday.

The day was wretchedly gloomy. On the whole we have had a delightful Summer which has however been terminated by the most unpleasant Autumn that I remember. This much diminishes my feeling of regret at leaving Quincy.

We dined with my father who is tolerably lonely. Evening, Conversation about the character of General La Fayette.

THURSDAY. NOVEMBER 1ST.

Weather changed during the night to sharp cold. I went to town. Return to my fathers where I remained the night. Visits.

Up early to get off the family and moveables and to complete the shutting up of the house. Went to town accompanied by my manservant, leaving the rest of the people and the three younger children to go in the Carriage. Mrs. Adams and Louisa propose to stay with me at my father's until Monday. A severe ride to town, and constant occupation there in the various little duties necessary to prepare the family.

Afternoon went to shut up. I do not know why I felt so melancholy. Perhaps man never looked forward with more hope of enjoyment to a summer residence, and never had his hopes better fulfilled. It is needless to moralize nor to look to the future. Time will roll on and bring with [it] that apportionment which is ordered by Providence to each of us. If mine has been hitherto beyond my deserts, I hope I may not forfeit it by my failure to attempt to be worthy of it.

We visited in the evening Mr. and Mrs. Appleton, Mr. and Mrs. T. Greenleaf and Mr. Beale and his daughter, being all to take leave prior to our departure for town.

FRIDAY 2D.

A very fine day. Devoted to arrangements for the winter and planting. Evening visit.

I have no special account to give of my day's work. My reading was somewhat desultory and divided by conversation upon various topics with my father. Dipped into the new publication of letters and papers of General La Fayette.[1] There is much interesting matter here for we have the testimony in it of a witness and an actor by his situation very far removed from the immediate passions acting upon others engaged in the contest.

La Fayette was not in my eyes a very great man. His powers of mind do not range upon that level which all classes incontestably admit to be above them. But he had the elements of goodness in a large proportion with enough of human weakness to keep sympathy excited.

Transplanted this afternoon two Maple trees of my fathers to the foot of my new inclosure. Mr. Lunt called and in the evening my Wife and I went to see him and Mrs. Lunt.

¹ CFA's bookplate is in the copy in MQA of Lafayette's *Mémoires, correspondance et manuscrits*, 6 vols., Paris, 1837–1838.

SATURDAY 3D.

A lovely autumn day. To town in the morning and in the Afternoon to Weymouth. Evening at home.

I rode to town this morning and devoted my time to the pursuit of the usual occupations. Called to see my children who looked comfortable and the general appearance of the house was such as to make me feel desirous of returning. The day looked so sunny and things looked so cheerful that I felt a lightness of spirits for which I can account as little as for my occasional depressions. They are the results in both of the most trifling causes.

After dinner as my Wife had a little commission to Weymouth I went with her and this took the whole of the Afternoon. Read a little of La Fayette which took up the remainder of the evening.

SUNDAY 4TH.

Rain. Attended divine service as usual, and the rest of the time passed at home.

It does seem as if we could have only one or two dry days at a time. The quantity of humidity in the atmosphere is so overpowering. From noon it rained pretty constantly.

I heard Mr. Lunt preach from the Wisdom of Solomon 1. 6. "For wisdom is a loving spirit," a sensible discourse upon the connexion of true Wisdom with benevolence, as distinct from selfishness or dishonesty. Also in the Afternoon from Titus 2. 11.12. "For the grace of God that bringeth salvation hath appeared to all men, teaching us, that denying ungodliness and worldly lusts, we should live soberly, righteously and godly in this present world."

As I had accidentally sent the volume of the English Preacher to town I took up a volume of Tillotson¹ and read a Discourse from Ecclesiastes 9. 10. "Whatsoever thy hand findeth to do, do it with thy might; for there is no work, nor device, nor knowledge, nor wisdom in the grave whither thou goest." I like this text and hence read the Sermon. It has been the principle of action with me for many years in the limited sphere in which action has been allowed to me. It is true there are to many others ideas of creating work to do which never appeared to my mind within the scope of the text. The hand must find it but must not make it.

Dr. Tillotson considers the text in two points of view as it regards religious benevolence and also the particular calling of the individual, in both of which undoubtedly there is much profit to be found. The great duty of man is the cultivation of the moral affections, then comes the collateral developement of the intellectual powers and the duties of active life. Mr. Degrand was here on a visit to my father until late in the evening.

[1] *The Works of the Most Reverend ... John Tillotson*, 10 vols., Edinburgh, 1748, are in MQA.

MONDAY 5TH.

Heavy rain all day. Confined to the house. Nothing material.

This was the day fixed upon for our return to town, but the rain was so heavy and so incessant that we could not stir a step. My time was principally taken up with Revolutionary History, now dipping into Sparks' Life of Washington and now into the Memoirs of La Fayette. There is something to be gathered from both. Mr. Sparks is a very laborious man and he has managed to get under his control a considerable proportion of the MS papers of our Revolution, but he is also a dull man and has a set of political notions which are not exactly in accordance with the theory of our system. He does not appear to have added many material facts but he has new details.[1] Before night I got tired of both books and the time hung a little heavy.

[1] Jared Sparks' *Writings of George Washington* in 12 vols. had been published 1834–1837; see vol. 4:xii–xiii and index for further comments on Sparks by CFA.

Boston

TUESDAY 6TH.

Clear. Removed to town. Office, and afternoon at home.

Shortly after breakfast I started with my Wife and Louisa from Quincy for the town. Thus terminates a residence than which I do not believe man can enjoy a much pleasanter. The Summer has been sunny and will perhaps make the happiest spot to look back upon if I live. There may have been times of more noisy pleasure or brilliant dissipation but none of more uninterrupted enjoyment.

I went to the Office and passed some time. Afternoon tolerably cheerless at home. Read part of Swift's Tale of a Tub which I have never read before[1] and which I do not much enjoy now. There is not method enough in the Satire. It mixes until the brain becomes confused and tired and will not follow longer.

Tried to write in the evening but could not find the materials to do it easily. It is surprising how easily these little trifles check me.

[1] See the entry for 7 Dec. 1836, above.

WEDNESDAY 7TH.

Very pleasant. To Quincy all day. Evening at home.

I started early this morning for Quincy in order to make a good day of it. Occupied most of the time in transplanting two trees. One an English Oak of some size which I placed in a conspicuous position and one a native Oak on the line below. This consumed all of the time not devoted to my father and brought me to town rather later than I wished. The darkness was such that I determined not to be caught so again. Evening much alone at my house. Worked hard upon my papers.

THURSDAY 8TH.

Another heavy rain. At Office. One hour before dinner devoted to Greek as customary in town. Afternoon, reading and evening, writing.

This succession of rainy weather prevents any thing like agreeable motion even when it becomes occasionally fair. I had intended going to Quincy but was obliged to remain and work at the Office upon accounts as usual.

I today began my Greek studies for the winter with the Alcestis of Euripides. Also Swift's Tale of a Tub. Evening at home reading aloud one of the Waverley Novels and then writing upon my papers.

FRIDAY 9TH.

Clear. Ride to Quincy for the day. Return home to tea and evening to the Theatre.

The mud was quite deep today but I went to Quincy and was occupied in various little matters which required my attention. The town was thrown into a great state of excitement today by the arrival of accounts from New York of the triumph of the Whig party.[1] This was not anticipated by either party and puts a very different face upon the aspect of political events. Mr. Van Buren now has to face the probability of a majority in the next Congress against him and the prestige of the democratic strength is much more broken. Well, it only keeps up the bubbling. One thing is pretty clear to me that nothing holds up the present Administration one bit but the little hold on the popular feeling of the other side.

Returned home by the old road through Milton and Roxbury as being more dry. Found Mr. Brooks at my house to tea. Went to the Theatre with my Wife and heard an Opera by Rooke called the Love Test, somewhat German in its character but with rather feeble music. The parts however very respectably sustained. After piece Truth or a Glass too much, better than usual.[2]

[1] The whig sweep was featured by the defeat of C. C. Cambreleng, chairman of the House Ways and Means Committee, and by the election of William H. Seward as governor (*Boston Courier*, 10 Nov., p. 2, col. 5 – p. 3, col. 2).

[2] *Amilie or The Love Test* and *Truth!*, given at the Tremont Theatre, had as performers Edward Seguin, John Wilson, and Jane Shirreff, current favorites in the New York theater (*Boston Atlas*, 9 Nov., p. 3, col. 3; below, entry for 30 April 1839).

SATURDAY. 10TH.

Cold and clear. At the Office. Athenæum and home. Evening quiet.

I have not much to record of my morning experiences. Called to see T. K. Davis at his Office having seen him at the Theatre last evening. He was not entirely cordial. There is some difficulty in his mind but what I do not know. His political feelings have probably led him off where I cannot follow him and he does not quite like it that I do not. Yet there was only such a nice shade of difference apparent in his manner as could be perceivable by a very practised eye. I hope this will be remedied.

My Afternoon was spent in re-instituting my collection of coins and in receiving my father who removed from Quincy to my house today. Evening, Mr. Brooks came in for an hour.

SUNDAY 11TH.

Moderate and clear. Divine service both parts of the day and an evening visit to the Governor.

Attended divine service and heard Dr. Harris preach from Isaiah 33. 9. "The earth mourneth and languisheth; Lebanon is ashamed and hewn down; Sharon is like a wilderness and Bashan and Carmel shake off their fruits." A sensible but not very interesting discourse. Afternoon Mr. Austin from Matthew 6. 9. "Thy kingdom come." Quite flat and on the whole I was sorry that my father had not a better opportunity for edification.

Read a discourse being the first in the second volume of the English Preacher, by Tillotson from John 1. 47. "Jesus saw Nathaniel coming unto him and saith of him, Behold an Israelite indeed in whom is no guile." Very sensible. In the evening I accompanied my father to Governor Everett's to pay a visit. Nobody there but the family, Mr. Brooks and a relative of the Governor's. Conversation of no interest.

MONDAY 12TH.

Fine day. General Election. Office. Athenæum. Afternoon at home. Evening at the Play.

I passed my time at the Office much as usual. It being the day for the choice of State Officers, I voted. My position has been somewhat varied during the last year. The course of the Administration in yielding to the eccentricities of Mr. Calhoun has placed me very much upon the other side and yet I have an innate aversion to the dirty dictation of the Whigs of this place. My opinions agree nearly with those of no body here and hence I am obliged to stand entirely upon what I hold to be right for my justification. I therefore selected the names which I held to be the best on the whole, out of the lists presented and voted it with perfect conscientiousness.

There was much excitement on account of the license law of the last Session which bears with peculiar severity upon the spirit dealers in this city. This has distracted the Whigs and hazards their County ticket. In such matters I feel little interest, but as bearing the best list of names I voted the Amory hall ticket which is considered as favouring the law.[1]

At the Athenæum I took out Davis life of Aaron Burr[2] with a view to future use for Dr. Palfrey. Afternoon, finished Swifts Tale of a Tub. There is so much of the vulgar and coarse about Swift, it is wonderful that his writings remain at all. A kind of bull dog mind characteristic perhaps of the lower orders of the English people.

Evening with my father to hear the Somnambula. Miss Shirreff as Amina, Wilson for Elvino and Seguin as Rhodolpho. The piece very well got up. And perhaps as well done in all but the prima donna as I ever knew it to be. Miss Shirreff is not the singer that Mrs. Wood or Caradori is but she is respectable. Her acting borders upon excess which is better than tameness. Afterpiece, the same as Friday.

[1] The Massachusetts legislature, under pressure of temperance advocates, had passed earlier in the year what was known as the License Law of 1838. Insistent demands for repeal made the law's future a crucial issue in the current electoral campaign, splitting the whig party. The dominant wing of the party was pro-repeal, the "Amory Hall" wing anti- (*Daily Centinel & Gazette*, 9 Nov., p. 2, cols. 3–5; 12 Nov., p. 1, col. 2, p. 2, col. 6).

[2] M. L. Davis, *Memoirs of Aaron Burr*, 2 vols., N.Y., 1836–1837.

TUESDAY 13TH.

Fine day. Ride to Quincy. Return to dine at Mr. Brooks'. Evening at home.

Immediately after breakfast my father accompanied me to Quincy. I took the opportunity to go and see Mrs. T. B. Adams about the settlement of the Estate of her son.

The town in a tremendous struggle about the election. It seems that Dr. Duggan has worked with some effect upon the town so that this year it is tolerably democratic. He procured his own election as a Representative and almost surprised a vote against my father for Congress. Today they were attempting to choose two more and doubted their result. Such are the humours of elections to produce what result! I am afraid to look at that part of the Picture. The Democrats without opposing my father openly have endeavoured to throw a combined vote on another candidate so as to weaken the force of his position.[1]

We returned to dine after I had accomplished my business, with Mr. Brooks. Nobody there but the family and Governor Everett and Edward. Pleasant dinner enough and home in the evening.

[1] "In the 12th Congressional District, there was no nomination of a candidate in opposition to me. But an opposition was secretly organized throughout the District, utterly unknown in many of the Towns until the opening of the polls. No preparation had been made for such resistance, and multitudes did not vote from the mere presumption that as there would be no opposition it would be useless. To play the game with more effect a highly charged democratic abolitionist was selected for the Candidate, and the whole Van Buren phalanx in every town of the District voted for him. Instead of an unanimous vote, my majority in the District will be but a few hundreds" (JQA, Diary, 13 Nov.). Official returns would show that JQA received 4,100 of the 6,951 votes cast in the District (*Daily Centinel & Gazette*, 27 Nov. 1838, p. 2, col. 1).

[*Quincy*]

WEDNESDAY 14TH.

A beautiful day. Office. After dinner to Quincy. Tea at Mrs. Adams' and delivered a Lecture. Sleep at Quincy.

I passed the morning at the Office in the usual course of things. My time flies with even greater rapidity than ever and to as little purpose.

After dinner my father accompanied me to Quincy in as fine a day as I ever knew at this season of the year. We reached there at five and went to Mrs. Adams' to take tea. They had sent me word in the morning that the Lyceum expected a Lecture from me although there had never been a distinct assent on my part. Still as I was anxious that my father should hear me I agreed to take the summons and accordingly we went to the hall where I read the Lecture delivered before the Historical Society last winter.[1] Returned home to my father's where we slept.

[1] "The Hall was crowded and more than half the auditory were women. The most perfect silence was observed and the deepest attention paid throughout the reading, which occupied an hour and a quarter" (JQA, Diary, 14 Nov.). The lecture was that delivered on 23 January.

Boston

THURSDAY 15TH.

Heavy rain. To town. Office. Afternoon at home. Nothing new.

My father concluded to remain at Quincy today so that after transacting a little business of Administration I returned alone to town. At the Office.

I find the Courier has this day commenced the publication of my papers.[1] The point has been gained of my admission to the press on my own terms. And hence I feel encouraged in the hope of establishing a reputation which will sustain me. Afternoon I finished and despatched two more papers which make five. Evening at home.

[1] "Political Speculation upon the Carolina Policy," unsigned, would appear in the *Boston Courier* in seven installments on 15, 16, 19, 20, 22, 24 Nov. and 1 December. In each issue it was given position as leader, p. 2, cols. 1-2, except on the 19th, when it was placed on p. 3, cols. 1-2. Drafts, incomplete, in CFA's hand are in the Adams Papers (M/CFA/24.17, Microfilms, Reel No. 320). The thrust of the articles, directed against both Van Buren and Calhoun, is reported in Duberman, *CFA*, p. 64-65.

FRIDAY 16TH.

Cloudy. Office as usual. Home. Afternoon reading and evening visit to Mr. Frothingham's.

Mr. Buckingham published my second number today which I like much better than the first. At the Office occupied in the making up of

In reflecting upon those memorials of Revolutionary times which have thus far made their appearance before the public, upon which the ideas of those who come after us as well as our own must be formed of the character and manners of the generation of that day, it seems a little remarkable that the acts and the language of men in their public capacities under the restraint which the eye of the world always imposes should so exclusively demand our attention. We all know how much the political condition of society depends upon the degree of its moral advancement, and that this moral advancement is manifested far more certainly in the tone of the domestic relations perceived generally to prevail than in the more elaborate published expositions made by individual statesmen or philosophers. The practical morality of States, that which is interwoven in the very texture of social existence depends for its excellence upon the prevailing habits of thought among the great mass of the men and I must particularly add, of the women also of the community. The precepts at the bottom of all well regulated society by which from infancy we are directed to love virtue and to shun vice receive their main impulse from the lips of the mother who teaches infinitely less than she instils. Hence love of country is in general but a late deduction of maturer minds from the early affection which makes home the delight

3. THE FIRST PAGE OF THE LECTURE "MATERIALS FOR HISTORY"
See pages ix – x

arrears of Diary and of Accounts which my way of passing time while my father is here has a tendency to accumulate.

On my return found my father who had been met and complimented by the Committee of his friends who had had his picture painted by Mr. Page.[1] The feeling in the City is much more favourable to him than it has been for many years.

Afternoon, I began the life of Aaron Burr by Matthew L. Davis. Evening, called to see Dr. Frothingham who has been confined to his house unwell. Conversation with him upon various subjects metaphysical and moral quite edifying. He spoke of my papers with commendation.

[1] The *Boston Courier* (17 Nov., p. 2, col. 2) carried an account of the ceremony of presentation and listed those who had contributed. The painting is reproduced and the attending circumstances recounted in Oliver, *Portraits of JQA and His Wife*, p. 197–200.

SATURDAY 17TH.

Day fine. Office with Accounts and visitors. Dine at I. P. Davis'. Evening at home.

I was taken up almost all of my time by W. Spear who came with his long Account to settle and with Mr. B. V. French of Braintree who was here about a piece of fence he wants made on the Mount Wollaston farm. There was some vexation in both. These improvements at Quincy are not without their heavy charge. Mr. French's business is an expense purely to gratify his own vanity and pique against the Tenant.

Home. Then with my father to dine with I. P. Davis. Judge Davis with T. K. Davis and Mr. Bancroft came in after dinner. Pleasant talk and a comfortable dinner. Judge Davis is a man of extensive information and strong natural sense.

SUNDAY. 18TH.

Cool day. Attended divine service as usual. Evening at home.

Read part of Milman's History of the Jews of which I have now the second volume. Attended at the Church in Chauncy Place and heard Dr. Gray preach both parts of the day. Morning from Colossians 3. 1. "Seek those things which are above where Christ sitteth on the right hand of God." Afternoon from Matthew 7. 1 and 2. "Judge not that ye be not judged. For with what judgement ye judge, ye shall be judged: and with what measure ye mete it shall be measured to you again." Dr. Gray is not very interesting and even if he was my mind is in such a state as to prevent my giving him much deliberate attention.

Read a Sermon in the English Preacher, by Tillotson. Titus 3. 2. "Speak evil of no man." The best discourse of his which I have read. Thus passed the day rapidly enough. The evening spent at home. Nothing of interest.

MONDAY 19TH.

Day pleasant. Morning spent at the sale of South Cove lands. Afternoon at home. Evening, Mr. Lawrence.

My time during the morning was taken up by the attendance upon the sale of the South Cove lands. This is a matter into which I have gone with a hope that it may benefit my children, although originally merely drawn in upon a point of honour. I purchased a number of the lots on the judgment of Mr. Nathl. Curtis and my own. The sale generally went off well, I thought and may enable the company to get clear of it's difficulties provided they will not incur any more. This is the rub.

Afternoon Life of Burr. Evening Mr. Abbott Lawrence came in to see my father who was out. Talk about indifferent matters. Continue work.

TUESDAY 20TH.

Day cloudy. Office as usual. Afternoon and evening at home.

I passed the morning in endeavouring to fill up the arrears of my Diary which are now constantly going on. I was also occupied in Accounts. Mr. Buckingham publishes this morning another number of my papers which are treated like all the rest. A little casual talk in private circles but not a whisper about them in the press. I have done my best with these and if they make no sensation will do no more. Exertion can scarcely go farther. Not that it has not produced some result, but it is so gradual as scarcely to be perceptible.

Home. Afternoon, reading the Life of Aaron Burr. Curious and on the whole more interesting than I could have expected. Evening quietly at home. Nothing of interest. Tried to write another paper but found myself dull.

WEDNESDAY 21ST.

Clear day but cool. Morning to Quincy. Return to dinner. Evening at home.

Immediately after breakfast, my father accompanied me to Quincy.

After an hour's stay at the house where every thing looked cheerless enough we went down to Mount Wollaston on the reference as to bounds which had been agreed upon. Mr. French came late but the Surveyor and other parties were present and we proceeded. No more vexatious affair could occur. The whole thing was cheerless in the extreme, and I was glad to hurry off my father to make good his engagement to dine at Governor Everett's. As it was, we did not get there until half an hour after the time. No body present but the various members of the family and I. P. Davis. The dinner was pleasant and we stayed late. My father then went to a club and I stayed at home. Difficulty again in writing.

THURSDAY 22D.

Cloudy threatening rain. Office. Athenæum. Afternoon and Evening at home. Mr. Degrand.

Another of my papers today making the 5th. The Courier publishes much faster than I can write. I went to the Office and after doing a certain amount of business, to the Athenæum where I met my father and we went into the studio of a Mr. Clevenger who was taking a bust of Mrs. Webster.[1] Then to see the new pictures in the Gallery and then home.

Afternoon, Davis's life of Aaron Burr. I am much interested as I proceed. There is a fine opportunity presented for impartial and yet severe criticism. Evening, Mr. Degrand in to see my father. Still unsuccessful with my seventh number.

[1] Shobal Vail Clevenger, a year before, had completed a bust of JQA in plaster; see Oliver, *Portraits of JQA and His Wife*, p. 192–195.

FRIDAY 23D.

Clear and cool. Office. Afternoon at home reading and in the evening to Mrs. Gorham's.

Morning devoted to the Office as usual. My father dined out at Mr. Bancroft's, who did not invite me because I have not visited him. I do not like the man's character but I suppose I ought to visit him.

Read Aaron Burr. His Wife an English woman apparently of some intellectual power. He seems to have had the art of gaining female affection perhaps because he made it a study.

Evening, a party at Mr. B. Gorham's to the Wife of Mr. G. Gardner. Mostly Lowells and that connexion.[1] Rather dull. Home early and fatigued from a long walk taken in the course of the day to see my investment in lands at the South Cove.

[1] George Gardner had married Helen M. Read on 24 Oct. (*Columbian Centinel*). He was the son of Rebecca Lowell Gardner, a daughter of Judge John Lowell; his sister had married Francis C. Lowell (*NEHGR*, 25 [1896]:50).

SATURDAY 24TH.

Day cold. Ride to Quincy. Return to dinner at home with company. Evening, Concert.

At the Office and from thence to Quincy. Transacted business at the Bank and then returned directly to town accompanied by Kirk who drove the horse back from the South Boston Turnpike, where I got out and walked home. The air was very keen. Mr. Buckingham published today the sixth number of my papers and I am greatly doubtful whether it would not be most expedient here to stop.

I had to dine with me six gentlemen — Mr. Brooks, Governor Everett, Dr. Palfrey, W. Lee, Mr. Lothrop and Col. Quincy. Tolerably pleasant. After it was over, I went to a Concert to hear De Begnis, an Italian Opera Buffa singer. He was assisted by Russel and a Mrs. Franklin.[1] The singing was good.

Home where I found Edmund Quincy talking with my father upon Abolitionism. It was somewhat dull to me as I thought my father's trouble was all thrown away. Quincy like all the other persons of that stamp in this State is somewhat impracticable. He has got hold of a good principle but does not know how to use it.

[1] The great Italian singer Guiseppe De Begnis had made his American debut in New York in September. Henry Russell and Mrs. Franklin had sung frequently in New York concert halls since 1836, Rus- sell attaining popularity as a ballad singer (Odell, *Annals N.Y. Stage*, 4:291 and index; a likeness of Russell appears facing p. 518).

SUNDAY 25TH.

Severely cold. Service all day. Reading and evening to see Mr. Brooks.

The thermometer was near zero this morning. I read some of Milman's History of the Jews and attended as usual divine service at Chauncy place. But the exercises were interrupted in an unusual manner by an alarm of fire which scattered the congregation. The Stove having been heated overmuch caught the [. . .] on fire and was burning with great rapidity. After seeing it put out, I returned home.

Afternoon to Mr. Lothrop's where I heard him preach from John 9.

5. "I am the light of the world." Christianity considers man in four relations — as a social, intellectual, physical and moral being, and acts upon him in all.

Read a Sermon by a Mr. Trebeck from Ephesians 4. 26. "Be ye angry and sin not." A reasonable examination of the real nature of anger, its bad effects and its allowable limits. The evening was taken up by a call at Mr. Brooks'. Nothing material. Miss Harriet Welsh and Mr. Degrand at my house.

MONDAY. 26TH.

Cold and clear. Office. Afternoon my father off. Evening quiet at home.

My time today was taken up scarcely with my knowing how. Engaged in Accounts at the Office until noon when I went home and made the arrangements for my father's going off. After an early dinner I accompanied him with my two boys John and Charles to the Railway depot. It was piercing cold but the Cars were close and comfortable.

My father has been with me two days over a fortnight during which time I have enjoyed his society as I always do.[1] Indeed I shall miss him very much as now I have not one single friend of any intimacy in the City. Davis appears to be in irrevocable eclipse, Walsh has vanished and I never had any others. Well, I must seek in the amusement of literary occupation for the substitutes, and in the growth of my family affections.[2]

Read Burr, and after an unsuccessful attempt at a visit, made another effort at a concluding paper.

[1] "I have been living more than a fortnight in indolent enjoyment at my Son's house, without being troubled with the distracting cares of a family, without being dunned, and without disturbance of any kind. From this delightful dream . . . I was this day compelled to awake" (JQA, Diary, 26 Nov.).

[2] Writing to his mother some weeks later, CFA returned to reflection on his situation with a conclusion recollecting *Paradise Lost*, XII, 646: "The few persons who formerly visited me socially and in a quiet way have taken other courses so that I am driven to form a taste for crowds. T. K. Davis has cut 'the fus colored circles' as too aristocratic, and me as being a consolidationist in politics, so that I see nothing of him. Walsh has evaporated for all that I know to the contrary, and [Edmund] Quincy has banished the intemperance of conviviality for the intemperance of Abolitionism. A. H. Everett is vegetating in Roxbury or elsewhere and never comes near me. So that the world is all before me where to choose just as if I was beginning it anew" (6 Feb. 1839, Adams Papers).

TUESDAY 27TH.

Cold and clear. Usual division of time. Evening, visits.

At the Office today making up arrears. The division of occupation now becomes so monotonous that I hardly deem it worth while to record it. I resumed the Alcestis of Euripides going over what I had already read. This practice must be adhered to.

Continued Burr, and resumed my voluntary task of making a Catalogue of the Athenæum coins. In order to remove them from danger, when my house was entered, I put them into a trunk in great disorder, which will cost me some additional labour.

Made another unsuccessful visit to Mr. and Mrs. Edward Blake and then went to see Mr. and Mrs. Frothingham with whom we spent an agreeable hour. Finished the last of my numbers. They will not pay the cost.

WEDNESDAY 28TH.

Milder and clear. Usual division of time. Evening Mr. Brooks and Mr. and Mrs. Frothingham and Thomas with us.

Nothing of moment to record of my morning which seems to be doomed to the same kind of worthless waste that has always so fretted me in Boston. Went to the Athenæum but found nothing.

Mr. G. Whitney the minister of Jamaica Plains called to ask for a Lecture there. I told him my principles and he fell into them. This business of lecturing is attended with mighty little profit. I do it only because it enables me to gain some foothold in the Community.

Euripides. Coins and Burr. A very pleasant visit from Mr. and Mrs. Frothingham and Mr. Brooks, after which I tried to revise my Lecture upon Northern Adventure with little success.

THURSDAY 29TH.

Clear and mild. Thanksgiving day. Service and evening at Mr. Frothingham's, family.

I read today the greater part of a volume of travels by Mr. Stephens of New York.[1] They are amusing and superficially instructive.

Attended divine service and heard Mr. Frothingham preach from Psalms 89. 15. "Blessed is the people that know the joyful sound." A very good discourse upon the connexion of the Institutions of Religion with Government and politics as contributing to cherish the true moral tone which is the salvation of all temporal blessings. An occasional hit at Mr. Emerson not without effect and well done. On the whole, the best Thanksgiving sermon I have heard.

At home today with my family. Afternoon, coins and Burr. Evening, the Brooks family at Mr. Frothingham's where we had a pretty Supper and finished the evening.

[1] Probably, John Lloyd Stephens, *Incidents of Travel in Greece, Turkey, Russia, and Poland*, 2 vols., N.Y., 1838.

FRIDAY 30TH.

Mild and clear. Office, and the usual record.

I made up my Arrears very bravely at the Office today and put myself somewhat at ease respecting my occupations. Then to the house for the sake of paying some visits due. Succeeded only in one but made good progress in Alcestis.

After dinner I resumed the Catalogue of coins and read Burr which interests me very much. His character is worth analyzing.

Resumed the examination and revisal of my Lecture, in which I put some new things and took out some old ones. The great obstacle is in it's length and yet I cannot well shorten it. The danger rather lies on the other side. Up until late.

SATURDAY. DECEMBER 1ST.

Mild and cloudy. Office, thence to Roxbury. Evening, Concert.

My Wife was taken suddenly sick in the night and continued so through the day. Her health is my greatest cause of anxiety. At the Office where my time was taken up by Deacon Spear, Mr. Stanwood and others. Buckingham publishes my last number today. Much ado about nothing.

Instead of dinner, I was obliged to go to Roxbury today to make my return of Inventory and Affidavit of Notice[1] both of which I succeeded in accomplishing and returned home by three.

Continued my work on coins, and in the evening attended a Concert of Mr. Russell. The music by him and De Begnis. Hardly variety enough. Mr. Russell is too much of a mannerist so that his style palls upon too frequent repetition. De Begnis is a very good buffo singer and several of his pieces pleased me much. There were one or two glees well sung but not in themselves remarkable. The house was very full.

[1] Tax levying procedures.

SUNDAY 2D.

Weather pleasant, divine service all day, time divided as usual.

Continued Milman's History of the Jews, and finished Davis' life of Burr. It is difficult to tell whose moral obliquity is the greatest the author's or his subject.

Attended divine service and heard Dr. Frothingham from Proverbs 8. 3. "Wisdom crieth at the entry of the City." A series of reflections upon the character of city life and the ordinary impression that it is unfavorable to religious impressions. Mr. Frothingham's mind is a curious one and partakes of the influences around it. He sees little in the external world upon which to throw himself and his feelings. Associations fix themselves with difficulty. To him the holy land is nothing, the green face of the earth nothing. Art delights him more than nature. These are not my feelings, who regard nature in all her forms as beautiful and who think more of a thing from its imaginary than from it's real value.

H. Ware in the afternoon from Romans 3. 5.6. "Is God unrighteous who taketh vengeance? God forbid: for then how shall God judge the world." A sensible discourse upon the question so frequently discussed of rewards and punishments in this life as in the place of a future retribution. Mr. Ware articulates with difficulty so that I could hardly hear him.

Read a Sermon of Dr. Clark from Proverbs 9. 10.11. "The fear of the Lord is the beginning of wisdom: and the knowledge of the holy is understanding, for by me thy days shall be multiplied, and the years of thy life shall be increased." Length of days the result of virtuous conduct. True as a consequence of the opposite proposition that vice shortens life. Evening quietly at home.

MONDAY 3D.

Cold and clear. Office and regular distribution of time.

My morning runs away in reading the Newspapers at the Insurance Office. Received a letter from my father[1] announcing his safe arrival at home and his having been to see the President who is polite as usual. Made up arrears and accounts. Alcestis as usual.

After dinner the Catalogue of coins, I finished Nero. It will be of use to me to look over the Roman History in the mean time. Began Crevier but think I shall go to Cook.[2] In the evening made a call upon Mr. John Parker, but not finding him at home, stopped for an hour at Dr. Frothingham's.

[1] 29 Nov., Adams Papers.
[2] At MQA are copies both of the 12-vol., Paris, 1749–1755, and of the 6-vol., Paris, 1818, edns. of J. B. L. Crevier's *Histoire des empereurs romaine.* For Cook, see the entry for 24 Feb., above.

TUESDAY. 4TH.

Clear. Office. Accounts, division as usual. Evening out.

My morning was very much taken up in accounts. I transacted business with the Treasurer of the South Cove Corporation, and took deeds and gave Mortgages for the lands which had fallen to my share. This operation involves me in a considerable debt, in addition to that which the original shares create. But in looking upon the probabilities of the future, and the transition state in which all kinds of property are likely to be while the question of the currency remains unsettled, I think the probabilities of permanency and ultimate value are in favor of land so that I intend as fast as possible to convert my personal property into that shape. I do not know whether I have been fortunate in my selections. Time can only determine that. And my children may perhaps draw the benefit.

Home. Alcestis. After dinner coins as usual and now and then Crevier. Evening. Visit to Mr. and Mrs. Tarbell. I had not been to see them for many years until I thought they began to feel it, so I made up my mind to go. Miss Anna Thaxter there.[1] Wrote a letter to my father.[2]

[1] Mrs. Thomas Tarbell (Lucy Tufts) and Anna Quincy Thaxter (1796–1878) were cousins and also, through AA, related to CFA; see entry for 16 Aug. 1836, above.
[2] Adams Papers.

WEDNESDAY 5TH.

Cloudy. Office, division as usual. Evening at home.

Morning taken up at the Office. Accounts becoming somewhat complicated and therefore require to be placed in full. Nothing further of interest. Alcestis. Coins and Crevier.

My life is now extremely regular and hardly seems to justify much recording. I find my amount of work is not nearly so much as when I am at Quincy. The morning and evening are both against my present arrangement. Yet time passes very fast and as it seems to me almost without impressing a moral with it. I grow older and as this impresses itself upon me I feel now and then on a dull day at this season of the year a moment of depression. Such was the case today.

Read to my Wife a farce called High life below Stairs. Finished my letter.

THURSDAY 6TH.

Clear and pleasant, division as usual. Evening out. Office.

Much interest is now excited by the movement of Mr. Biddle and the Bank of the United States at Philadelphia, in holding up the price of cotton. There is cause for serious apprehension, I think, of the consequences of these operations. Perhaps it may be croaking but it does not look right. Yet I perceive that the President congratulates himself in his new Message upon the present state of security as if it was established upon a permanent basis. Talked with Mr. T. W. Ward about it who is a well informed merchant and who as Agent of a great London banking house is much interested in watching these operations.

Mr. Lunt dined with me from Quincy and thus cut off Alcestis. Coins as usual. Went to a party in the evening at the house of Mr. Charles Brooks, a cousin of my Wife, where however I saw only the members of the family whom I knew.

FRIDAY. 7TH.

Clear, mild and pleasant, time divided as usual. Evening to Medford to deliver a Lecture.

The public mind is at present agitated by the receipt of the Presidents annual message, by the alleged operations in Cotton of Mr. Biddle and by the course of violence adopted to secure the Majority of the Legislature at Harrisburg. These are all aggravated by reports of immense defalcations in the collecting department of the Revenue at New York.[1] The Administration has an immense weight pressing upon it from the re-action of its own principles, and to sustain itself can only go into the extremes of the Slavery principle and of the demagogue agrarian spirit. I am but a poor worm incapable of seeing an inch before me, but I cannot help apprehending that some fearful scenes are in store for us.

Accounts. Alcestis. Afternoon coins, but interrupted by visitors.

Rode to Medford to Mr. Angier's, having been requested to deliver a Lecture before their Lyceum. After tea, we went to the Hall where I found a small collection, the smallest I had ever seen. Before them I delivered my first Lecture upon Northern Discovery, to which if I could judge from the attention with which it was listened to they gave success. But they are not so moveable an audience as that at Quincy. Home by nine. Crevier.

[1] The President's annual Message to the Congress is printed in the *Boston Courier*, 7 Dec., p. 1, col. 3 – p. 2, col. 3. The operations of the United States Bank by which excess surplus cotton would be held to prevent a drop in price were reported in same, 8 Dec., p. 2, col. 4. Violence, then rioting, in Harrisburg over abuses in the certification of elected members attended the opening of the Pennsylvania legislature, same, 8 Dec., p. 2, cols. 2–3; 10 Dec., p. 3, cols. 3–4. Samuel Swartwout, collector of the port of New York, was charged with large defalcations, same, 7 Dec., p. 2, col. 3.

SATURDAY 8TH.

Fine day, time divided as usual. Evening, Mr. Brooks at home. At the Office nothing new.

But the political accounts are very interesting. The departure of the District Attorney of New York for Europe in the Liverpool gives rise to conjectures of new deficiencies in Revenue.[1] And the accounts from Harrisburg appear to be of a last appeal to force. The workings of our system are peculiar, but the occasional appearance of this popular feature is somewhat ominous. It remains to be seen how they will get out of the scrape into which they have got.

I read a good deal of Alcestis which is quite easy and very touching. Coins as usual. Mr. Brooks spent an hour with us in the evening after which I read Crevier. Rather out of work now.

[1] William M. Price, district attorney for New York, faced with the obligation of supervising proceedings taken against Swartwout, pleaded inability to do so because of his prior relations with the defendant, resigned his office, and took passage on the *Liverpool* for Europe. There followed reports of his great gambling losses and rumors of further defalcations (*Boston Courier*, 10 Dec., p. 3, col. 2).

SUNDAY 9TH.

Day fine but cold. Services as usual. Evening out.

I read more of Milman's history of the Jews, relating to the disturbances in Judæa and the reduction of the country under Vespasian. This is a very interesting portion of the Roman history of which I hardly recollect enough.

Attended divine service and heard Mr. W. Ware all day.[1] John 17. 15. "I pray not that thou shouldest take them out of the world, but that thou shouldest keep them from the evil." A sensible discourse upon the necessity of keeping among men and avoiding temptation, which can be done under the guidance of religious feeling alone. Romans 8. 24. "For we are saved by hope." The power of hope. Mr. Ware is not interesting as a preacher but he has evidently a sound and cultivated mind.

Read a very sensible and excellent discourse by Dr. Evans in the English Preacher from Ephesians 4. 25. "Wherefore putting away lying, speak every man truth with his neighbour: for we are members one of another." With a great deal of legal acuteness, he distinguishes the precise moral wrong after which he enforces the value of the precept. This appears to me the best Sermon I have yet read in this collection. I read also some of Crevier.

Evening my Wife and I went to Edward Brooks' and spent an agreeable hour in conversation. Home to continue Crevier.

¹ On Rev. William Ware, see vol. 6:22.

MONDAY 10TH.

Fine day though cool. Usual division of time.

I was at the Office as usual. Making up arrears of Diary. The accounts from Washington contain nothing new, but the insurrection at Harrisburg continues. It is yet questionable on which side the result will turn whether on that of order or of anarchy. Walk to the Athenæum and then home. Alcestis with which I am quite delighted.

After dinner, attended a meeting of the City Hotel Corporation a pendant of the South Cove. The undertakers made it more extensive than they could execute and therefore left the building half finished and subject to a debt. It was now proposed to create more stock and go on. I listened to the arguments of the Speakers and only regretted that they were not cogent enough to overrule my determination not to go into that slough.

Home before the decision. Evening, read Miss Martineau's last book aloud,¹ and after it, Crevier and coins.

¹ Harriet Martineau, *Retrospect of Western Travel*, 3 vols., London, 1838.

TUESDAY 11TH.

Fine day. Usual division of time.

I was at the Office, but the Editor of the Courier sent me an article from the Globe bringing up the whole story of my papers of the Conservative criticizing the doctrine much in the manner it formerly did.¹ I think it a good opportunity for throwing in another dose to rectify public opinion, which has been operated upon, I perceive although without any immediate outward demonstration, by what I have already written. I therefore occupied myself both morning and afternoon in producing something which I think would answer.²

Went also with my Wife to make a formal call upon Mr. and Mrs. Webster, he having left a card for me when he returned my father's visit. This is a poor business. Also called upon Mr. and Mrs. Seaver at Mrs. Carter's. And did not omit Alcestis. In the evening continued a goodly portion of Miss Martineau who is amusing and egotistical. And sat up late doing the revise of my Article.

[1] *The Globe*, on 4 Dec. (p. 3, cols. 4–5), reasserted the interpretation of CFA's papers it had made earlier (cf. the entries for 15 and 17 Aug.).

[2] To *The Globe*'s reiterated charge that "A Conservative's" articles in the *Courier* were an expression of Webster's views and were representative of northern whig positions generally, CFA, again signing as "A Conservative," replied that the administration organ lumps together all varieties of whig opinion "to drive the South into a concentrated support of the only Northern man who dares in high office to think and act as if he was a slaveholder." To demonstrate the lack of validity in *The Globe*'s position, he reveals his support of Van Buren over Webster in the last presidential election. That support ended, however, when Van Buren, in his inaugural address and after, "made himself the instrument for perpetuating the slaveholding policy" (*Boston Courier*, 14 Dec., p. 2, cols. 1–2).

WEDNESDAY 12TH.

Day fine, distribution as usual, ball in the evening.

I had for once a morning of entire leisure, interrupted only by a visit from Mr. Jones of Weston about some wood, which he wishes to buy of me. I cannot deal with these acute Yankees.[1]

Read a historical account of the Chapel and of Episcopal service made some years since in a series of Sermons by Mr. Greenwood.[2] It is full liberal to the Royalist doctrines. The educated class here are generally rather hightoned. One remarkable circumstance struck me, that is, the entire absence of names well known here. It would seem as if the race had been pulled up by the roots which had been cherished by Episcopacy, at the critical time of the Revolution.

Finished Alcestis. I will now go over one of the most touching dramas that ever was written. Coins and Miss Martineau. But we went to a ball at Mrs. S. Appleton's which was lively and pleasant. Her house is well adapted to entertaining company, and her parties are usually as tolerable as such vapid things ever are any where.

[1] On Col. John Jones of Weston, see vols. 2:251 and 4:index.
[2] Probably Francis W. P. Greenwood's *History of King's Chapel, Boston*, Boston, 1833. After the Revolution the Chapel became Unitarian.

THURSDAY 13TH.

Fine weather, usual distribution. Evening at the Theatre.

I was occupied at the Office in the morning for the most part in looking over papers connected with the long delayed matter of the mortgaged Estate of Mr. Thorndike. At last we have pressed up the execution of the conditions, but have not yet executed the papers. Tomorrow was assigned for the purpose.

Read the whole of Potter's translation of Alcestis previous to a review of the original. There are passages of no meaning in the translation which manifestly result from mystery in the text. After dinner coins.

Mrs. Adams and I carried our two children Louisa and John to the Theatre for the first time. Hackett in the parts of Solomon Swap and Monsr. Tonson, and the Spectacle of the Forty Thieves.[1] The first impressions of children are always curious subjects for philosophical observation. They depend much upon temperament and as it respects these two were entirely and singularly different. While the one seemed affected in an extreme and almost hysterical manner, the other appeared overwhelmed into silence by the rapidity of his ideas. Hackett is a perfect specimen of the Yankee character throwing out its characteristics in a very striking and laughable manner. He overacts less than I had been formerly led to suppose.

[1] Solomon Swap in *Jonathan in England* and M. Morbleu in William Thomas Moncrieff's *Monsieur Tonson* were among James Henry Hackett's most popular roles. *Jonathan in England* was Hackett's title for his condensation of George Col- man's *Who Wants a Guinea? The Forty Thieves* was a concoction devised by Stephen Price, manager of the Park Theatre in New York, from a variety of sources (Odell, *Annals N.Y. Stage*, 2:315; 3:49, 386; on Hackett, see vol. 4:viii–ix).

FRIDAY 14TH.

Fine weather. Distribution as usual omitting Greek.

My morning was entirely taken up by the various little forms incidental to the execution of the papers of Mr. Stanwood. I have been so long delayed that I determined if possible to push the matter right through to it's termination. Having therefore got Mr. Goddard and Mr. Stanwood together, I waited until all the papers connected with the subject were ready drawn up and all the difficulties and impediments were removed and then we got through thus terminating this business. A very disagreeable affair from beginning to end, and my delay prevented my Greek. Coins, and Evening Miss Martineau and Crevier.

SATURDAY 15TH.

Fine day. Distribution as usual. Concert in the evening.

My time at the Office was taken up in a great degree by a visit from Mr. and Mrs. Kirk who had come into town for a settlement of their Summer wages Account. This took up a great deal of time.

Home where I began Alcestis over again. After dinner, coins and looked over parts of Cook's Medallic History of Rome which is rather a superficial affair.

Mr. Brooks came in to tea and after it Mrs. Adams and I attended another concert of Mr. De Begnis. The music by himself and Russel, most of the latter old songs, the former is good as a comic performer. He sung an air from the Fanatico per la Musica very well, as also a duett from the Matrimonio Secreto.[1] Strange that the Italians should be so musical a people. All other music sounds thin and poor, contrasted with their's.

[1] *Il Fanatico per la Musica* by Gaetano Rossi and *Matrimonio Segreto* by Cimarosa were operas, often performed.

SUNDAY 16TH.

Fine day. Services and reading. Evening at home.

I finished today the second volume of the History of the Jews which ends at a time of great interest, the famous siege of Jerusalem. The whole of the Jewish War is one of the most fearful records ever made. No people probably ever suffered more from the date of the denial of Christ than have this and even now they are subjected to a degrading distinction nearly all over the East. Trampled upon by the Turkish and the Christian almost alike.

I heard Dr. Frothingham preach from Matthew [*i.e.* Luke] 8. 12. "Then cometh the devil." A singular text but remarkably well treated —the temptations of the fiend are not to be found in any palpable shape but must be looked for in the soul itself and that when it is least on it's guard and most unaware of the evil.

Dr. Parkman from 1 Timothy 5 and 6. [*i.e.* 4. 4.5.] "Every creature of God is good and nothing to be refused if it be received with thanksgiving, for it is sanctified by the word of God and prayer." The Dr. made sundry remarks upon the expediency of moderation and temperance in all things, and applied them to the principal errors of the Community.

Read a Sermon of Bishop Smalridge from Isaiah 51. 12.13. "Who art thou, that thou shouldest be afraid of a man that shall die and of the son of man which shall be made as grass? And forgettest the Lord thy maker that hath stretched forth the heavens and laid the foundations of the earth." Directed against a vice not often seen here, that of fearing to be religious because of the ridicule of the world. In this community there are more who fear to be otherwise from the same cause. This might give rise to a train of reflection but I forbear.

Read Crevier and in the evening, heard my Wife read French. She is desirous of mastering the language in which she is already well founded.

MONDAY 17TH.

Fine day though cold, distribution as usual. Evening visit.

My morning at the Office was consumed in looking up Title deeds and in making settlement with Mr. Brooks of his interest in Mr. Johnson's Affairs. Thus a large sum is now in my hands which will require re-investment. I must try to be cool and cautious.

Continued Alcestis picking up much in my review. Coins, comparing with Cook and Crevier. I am improving and refreshing my acquaintance with the Roman Empire.

Evening Mrs. Adams and I to see Mr. and Mrs. R. D. Tucker. He was out but we were admitted and saw her and Mrs. Gray her daughter. After a pleasant half hour we went home. Mr. Tucker is one of those gentlemen who has manifested some little kindness towards me and therefore it is that I do this.

TUESDAY 18TH.

Clear. Time as usual. Evening to Jamaica Plains to lecture.

A little snow had fallen during the night but the day was clear and pleasant. At the Office I hardly know how I occupied myself but the time went. Finished my arrears of Diary which will grow upon my hands now and then and corrected my Account books. Home where I went over much of Alcestis. Coins.

At six o'clock Mr. Richard Greenleaf called for me to go to Jamaica Plains where I had been engaged by Mr. Whitney to deliver my Lecture. We reached his house early and after warming ourselves were escorted to the hall, a small building apparently erected for the purpose in which I found a large number of persons among whom were many of my acquaintances. To them I delivered the Lecture which has heretofore been so successful, in quite as animated a manner as before. It appeared to take with them quite as much as it had ever done elsewhere and I received many congratulations. After taking a cup of coffee at Mr. Whitney's we returned and I got home much fatigued by half past nine.

WEDNESDAY 19TH.

Fine day. Distribution as usual. Evening visit.

My time at the Office was taken up in finishing various little duties which I recollected still to remain unperformed. Wrote to Mr. Frye respecting the execution of the Will of T. B. Adams, sent a letter to the publisher of the Concord paper and left one for an old tenant Miss Oliver,[1] besides calling upon the painter Kauffer. These little details it is pleasant to get rid of. I then walked round to take a look at the South Cove.

Home. Alcestis. Coins and Crevier. A visit in the evening to see Mr. and Mrs. Frothingham and a pleasant talk for an hour. A very agreeable place to visit in a sociable way. Nothing new.

[1] LbC of the letter to Nathaniel Frye is in the Adams Papers; the other two letters are missing.

THURSDAY 20TH.

Mild, pleasant day. Distribution as usual. Evening party.

At the Office pretty lazy. Having now accomplished all the morning work I have to do, my time is unoccupied and I must look around me for some occupation. I am waiting for Burr's new work before I review that,[1] and also to get through with my job for the Athenæum.

Continued Alcestis, and coins. The afternoons are so short I make no very rapid progress. I have reached the time of Aurelius which may be considered as the palmy days of the Roman Empire, and now there is the long tale of decline to be told.

In the evening after French, we went to a small party at Mrs. H. B. Rogers'. Principally consisting of the Mason connexion which is very large but of whom I know extremely few. T. K. Davis there and barely recognized me. So much for political theories. They have changed the man.

[1] See entry for 30 Jan. 1839, below.

FRIDAY 21ST.

Fine day. Distribution as usual. Evening at home.

Office as usual where I had a variety of little matters but no regular nor useful occupation. Alcestis the review of which is very interesting.

Coins after dinner. And Crevier. My ignorance of the History of the Roman Emperors strikes me very much now I am upon it. The little I got from a careless perusal of part of Tacitus at Cambridge is nothing at all. What is the knowledge got at College? A negative quantity I say.

Reflecting today upon the subject of yesterday and more and more struck with the fact of the entire isolation of my position in life. And yet perhaps this is one incident in my good fortune. Who knows? In my system of reliance I draw great comfort from this idea.

SATURDAY 22D.

Day fine. Office, dinner at Mr. Brooks' and evening at Dr. Frothingham's.

My time at the Office today was very much taken up by business accounts of Deacon William Spear who came in as usual charged with a great variety of bills. Received also letters from Washington from Mr. Johnson.[1]

Alcestis and then to dine with Mr. Brooks, family and Sidney Brooks who is here with his Wife for a few days. Dinner as usual. After return home go back again as far as Dr. Frothingham's to meet some of the same persons. Not much conversation nor very interesting. Returned home in good season somewhat tired by the doing of nothing but feasting and saying useless things.

[1] Missing.

SUNDAY 23D.

Clouds and snow but cleared off cold. Services as usual. Evening at Governor Everett's.

Worked upon the Athenæum collection, having finished Mr. Milman, until time for divine service, when I attended as usual. Heard Dr. Frothingham preach from Acts 20. 35. "It is more blessed to give than to receive." A sort of Christmas Sermon upon the value of charity to the dispenser of it. In the Afternoon John 1. 19. "Who art thou," to which my attention rather failed.

Read a discourse of a certain Mr. Grove upon the reasonableness of Religion[1] drawn as well from a consideration of the nature of the Creator as from that of man and the relation between them. Job 21. 15. "What is the Almighty, that we should serve him?" Sensible but not striking.

Evening to see Governor and Mrs. Everett. Sidney Brooks and his wife, Mr. Brooks and Chardon there and a pleasant evening enough. Home early.

[1] The name Grove does not appear in *The English Preacher*; the reference would seem to be to Rev. Strickland Gough.

MONDAY 24TH.

Very cold and clear, distribution as usual. Evening at Mr. Brooks'.
At the Office where I found John Kirk with an announcement that

his stable was broken open and the harnesses were gone. Lucky that it was not the horses. Mine however escaped. We have had rather singular fortunes in the way of robbery this year. Two other men applying for the farm at Weston. Nothing new. Alcestis, and Coins. Sidney Brooks came in and took tea after which we went down to Mr. Brooks in Pearl Street and found there a party of the family. Tolerably pleasant. Home early.

TUESDAY 25TH.

Cold but it moderated before night. Distribution as usual.

Christmas day but with us commonly the quietest day of the year. I saw nobody and went on with my usual avocations just as regularly as ever. How different it used to be when I was a boy and knew not the meaning of the days. Perhaps this is the greatest point of contrast between the pleasures of boyhood and man's age.

At the Office in Accounts. Then to the Athenæum where I picked up a book or two more upon coins. Alcestis and Coins. My Wife dined out at her sick friend's Mrs. Gorham's. Evening French and a visit from Mr. Brooks for an hour. After which Crevier. Thus I have about as monotonous a record to make as if it was the commonest day of the year.

WEDNESDAY 26TH.

Pleasant day, distribution as usual. Evening at home.

I passed my day quietly enough. At the Office I began an examination of my Accounts for the last six months to see the reason of some discrepancies which I could not understand, but was interrupted by Mr. Angier who came on Account of his last Quarterly demand and by Mr. Stanwood about Mr. Johnson's affairs.

Athenæum and home. Alcestis. After dinner coins in which I now make visible progress. I have got to the time of Heliogabalus. An hour of time is consumed by the children's lessons and another in the evening by Mrs. Adams' french. After which we read a little of Miss Martineau and then I continue Crevier. The records of the times of Nero and Caligula.

THURSDAY 27TH.

Pleasant day, usual course, evening visit Mr. Brooks.

At the Office I executed my entire revision of the accounts of the last six months and rectified two small errors which had crept into the arrangement. But it took up my time excepting a visit to Kauffer and to warn him out of the premises,[1] and a walk. Then Alcestis the review of which I finished today and with which I am as much pleased as with any Greek drama I have yet read. Coins and Crevier. Mr. Brooks was here in the evening and talked pleasantly for a couple of hours. Miss Martineau and French.

[1] CFA had employed John T. Kauffer, a painter, two years earlier; see entry for 1 Oct. 1836, above. The circumstances of an ensuing quarrel are not known to the editors, nor of what property he became a tenant; entry for 31 Dec., below.

FRIDAY. 28TH.

Cold and clear. Time divided as usual. Evening at home.

At the Office I was engaged in writing Diary and then beginning the re-examination of the Life of Burr with a view to writing a review. This is a business I do not much take to, but as I have nothing on hand at present, it will save me from idleness. I must first however notify Dr. Palfrey of the same. Walk.

Began today the Electra of Sophocles, an unfinished work of last Spring and drew some conclusions in favour of my progress from the facility with which I read it.

After dinner coins down to Pupienus. I go too fast for my historical study which has not as yet gone farther than Galba. And what a record for the mind of a philosophical observer of human affairs. And what mere puppets are men and women when they give up the guidance of noble thoughts. Evening, French and a chapter of Miss Martineau's amusing book.

SATURDAY 29TH.

Snow and rain with clouds. Time as usual. Evening at home.

At the Office today as usual. Nothing material. I read some of Aaron Burr's Life and made notes of it. The weather was dull and at the close of the year one feels always slightly inclined to melancholy. I have however experienced very little of it this season. A walk, and then Electra. Coins getting through Philip. So we go. French and Crevier. Thus a very quiet, uninteresting day.

SUNDAY. 30TH.

Clear and cold. Usual exercises. Evening out.

I continue Crevier with diligence in order to get up in my historical commentary upon the coins. But I cannot do so, being now with Vespasian in the one and Gallienus in the other.

Attended divine service all day and heard Dr. Frothingham preach from 1. Samuel 16. 45. "And Samuel came to Bethlehem and the elders of the town trembled at his coming and said comest thou peaceably? And he said Peaceably." A discourse upon the character of the Christian doctrine emanating from the same town described as the scene of the words in the text, with some pretty pointed allusions to the benevolent fanaticism of the day which is militant. No doubt it is true that the spirit of the Christian system is thoroughly peaceful, and yet no man can forget the memorable saying of Christ that his doctrine would prove a sword even in the midst of families. Truth and right cannot always be retained without contention even when the spirit of proselytism is not existing. All maxims in short have their qualifications and sometimes very important ones, particularly when they lead to indolence and self excuse from the support of truth. Afternoon, Philippians 3. 13 "forgetting those things which are behind." A discourse upon the close of the year, very appropriate and judicious.

Read a Sermon by the Rev. J. Tidcomb, from 2 Timothy 1. 10. "But is now made manifest by the appearing of our Saviour Jesus Christ, who hath abolished death, and hath brought life and immortality to light through the gospel." A discourse upon the value of Revelation, neither new nor original.

In the evening my Wife and I went to see Edward Brooks and his Wife and we had a pleasant evening enough. Home at ten.

MONDAY 31ST.

Cold and clear. Distribution as usual. Evening Assembly ball.

The time passed at the Office is not easily to be accounted for because I interrupted my pursuits for this and that little commission in the shops. The procuring of little remembrances for the children took much time. And after all I missed my hour for Greek. J. T. Kauffer one of the Tenants came with his bills manufactured in a very curious manner. I must get rid of him but it will be hard work I foresee. Coins and Crevier.

Evening to the first of the Assemblies which some gentlemen have gotten up here at Papanti's rooms.[1] There were about two hundred persons present I should think, among whom were the principal people in the place. The hall is a good hall, and the collection was very well made, but there are great difficulties in all such cases from the impossibility of drawing any lines in this Country. There were lines in this case attempted and that very strictly which could not fail to give much offence. Another subject of grievance arose among those admitted. The managers were self appointed and had proscribed wine, at which every body rebelled whether they wanted it or not. The result was they had to give way and Champagne was brought at midnight.

Thus ended the year 1838, and in looking back upon it I can scarcely trust myself in the expression of my feelings. Few of the Community enjoy what I enjoy, and in this sense I am constantly grateful I hope properly so for my advantages. Yet what can be the measure, when a kind Providence has dealt so kindly and bountifully by me. I close this book as the record of mingled feelings of gloom and joy, of pleasure and pain, which nevertheless have left behind them no mournful reminiscences and very many highly delightful ones. May it be so ever is the prayer of one who relies far more upon the benevolence of the Deity to us unworthy mortals than upon any foundation of hope or fear in his own heart.

[1] "Papanti's rooms" were and remained over two generations a center for balls, "assemblies," dancing classes, and the like in Boston. Located at 23 Tremont Street, the hall was presided over by Lorenzo, the first of the Papanti family to settle in the city (Mary Caroline Crawford, *Romantic Days in Old Boston*, Boston, 1910, p. 314–315; Abigail Adams Homans, *Education by Uncles*, Boston, 1966, p. 100).

No. 13. Diary

1 January 1839

23 May 1841[1]

"It is not worth while to be concerned, what he says or thinks, who says or thinks only as he is directed by another."

Locke

"Every man that striveth for the mastery is temperate in all things."

1. Cor. 9. 25.

> Would you then learn to dissipate the band
> Of these huge threatening difficulties dire,
> That in the weak man's way like lions stand,
> His soul appal, and damp his rising fire?

Resolve, resolve, and to be men aspire.
Exert the noblest privilege, alone
Here to mankind indulg'd: control desire:
Let godlike reason from her sovereign throne,
Speak the commanding word, *I will*— and it is done.

Thomson

[1] Titlepage of D/CFA/13 (Adams Papers, Microfilms, Reel No. 65), which begins where D/CFA/12 ends and in which are contained all the journal entries CFA made between the terminal dates indicated here. An explanation of the discrepancy between CFA's number- ing of his Diary volumes and the Adams Papers serial numbering is given at vol. 1:xxxviii–xl. For a description of this Diary MS and of the other MSS from which the printed text of vols. 7 and 8 of the present edition is derived, see the Introduction.

JANUARY 1839.

TUESDAY IST.

Here is a new volume with which to begin the New Year and a very fine opportunity to moralize upon the passage of the years, the prospects of the future and the vicissitudes of this world, all of which new and interesting topics might furnish some pages of reflection. To each man, this new subject never loses it's interest. However often he may have seen and heard the truism that time flies, he cannot yet resist the chain which binds him to the recollection of its force upon him. The words of Terence carry their moral with them, that which appertains to the lot of humanity as a race cannot lose it's attraction to the individual. He feels himself changing from year to year without the power to resist or to control it. The hair will turn grey and the flesh will grow harder, inspite of the wishes or the prayers of millions.

For myself I can say with truth and sincerity that my anxieties are not upon such matters. I am now in my thirty second year and as yet have done little either for myself or for the world. I have picked a little hole in the sand wherein I have attempted to lay small stores for future use, altogether doubtful as yet whether they will ever prove more than a buried treasure. The consolation always is to me that I have done my best to improve my opportunities of usefulness which have not been great, while I cannot say the same of the use of my means of instruction. Favoured as I have been more than is common, I have gathered only here and there a light faggot, where I might have got a tree. But repining is foreign from my nature. I have so much of the prosperity of this life that I would not be understood in wishing to be more useful, to wish myself more happy. This can hardly be. I am rich in the enjoyment of domestic happiness and worldly fortune, and wish to add to it the earning of a good name rather to relieve myself from the inequality in the proportion between my acts and my rewards or gifts, between that which has been bestowed upon me and that which I have deserved. To this end I will still continue to try to the best of my abilities. I will endeavour at least to avoid the self reproach of not doing any thing at all of that great part which I ought perhaps to have done all.

We opened the year at the Ball as I noticed in my yesterday's record. Up late of course and day distributed as usual. Evening at Dr. Frothingham's.

New Year's day is always a day of money transactions and a day of congratulations and mutual presents. Children delight in it often to the disturbance of their happiness. I worked as usual with little variation, upon accounts, upon Electra and the coins. In the evening the children of the various families met at Mrs. Frothingham's and had a cake with a ring in it and a scramble for presents which diverted them much. The elder members of the society conversed as usual, and returned home before ten. Such is the record of New Year's day in 1839.

WEDNESDAY 2D.

Pleasant morning. Distribution as usual. Evening at Governor Everett's.

I was very much occupied at the Office by the making up of my Accounts and the business of paying money which becomes more extensive with me every year. The multiplication of my engagements is by no means a favorable sign with me of the improvement of my property, but having now arrived at the end of the first outlay upon my country house and furniture, I hope to correct my course in future.

Home to read Electra parts of which I remember very well but other parts did not impress themselves upon me at all. Coins as usual.

Evening to a small party at the Governor's. Made apparently for Mr. Chapin and his Wife who are here from Vermont and who on account of his kindness to poor Horatio Brooks who is there,[1] is treated with civility by the family. Also for Col. Howard of Springfield, who is a member of the Council and has a daughter with him now.[2] There was as usual an entertainment to profuseness. Nothing of interest and home early.

---

[1] Apparently no improvement in Horatio Brooks' condition was to be expected (above, entries for 1 Sept. 1837, 6 Sept. 1838); he remained alive, however, until 1843.

[2] John Howard of Springfield, a member of the Governor's Council.

THURSDAY 3D.

Fine day. Distribution as usual. Evening at home.

My practice is to go down and read the Newspapers at the National Insurance Office where I commonly meet with a few gentlemen of commercial information and talk with them. To day I found there Mr. Henry Lee and had quite a free and long conversation with him upon the present state of the currency and the prospects of the Country in relation to it. I think he is the most intelligent gentleman that I meet with in mercantile circles where they are apt to be swayed by rather narrow notions. This made me late at the Office and but a very short time there.

Electra, and coins after dinner. An evening at home divided between my children with whom I play an hour after tea, my Wife who has her French lesson, and Miss Harriet Martineau.

FRIDAY 4TH.

Cloudy day. Occupation as usual. Evening at home.

At the Office I finally got rid of the large sum of Mr. Johnson's which has been upon my hands for some time.[1] These operations are always a relief to my mind. Perhaps it would have been better if I had never charged myself with such heavy responsibilities in managing the affairs of others, but man is required to be useful for something and perhaps that is the wherein[2] I may be considered most so.

Electra. I have got my Catalogue of Coins into the lower empire, where they are more confused and of less value and interest. Evening, Mrs. Adams and I attempted to pay a visit to Mrs. Quincy without getting in and to Mrs. Edward Blake where there was company, so we returned home and travelled up the River Mississippi with Miss Martineau. Crevier.

[1] CFA had invested $7,000 of T. B. Johnson's funds, with his approval, in a mortgage on 22 Beacon Street (CFA to T. B. Johnson, 4 Jan., LbC, Adams Papers).
[2] Thus in MS.

SATURDAY 5TH.

Day cloudy but it cleared. Distribution of time as usual. Evening at home.

I am commonly more occupied at my Office on this day than on any other as my Quincy business commonly is done on this day. Deacon Spear came in and returned me my Note to the Quincy Stone Bank which I hope is the last of the list of incumbrances upon me by virtue of my Country house.

Returned home as usual and read a portion of Electra which is more difficult Greek than Alcestis, but which is nevertheless a very powerful play. After dinner, worked upon coins as usual, and Crevier. Evening at home quietly, but passing rapidly by force of French, of Miss Martineau and a visit from Mr. Brooks which was however very brief.

SUNDAY 6TH.

Day cloudy with snow. Usual division on Sunday. Evening at J. Quincy's.

The greater part of my day was taken up in continuing the third volume of Milman's History of the Jews which had been sent to me by mail from Washington. The first part is the account of the siege of Jerusalem which I had already read in Crevier. The accounts being both drawn from Josephus are substantially the same, and it is a wonder to me how ignorant I have heretofore been of the most fearful detail of human suffering that ever has been made.

Attended divine service and heard Dr. Frothingham preach from 2. Samuel 23. 15. "And David longed and said, Oh, that one would give me a drink of the water of the well of Bethlehem, which is by the Gate!" Of wishes and of hopes in human life, their effect upon the sum of human happiness. Matthew 11. 7. "What went ye into the wilderness to see? A reed shaken with the wind?" I also read a discourse of Bishop Hoadley from 2. Timothy 3. 4. "Lovers of pleasures more than lovers of God." Sensible enough but not extraordinary. The Church of England is not so eminent for it's developing talent as nourishing good sense.

Evening my Wife and I went to see Mrs. Josiah Quincy in consequence of her application to us in favor of a new female instructress of children. Mr. and Mrs. Minot came in and strange to say, Mrs. Davis and her son Thomas K. The awkwardness of the meeting was amusing enough. I could not help a little coldness and my Wife as well as all the persons present manifested a little of it. It seems that Davis has acted upon all his old acquaintances in the same manner that he has upon me, and they all resent it, especially as implying a sense of personal importance which does not belong to him. I think in this they do him injustice. But his is a species of wrongheadedness it is difficult to treat justly with due regard to that kind of self respect indispensable to correct conduct in life. I am personally as friendly in feeling to him as ever I was and yet I cannot consider him as justified in trespassing upon kindness in the manner he has done.

MONDAY 7TH.

Morning cloudy which ended in rain. Distribution as usual. Evening party.

At the Office my time engaged in Accounts as usual. The commencement of this year has been an unusually busy one in this regard and that scarcely with my knowing wherefore. I have been utterly unable to prosecute my design upon Aaron Burr's history, and much of the ordinary business of the agency is behind hand. Also my correspondence, but I was glad to receive from Washington today some papers from Mr. Frye which smooth the difficulties in the way of the settlement of T. B. Adams' affairs. These hang on exceedingly, and through Mr. Harrods apparent inattention seem likely to do so still more.[1]

Electra and in the afternoon working on the Catalogue of coins which absorbs much time I should otherwise have better employed perhaps. And yet I have acquired an amount of positive knowledge which may be useful and in which I was shamefully deficient.

Evening we went to a party at Mrs. Thayer's stated to be a small party but in fact a ball. Almost all the fashionable people there and altogether a brilliant, well arranged affair. Home a little after eleven.

[1] Through Nathaniel Frye Jr., CFA was able to obtain the signature of Isaac Hull Adams, a co-executor of the estate of Lt. T. B. Adams Jr., on documents necessary to the settlement of that estate (CFA to Frye, 19 Dec. 1838, LbC, Adams Papers). Charles Harrod of New Orleans had been charged with arranging the removal of Lt. Adams' body to Quincy; CFA's letters to him had brought no response (to Charles Harrod, 16 Nov. 1838; 3 Jan. 1839; LbC's, Adams Papers).

TUESDAY 8TH.

Morning clear, and a pleasant day, time as usual. Evening at Edward Brooks'.

There is no very important record to be made of my mornings. They pass in conning over newspapers, reading accounts and paying money the whole process of which however interesting does not make much figure in a Diary.

Electra in which I make rather slow progress also. After dinner, continue the coins which now come down to Maximin. I begin to see the end.

Evening, by request, went down to Edward Brooks to see his Wife who is without occupation and therefore catches events to be delighted with such as that of the marriage of Miss Sumner this day to Mr. Nathan Appleton.[1] Here is one of the Revolutions of this life, a transfer at a bound from extreme penury to unlimited abundance. Miss Sumner yesterday a lady of a certain age with little attention but from her rather oldish friends, is today Mrs. Appleton the Wife of a millionaire. Conversation with Edward very pleasant as it always is. Home at ten. Crevier.

[1] Nathan Appleton had taken as his second wife, Harriet Coffin Sumner (*DAB*).

WEDNESDAY 9TH.

Fine day. To Cambridge. Afternoon at home, coins. Evening Mr. Dexter's.

I was up early to be off on the examination of one division of the Junior class in Cambridge University. The arrangement has been much altered, and now imposes upon the Committee much heavier burdens.[1] A Carriage called for me which contained Mr. Forbes and Mr. Hillard, and at Cambridge, we found T. K. Davis had come *in another carriage* with the Latin Committee. Was this accident or a desire to escape me? I neither know nor care which. He seated himself at dinner at the other end of the table which also betrays very much the nature of his feelings. In other respects however there was no difference in his manner, and we were all as pleasant as usual, with due regard to distance.

The examination was an indifferent one. The class is the same with which I first entered into the examinations and does not appear to me to have gone a step forward since the close of the Freshman year. The Professor himself appears to me to be a good scholar but not an effective teacher. We returned to town immediately after dinner, having as a fourth Professor Longfellow in the carriage. Continued coins as usual.

Evening, attended a circle of ladies who form a charitable gossip society and meet at each other's houses at stated periods. This was by invitation of Miss Catherine Dexter at her brother's, George M. Dexter's. A great number of ladies and very few gentlemen. However I got along pretty well, home early.

¹ CFA here seems to have reverted to
the usage of his grandfather who in his
draft of the Massachusetts constitution
had been the first to speak of Harvard
College as the "University at Cambridge"

(Morison, *Three Centuries of Harvard*, p.
160). The new arrangement for the examiners was communicated to CFA in a
letter from President Quincy (1 Jan.,
Adams Papers).

THURSDAY. 10TH.

Morning mild. Again to Cambridge returning by dinner time. Evening at Mrs. Shaw's.

I was rather a volunteer today in going to Cambridge having already
done as much as I ought for the week. But as Judge Merril was the
only other member of the Committee who could go, I entered the carriage where I found Mr. Gould and Mr. Hubbard of the Latin Committee also. We today finished the examination of the Junior Class, this
being the second section. It was much better than that of yesterday
although it confirms me in my impression that the classes do not improve in their application as they advance. The young men today did
not make out as well as they did in Thucydides a much harder author.
Indeed my impression is that the facility of extracting the literal sense
of Homer is one of the temptations to slight the study. We dined as
usual, and returned by the time of my dinner at home.

Afternoon employed upon coins as usual. Evening to a great ball at
Mrs. Shaw's house in Beacon Street.¹ This has been talked of a long
while, and great preparations were made for it. The throng was so
great as to fill all the rooms even of that spacious building and to make
a degree of confusion not very pleasant. The disposition this winter
seems to be towards a great deal of social amusement. People are re-
viving from the pressure of the past and hope is the prevailing feeling
for the future. We came home at midnight.

¹ In 1838, the Israel Thorndike house at the corner of Beacon and Belknap (now
Joy) streets had been purchased by the elder Robert Gould Shaw (Chamberlain, *Beacon Hill*, p. 131, 139).

FRIDAY 11TH.

Morning clear. Time distributed as usual. Evening at home.

This was a quiet day and I confess I relished it somewhat. My time
at the Office taken up in Accounts and settling bills. Nothing of importance going on at present. Home where I continued Electra. This is
about the only profitable hour which I spend in the course of the
twenty four, and in this I think that I make progress in the language.
The coins still go on and I reach in them the age of Constantine while

in Crevier I remain with the Antonines. Quiet evening at home reading Miss Martineau.

SATURDAY 12TH.

Mild day. Time as usual, dinner company at home, quiet evening.

My time passed this morning quite in a bustle, first with various little commissions second with tenants and business people at Office. The payment of bills seems to be quite an important part of existence. Home where I continued to read Electra.

Company to dine. Allyne Otis, T. Dwight, F. H. Story, W. Gorham and Dr. Frothingham. Very pleasant and just what a dinner ought to be. They did not remain long and I had a quiet evening at home.

To think that Davis is now among the self banished from my table because he chooses to cultivate wild theories action against which he dreads.[1] So be it. We had much talk about him and the other gentlemen were rather unjustly severe upon him, but this is the fate of dissentients. I continued reading Crevier.

[1] The meaning would seem to be: he chooses to cultivate wild theories, any opposition to which he dreads (or resents?).

SUNDAY. 13TH.

Pleasant day. Services as usual. Evening at Mr. Brooks'.

I passed my time as usual, continuing the History of the Jews by Milman which is my Sundays reading besides one Sermon and the regular devotional exercises. Dr. Frothingham preached in the morning from 1 Timothy 2. 4. "Who will have men to be saved and to come unto the knowledge of the truth." A discourse upon the probable design of the deity, in signifying the spread of the gospel and the universality of the Christian Religion which had not as yet taken place.

Afternoon Luke 16. 24. "I am tormented in this flame." Dr. Frothingham is one of the class who draw every thing into the vortex of fancy. I for one am not prepared to pronounce that hell is a place of fire where flesh is burnt, but then on the other hand I am not prepared to maintain it's impossibility or that after admitting for once the resurrection of the body, there is any sort of improbability in it. After all, the subject is beyond us.

Read a Sermon of Dr. Holland in the English Preacher, Psalm 34. 19. "Many are the afflictions of the righteous but the Lord delivereth him out of them all." The favourite subject of the action of the Deity

171

upon good and bad alike, which is puzzling to many but plain enough to any one who believes in a future state. The one proposition hangs upon the other.

Evening, as my Wife had a cold I went down and paid a visit to Mr. Brooks. Found there Mr. and Mrs. Story and after a pleasant hour walked home with them in company.

MONDAY 14TH.

Morning pleasant, time divided as usual. Evening Assembly.

I went to the Office and from thence attended the annual meeting of the Stockholders of the Suffolk Insurance Co. The President Mr. Perkins was understood to be about to give in his resignation upon which the question of continuance was to depend. There was a large attendance and a letter from him was submitted. The substance of it was that there was a deficiency in the capital Stock to the amount of twenty five per cent during the last year, occasioned by losses, that during his management of twelve years one hundred and three per cent had been paid in Dividends and that he left it now because if to be redeemed at all, it should be redeemed by younger direction. This was a doleful account particularly when an exposition of the invested capital showed that the bank stock was rather estimated at cost than at value. It was evident that there were dissenting opinions from that of the existing board of Directors but a motion was made to appoint a Committee to examine and report upon the state of the Office and this carried the majority. Adjourned to meet again a fortnight hence.

Insurance property generally is in a very bad way here and there is a movement to reduce the amount of capital concerned in it. I have always heretofore considered this my best property but such are the fluctuations of it, I shall probably have eaten up at the end twenty per cent of my investment.

Read Electra and worked upon coins. Evening alone to the second assembly which was very pleasant. Returned about midnight. Mrs. Gorham's funeral.[1]

[1] See entry for 20 Jan., below.

TUESDAY 15TH.

Cool day. Division as usual. Evening at home.

Every thing falls now with me into arrears so much that I refused to day going to Cambridge upon the examination of the second section of the Sophomore class. And in the evening, received a slightly complaining letter of the same, from the President,[1] as none of the Committee had come. At the Office I did not execute great things neither.

Continued Electra and made some progress in coins. While reading Crevier I glance off to read Gibbon's opening chapters of his history which never struck me so masterly as now. He is certainly in most respects unique. Evening we were quietly at home. Edmund Quincy stopped in to take tea and talked for an hour. After whom, Mr. Beale and his son George.

[1] Letter missing.

WEDNESDAY 16TH.

Fine day though cold. To Cambridge, returning to Mr. Brooks' and in the evening to Mrs. N. Appleton's.

I went on my division to Cambridge today and found myself in a carriage with Mr. Hillard, and Messrs. Gould and Hubbard of the Latin Committee. We had the first division of the Sophomore class before us in six books of the Iliad and four of the Odyssey of Homer. And a very bad recitation they made of it, so much as to satisfy me that the deficiency of training could not be supplied.

The complaint now is that nobody goes to Harvard because it is dear. Sure enough, nobody will buy an article dear when the same can be got cheap, but the secret not yet found out at Cambridge is that they should provide a better article than can be got elsewhere, and then see if even in these economical times they would not have abundant demand.

The dinner was dull and I was glad to get back to town to a second at Mr. Brooks' where were assembled Mrs. Gray and Mrs. Hall, Mr. and Mrs. Sargent and my Wife. We had a pleasant time and then home.

Evening we went to pay the wedding visit to Mr. and Mrs. Nathan Appleton. She is at once transferred into wealth and station, and becomes it well. If an old man like Mr. Appleton must marry, it is as well that he should act with discrimination as to the person he is about to admit into his family. A great crowd from which we were glad to go home.

THURSDAY 17TH.

Fine day. Morning as usual. Dinner late at Mr. Otis's. Evening at home.

I was occupied as usual this morning upon my Arrears of Diary which keep growing in spite of myself and upon the accounts the end of which is not yet. I take no exercise this year excepting such as I can get by going out to various places. Home to read Electra. And as Mr. Allyne Otis had invited me to a late dinner I occupied my intervening time in my pursuit of the coins. Miss Louisa C. Smith spent the day with my Wife.

At five I went down the street to the place of invitation and was ushered into a room where were assembled a company among whom I was most surprised to see myself. T. H. Perkins Jr., W. Amory, R. S. Fay, J. L. Stackpole, W. Lee Jr., Mr. Crowninshield, T. Dwight, Copley Greene, T. Motley Jr., P. Grant, J. M. Warren, F. Codman, besides Mrs. Ritchie, Mr. Otis the elder and his two sons. These are the members of the club to which Otis had called my attention. A poor business enough. I felt much out of my element, but was treated with great civility and left the table at eight.

Mr. Otis feels aggrieved by my father's political career. He thinks it destroyed him and probably is correct insofar as this, that he was made by it to pay a heavy penalty for his own faults. He has always treated me with attention and though I cannot admire nor respect the motives of action which have gone through his life, yet I think his age and his private character are entitled to respect.[1] Evening at home, reading Miss Martineau.

[1] The long maintained but often unhappy relations of Harrison Gray Otis, now 73, with JA and JQA are chronicled in Morison, *H. G. Otis,* 1969, p. 190–193, 272–274, 446–448. These connections spanned the years of controversy among the Federalists and between them and the party's opponents, from the Hamiltonian break in 1799 through the charges of disunion conspiracies in 1804 and 1814 to the breakup of the Federalists in 1828. The stormy relationship was punctuated on several occasions by pleasant dinners at which Otis was a genial host to an Adams. Of the present occasion, CFA wrote to LCA: "Among other wonderful events is the rapprochement between us and the O's. We have talked and becarded and bedined and are mighty friendly" (6 Feb., Adams Papers).

FRIDAY. 18TH.

Day pleasant. Quietly divided. Evening at home. E. C. Adams here.

Otis's wine was a little too strong for my head, I think, for I suffered a little from head ach this morning for the first time this winter. But it did not turn out very severe as with fasting I got over it before night.

I made little head way in my Office matters notwithstanding my leisure and as to my bill department it is very far behindhand. Home where I went on with Electra.

Mrs. Angier dined here with Elisabeth C. Adams who passed the day. I continued upon the coins finishing the reign of Constantine the great with which the heaviest part of the labour finishes. I shall not be sorry to have it completed for it takes all of my disposable time, and I am to consider the winter as in other regards profitless.

SATURDAY 19TH.

Day clear. Distribution as usual. Evening uninterrupted at home.

My morning was taken up very much by my country business. Received a letter from the Cashier of the Bank at Quincy offering a purchaser for my Shares and answered it immediately accepting. This will I hope facilitate my efforts to put my business affairs upon a different footing. I have made myself a new rule to avoid holding in joint stock and to throw my property as much as I can into real estate. The sale of these shares and the winding up of the Suffolk Insurance Company will thus furnish me a sum to redeem my mortgaged South Cove Investment in part. This will be converting productive into dead property but as I do not absolutely need the income, perhaps the operation may be one of accumulation. At any rate, it will simplify matters much. And I feel anxious whenever I am in debt. Deacon Spear came in and I gave him the necessary orders and papers.

Finished Electra today and committed an extravagance in purchasing a new copy of Sophocles with which to review.[1] My father's library is deficient in this book. Coins and quiet evening at home reading Miss Martineau, French and Crevier.

[1] See above, entry for 22 Jan. 1838.

SUNDAY 20TH.

Cold day. Services and studies as usual. Evening at home. H. G. Gorham.

I read much of Milman's History of the Jews, in the latter part of which I find some confusion. Perhaps this arises from the great difficulty of the subject. When the Jews ceased to be a united people and to have as such a local habitation, they could of course have no unity in historical treatment. This dispersion of a people, and yet its preservation of its distinctive character in the midst of others are curious facts, and well worthy of meditation.

Attended divine service as usual and heard Dr. Frothingham from 16 Psalm 11. "Thou wilt show me the path of life: in thy presence is fulness of joy; at thy right hand there are pleasures for evermore." My attention was so little fixed that I can give no great account of this discourse. That of the afternoon attracted me more. Matthew 7. 1. "Judge not that ye be not judged." A very accurate delineation of the proper rules of judgment of the conduct of others. The objections to hasty to censorious and to envious judgment, while the construction of motives should always be made to depend upon the strict application of the rule of right. Perhaps there is no subject upon which the mind requires to be trained in the true principles so much as in moral judgments.

Read a good Sermon of Dr. Atterbury from Matthew 14. 23. "When he had sent the multitude away, he went up into a mountain apart to pray." Upon solitary religious meditation as an improvement of the character. How much the world has changed within a thousand years as to this subject.

Evening H. G. Gorham came in, the first time since his Mother's death. By an oversight consequent upon suffering my Diary to run into arrear, I omitted a notice of my attendance last Monday afternoon at her funeral. By a curious coincidence I have followed to the tomb three members of this same family since I came to Boston to settle. And in all my experience of life I have known nothing to compare with the rapid decline of perhaps as prosperous a family as existed at that time. The death of Dr. Gorham exactly at the summit of his medical reputation, threw his children out of the expectations they might reasonably have formed. The death of his only daughter in childbed broke the heart of her mother, and now three sons are left to make their own way in the world. And this is real life and no romance. Contrast the scene with the late wedding visit and what a fund for moral and religious meditation.[1]

[1] Dr. John Gorham, Erving professor of chemistry at Harvard, had died in 1829. He was a cousin of ABA's mother, and the families were close. Among the Brooks and Gorham children, ABA and Julia Gorham were intimates. Julia had married Richard Robins in Oct. 1835 but had died at the birth of her first child in Nov. 1836. With Mrs. Gorham's death, three sons, Gardner, Warren, and H. G., remained. See vols. 2:167, 195, 360–361; 3:55; 6:254–255; and above, entries for 20 and 22 Nov. 1836.

MONDAY 21ST.

Cold day. Time divided as usual. Evening at home.

I have no account to give of my day. Worked with some diligence upon my arrears and also upon the accounts. But the mornings are so short as to pass away like nothing. Home where I began Electra in my new edition and read sixty lines *thoroughly*. I think I make progress in mastering the details of the language. The prepositions and adverbs are the most curious and neglected portion.

After dinner, coins. I propose to labour through these with diligence and steadiness. Evening at home. French and Miss Martineau. A curious mixture of shrewdness and absurdity about her. Crevier and Gibbon. Eliogabalus and his antics.

TUESDAY 22D.

Cloudy day with a light fall of snow. Time as usual. Mr. Stearns and coins. Evening ball at Mr. Appleton's.

I prosecuted my work of arrears with some diligence and had the gratification of seeing some progress. I have a parcel of letters on hand which I scarcely know what to do with and which yet will require answers. One from Mr. Downing requesting me to get a picture of mine copied on his account.[1] Home to read Electra.

Mr. Stearns a lawyer in practice here has written to ask to see my coins and upon my answer,[2] had fixed this afternoon to see them. I was with him most of the time until sunset. He takes great interest in modern coins and not much in the ancient which are incomparably superior in point of interest. He has a collection of his own of some extent.

Evening, a visit from Dr. and Mrs. Frothingham, prior to our going to a ball at Mrs. W. Appleton's given to the bride. Not a large but quite a choice party at which I enjoyed myself about as much as I commonly do. Home at midnight.

[1] The letter is missing. The likelihood is that Andrew Jackson Downing of Newburgh, N.Y., architect and landscape gardener and the husband of Caroline Elizabeth de Windt (above, entry of 19 June 1838) was the writer. Also, that the request related to Gilbert Stuart's 1823 portrait of JA, which JQA had given to CFA. Subsequently, the painting *was* copied for Downing by Samuel S. Osgood; see below, entry for 10 Nov., and Oliver, *Portraits of JA and AA*, p. 191, 259.

[2] W. G. Stearns to CFA, 14 Jan., Adams Papers; CFA to Stearns, 18 Jan., CLU:Gerson Autographs.

WEDNESDAY 23D.

Cloudy but turned excessively cold by night and clear. Division as usual. Dr. and Mrs. Frothingham and Thomas in evening.

I continued my work this morning and began to see light in my accounts by virtue of the annual Dividend of the Middlesex Canal. With this I propose to pay off my Mortgage on account of the South Cove land for my father and thus put that affair in train of settlement. I have for some years past been able to lay that Dividend up out of his Income, which is I suspect the only increase that happens to his fortune. And this he is hardly conscious of. This particular direction of his funds is perhaps better calculated for him than any other as it may be an accumulating fund, without anxiety.

Electra which I read now satisfactorily. Coins down to Gratian which is very near the end. Evening Dr. and Mrs. Frothingham and Thomas, notwithstanding the severe cold. Pleasant evening and conversation.

THURSDAY 24TH.

Severely cold night and morning. Office. Time as usual. Evening ball at Mrs. J. Welles'.

I made up my arrears this morning and filed up all my bills, besides releasing the Note upon the South Cove Property owned by my father. This was doing more than I have been able to compass before. Electra.

In the midst of the excessive cold of last night was a fire which burnt a whole street of carpenters' shops, and some other buildings of more value. Thermometer at ten degrees below zero. Continued the coins until I got down to the region of barbarous symbols which nearly finishes the sequence.

Evening at a ball at Mr. John Welles. Very handsome and pleasant because large without being crowded. Home at midnight.

FRIDAY 25TH.

Mild and pleasant. Division as usual. Evening at Dr. Frothingham's and Governor Everett's.

The cold proved but a short blast of the keen polar wind, and today was mild again. My time was taken up in part by finishing arrears of business at the Office and by a wild goose chase in quest of one of my departed tenants, who has not merely vacated the house but like the dog in the manger policy refuses to let any one else into it.

Continued the review of Electra and after dinner finished the remainder of the Athenæum collection of coins. This has been a very long work and I am not sorry it is well over.[1] I propose to number them and send them home.

Evening I went to Dr. Frothingham's and there talked until nine o'clock when I crossed over to the house of the Governor's to a meeting of the members of the Legislature by invitation. As I had no acquaintance with most of them I felt disposed to make my visit very short. And I got back in a few minutes. Home by ten.

[1] CFA had completed the "Catalogue of Brass Coins of the Roman Empire belonging to the Boston Athenæum" in 120 pages and would dispatch it, along with the coins "assorted" and "in covers," and a letter to the Trustees on 31 Jan. (MBAt). On 11 Feb., Nathaniel I. Bowditch, secretary *pro tem.* of the Athenæum, wrote him on behalf of the Trustees that the "Gentlemen were very much pleased with the manner in which the coins were arranged and directed the Standing Committee to have the catalogue bound" and that the board had ordered recorded their thanks for the "skilfully prepared" catalogue (Adams Papers). The catalogue remains at MBAt; a photocopy is in MHi.

SATURDAY. 26TH.

Warm with rain which continued until night. Time as usual. Evening at home.

I went to the Office in good season for the sake of doing business. As I expected W. Spear came in from Quincy and I received the proceeds of the sale of my Bank Stock which I have converted into land. I redeemed immediately two of my Notes which now leaves three more which I hope to cover before the end of the year. This is but one half however of my general engagement. The reflux[1] seems now to be beginning to be visible and perhaps I may rely upon that for a little farther assistance. Electra.

After dinner made up a list of the catalogued coins being in all about 840, not so many as I had supposed, but the trouble has nevertheless been great. I wish to keep them for a few days for the sake of rectifying my own list of my collection which having been made when I knew little of the subject is defective. It is here that I see the advantage that it has been of to me. Evening at home. Luxuriated in an article upon Horace in the London Quarterly Review sent to me by Dr. Frothingham.

[1] "A flowing back, return, refluence" (*OED*); perhaps here in the sense of economic recovery.

SUNDAY. 27TH.

Fine day. Exercises as usual. Evening at Edward Brooks'.

The morning was clear and pleasant. I read some of the London Quarterly Review. My tendencies are not towards the cultivation of periodical literature but when I do I am struck with the superiority in fulness of scholarship in the English articles over our stupid, thin productions in the same way. I finished a Review of Mr. Milman's edition of Gibbon written with much force.

Attended divine service all day. Heard in the morning Mr. Greenwood from Ephesians 4. 30. "Grieve not the holy spirit of God whereby ye are sealed unto the day of redemption." In the afternoon Mr. Gannet, Luke 2. 11. "Unto you is born this day in the city of David a Saviour which is Christ the Lord." The latter written apparently for a Christmas Sermon, and neither of them of much interest to me.

Read a discourse of Dr. Butler in the English Preacher from Numbers 23. 10. "Let me die the death of the righteous and let my end be like their's." Upon the character of Balaam, one of the least comprehensible histories of the old Testament. It is manifest that the account of him is deficient in materials for full judgment.

In the evening Thomas Frothingham came in and took tea after which Mrs. Adams and I went down to spend an hour at Mr. Edward Brooks'. Finished Milman's History of the Jews, the last part of which is rather lame. But on the whole it is a valuable work and has furnished me much good information.

MONDAY 28TH.

Cloudy and snow in the evening. Time as usual. Evening, Third Assembly.

I went to the Office and brought up my Accounts, though not before attending a meeting of the Suffolk Insurance Co. to hear the report of the Committee raised at the last. There was a large attendance and evidently much interest felt in the result. The Committee reported unanimously in favour of winding up the present concern, with a clause of provision for such Stockholders as being unwilling to stop might take the property at an appraisement and supply the places of the withdrawing persons. The question being upon the acceptance of the report, a motion was made to lay it on the table which after discussion was carried. This was followed by a proposition to raise a Committee to procure an appraisement of the property and propose to each Stockholder a question whether he will take the appraisement or go on, which was carried thereby procuring another delay of a fortnight. Very manifestly there was a great deal of feeling in the business on both sides, and as yet it has proved a drawn game. I was much at a loss to know the motives of the persons who advocated continuing a business which had lost for the company one third of their capital in twelve months.

Electra. Afternoon, luxuriated in the Quarterly Review. Evening at the third Assembly which I enjoyed as well as any. But I heard a rumour that I was myself about to give a great ball at these rooms which accounted for the change in the manner of some to me tonight.[1] What a thing is human nature! Home at about midnight well pleased.

[1] "The world ... no doubt inferring that because [the Adamses] go out they are to open house themselves, they have fixed the day, the hour and place when ... A. et ux are to entertain their one thousand newly revived acquaintances in a manner unexampled in the annals of Boston extravagance. Here is the march of mind! At this rate we bid fair very soon to be at the pinnacle of social greatness.

"We have at last found out that we have a fine dancing hall at which certain assembly balls of an exceedingly select description confined to 'de fus colored circles' have been held. . . . It was here that I was to follow suit, but I cannot afford a thousand dollars and so my one thousand friends must have their trouble for their pains. *Je ne m'en soucie guère* [I hardly concern myself about it]. They must feel mortified at having thrown away so much civility in so vain a cause, and will probably revenge themselves upon me forthwith. But I care as little for that" (CFA to LCA, 6 Feb., Adams Papers).

TUESDAY 29TH.

Fine day. Distribution as usual. Evening Mr. R. Robbins.

I occupied my morning in returning my answer to Mr. Downing[1] and other work remaining on hand at Office, which with a country man applying for the Weston farm took up my time. Call in at Warren's and buy coins at an exorbitant price.[2]

Electra. The time after dinner spent in reading the Quarterly, but I am bitterly sensible of my misuse of time. A visit this morning from Dr. Kirkland ostensibly to inquire about a copy of my father's letter to Baltimore, for Mrs. Cabot.[3] He is a very wreck and it is melancholy to look upon him when put to so base a use by intriguing women, for I cannot help connecting in my mind his visit with the rumor of last evening. And here again is human nature! Evening, a visit from R. Robbins who talked more sensibly.

[1] Missing.
[2] Perhaps John Warren, "conchologist," at 186 Tremont Street (*Boston Directory*, 1839), also dealt in coins. CFA, recording later visits, calls him "old Warren, the coin collector" and "the virtuoso" (see entries for 9 July, 4 Dec., 11 Jan. 1840, below). Warren did not become a principal supplier for CFA's collection (MHS, *Procs.*, 86 [1974]:7).
[3] Dr. John Thornton Kirkland, former president of Harvard, had, in his retirement, married Elizabeth Cabot, daughter of Mrs. George Cabot (vols. 2:226; 4:395).

WEDNESDAY 30TH.

Snow showers but on the whole clear. Time as usual. Evening, Diorama.

Finished the balance of occupation at the Office and now I promise to go on seriously with Burr and to try to squeeze something out of him. To this end went to the Athenæum where I found the Private Journal and took it home with me.[1] The afternoon was then devoted very much to the study of it which fills me with disappointment. What a mere parcel of emptiness it is.

Evening I accompanied Mrs. Adams, and the two elder children with E. C. Adams whom we called for at Mrs. Miller's to the Diorama of the Battle of Bunker's hill. This is an imitation of the Conflagration of Moscow, and represents three scenes — the march of the insurgents to take the heights, the preparation of the troops to go from Boston, and the action and burning of Charlestown. It is ingeniously done and carefully prepared, on the whole well worth seeing.

[1] Aaron Burr, *Private Journal during Four Years in Europe*, 2 vols., N.Y., 1838.

THURSDAY 31ST.

Clear and cold. Time divided as usual. E. C. Adams in the evening.

I sat down today in earnest both at the Office and at home to reading Aaron Burr. The biography at the former[1] and the private Journal at the latter. In this way I made great progress in both and as my time was less interrupted than usual, gathered some materials for criticism. Read Electra too and this constitutes the whole of my work for the day. E. C. Adams spent the day here very quietly and I returned with her to Mr. Miller's. Otherwise, nothing remarkable.

[1] See entries for 12 Nov. and 20 Dec. 1838, above.

FRIDAY FEBRUARY IST.

Cloudy with snow. Morning as usual. Dine at Mr. Brooks'. Evening at home.

Continued my labour at the Office in reading Burr all the morning and made some progress. I think I shall yet screw something useful out of this dissipated winter.

Home, to read Electra and then to Mr. Brooks' house to dine in company with Dr. David Gorham, a nephew of his settled in Exeter as a physician, whom I recollect at Cambridge graduating in the year that

I entered. He has much of the manner of that family and some of the face.[1] Home to tea and quiet evening. Records nowadays insignificant.

[1] Dr. David Gorham must have been the son of a brother of Mrs. Peter C. Brooks (Ann Gorham). The family resemblance would refer to the Gorhams of Charlestown.

SATURDAY 2D.

Clear day. Office. Time as usual. Evening at home.

This is a period of such profound quiet in all affairs domestic, political and literary that my Journal is in very poor case. Read Burr today at the Office finishing the first Volume, and the Journal in the afternoon. There is a marked defect of principle running through his whole conduct and yet a singular privation of complaint in his Record. He experiences bad treatment more often than good but abstains from censure in most cases even when he feels most strongly. This excites sympathy.

Read Electra with which I am refreshed. Classical study is like drinking wine. A stimulating pleasure. Evening sat down to make a draught of a paper upon the currency. Found thoughts enough but not facts and hence a difficulty.

SUNDAY. 3D.

Cold and clear. Exercises as usual. Evening at Mr. Brooks'.

I have finished Milman and am now in want of some substitute. In the mean time and not to be idle, read the last number of the North American Review, two leading articles with neither of which I was entirely pleased.

Attended divine service and heard Dr. Frothingham preach from Proverbs 3. 5 and 6. "Trust in the Lord with all thy heart; and lean not unto thine own understanding. In all thy ways acknowledge him and he shall direct thy paths." A good Sermon pointed at the extremes very prevalent in these times of utter incredulity and of extreme confidence. If there is any portion of my religious feeling to which I adhere constantly it is to my reliance upon a power in comparison with which the intellect of man is a cipher. After dinner, Matthew 12. 33. "Make the tree good and his fruit good."

Read as usual a discourse from the English Preacher. Proverbs 3. 17. "Her ways are ways of pleasantness; and all her paths are peace." A discourse by Dr. Foster upon the value of religion as productive of happiness a variety of the old doctrine of honesty the best policy.

Evening, Mrs. Adams and I to Mr. Brooks'. The usual family and C.

Brooks and F. Gray. Rather dull. Home where finished Burr's first Volume of Journal and began second.

MONDAY 4TH.

Cool day. Distribution as usual. Evening at Dr. Frothingham's.

I have only to repeat that I worked upon Burr today, attending however the annual meeting of the stockholders of the Middlesex Canal. No report this year, the agent being sick, so adjourned for one month, after renewing the direction, and raising a committee to make a protest against the water project of the City from Long Pond.[1] I am afraid the managers are losing their interest in this property, yet to me it has been very productive.

Electra. Steady at the Private Journal of Burr which wants positive interest and yet is amusing. How to reconcile these.

Have I mentioned having a curious visit from Russell Freeman entirely laudatory of the letters to Biddle, the papers of the Conservative, and requesting a copy of my Pamphlets. What does that mean? He is as usual upon the world, has thrown off the Administration only because they do not want him. Evening at Dr. Frothingham's. A very pleasant supper.

[1] A project that would divert water from Long Pond, lying between Billerica and Tewksbury and close to the Middlesex Canal, would affect the canal unfavorably.

TUESDAY 5TH.

Cool and clear. Distribution as usual. Evening visit Mrs. Bates at Papanti's.

At the Office I am often bored by countrymen who come in about the farm at Weston. They seem to have little or no idea of the value of time. I suppose a farming life rather begets indolence.

Continued Burr, and today wrote a note to Dr. Palfrey proposing to him a review of the same.[1] So now my head is in for it. The truth is that I am conscious of being eaten up by indolence and luxury.

Home reading Electra. Average about 110 lines of review in the hour. This is slow. But I read most of the Greek Scholia.[2] Finished the private Journal of Burr. Quite a tragedy finale. A case entirely unexampled in America and perhaps in the world.

The ball at Papanti's was as splendid as money could make it, and on the whole quite pleasant, although by no means so much so as the Assemblies. We returned at one o'clock in the morning of [Wednesday 6th.].

¹ To J. G. Palfrey, Adams Papers.

² Marginal notes to Sophocles' text, commenting either on language or subject matter, and originating in the first cen- tury B.C., or earlier. N. G. L. Hammond and H. H. Scullard, eds., *Oxford Classical Dictionary*, 2d edn., Oxford, 1970, p. 960–961.

WEDNESDAY 6TH.

Severe cold. Time much as usual. Evening at home.

The morning was devoted to Burr. The whole account of the Presidential Election of 1800 is interesting although it may be questioned whether the time has yet arrived to analyze it critically. I shall not begin until I get an answer from Palfrey.

Continued Electra which I probably finish tomorrow. Devoted the afternoon to writing an answer to my Mother, the first letter I have written to her this winter.¹ My time has galloped away in a most remarkable way, and I have done nothing but the Athenæum coins. In the evening, a quiet time at home and being fatigued, retired betimes.

¹ Adams Papers. A reply to LCA's letter to him of 22 Jan. (Adams Papers). Passages from CFA's letter are quoted in the Introduction to the present volumes and in notes to the entries of 26 Nov. 1838; 17, 28 Jan., above.

THURSDAY. 7TH.

Very severe cold, but moderated afterwards. Time passed as usual. Evening at Mrs. Parker's.

Morning devoted to Burr, excepting always time given to applicants for farm at Weston. Called by request at the Suffolk Insurance Office to see the return of the Appraisers and to vote on the subject of the dissolution. The deficiency is estimated at 71,000 dollars or about twenty four per cent of its capital, and yet the list of those who wish to go on is so large that I think they will carry it. It is hard to kill a corporation. The vitality is greater than one would at first sight suspect.

Finished Electra, a play of much power. There is an idea afloat that the Greek drama is cold and statue like, which I hold to be very erroneous. Electra for example is the personification of intense passion.

After dinner, wrote a letter to Mr. Peacock condoling with him. He has lost his Wife and one daughter since the period of our journey.¹ At a small dancing party at Mrs. D. P. Parker's given to Mrs. Appleton. Nothing particularly interesting, the company appearing rather languid. Home early.

¹ On James Peacock and his family, companions of the Adamses on their trip to Niagara, see the entries beginning 30 June 1836, above. CFA's letter to Peacock is missing.

FRIDAY 8TH.

Mild and cloudy. Time as usual. Evening at home.

My morning was taken up by a succession of persons calling, principally applicants for the Weston farm. I was therefore obliged to omit Burr as well as Diary and accounts. Read Antigone, forty five lines, rather a small but a difficult lesson. I think I will go through with the seven plays of Sophocles. They improve the taste.

After dinner, having as yet no answer from Dr. Palfrey and being on my oars, I went to work upon the A[dams] MS and prepared nearly one volume more for binding. This work is very necessary but it drags.

Read aloud to my Wife a little of a new novel called Oliver Twist[1] wherein the Author seems to indulge a propensity to abuse human nature. This has two sides after all, and it is best for us not to think too much of the bad one. Tried to write but could not so that I concluded to refresh my recollection of what I had done before, and read over my two last Pamphlets.

[1] *Oliver Twist* appeared in book form in 2 vols., London, Oct. 1838, after earlier serial publication in *Bentley's Magazine* beginning in Jan. 1837.

SATURDAY 9TH.

Clouds and light snow. Time as usual. Evening at home.

My morning went rapidly. W. Spear came in from Quincy without any particular business and took much time. I therefore did little with Burr, but got an answer from Dr. Palfrey which makes my work somewhat obligatory.[1] Continued Antigone, the first part of which is difficult and the lyric poetry highly elliptical.

I sat down in the afternoon to write upon the state of the currency but found myself at fault for information. I therefore directed my attention to the balance of the A[dams] MS. Finished the arrangement of the collection of the State Department which goes far towards two volumes.

Went out too and spent an hour with Edmund Quincy who certainly has the appearance of a very sick man. He was lying on a sofa reading, says he has lost blood and is too weak to go upstairs. Our talk was of indifferent topics. In the evening, French, and Oliver Twist which is interesting however disagreeable.

[1] John G. Palfrey to CFA, 7 Feb., Adams Papers.

SUNDAY. 10TH.

Cold and clear. Services as usual. Evening to Edward Brooks'.

I continued my attempt at composition this morning without success. One thing is certain, my dissipated way of life entirely kills connected thought or I am not as well charged with ideas upon the subject as I apprehend.

Divine service as usual. Dr. Frothingham from Psalms. 131. 2. "My soul is even as a weaned child." I had heard of this sermon and text some time ago, but gained little from it I regret to say. Afternoon, S. K. Lothrop from Exodus 20. 3. "Thou shalt have no other gods before me." Upon idol worship of this age, more refined but equally marked with that of antiquity. The ancient mythology personified passions and gave them divine attributes and then worshipped them. We do so without personification. It was a good but not a new discourse in invention delivered with the peculiar artifice which deadens the effect of his performances.

Read a discourse in the English Preacher from a Mr. Bourn, Psalm 103. 2. "Bless the Lord, O my Soul; and forget not all his benefits." Upon religious gratitude, a respectable discourse. Made a pleasant visit in the evening at Mr. Edward Brooks'.

MONDAY 11TH.

Cloudy and more mild. Day spent in attending corporation meetings. Evening Assembly.

I was entirely unable to be at my Office this morning as I was first called to attend a meeting of the Directors of the Middlesex Canal to organize, then to the Suffolk Insurance Company where the struggle between the Stockholders about the continuance of the charter was at length brought to a close, those who favored a continuation having the majority by a small number of votes. I was of the minority but am satisfied with the result if by it I am any better protected from loss. But my confidence in joint stock companies grows less every day so that having now nearly got myself out of Banks I propose to begin the same operation with Insurance companies, which are now at so low an ebb as to make it a more slow and dangerous process.

After the meeting I got into a conversation with Mr. H Cabot upon the subject of joint stock and expressed opinions which find very little currency here. I might have saved my labour.

Afternoon to the Annual Meeting of the South Cove Corporation. No subject of much interest agitated. Directors elected, but I found the feeling much firmer as to the success of the undertaking. I hope it is well founded for I have now too great a stake to be trifled with in that corporation, which I hope will not try it's vitality as others do but die gently and gradually. Evening to the Assembly, thinner than usual, but very pleasant. We remained until after midnight.

TUESDAY 12TH.

Clear and mild. Time as usual. Evening, friends at home.

At the Office I continued Burr, as steadily as applicants for the farm at Weston would let me. A walk to the South End about tenants and money and then home.

Felt exceedingly fatigued from the exercise and late hours of last night. Antigone as usual. I did not remit the study of Burr throughout the Afternoon.

Evening a few friends. Dr. and Mrs. Frothingham, Governor and Mrs. Everett. Eliz. C. Adams and J. H. Foster with his young sister. Nothing material.

WEDNESDAY 13TH.

Lovely day. Division as usual. Quiet evening.

More applications for the farm at Weston. Time at the Office spent in Accounts reviewing the state of the last two years, and especially six months back. Tried to find the Report of Burr's trial at Richmond but without success. What difficulty always about books. I ought to go to the Athenæum and study, Wood's book, and Jefferson and many others.

Home. Antigone in which I make progress. Finished in the afternoon the review of Burr's Life. And now I must positively go on to write. Inconceivable how sluggish I am. My ambition is almost dead within me. Evening, trying again upon the currency, and better.

THURSDAY. 14TH.

Cloudy and wet. Time as usual. Quiet evening.

Not long at the Office today as I felt obliged to go down to the Athenæum and make an effort to procure the volumes of the trial of Burr.[1] I am so languid about this that it is eminently doubtful whether I shall make any thing at all of it. Procured the necessary volumes, and also one of General Wilkinson's life[2] with which I went home after looking over Wood's Administration of John Adams[3] and Jefferson's letters about the period of the election.[4] I want also the report upon John Smith[5] and the Ana in Jefferson[6] which were not in.

Antigone after which the report of the trial. It seems to be a contest of technicalities and an extremely vehement one. Quietly at home. I continued upon currency and begin to see my path.

[1] At the Athenæum were Thomas Carpenter, *Report of the Trial of Aaron Burr for Treason*, 3 vols., Washington, 1807–1808; David Robertson, *Reports of the Trials of Burr for Treason and Misdemeanor*, 2 vols., Phila., 1808; *Trial of Burr including the Arguments during the Examination and Trial of Gen. Wilkinson*, 3 vols., Washington, 1807.

[2] Gen. James Wilkinson, *Memoirs of my own Times*, 4 vols., Phila., 1816.

[3] John Wood, *The History of the Administration of John Adams*, N.Y., 1802.

[4] *Memoir, Correspondence and Miscellanies of Thomas Jefferson*, ed. Thomas Jefferson Randolph, 4 vols., Boston, 1829. The letters of 1789–1803 are in vol. 3.

[5] *Testimony in Connection with the Investigation of Senator John Smith* [of Ohio] ... *Queries Addressed by the Committee, Dec. 9, 1807, to Mr. Smith*, ordered printed Dec. 31, 1807, Washington, 1808.

[6] Vol. 4 of the edition of Jefferson, above, contained the Ana.

FRIDAY 15TH.

Cloudy and wet. Time as usual. Evening to see Edmund Quincy.

I devoted much of my time to the reading of the trial of Burr. Never was a case so embarrassed with preliminary motions, challenges of jurymen, questions of bail &ca. I have as yet no idea of the merits. A struggle of wit among acute lawyers seems the only characteristic of the work.

Antigone, and went in the evening to see Edmund Quincy who is recovering. Mrs. Quincy was not there but he was, and we sat an hour. Letter from my Mother today covering some bad intelligence.[1] The public news is also of great disaster from a furious storm in the British Channel.

[1] LCA, in her letter to CFA (11 Feb., Adams Papers), reported "a disgusting tale" involving Thomas Baker Johnson Frye, son of the Nathaniel Fryes: "You and Abby will start with astonishment and disgust to learn that he has been married *some time*, and is the Father of a Son by Miss Catherine Johnson, the immaculate Saint of thirty three, who was a visitor at Mrs. Frye's when you were with us last April [see entry for 20 May 1838, above]. He is 19 next June.... The dark despair of the poor Father rends my heart, and who can offer consolation?"

SATURDAY 16TH.

Weather dull and foggy. Much the usual distribution. Evening at home.

At the Office this morning where I was occupied by Deacon W. Spear who came from Quincy with the usual amount of applications. This day of the week is commonly frittered away in things of this kind. Home to read Antigone. Mr. Brooks and P. C. Jr. dined here today by way of remembering the birth day of my youngest boy Henry who is a year old. There is no intelligence of any kind, and on the whole we are growing very dull. Evening passed very quietly at home. Finished the first draught upon the currency not at all satisfactory.

SUNDAY. 17TH.

Snow and drizzle. Exercises as usual.

I follow up my investigations respecting Aaron Burr during my day light hours and write upon the currency in the evening. Attended divine service all day and heard Dr. Frothingham preach from 1 Thessalonians 4. 1. "We beseech you that as ye have received of us how ye ought to walk and to please God, so ye would abound more and more." And from Matthew 25. 13. "Watch therefore, for ye know not the day nor the hour wherein the son of man cometh." I paid rather a languid kind of attention.

A Sermon of John Balguy from Esther 5. 13. "Yet all this availeth me nothing, so long as I see Mordecai the Jew sitting at the King's gate." The story of Haman as illustrating the restlessness of human desire. There is something a little extravagant to us in this excess of Haman's and yet not at all inconsistent with the passions we know to exist in man when left as in Eastern countries entirely unbridled.

Evening at home the first time for several weeks. Writing afterwards but I know not how it is I can by no means satisfy myself.

MONDAY. 18TH.

Still dull and cloudy. Division as usual. Evening to the Theatre.

This gloomy weather continues long. At the Office not having any other definite occupation, I made an overturn in my collections of old papers and began to destroy with very little mercy. Home where I continued Antigone. I felt extraordinarily unwell all day and began to apprehend being taken sick but as I fasted, towards evening grew better.

Went to the Theatre to hear a play called "Il Giovanni" being an English hash of Mozart's music. Mrs. Bailey sung as Zerlina.[1] But nothing could well be poorer. This piece I had always expressed a great wish to hear, never having had an opportunity, but either this gives no sort of idea of it or I should not like it. Returned home much disappointed and resolved not to go to the Theatre again with such performances.

[1] At the Tremont Theatre, Mrs. Bailey, the former Charlotte Watson, also sang the principal role in the comic afterpiece "Pet of the Petticoats." In "Il Giovanni," Joseph Pearson was Don Octavio and Miss Morgan was Donna Leonora (*Boston* *Evening Transcript*, 18 Feb., p. 3, col. 2). "Il Giovanni" may have been the extravaganza titled "Giovanni in London," which was introduced in New York in 1827 and was popular for many years (Odell, *Annals N.Y. Stage*, 3:246).

TUESDAY 19TH.

Clear and pleasant. Time as usual. Quiet evening at home.

It was a fair and bright day today but I felt not quite well and rather uneasy at some symptoms of pain in my left side. At the Office I continued the burning system and managed to destroy most of the remaining papers of the last ten years. What a dreary sensation it is to look back over the minutiæ of life, see accounts of this or that incident made by persons no longer living, and to ponder on the vanity of their existence.

Home to read Antigone. Devoted all my leisure after dinner to writing upon the currency in which I made much more satisfactory progress. It is remarkable how easily I can write when once warmed and how badly when I labour.

WEDNESDAY 20TH.

Cloudy. Time regularly divided. Evening at Edward Brooks'.

At the Office, feeling better but still not quite free from my trouble. Finished off the clearing work and then to the Athenæum where I looked over many papers for some more information respecting Burr, then a walk round the South Cove where I find are some preparations for building. I must observe more. Met Devereux whom I formerly knew and asked him to call and tell of Burr.[1]

Home. Antigone. Went on with my labour after dinner. These articles upon Currency are as bad as Burr. Evening, after a visit from Mr. Brooks, we went down to pay a visit to Edward Brooks and his Wife where we spent the evening and brought home with us Miss Mary Hall.[2]

[1] On John Devereux, see vol. 5:403–404.
[2] Mary Brooks Hall, a niece of Peter C. Brooks (vol. 5:122).

THURSDAY 21ST.

Mild and clear day. Time as usual. Evening a family party at home.

My time at the Office a little wasted. J. Kirk from Quincy came in and bothered me. He had not much to say but country people idle. Walk and home where I made great progress in reading Antigone which becomes much easier as we go on. The lyric poetry is not so difficult and perhaps a little more common place than in the other pieces. Went on with the currency.

The family met this evening at my house together with a few of the more remote branches of the connexion. The party was much as they all are, and they separated as usual about eleven o'clock. The accounts from the State of Maine portend some spark of War in that quarter. Our boundary questions are becoming very troublesome.

FRIDAY. 22D.

Clouds and rain. Distribution regular.

The profound quiet of my life is interrupted only by tenants from Weston. I this morning managed to settle the question, and was occupied in writing instructions to an attorney at Concord to recover damages from Conant.[1] Also writing to New Orleans and to Florida with a view of finishing the long standing accounts of T. B. Adams at those places.[2] Went on with Antigone which I read fast. The rest of the day was taken up with my essay which after all makes no great headway.

[1] Letter missing.
[2] CFA to Charles Harrod; same to Lt. J. C. Casey; both LbCs, Adams Papers.

SATURDAY 23D.

Clouds and fog. Division made as usual.

At the Office today I concerned myself with Accounts, but got into an examination of Mr. Woodbury's last report where I found some things which require notice in my proposed publication. The public here is now in great excitement from the accounts of a collision likely to take place between our people and those of Great Britain.[1] What a strange jumble of elements in our political world and what very ordinary persons are those who have the management of it in their hands.

Home, where I finished Antigone. I have read this play in thirteen days, one hour of each day, which is encouraging although I do not mean to pique myself upon fast reading. I shall now review, and be more thorough. After all, this hour's occupation though perhaps the least profitable in a mere worldly estimate of my time, gives me the most unmixed pleasure. My labour upon the Currency still going on, but rather hesitatingly for I have to write over much. Evening, Miss Mary Hall who had been staying here is gone.

[1] The simmering dispute between the United States and Great Britain over ownership of a substantial portion of Maine lands, usually called the northeast boundary dispute, would appear to reach a boil on several occasions before the alarms would give way to serious diplo- matic attention in 1841–1842. In the new administration, with Webster as secretary of state and JQA as chairman of the House Committee on Foreign Affairs, conditions prevailed which permitted the negotiation and ratification of the Webster-Ashburton Treaty.

SUNDAY. 24TH.

Day pleasant. Exercises as usual. Evening at Mrs. Quincy's.

I am working upon my papers respecting the currency in order to get them out of the way of Burr. But they do not suit me. And the public mind is now so entirely taken up with the threatening aspect of affairs at the Eastward as to make publication at present quite inexpedient.

Attended divine service and heard Dr. Frothingham preach from Ephesians 3. 21. "Unto him [be] glory in the church by Christ Jesus, throughout all ages, world without end." A very sensible and beautifully composed discourse upon the necessity of a visible church and the preservation of external observances, together with the duties inculcated by its ministers, of attention to religious feeling and not to extravagant fanaticism.

Mr. Young gave us in the afternoon from Hebrews 11. 13. "These confessed that they were strangers and pilgrims on the earth." A noisy sermon upon the vanity of earthly pleasures and occupations. Mr. Young writes well but thinks wordily.

Read a discourse by Archbishop Tillotson. Psalm 119. 59. "I thought on my ways and turned my feet unto thy testimonies." Upon the necessity of reflection and consideration of religious truth. A good sermon.

Called to see Mrs. Josiah Quincy in the evening. Found her a little nervous, but had a pleasant evening enough.

MONDAY 25TH.

Snow but cleared by night. Time as usual. Evening, Assembly.

At the Office this morning I devoted my time to business and making out my quarterly account, in which I have been backward. This took all my leisure. Read the translation of Antigone by Francklin, and Brumoy's analysis of it as well as Potter's version of the choruses,[1] after which I began my review.

The afternoon was devoted to currency my last draught of which I finished without satisfaction and then laid them away. I have rarely in composition experienced so much of difficulty.

We went this evening to the fifth Assembly. It was more full than the last and was quite pleasant. I have enjoyed these parties as much as I can ever enjoy society of this kind which is after all to a person who feels himself equal to better things but a vapid pleasure. Home at midnight.

[1] Of Pierre Brumoy's *Le théâtre des Grecs* and the translations of Sophocles by Thomas Francklin and Robert Potter, see vol. 3:93, 119, 121.

TUESDAY 26TH.

Lovely morning but rain at night. Usual division. Evening, ball at Mrs. Miller's.

Finished the work of my Quarterly Account. I believe I am now free from all further duties of any sort in business, having written and despatched the necessary letters. A good deal fatigued by the labour of last nights party.

The accounts of the frontier difficulties still appear to engross most minds. I cannot believe a war will grow out of it. Neither Great Britain nor the United States are in a condition to make war. Our people however want an experience of what it is, and our boundary difficulties must be admitted to be extremely embarrassing.

Antigone. The first chorus is noble, but they generally have too little relation to the piece, and though fine, poetical conceptions are without any but the commonest moral.

After dinner, resumed the work upon the MS and arranged another volume for binding. I keep off from Burr. Evening, notwithstanding the rain we went to a ball at Mrs. Miller's, a mixed company but not unpleasant. Home at midnight.

WEDNESDAY 27TH.

Morning fine but it clouded over by night. Time as usual. Evening at Mrs. Thorndike's.

I am so much dissatisfied with my papers upon currency that I have determined to bring them down to the Office and try to build up an improved set. I began upon this work today, and thought I did well.

Antigone in review. Afternoon devoted to the MS, finishing the arrangement of the Executive Correspondence which in itself makes four large volumes. This is a work too long delayed, and one which is among the most necessary. I am not very constantly occupied and yet how perpetually I am delaying this, and giving to almost any other duty a preference. I made a great step today.

Evening, Mrs. Adams was so much fatigued with the exertion of the last two nights that tonight she was compelled to remain at home. So I went alone to Mrs. Charles Thorndike's. It was a small party, indeed perhaps the smallest of the sort I have been to this winter, but was very handsome and very pleasant.

THURSDAY 28TH.

Cloudy but it cleared fine. Time as usual. Evening, Mr. Brooks at home.

The children have been more or less out of order for a week or two past and today the baby drooped much. We have been exceedingly dissipated of late and I think it is high time for us to lay by and be quiet. Since my residence in Boston I have never known so gay a winter, and by a singular coincidence it has been the season I have selected to extend my acquaintance. This I have done partially but not generally.

At the Office continuing my papers. The boundary troubles still the prominent topic. Antigone, and an afternoon of relaxation with Crevier and Gibbon.

Mr. Brooks took tea with us and mentioned a suggestion of my father's appointment on a special mission to England, which is no otherwise worthy of notice excepting as going to show the public estimate of his value in times of difficulty. Began Burr.

FRIDAY, MARCH I.

Day cloudy. Time divided as usual. Evening at home.

At the Office today I was so busy in attending to business that I could not go on at all with my papers. Wrote an answer to Mr. Johnson's letter received yesterday as also a letter to my father covering an Account current for the last Quarter.[1] This with a walk up to the house in Tremont Street on a dunning expedition took much of my time.

Antigone as usual. Afternoon, indulge in reading Crevier and Gibbon. The whole history of the Roman Empire ought to be a profitable one to the thinker, but I have great doubts whether any existing generation draws much of instruction from any past one excepting in the sciences which yield palpable results and mathematics.

Evening at home. Continued my Essay upon Burr. I write easily but as usual now with me dislike what I write.

[1] The letter from T. B. Johnson is missing; CFA's letters to him and to JQA (LbCs) are in Adams Papers.

SATURDAY 2D.

Lovely, spring day. Time as usual. Quiet evening.

The season appears to open quite early. Office doing business with William Spear and others. The sensation here about the English War becomes greater in consequence of the reaction produced by the debates in Congress. Parties are agreed upon the subject. And a belligerent tone runs through all the proceedings. There appears to be no foundation for the suggestion respecting my father. The danger seems to be so imminent that in my opinion Mr. Van Buren could not do a wiser thing than to avert it by the measure proposed but it would be a concession to his superiority which can not be expected from a man who builds on party walls his defences. We are too commercial here to be warlike, and this news strikes like Ice.

Walk round by the South Cove to see the improvements which are already beginning. Antigone. Also at work finishing the fifth volume of Crevier and upon Burr.

SUNDAY 3D.

Snow but cleared off very cold. Exercises as usual. Evening at Edward Brooks'.

I spent half an hour this morning over my cabinet of Medals. Attended divine service and heard Dr. Frothingham preach from Luke 22. 8.9. "And he sent Peter and John saying Go and prepare us the passover, that we may eat." A communion sermon. I noticed that the Dr. in his prayer alluded to the threatening political appearances of the day. What a nation of excitements are these United States! Two weeks ago and who would have earned any but a character of a madman in proclaiming the least possible chance of war. Now it is so familiar an idea as to call forth a prayer to Heaven to avert it. I cannot yet persuade myself there is danger, but I find myself very ill informed of the true merits of the question.

Afternoon, 1 Kings 17. 14. "For thus [saith] the Lord God of Israel

The barrel of meal shall not waste neither shall the cruse of oil fail until the day that the Lord sendeth rain upon the earth." Trust in the Lord as exemplified in the instance of the widow and Elijah. A trust which with me has been, I believe, perfectly uniform though I ought to take no credit for any trial.

Read a sermon of Tillotson. Psalm 119. 60. "I made haste and delayed not to keep thy commandments." Immediate obedience inculcated with calmness and good sense. Evening to see Edward Brooks and his Wife. Found there Dr. Bigelow. Conversation, the frontier question and the fancy ball.

MONDAY 4TH.

Very cold. Distribution as usual. Evening at home.

At the Office as usual. Much of my time taken up in examining the question of the boundary which excites such deep interest at the moment. Read the greater part of the Report of the Legislative Committee of this State upon it at the last Session which gives the substance of the question, and I think it pretty conclusive. The debates in both houses are very spirited but unanimous and as usual I see much conceded to my father's position the moment difficulty occurs.[1]

Antigone. Crevier and Gibbon. Evening after reading French with my Wife, continued Burr. But my style is slovenly. G. Gorham here.

[1] The long-standing dispute with Great Britain over the boundary between Maine and New Brunswick had reached a level of crisis in consequence of recent intransigent assertions of jurisdiction by both claimants to the territory. The Maine legislature had addressed appeals to the federal government to assert the national interest and to the Massachusetts legislature to support Maine's case in Congress. After lengthy debate, the legislature in Boston enacted four resolves addressed to Massachusetts' senators and representatives for presentation to Congress entirely supportive of Maine's case and opposing submission of the quarrel to outside arbitration. Of the four resolves, the first was passed unanimously, the third and fourth by votes of 28 to 1. Significant opposition was encountered only in the vote on the second, which asserted that "the *active* measures authorized by the Maine legislature ... were required by the exigencies of the case." In the course of the debate reliance was placed upon President Adams' message to Congress in 1828 in which he held that "the claim of exclusive jurisdiction [in the disputed territory] on the part of Great Britain is incompatible with the understanding between the two governments." What JQA's position would be on the resolves when presented is not clear (*Daily Advertiser*, 28 Feb., p. 2, col. 3; 4 March, p. 1, cols. 5–6; JQA, *Memoirs*, 9:542).

TUESDAY 5TH.

Still cold. Time according to custom. Evening at Dr. Frothingham's. At the Office, I went on with the examination of the papers respecting the frontier and obtained a pretty clear notion of the points of controversy. They are very certainly with the United States but the adherence of the British to their side of the matter and the pertinacity with which they have continued to support their claim and push it whenever they reasonably could make the chance of amicable settlement more doubtful than I had supposed. God only knows what the result will be. I cannot believe it will be a war.

Home. Antigone. After dinner, Crevier, the Roman Empire in its decay—Gallienus, Claudius, and Aurelian—still some vigour left. Went in the evening to see Dr. and Mrs. Frothingham and we had a pleasant conversation. Afterwards, creeping with Burr.

WEDNESDAY 6TH.

Clear and more mild. Distribution as usual. Evening at home.

We have accounts of the breaking up of Congress as usual in a great hurry. They have passed a bill providing for contingencies in Maine and for a special mission to England about it. Public opinion points to Mr. Webster or to my father, and there is so obvious a fitness in the selection of the latter that I cannot help thinking of it though my judgment leads me to suppose it impossible. Mr. Van Buren will appoint a partisan. I am sorry my father has been named[1] because it unsettles my thoughts. The probabilities of difficulty do not diminish.

Occupied at Office in making up Diary. Walk, and Antigone. After dinner, Crevier and continue busy upon Burr. I find the subject fruitful but difficult to handle.

[1] That is, suggested.

THURSDAY 7TH.

Mild and pleasant. Time as usual.

The difficulties with Great Britain still continue to be the general topic. I received today a letter from my father dated at Washington on Sunday,[1] from which it is clear to me that he had not the remotest idea of being called upon at this contingency. I therefore dismiss it from my thoughts.

Devoted myself to the currency papers which have been languishing for some time. Finished one and began a second. The afternoon attending to Crevier and after a quiet evening at home, finished the first draft of Burr. I hope I shall be able to make something creditable to me out of this.

[1] 3 March, Adams Papers.

FRIDAY 8TH.

Mild but easterly cold. Division as usual.

I was pretty assiduous this morning in the continuation of my work upon currency and made a good deal of progress. But affairs have taken so novel a turn that it is very questionable on the whole whether any attention would be paid to similar speculations until the war fever is over.

Walk and Antigone. After dinner, a chapter of Crevier and two of Gibbon. I think his power over his subject is one of the most remarkable things I have ever noticed. The exactness with which he mentions all important facts in very small compass, and the service to which he puts all his adjectives. Is this worth studying for imitation? Quiet evening at home. Began upon the last draught of Burr. Heavy work is writing.

SATURDAY 9TH.

Fine day. Time as usual. Evening out without success.

I was much engaged at the Office all the morning with various interruptions common on this day of the week but managed on the whole to be satisfied as I recruited my almost exhausted funds considerably thereby. Walk.

Finished Antigone with which I have been much pleased. The drama is a deeply pathetic one from the self devotion of the heroine, and is remarkable as introducing love as one of the moving forces though not the principal in the piece. I now go on to Philoctetes.

Afternoon, Crevier, and in the evening we went out to pay an evening visit to Mrs. Webster but found her not at home. Went on a little heavily with Aaron Burr.

SUNDAY 10TH.

Colder. Exercises as usual. Evening at home.

I devoted an hour to my collection of medals this morning. Attended divine service as usual. Heard Mr. Robbins preach from 1 Kings 4. 13. "And she answered, I dwell among mine own people." Upon domestic harmony and the practice of exercising the family affections. This history of Elisha and the Shunnamite woman had been the topic of a discourse of Dr. Frothingham's last Sunday far superior in pathos and force to this of Mr. Robbins'.

Afternoon, Mr. Barrett. John 8. 12. "Then spake Jesus again unto them saying, I am the light of the world." This speech coming from such a person, whose station in life and mode of education by no means justified its being made, wonderfully verified as it has been by the spread of the Gospel satisfies the preacher that he could have been no mere mortal. The point is a strong one and was not badly put, but Mr. Barrett is so unfortunate in his delivery as to make listening to him positively painful.

Dr. Hayley furnished the day's sermon from the English Preacher. Colossians 3. 14. "Above all these things, put on charity which is the bond of perfectness." Upon charity and sensible. Evening at home. Went on with Burr.

MONDAY 11TH.

Fine day. Time as usual. Evening sixth Assembly.

At the Office where I dispatched two of my papers upon currency to Mr. Buckingham. I hope this will stimulate me to further exertion although I am afraid not for even in this first instance of it I failed to go on. My ambition is dead. It is injurious to me even to hope for any distinction in this life as the elevation is followed by as instantaneous a depression. My duty however is to try, and so I continue at brief intervals to throw out some thing with a consciousness perpetually falling in its estimate of my power of acting upon others. The position which my father has assumed and in which I follow him is not one of very easy attainment. I fear that I shall utterly fail in making any thing out of it.

Reading today one of my Grandfather's MS reflections upon Government I found a very deep and wise discussion of the parties which agitate our country. And in it I saw my own fate as a politician clearly marked. Began Philoctetes being the fifth play of Sophocles that I have attempted. After dinner Crevier, and resuming upon the MS.

Evening, the sixth Assembly, as pleasant as any of it's predecessors. These have made an agreeable impression upon me of Boston Society, which though not so very brilliant and hightoned as that of more fashionable capitals has perhaps a more quiet and well regulated spirit.

TUESDAY 12TH.

Fine day. Time as usual. Evening small party at Miss Scollay's.

At the Office I busied myself very assiduously in my work upon my articles but made slow progress. The public news is stationary. The rumor of Mr. Calhoun's appointment turns out to be thin air. The

Whig newspapers as usual are busy in carving out for the President what he shall do, while those of his side are holding back uncommitted in order that they may approve whatever he does. I see not a symptom of probability that my father will be selected although I am more and more convinced he is the man who should go. The probability now is that nobody will be sent for the present, and while it will do any good. In the mean time, however, things upon the frontier look rather better.

Read Philoctetes which is easy Greek. After dinner, Crevier and further work upon the MS.

Evening to Miss Scollay's. She piques herself upon uniting at her house the most cultivated people and commonly makes dull parties. Met Dr. Channing there and had some conversation with him about general matters of speculation. He is undoubtedly an able man and I believe a sincere one but I apprehend he does not live enough among his fellows to understand fully the extent of their moving impulses. He treated me however with very great civility and asked me to call and see him which I do not know but I may do.

WEDNESDAY 13TH.

Fine day. Usual division. Evening small party at Mrs. E. Blake's.

I continued my work at the Office which gives me satisfaction as it keeps me employed. My sct of articles however are very slow in their progress. I began to write one over the fourth time this day.

Philoctetes as usual. It is very easy to read and I begin to think I am really mastering Greek. After dinner, Crevier and MS. upon which I propose to be again engaged.

Went to a small family party at Mrs. Blake's in the evening. The Parkmans and Dehons, rather dull. Home. Burr is dull.

THURSDAY. 14TH.

Rain. Time divided. Evening at Mrs. H. G. Rice's.

My first number on the currency appeared today.[1] I read it with some interest and liked it much. But it comes at a wrong season. Nobody knows or cares for it. Perhaps it is worth nothing.

Read Philoctetes, the only pursuit that gives me rich satisfaction. The rest are all in the performance of a heavy duty. Crevier, History of Constantine. His catholic feelings influence the latter portion of his history much. The struggles of the christian religion over the passions of men would make perhaps a most interesting subject of investigation.

They were terrific during the middle ages. And yet they remain working upon generation after generation with improving force but very gradual success. Ms.

Evening at Mrs. H. G. Rice's. A new acquaintance. Company as usual. Returned at ten.

[1] CFA's series, "The Prospect for the Currency", in which he took issue with Secretary Woodbury's Report, appeared, unsigned, in the *Boston Courier* in four parts on the 14, 16, 19, and 23 March, all at p. 2, cols. 1–2.

FRIDAY 15TH.

Clear and fine day. Time as usual. Evening at home.

I felt this morning a little the worse for the week's dissipation and was glad to think that it was now probably at an end. At the Office where I was so engrossed with business matters that I was unable to touch my papers. I left it sooner than usual for the purpose of putting into the hands of Mr. Hosmer of the Council who is a lawyer the very abominable case of Conant's trespass. A person who applied for the place came to me today and told me they were going on with a high hand there. This has reanimated my courage which had been wavering since Mr. Cheney's declining the business. I hope it will now turn out for the best. But I dread the law.[1]

Walk round the South Cove. Philoctetes as usual. Afternoon, finish Crevier which is rather a lumbering book after all. MS, upon which I make gradual advances. I purpose to touch a little upon Gibbon and then devote my Afternoons for the remainder of the season to vigorous pursuit of it.

Quiet evening. My head felt so dull and achy that I had an insurmountable repugnance to taking up Burr, so I wrote an answer to my Mother's letters received yesterday and today.[2]

[1] Silas and Amory Conant had been tenants of JQA's woodlot and farm in Weston since 1829. Under CFA's direction, they had seen to the necessary preliminaries to the periodic auctions of wood selected for cutting, collected from purchasers, and brought the proceeds, along with their own rents, to CFA with fair regularity (see vols. 3:17, 19–20, 74–75; 4:169, 294, 397–398; and indexes to vols. 3 and 4). The diary entries do not record a termination of their tenancy nor the nature of their trespass. Possibly it was to replace them in matters relating to the timber that CFA approached Alfred Cheney of Cheney and Spaulding's woodwharf in Boston (*Boston Directory*, 1839), but without success. His decision to seek redress at law led him to engage Rufus Hosmer, an attorney of neighboring Stow and a member of the Governor's Council (*Mass. Register*, 1839, p. 32, 78). The threat of legal action proved effective (see entry for 26 March, below).

[2] LCA to CFA, 12, 13 March; CFA to LCA, 15 March; all in Adams Papers.

SATURDAY 16TH.

Morning fine. Time divided as usual. Evening at home.

I spent my time at the Office today in writing my fourth and last number of my papers upon currency but without satisfying myself. The second appeared, and Mr. Brooks expressed to me his gratification with it. I am glad any body reads them with pleasure.

J. H. Foster called to tell me that the body of poor T. B. Adams had at last arrived and I made an arrangement with him about the details of interment.

Read Philoctetes as usual. Afternoon Gibbon, and MS, but this is lazy work. Next week I must begin in earnest upon Burr. Evening very quietly at home. Lazy with Burr.

SUNDAY. 17TH.

Lovely day. Time devoted to the ordinary exercises. Evening at E. Brooks'.

I began this morning a series of Sunday Morning readings which I purpose to continue with my daughter Louisa. She read today the two first chapters in the book of Genesis and committed a hymn of Dr. Watts.[1] She is now old enough to begin to think for herself upon matters of conduct and I wish to instil into her a sense of right which shall help her to govern the impetuosity of her character. She is a fine child with noble powers of mind and a good heart, but like all such she has strong impulses and a fiery temper. Religious and moral affections are what I rely upon to correct these.

Attended divine service and heard Dr. Frothingham in the morning preach from Galatians 5. 7. "Ye did run well; who did hinder you that ye should not obey the truth?" Upon the discouragements under which men often relax their hold upon good. I liked the afternoon discourse the best. Matthew 9. 16. "And the rent is made worse." A curious text upon which to work a discussion of the projects of moral reforms in the present day which have such extensive approbation and which yet are as the preacher said, calculated for the most part upon a mistaken estimate of man.

Read a discourse of Bishop Smalridge. Psalm 42. 11. "Why art thou cast down, O my Soul? and why art thou disquieted within me? Hope then in God, for I shall yet praise him, who is the health of my countenance and my God." A text I have often read with a deep sense of its consoling import although I have never yet been tried by affliction. This was a sensible discourse upon the subject.

I tried Burr but failed and much dissatisfied. Evening, we went to Edward Brooks' where we passed an hour much in the usual way.

[1] *The Psalms, Hymns, and Spiritual Songs* of Isaac Watts were published in countless editions from 1719 onward.

MONDAY 18TH.

Cloudy day. Time occupied as usual. Evening at home.

I devoted some time to the arrangement necessary for removing the body of T. B. Adams and had a little left for writing. But I did not satisfy myself. When do I? The day was foggy and drizzly and I felt dull.

A Letter from my Mother with no news in it.[1] Philoctetes, making great progress. It is the easiest Greek tragedy I ever read. Continue to work on MS and Gibbon, so I did *not* do as I said on Saturday. Evening, French, and Burr which I worked over as usual.

[1] 14 March, Adams Papers.

TUESDAY 19TH.

Clouds and cold with a high Easterly wind. To Quincy. Afternoon and evening at home.

After going down into State Street for half an hour, finding that Mr. Hobart had come in as I had arranged,[1] I immediately proceeded to Quincy. I went time enough to give me half an hour to look about my place at Quincy, but it seemed so cheerless I was glad to get away. There is no attraction to me in the country in the winter season, however much I delight in it in summer.

At the appointed time I went to the vault in the grave yard, and found there Mr. Hobart just arrived with the body. Mr. Harrod and I. Hull Adams soon joined us accompanied by Mr. Lunt. This gentleman made a short and feeling prayer and then the remains of Thomas were gathered to those of the rest of his family. Poor fellow, no more deserving member is to be found there. I could not avoid reflecting upon the vanity of human expectations and the necessity of unlimited submission and trust in the divine decree.

I went into the vault and saw there the coffins as they remain still in very good preservation of the various members of the family who have died during the present century, with the exception of my grandfather and grandmother who lie under the Church. There are my two brothers both of whom died far from this place and both of whom have been returned to it as Thomas is. My uncle Thomas, and aunt Smith, Louisa Smith's mother, and a child of Mrs. T. B. Adams, and two besides whom I do not remember.[2] As Hull told us his mother was not yet informed of this event and he feared the effect of her seeing us, we returned directly to town. I got home chilled at three o'clock.

Afternoon reading Gibbon. Did nothing else. I shun writing. Evening W. C. Gorham called and spent an hour. He is a thinking young man but is in a bad school for this country. He is too English.[3] Read Gibbon's celebrated fifteenth Chapter. What a labour it must have cost to overlook the primary causes of the spread of the Christian faith in order to magnify the secondary ones.

[1] Hobart, or Hubbard, was the sexton of the First Parish, Quincy; see vols. 3:84; 6:107.

[2] The remaining two were AA's sister, Mary Smith Cranch, and her husband, Richard. "Aunt Smith" was Mrs. William Stephens Smith (AA2); Louisa Smith's mother was Catherine Louisa (Salmon) Smith. CFA had earlier had to preside at the interments of GWA, TBA, and JA2; see vols. 3:85; 4:260; 6:107.

[3] An earlier view of W. C. Gorham is at vol. 6:109.

WEDNESDAY 20TH.

Cloudy and dull. Time divided as usual.

I was very busy all the morning in making up the fourth and last of my numbers which has been long delayed. I perpetually ask of myself why I write them at all for nobody in this country cares a sixpence about any thing but his personal advancement. And the ambitious men jostle one another all the time to the edification of all lookers on.

Philoctetes. Gibbons, sixteenth chapter. An amazing master of his weapons but used in a bad cause. The History has failed in it's effect upon the Christian religion. Evening at home. Reading to my Wife of Nicholas Nickleby, part of a fashionable novel.[1] On with Burr.

[1] Charles Dickens' *Life and Adventures of Nicholas Nickleby* had been appearing in monthly numbers in London since April 1838. The numbers would end in Oct. 1839 with book publication in the same month.

THURSDAY 21ST.

Rain and clouds and darkness. Time as usual. Evening at Mr. Brooks'.

I worked hard this morning and made out to finish the fourth and last number of my papers, which after once reading over I sent to the

Courier. It pleases me much but I do not find that it pleases any body else, or excites even a passing thought. Was there ever a young man who exerted his powers to so little purpose? I have laboured much upon these and yet not a soul will feel the wiser.

Home to read Philoctetes. Afternoon finished the sixteenth chapter of Gibbon which excites in me nothing but disgust, and continued at work upon the MS. I have now disposed of all of the first class of papers.

Evening, notwithstanding the rain I went to see Mr. Brooks, hearing he had been confined two days at home with a cold. He seemed very well and cheerful. Home, on with Burr.

FRIDAY. 22D.

Cloudy but clearing. Office. Nickleby. Philoctetes. China. Evening at Mr. Brooks'.

My day at the Office today was full of laziness. This I took out of pure revenge for my work on preceding days and more particularly yesterday. Read part of the Novel of Nickleby which is much after the style of all other of the works of that writer, highly unnatural, and overdrawn. It is the sardonic laugh at the miseries of human kind.

Continue Philoctetes. I. Hull Adams and his friend Campbell dined with me. Read a portion of an Essay upon the Chinese in the Library of Entertaining Knowledge, prepared in so very slovenly a manner that I confess I wonder a little at its being ushered forth in such presence. The subject is curious.

Evening, Mrs. Adams and I to Mr. Brooks' where were the female branches of the family. On with Burr.

SATURDAY 23D.

Clear. Office. Time as usual. Evening at home.

At the Office I did little or nothing. My last paper upon Currency was published and adds one more to the list of fruitless efforts. I read it over today and am confirmed in my belief that it is good, even though I stand alone in it.

Walk round the South Cove to watch the improvements going on in the property. My stake in it makes me feel anxious in these times of difficulty.

Finished Philoctetes, a remarkable specimen of the ancient Greek drama as it has hardly any plot at all. The dialogue is extremely rapid and the text easy. I shall therefore omit a Review of it and instead, go on to the Trachinians with a view of reading all the rest of Sophocles this winter. Afternoon, the Chinese. On with Burr.

SUNDAY 24TH.

Fine day. Exercises as usual. Evening, visiters at home.

I continued my exercises with my little girl this morning, and she read two chapters of Genesis and committed another part of a hymn of Watts. I also went on with Burr. I find the morning the best time for composition and hence I shall take down [to] the Office this draft of my Article which does not satisfy me as it now stands and write it over there.

Attended divine service and heard Dr. Frothingham preach from Matthew 21. 8. "And a very great multitude spread their garments in the way. Others cut down branches from the trees and strewed them in the way." An occasional discourse in commemoration of Palm Sunday, very beautifully composed. Also from the same chapter in the afternoon four verses below, relating the act of Christ in driving the money changers out of the temple at Jerusalem. I recollected this sermon well, and it's peculiar view of the energy, zeal and activity of the Saviour.

Read a sermon of Dr. Herring, in the British Preacher from Luke 10. 36.37. "Which now of these three thinkest thou was neighbor unto him that fell among thieves? And he said, he that showed mercy on him. Then said Jesus unto him, Go and do thou likewise." Upon the parable of the good Samaritan which has much of a lesson in it to every man at this day.

Evening, Edmund Quincy took tea with us and after he went, H. Gardiner Gorham spent an hour or two in conversation. After which I on with Burr. Heavy. Heavy. Heavy.

MONDAY 25TH.

Day fine. Time divided as usual. Evening at Mrs. Everett's.

My time at the Office is now a little on my hands and I am not sure that I make the very best use of it. Walk and Accounts. Began today the play of the Trachinians, founded upon the death of Hercules the great giant killer of antiquity.

Afternoon the Chinese, a remarkable people whose history is really worth studying. There is something a little extraordinary in the fact of the opposition of the habits and manners and customs of the two most civilized races of the world, the European of the Caucasus, and the Asiatic Mongol. We settle it however in America that we know every thing, and the rest of the world is benighted. Happy self-complacency which each Nation cultivates towards all the rest.

Evening at Mrs. Everett's where we had a few of the family and nothing new. Burr.

TUESDAY 26TH.

Fine day. Office. Conant to settle. Evening at home.

At the Office. Call at Mr. Foster's Store to settle the charges of freight for poor T. B. Adams and to bring his affairs more gradually to a close. Accounts, home, the Trachinians. Miss L. C. Smith at our house to dine.

Silas Conant kept me all the afternoon discussing the question of his damage to the Weston farm. The attachment has brought him up as I expected it would. He was accompanied by his under tenant Fuller. After a full discussion of the merits of the case, he paid me my demand being two hundred dollars besides the year's rent, and I gave him a receipt in full. Thus is that matter off my mind. But I fear I shall yet have some trouble with it and seriously meditate recommending to my father a surrender to the reversionary heirs.[1]

Mr. Brooks spent the evening with us. On with Burr.

[1] That is, to the heirs of Ward Nicholas Boylston, from whom JQA had received the devise; see vol. 2:228, 244.

WEDNESDAY 27TH.

Mild day. Office. Time as usual. Evening to Mr. Shaw's.

Called for Mr. Brooks and we went to see a collection of plants from France, some of which I desire to buy for Quincy. Then Office where I did not much. Looking over Accounts and into probabilities. I undertake rather more than I ought.

Trachinians. Afternoon, Chinese. I am much interested in them and think I will make them the subject of a Lecture if I should ever again be expected to deliver one.

Evening at Mr. Robert G. Shaw's at a Levee made by him of members of the Legislature and others. I found there many gentlemen who greeted me with great cheerfulness and one or two spoke to me of my papers. So that I have not entirely thrown away my labours. My headway is not rapid but it is gradual and safe. Abbott Lawrence *puffed* which seemed to me hollow. T. W. Ward less fulsome but I think more sincere. Home early. On with Burr.

THURSDAY 28TH.

Fine day. Fast. Morning service. Afternoon at home. Evening visit at Mrs. Minots.

The day was pleasant as is almost always the case so far as my experience is concerned when the annual fast has been appointed. But it did not seem to me so lively. The streets were less full and the common less animated.

Attended divine service in the morning and heard Dr. Frothingham preach a Sermon from Isaiah 22. 12.13. "And in that day did the Lord God of hosts call to weeping and to mourning and to baldness and to girding with sackcloth. And behold joy and gladness slaying oxen and killing sheep, eating flesh and drinking wine, let us eat, and drink for tomorrow we shall die." The misuse of the purposes of this day has been frequently the topic of the Drs. late discourses on this occasion and very justly. The people of this State are by no means a people who now feel what the Puritans two centuries ago felt, the necessity of self-mortification. Yet I have liked the day for its quietness and for the appearance of sports among the male population which we so seldom else see.

I took a walk, but my dinner was quiet and simple and not as it has been for some preceding years attended by friends. Davis and Walsh are both gone from us, and the reflection made me feel a little melancholy. I made good use of my afternoon however in a long stretch upon Burr.

Evening Mrs. Adams and I paid a visit to Mrs. Minot who has made her acquaintance. Home early. Burr.

FRIDAY 29TH.

Dark and damp. Distribution as ordinary. Evening at home.

The accounts from Maine are at last pacific, but the apprehensions now are respecting all the intelligence to arrive from Great Britain. Stocks are falling, there is much want of confidence in the money market and evidence of serious derangement in the Banking system of the Southwest. Well, the game is not yet out. ·

Time at Office rather wasted. Walk and purchase plants for Quincy. The Trachinians. After dinner, the Chinese, and in the evening, French and Burr. Nothing can be more quiet than the present state of our life. When I finish this interminable review my Winter's work is done, and Heighho for Spring labours.

SATURDAY 30TH.

A beautiful day. Time divided as usual. Evening spent at home.

I do not well know what I did with my time but presume it was usefully employed. Nothing of much interest occurred today and I have no particular record to make. At home studying the Trachinians. After dinner the Chinese, and evening Nicholas Nickleby and Burr.

SUNDAY. 31ST.

Clear and cool. Exercises as usual. Evening at Edward Brooks'.

I devoted the morning hour as usual to my little girl who read two Chapters in Genesis, committed to memory a hymn of Watts and read one of Mrs. Barbauld's Hymns for children in prose.[1]

Attended divine service and heard Dr. Frothingham preach a Sermon concerning Easter. Revelation 1. 10.18. "I was in the spirit on the Lord's day and heard behind me a great voice saying I am he that liveth and was dead, and behold I am alive for evermore. Amen." The anniversary of the Resurrection is among the most interesting of the church festivals. It recals the history of those three days during which all of the hopes of mankind drawn from a positive revelation of a future state were and are founded. After dinner a dull discourse upon the evidences from Mr. Green. John 20. 29. "Jesus saith unto him Thomas, because thou hast seen me, thou hast believed; blessed are they that have not seen and yet have believed."

Read in the English preacher a sermon by Mr. Fothergill from Genesis 20. 11. "And Abraham said, because I thought surely the fear of God is not in that place: and they will slay me for my Wife's sake." A discourse upon the foundation of society which he maintains to be religious feeling. No doubt, moral restraint is the greatest help to the civil authority.

Evening to Edward Brooks' as usual. The town much surprised to hear of the resignation of Nicholas Biddle and withdrawal from the Bank of the United States.[2] This is very extraordinary and needs explanation.

---

[1] A copy of Anna Letitia Barbauld's "Hymns in Prose for Children" is in her *Works* (vol. 3, Boston, 1826) at MQA.

[2] Nicholas Biddle's letter of 29 March, resigning as president of the Bank of the United States in Philadelphia, appeared in the *Boston Courier* on 1 April, p. 3, col. 3.

MONDAY. APRIL 1.

Cool and extremely windy. Office. Afternoon to a funeral at Charlestown.

As this was the first day of a new quarter I was much occupied in collecting Dividends and in going over accounts. For this purpose took a walk to the Washington Bank as usual.

The letter of Mr. Biddle resigning is a quiet composed one as his always are. But taking into consideration the case of the Vicksburg Bank, the panic in Philadelphia, the fall of the price of Bank shares in New York since January I cannot help regarding the fact as of more importance than it looks. But it is clear we must find out for ourselves.

The Trachinians. After noon I walked over to Charlestown and attended the funeral of an Aunt of my Wife's, Mrs. Bartlett who died aged 72.[1] I have never seen her. She has been an invalid for many years and retired from all her friends. Home with Edward Brooks. Finished the Chinese. Evening at home. Robinson Crusoe to the children and finished Burr.

[1] Mrs. George Bartlett (Mary Gorham), a sister of Mrs. Peter C. Brooks; see vol. 2:168.

TUESDAY 2D.

Cool and clear. Distribution as usual. Evening at home.

My time at the Office was again much taken up in Accounts. Paid off one of my Notes of the South Cove Company making the third. There are two left about which I propose to make arrangement as soon as possible. For that debt worries me a good deal. The State of the Stock market is such as to disable me from converting any thing that I possess to advantage. I have nevertheless so far done wonders and hope I shall continue and persevere.

Continue Greek. After dinner read another publication of the Library of Entertaining Knowledge being the Search for Knowledge under difficulties. The instances are too much crowded for the memory. Evening at home. Read over Burr and was disgusted. O dear!

WEDNESDAY 3D.

Cloudy and cold. Morning to Quincy. Day as usual.

The day was not pleasant but I felt obliged to go and attend to my affairs at Quincy which now begin to press upon me. My Wife went with me and stopped at Mrs. T. B. Adams's. My morning was consumed in writing down tasks and seeing workmen. The ground however looks cold and the country ungenial. Called and transacted business with Mrs. Adams and Elizabeth and then glad to get home.

Afternoon, the pursuit of knowledge under difficulties, a work calculated to be somewhat useful. Evening at home. Read to my Wife a part of my Article upon Burr and was a little better pleased with it. Gardiner Gorham came in and stopped it. Afterwards, Read Sparks' Life of Washington.

THURSDAY 4TH.

Very fine day. Distribution as usual. Evening at home.

At the Office whither I transferred my Review with the design of writing it out and improving upon it. But I am yet so taken up with business matters as to be unable to attend to it. My father is to deliver an Address before the Historical Society at New York on the 30th inst. so that he will be here a day or two after.[1] I must therefore get ready for him.

Walk round to see the florists and purchase one or two more plants of them. Continue the Trachinians. After dinner, the pursuit of knowledge. It revives in me my ambition which prosperity will sometimes deaden. I have seen plenty of instances of the pursuit of knowledge under difficulties made by poverty and low birth but I wish to see more of those carried on under discouragements of a higher kind. Evening at home. Continued Sparks' dull book.

[1] This advice contained in LCA to CFA, 31 March, Adams Papers.

FRIDAY. 5TH.

Fine day. Distribution as usual. Evening, visit Mrs. Blake's.

At the Office where however I had a visit from I. Hull Adams which disabled me from doing any thing about Burr. Communicated with him respecting the affairs of T. B. Adams but settled nothing. Time in fact wasted.

Continued the Trachinians, and after dinner the pursuit of knowledge. A man may be learned and not be useful. The thing is to combine the two.

In the evening Mrs. Adams and I called at Mr. Otis' to see Mrs. Ritchie but finding her not at home we went to see Mr. and Mrs. Ed. Blake, with whom we had a very pleasant evening. And looked over some engravings of Paine's. There are a collection of Morghen's which are very valuable.[1] Heads of painters most of whom however I have in

the British Gallery, the collection of which is at Quincy.[2] Home at ten.
Sparks.

[1] The engravers are probably James Paine, English 18th-century delineator of city and architectural subjects, and Rafaello Morghen, Italian, who specialized in reproductions of masterpieces of paint-ing.

[2] *Gallery of Portraits: with Memoirs*, 7 vols., London, 1833–1837; CFA's bookplate is in the set.

SATURDAY. 6TH.

Fine day. Time as usual.

I have very little to say concerning my use of time today beyond what I must every day record. At my Office I had some business to transact and accounts to look over, and as usual time to waste. Went home in time to study the Trachinians. I certainly find much greater facility than formerly in reading Greek which satisfies me my time is not thrown away. This piece turns entirely upon love and jealousy.

After dinner, the pursuit of knowledge. This is a very interesting piece of composition. The more I reflect upon the matter the more my mind is led to the conclusion that political fame is not all in all. There appear to be so many barriers in the way of my progress in this direction that I believe I will cut all prospect of official success and enlarge my mind into the theories and practice of the world. I meditate now entering upon a course of study upon Government with a view to a series of lectures in two or three years.

Evening at home. Sparks.

SUNDAY 7TH.

Beautiful day. Time given to exercises as usual. Evening at Mrs. Frothingham's.

I spent the morning hour with my daughter, in reading two chapters in the book of Genesis, hearing her repeat a hymn of Watts and one of Mrs. Barbauld.

Attended divine service and heard Dr. Frothingham preach from Luke 6. 26. "Wo unto you when all men shall speak well of you." An admirable discourse upon the value of fame, with allusions to the classes of men some of which seek too much to run counter to the opinion of the world and others follow it implicitly. I could not help thinking the Dr. had in his mind as models for his description my father and Governor Everett who are indeed antipodes in this respect. He went on to recommend an adherence to the strict rule of uprightness in conduct respecting public opinion as often right without obeying it when certainly wrong which did me good because it encouraged me to persevere in a course of conduct which I have selected very much upon the principle laid down. Afternoon, Matthew 16. 6. "Then Jesus said unto them Take heed and beware of the leaven of the Pharisees and of the Sadduces."

Read a discourse in the English Preacher by Mr. Gough upon the necessity of virtue in all things. James 2. 11. "For he that said do not commit adultery said also do not kill. Now if thou commit no adultery, yet if thou kill, thou art become a transgressor of the law." A sensible discourse upon this difficult text. Finished the pursuit of knowledge, and on the whole have received an impulse from it.

Evening at Mrs. Frothingham's where were the Wales family. He goes tomorrow for a week or two to New York.

MONDAY 8TH.

Windy and cool. Distribution as usual. Evening at home.

I was at the Office this morning somewhat earlier and sat down resolutely to work upon Burr. Made a beginning which I liked and on the whole found an advantage in morning work. If I could, I would divide my day, into three parts. Morning, for the hard work of composition. Afternoon for relaxation, either by reading or exercise. Evening for reading and meditation. But business calls and money affairs, the newspapers and politics make sad interruptions. Never mind. I will keep on trying.

The Trachinians. Afternoon, Chevaliers book upon the United States,[1] very clever and very French. Evening quiet at home.

[1] Michel Chevalier, *Society, Manners, and Politics in the United States*, transl. T. G. Bradford, Boston, 1839.

TUESDAY 9TH.

Pleasant. Morning to Quincy. Afternoon at home. Evening, W. C. Gorham came in.

I went to Quincy this morning and was fully occupied in attending to the various people whom I am setting in motion. Found my drain in progress slowly, contracted with the man about my wall, directed the Carpenter and worked with Mr. Kirk in setting the plants which I have either had purchased or brought out to me. I had barely time to execute every thing and get into town to dinner.

Afternoon, Chevalier, with whose book I am pleased although it is more superficial than Tocqueville's. Evening, W. C. Gorham came in before going on a voyage. He is intelligent and pleasant.

WEDNESDAY 10TH.

Day fine. Time divided as usual. Evening Mr. Brooks.

I made another good morning's work upon Burr today and begin to feel encouraged. There is nothing more curious in the world than the alternation of hope and fear in the labour of composition. While the mind is fresh and warm it is all hope, cooler moments make the defects glaring.

The Trachinians, the least pleasant of all the Tragedies of Sophocles which I have read. The character of Hercules is a mingled one of virtues and defects in which the latter too much predominate, and his death hardly produces sympathy because accompanied with so little heroism in dying.

Afternoon reading a Novel called Fielding by a man who has done better.[1] He is over political and tory. Mr. Brooks spent an hour with us.

[1] Robert Plumer Ward, *Fielding*, 3 vols., Phila., 1837. Ward's earlier works included *Tremaine, DeVere,* and *Sterling.* However, CFA would seem to be alluding to his *Historical Essay on the Revolution of 1688,* 2 vols., London, 1838, and to his *An Enquiry into the Foundation and History of the Law of Nations in Europe,* 2 vols., Dublin, 1795. JQA's copy of the latter is in MQA.

THURSDAY 11TH.

Cloudy and warm but no rain. Distribution as usual. Evening at Mrs. Carter's.

Continued my work today. If I can go on at this rate I shall soon wind up this business. The times are again so quiet that I have only to strain a point a little to get rid of all trouble about this article before I go into the Country.

Finished the Trachinians which I shall not review at present, so that I shall be able to embrace the last of the plays of Sophocles within my winter's work. Well done. This is encouraging.

Afternoon the second volume of Chevalier, the first half of the first dissertation of Spanheim upon ancient coins.[1] Evening to Mrs. Carter's where my Wife was asked to drink tea. Mr. and Mrs. Seaver, and Miss Sigourney there.

[1] E. Spanheim, *Dissertationes de praestantia et usu numismatum antiquorum,* Amsterdam, 1671. JQA's bookplate is in the copy at MQA.

FRIDAY 12TH.

Heavy rain all day. Distribution as usual. Evening at home.

We had more rain today than we have experienced for a long time back. And it was acceptable both to the farmer and the citizen. I went on vigorously with my occupation and made great headway with Burr. The facility with which I write in the morning is among the curious things.

Home to Ajax which I began. In making a play out of the madness of a man who kills sheep while he thinks himself slaughtering men, Sophocles assumes for tragedy much the same basis which Cervantes takes for ridicule in Don Quixote.

After dinner, finished the first Dissertation of Spanheim de præstantia et usu numismatum veterum which is rather about the former than the latter.[1] Continued Chevalier also, who treats more of France than America in his later letters. Evening at home reading one of Theodore Hook's silly novels,[2] and finished Mr. Ward's Fielding which I think poor.

[1] That is, rather about the excellence than the use of ancient coins.
[2] Theodore Edward Hook's earlier novels included *Maxwell*, 2 vols., N.Y., 1831, and *Plebeians and Patricians*, 2 vols., Phila., 1836.

SATURDAY 13TH.

Continued rain. Distribution as usual. Evening at home.

I was little interrupted and therefore made good work upon Burr. The rain which continues as if making up for lost time kept people away and prevented any temptation to go out.

A shocking accident today upon the Worcester Railroad causing the death of Mr. Curtis the Railroad Agent. Chevalier's remark about the indifference to human life in the United States is very just. The public passes on over the bodies of the killed just like a regiment of veterans in battle. The railways will not transport a man less nor will people cease on account of this to put their heads out of the windows.

Continued Ajax. Afternoon Chevalier. Evening at home reading to my Wife.

SUNDAY. 14TH.

A continuation of clouds and rain. Division as on this day. Evening at home.

I devoted some time as usual to my daughter's morning exercises,

216

and began to read Professor Tucker's life of Mr. Jefferson. This work was written with a view to soften the effects of the publication of the papers by the grandson.[1] I must follow up my study of American history for after all if providence should continue my life, the great object of it will be perhaps to write upon it.

Attended divine service and heard a man by the name of Holland settled in Brooklyn, New York. John 6. 12. "Gather up the fragments that remain, that nothing be lost." An economical, prudential discourse much in the Essay style of the day and in the worst possible taste for the pulpit. John 17. 21. "That they all may be one." This was in a better spirit, and instead of viewing the text in a doctrinal way, he regarded it as promising unity of Christian feeling to the destruction of all sects. There is something just and for aught I know, original in this application.

Read a Sermon of Dr. Clarke. Revelations 3. 15.16. "I know thy works, that thou art neither cold nor hot: I would thou wert cold or hot." A good Sermon upon zeal. Evening quietly at home.

[1] George Tucker, *Life of Thomas Jefferson*, 2 vols., Phila., 1837. Jefferson's "papers" had been published by his grandson Thomas Jefferson Randolph in 1829; see entry for 14 Feb., above.

MONDAY 15TH.

Bad weather continues. Distribution as usual. Evening at home.

I worked again upon Burr, although neither so long nor so effectively as last week. As I proceed the task becomes more difficult and I am not so well prepared in my mind. Much that I think of, I reject.

At the Athenæum also where I procure books upon currency. I wish to extend my information upon the subject. Several pamphlets I find, which may be of some use. Home late and read Ajax superficially. This is bad.

Afternoon reading a part of Spanheims Second Dissertation upon the value of coins as a study, and the pamphlets already mentioned caused by the distress of 1837. Evening at home. I read Robinson Crusoe to the children one hour. Continue Tucker.

TUESDAY 16TH.

Cleared very fine. Distribution as usual. Afternoon, Athenæum. Evening to Mr. Brooks'.

I intended to have gone on with Burr this morning vigorously but I only did enough to convince me I must go backward and write over a sheet, and in the mean time go down to the Athenæum to get some more information in which I am deficient.

Several applications. Among others Mr. Freeman Hunt who is about publishing a new Magazine of Commerce in New York and who wishes to procure contributions from persons of reputation. He comes to me upon the recommendation of Henry Lee. I told him I would help him with pleasure but I had to finish first an article for the North American Review. He said his first number was to come out on the first of June. I told him that I might get an article ready in time for it, but could not promise as I must first get through Burr and must get my information. He promised to procure for me what I wanted and would see me again.

Winch here too, the new tenant from Weston, so I lost my hour for Ajax but made it up in the Afternoon. Against my custom I went to the Athenæum and supplied to myself the facts which I wanted to know. Fell upon the Cunningham Correspondence there and looked over the letters which are curious enough,[1] they however tell the truth, which has always been very unsavoury in America. Evening to Mr. Brooks' where were the family together.

[1] The partisan and impolitic letters written by JA between 1803 and 1810 to his cousin William Cunningham were published after Cunningham's death by his son as *Correspondence between the Hon. John Adams and the late William Cunningham, Esq.*, Boston, 1823. Publication opened old wounds and reopened bitter controversies; see vol. 1:146 and JA, *Works*, 1:628–629.

WEDNESDAY. 17TH.

Rain again. Distribution as usual. Evening at home.

Stormy days are favorable for me. I worked over the bad part of the last Sheet so as to please me much better, but did not after all quite get up to the place where I had left off. At this rate I do not know when I shall finish. The rain is very provoking. It puts back all my work prodigiously.

The Great Western has at last arrived and quieted the panic that has been raised about War. The accounts are not at all decisive however of the course which the British Government may pursue.

Ajax about one hundred and twenty lines. Afternoon the remainder of Spanheim's Second Dissertation, and part of a pamphlet treatise upon the system of coining in Great Britain. This is a subject which I must look into rather more fully than I have yet done. Evening, Tucker's Jefferson.

THURSDAY 18TH.

Morning cloudy but cleared. Division as usual. Afternoon Railway to Brighton. Evening at home.

I did something in the matter of my Review this morning although the ideas did not flow quite as freely as they sometimes do. Indeed the political history is the most difficult as it involves the reputation of the Review for fairness.

Saw Mr. Hunt again today who gave me Professor Tucker's new work on Banking with a request that I would look it over.[1] Home to read Ajax which was however clipped of it's fair proportion.

After dinner I executed my long meditated design of going to a Nursery for trees but instead of getting to Kenricks which I find some distance from the Railroad station, I went to Winship's at Brighton which is directly upon it. I did this only from a belief in it's necessity and by no means from inclination inasmuch as I had always much disliked the manners of the men who manage it. I succeeded better today in getting trees as I saw a nephew who was more accommodating.[2] My boy John went with me but we had a little superfluity of time before the train came back which hung upon our hands. We got home by seven where we found Mr. Brooks who passed an hour. Evening, Tucker.

[1] George Tucker was a long-time professor at the University of Virginia. The biography of Jefferson is the best known of his many published works on a variety of subjects (*DAB*). A copy of his *The* *Theory of Money and Banks Investigated,* Boston, 1839, is at MQA.

[2] For CFA's earlier experience at the nursery of Jonathan and Francis Winship, see above, entry for 13 April 1837.

FRIDAY 19TH.

Beautiful day. Morning to Quincy. Afternoon at home. Pamphlets. Evening, Dr. Gorham.

I expected Kirk with my horse early this morning so that I could make a long day of it but by a curious error, he did not notify me until I had given him up. I improved the time however to do some business, and more particularly to make use of a balance accumulated upon hand to pay off another Mortgage of the number upon the South Cove lots. This is the last but one. The money to be sure is not mine but my fathers and in doing this I only save myself the interest until July which is however of importance. If the time shall come when I can convert my Market Bank Stock without loss I may then free myself from this load and patiently bide the time when the land will realize something in compensation. Perhaps my children may benefit from it.

At eleven o'clock, Kirk came in and we went to Quincy. Found every thing only half done and looking very discouraging. I feel worried whenever I go out and see how my place looks compared with other places. Worked for the short time left in setting plants and then home which I barely reached by dinner time.

Afternoon finished one of the Pamphlets upon coinage, and looked over a publication made in Philadelphia last year and containing many important statistics for the year of the suspension. Evening, Dr. J. W. Gorham spent an hour. Finished the 1st vol. of Tucker.

SATURDAY 20TH.

Clear but cool. Office. Afternoon at Quincy. Evening, visits.

The day was fine though windy and cold. At the Office I continued my labours with great steadiness considering every thing, made some progress but not enough. Mr. Hunt again here and anxious to know if I had read Tucker which I have not. Promised him I would look at it tomorrow.

Ajax. After dinner, to Quincy with my boy John. Found nobody at work. But I set about my part of the labour vigorously and succeeded before night in setting all the trees that I had procured excepting one bundle which was put away until Monday.

Home at sunset after calling at Mrs. Adams for a moment. Although fatigued I called with my Wife upon Mrs. Ritchie and not finding her at home we went to Edward Brooks where we spent the evening. Home to read Tucker.

SUNDAY. 21ST.

Cold east wind but clear. Services as usual. Evening visit to Mrs. Everett.

I passed an hour this morning in my usual exercises with Louisa. Tried to teach her the ten commandments. But she learnt three only imperfectly.

Attended divine service and heard Dr. Frothingham preach from that beautiful text in Ecclesiastes 12. 7. "Then shall the dust return to the earth as it was; and the spirit shall return unto God who gave it." I was disappointed in the sermon which is natural. I incline to think that the most beautiful and pithy sentences in the Bible are not those best calculated to amplify into discourses. The starting post is too lofty. There were allusions to the late melancholy accidents here and at Lowell which destroyed two useful men.

After dinner Dr. Palfrey from James 4. 14. "Ye know not what shall be on the morrow. For what is your life." The strain of reflection upon the nature of life and the predominance of it's good over it's evil is encouraging.

Read a Sermon of Dr. Clark in the English Preacher. Job. 23. 15. "Therefore am I troubled at his presence when I consider I am afraid of him." The difference between Religion and superstition.

In the evening Mrs. Adams and I went to Governor Everett's to pay an evening visit. I had much talk with the Governor about the MS in my possession which he wishes to see for the sake of some information respecting the North Eastern boundary.[1] Home to read Tucker.

[1] Perhaps the allusion is to JQA's message to the Congress in 1828, referred to in the entry of 4 March, above. However, CFA may be speaking in a more general way of JQA's papers of the same period.

MONDAY. 22D.

A lovely day. At Quincy all day. Home late. Evening fatigue.

I went to Quincy as soon as possible after breakfast, and worked there all day with Kirk in setting trees and bushes. I find in this manner that I execute a great deal, when if the work is left to others I find it only half done. I took about half an hour for a little dinner at home which I brought out with me, and devoted the rest of the time to labour. I succeeded in setting the remaining bundle from Winship's and in transferring great numbers of plants from the other house to cover a naked fence on the South side. Thus it was sunset when I was about halfway home. And I found myself pretty well tired out by evening.

TUESDAY 23D.

Fine day. Morning, Office. Afternoon Quincy. Evening to Mrs. H. B. Rogers'.

I made a little more headway upon Burr but not much. I am almost discouraged about it. I must increase the number of my working hours. For at this rate I shall get nothing done. Ajax for an hour.

Afternoon to Quincy where I kept on my work transferring trees to the bottom of the slope in front of my house. But I had so short a time to do it in that I could not finish.

Home late where I found Mr. Brooks, who took tea. After which we went to a small party at Mrs. H. B. Rogers'. A few persons to meet Mrs. John Rogers from Northampton. Middling dull.

WEDNESDAY 24TH.

Fine day. Morning to Quincy. Dinner company. Evening at home.

I went to Quincy again this morning and continued my work of transplanting trees. I removed a great number of Firs from the low ground to the edge of my new inclosure and one or two larger trees. The men were at work upon the wall so that once again every thing seems to be in operation. I finished this morning the heavy part of the transplanting and have now only to replace some particular trees, which have died. The past week has advanced matters wonderfully at Quincy. We have been favored by weather and my personal attention has been beneficial.

Home to meet some gentlemen I had invited to dinner, to meet I. Hull Adams and Mr. Campbell. Present Dr. Frothingham, Mr. Joy, H. B. Rogers, Dr. Gorham and the two gentlemen. A pleasant dinner. They sung well but I am afraid nearly all of us drank a little too much wine for convenience. There is a sort of conviviality in music that renders it exceedingly dangerous. It makes one forget the limits of prudence a little.

THURSDAY 25TH.

Fine warm day. Morning Office. Afternoon Quincy. Evening at Mrs. Minot's.

It was a very agreeable morning, but I was not in much condition to enjoy it as I was slightly suffering from the excess of last evening. To me all the pleasure of a social meeting is very poor compensation for the feeling of dissatisfaction which it brings with it, the lassitude and inability to set about the usual occupations with relish. I was not able to do much of the work which is really pressing upon me, and so limited myself to accounts and reading a long letter of my father's which appeared in the Intelligencer, in which Mr. Otis is answered among others.[1]

Home. Ajax. Afternoon to Quincy, but my work was cut off by a heavy thunder shower. The improvements in the old house are going on simultaneously with all the rest. The shower prevented my getting home until quite late when we went to Mrs. Minot's. The Quincy family, but it was uncommon dull. Home at eleven.

[1] In the *National Intelligencer* for 23 April (p. 2, col. 1 – p. 3, col. 1) appeared JQA's letter "to the Citizens of the United States, whose petitions ... have been entrusted to me, to be presented to the House of Representatives ... at the Third Session of the 25th Congress." In it he reported that those 825 petitions had received "very little attention from the House" because by adoption of the Atherton Resolutions of 12 Dec. 1838 all antislavery petitions were required to be laid on the table "without reading, printing, or debating." He proceeded to attack the Resolutions as annihilating not only "the right of petition, but the freedom of speech in the House." Defending his position that the Resolutions were in violation of the Constitution, he undertook also to reply to arguments that had been advanced especially in state legislatures to defeat efforts to record their opposition to the "gag" rules.

One such formulation that had attracted favorable notice recently and that JQA addressed himself to was that made by John Whipple in January in a minority report to the Rhode Island legislature. On 1 March, Harrison Gray Otis had written to Whipple: "Had I been a member of Congress ... I should not have voted for the [Atherton Resolutions]. At the same time, I have no doubt of the constitutional power of the House to adopt them.... Had I been a member of the Rhode Island Legislature, I should have been found on your side.... It is one thing for Congress to refuse to act upon a petition, and another thing for a State Legislature to deny the right of the former to regulate its own proceedings." The *Intelligencer* printed Whipple's report along with JQA's letter (p. 1, cols. 2–6), and Otis' letter to Whipple on the 25th, p. 4, cols. 3–5. See also JQA, Diary, 17 April, and JQA to CFA, 23 April, Adams Papers.

FRIDAY. 26TH.

Fine day. Regular distribution. Evening Mr. Brooks, at home.

I was at the Office today and worked pretty vigorously upon my Review, but the work goes slow. I am not sure whether Dr. Palfrey will publish it after all.

Read Ajax which I am desirous to finish before I leave town. The play is remarkable as departing in many respects from the strict rules of the Unities, and also for its singular combination of power and absurdity. The speech of Tecmessa[1] strikes me as superior to the more celebrated one of Ajax to his sword. This is a soliloquy the only one in Sophocles that remains to us.

After dinner studying a Pamphlet by a Mr. Quin in the Financial Register.[2] Evening, my Wife went to Medford, and I devoted the time to a draft of a paper for Mr. Hunt's Magazine. Mr. Brooks spent an hour with me.

[1] In the *Ajax* by Sophocles, a Phrygian king suffers the loss of his domain and the captivity of his daughter Tecmessa, who is taken by Ajax, lives with him, and by him has a son.

[2] A periodical published in Philadelphia from July 1837 to Dec. 1838 by Condy Raguet, on whom see below, entry for 15 May.

SATURDAY 27TH.

Fine day and warm. Morning as usual. After dinner to Quincy. Evening at home.

I was at the Office but unable to execute as much of my Review as I wished. This matter now begins to press and I must resort to some mode of hurrying myself. What with Mr. Hunt and Dr. Palfrey and my House and the Agency affairs, I am rather driven.

Home to read a little of Ajax. I have now arrived very nearly the termination and yet shall probably find it more difficult to reach that than going all the preceding way.

After dinner I went to Quincy, the wind being mild and allowing a dismissal of the surtout. I however attended as well as I could to what was left to be done. The man to build the wall was there and announced a deficiency in material.

Home late. Short evening. I went to work upon the final draft of the paper for Mr. Hunt and executed a large part of it but not the whole. The deficiency is in the necessity of consuming much time, occasionally to hunt up small facts.

SUNDAY 28TH.

Cold east wind. Divine service as usual. Evening at home.

I occupied most of my leisure hours today in writing upon the Essay which I promised to Mr. Hunt. To this end I devoted the hours of the evening which I have formerly spent in the family.

Attended divine service and heard Dr. Frothingham preach from Luke 6. 19. "There went virtue out of him and healed them all." Also from 1. Corinthians 1. 27. "God hath chosen the weak things of the world to confound the things which are mighty." This last very good discourse, I have heard before.

Read also a Sermon in the English Preacher by   from 2. Samuel 19. 34. "And Barzillai said unto the King, how long have I to live that I should go up with the king unto Jerusalem." My mind was perhaps too much occupied with matters wholly foreign to pay so much attention as I should have done.

[*New York*]

MONDAY 29TH.

Cloudy and cold with rain. Morning to Quincy. After dinner to New York.

It was a cheerless looking day that I have rarely known worse at the season. I rode to Quincy and gave as many directions as I could respecting what was left to do but as the principal man upon the wall was not there I had to leave the procuring more stone until my return from New York. The rest of the details about the old house are also backward. Hurried them as much as I could and then returned to town.

The rain began and I felt particularly gloomy about going. It was ten years ago on this day that my poor brother George left this same place for New York which yet he never reached alive.[1] And I felt as if there was some danger in the coincidence. I yet felt that my father was alone and might need assistance if he found himself unable to do what he had engaged.[2] So the conflict between duty and inclination was quite trying.

I finally determined to go, being influenced quite as much by a wish to break down the superstitious fear of presentiment which in my life I never yet knew verified although I have often felt it as by the more obvious motives. Accordingly I started in the Railway cars for Providence and thence to Stonington, where we took the Steamer Rhode Island for New York. There were in company Dr. F Parkman, Rev. Messrs. Lunt and Robbins, and Capt. H. Oxnard, and I got along very pleasantly. General W. H. Sumner was also on board of the boat.

[1] See vol. 2:370–372.
[2] JQA had been in ill health, sometimes without voice, since the adjournment of Congress and while preparing his oration for delivery in New York (Diary).

TUESDAY 30TH.

Visits. My father's Address. Sidney Brooks. Evening, National Theatre.

I did not sleep much and could not help thinking when awake of the melancholy event which had happened ten years before on this route. It seemed to me as if some accident would happen to make the day memorable to the family. But the time wore away and at six o'clock we found ourselves at the foot of the Battery. Thus was dismissed one of those vain superstitious fears which when given way to would have an increasing force as we go on in life. I was glad to be rid of it.

Found my father at the Astor house. The morning was passed in making calls upon Mrs. DeWint, Sidney Brooks, A. Campbell and others, in which I was the longer that I knew not well the streets. This occasioned a delay of my getting to the Church where my father was to deliver his Oration. It was extremely full and I had to stand for some time, but a lady becoming tired in a Pew close by, I procured a seat comfortably. The oration of my father was more successful than I had expected. It was written with his usual force and inculcated his political doctrine with earnestness.[1] He was tolerably well heard and sustained his voice very uniformly to the end. The close brought down a continuation of loud applause. After it was over we returned to the Astor House.

I met Dr. Wilkes in the Church but upon my addressing him it seemed he had utterly forgotten me.[2] However upon our leaving his recollection had returned and he was correspondingly anxious to make up his error by pressing me to dine with him today and when I waived that he urged tomorrow to which I assented notwithstanding that I was to return to Boston in the afternoon. My father came in with President Duer of Columbia College and upon invitation I accompanied him to see the library of that Institution which seems a very respectable and carefully selected one. Thence home.

The Historical Society proposed to finish the day by a dinner but I received no invitation to it and did not think a ticket worth purchasing even if I had known they were for sale. I detest going as a mere pendant of another person and dislike dinners themselves too much to go myself. But my father who was anxious to have me invited went in a manner to give me reason to suppose I might be sent for, to avoid which I went out myself.

Called to see Mrs. Brooks and found her at dinner with her husband at a new French hotel in Broadway. They live in great luxury but I think are not happy from the restlessness of having no home. I spent a couple of hours with them in conversation and upon the coming in of two Italians, I left and walked up though tired enough to the National Theatre, where was performed the Mountain Sylph. Miss Shirreff, Mr. Wilson, Seguin and Mrs. Bailey. Some pretty airs but I was rather disappointed.[3] Home at ten very tired.

---

[1] JQA's oration before the New-York Historical Society, "The Jubilee of the Constitution," was published in the *Quincy Patriot* on 22 June; the MS is at MHi.

[2] An acquaintance made on CFA's trip to Niagara; see the entry for 30 June 1836, above.

[3] The new opera, *The Mountain Sylph* by Barnett, performed by Jane Shirreff, John Wilson, Edward Seguin, and Charlotte Watson Bailey, was one of the most popular theater pieces in New York during the 1838–1839 season (Odell, *Annals N.Y. Stage*, 4:20, 292–293, 301).

WEDNESDAY MAY 1.

Day dull and drizzly. Breakfast with Sidney Brooks. Visits, dine with Dr. Wilkes. Steamer Narragansett.

We went out, (that is my father and I) to breakfast by invitation with Sidney Brooks. A very pleasant time and a luxurious french breakfast. Leaving there, I passed the morning in making purchases and visits. Called to see Mrs. C. A. Davis, Mrs. E. Curtis and Mrs. N. Appleton. Saw them all. Also at noon accompanied my father to see the Exchange which is in no more finished condition for inspection than when I left it.[1] Glad to get out of Wall Street and home.

Went up at the time to Hudson Square the residence of Doctor Wilkes.[2] Found there Mr. and Mrs. Colden, Miss Wilkes of my former acquaintance, Mrs. Wilkes the elder, Mr. Hamilton Wilkes, his Wife and daughter and another brother. It seemed quite a collection of them. I felt a little awkwardly in being thus heralded into the midst of a family, but it was not to be helped so I did as well as I could.

My principle of late years has been always to try to feel at ease, which is hard struggling against my natural diffidence of temper. And circumstances throughout my life have always occurred to prevent my complete success. I never went out unexpectedly that it was not a contre temps, nor made a voluntary advance that it was not put down. Yet I have resisted the effects of these accidents and have been moreover assisted much in doing so by the happy event of my marriage. Without which I should have been incurably shy.

I was obliged to leave in the midst of dinner and hurry to the Steamer. It was the Narragansett and full of passengers. We started precisely at five and passed down the East River in a fog. Thus ended my visit to New York which seems to me to be growing a greater Babel than ever. Perhaps no city in the Union has made such unexampled progress, and if not put back by the bad elements of its poor population bids fair to be the London of America. I desire not to have much to do with it. The people are commercial, enterprising and industrious, but their moral tone is far from encouraging. Adventurers abound and the steady, old settlers occupy the back ground.

[1] The Merchants Exchange was being rebuilt after having been destroyed by fire a few days before CFA saw the remains on a visit to Wall Street and the surrounding area in 1835 (vol. 6:287; see also entry for 25 July, below).
[2] Hudson Square, then one of New York's most fashionable residential areas, was the site of St. John's Chapel, from which the square later became known as St. John's Park. The square was located on what is now Varick Street and was within the Trinity Church parish (Stokes, *Iconography of Manhattan Island*, 6 vols., N.Y., 1918, 3:608).

THURSDAY 2D.

Rain but afterwards cleared. Railway to Boston. Afternoon to Quincy. Evening at Mr. Otis'.

The fog was such that the boat could not attempt to enter Stonington until after daylight and indeed she only made her way along all night by soundings. There was thunder and lightning too. At about six we were transferred to the Cars and did not reach Boston until nearly noon. I went home directly and from thence to the Office.

Mr. Brooks and my father dined with me, after which the latter accompanied me to Quincy where I found things much in the same state in which I left them.

Returned home alone and went with my Wife by invitation to Mr. Otis's. Mrs. Ritchie had asked us again and I determined that this long delayed affair should be settled. It was a little company consisting of F. Dexter and his Wife, Mr. J. L. Motley and his Wife, Mr. and Miss Appleton, Mrs. Child, Mr. Inglis and T. G. Bradford. These were very few of my acquaintance and I felt awkwardly enough. But I was called to cards and this with a little supper finished the evening. Glad to get away however as I had slept little.

FRIDAY. 3D.

Clear day. Distribution as usual. Evening at home.

I devoted this day very much to the prosecution of my various occupations. Worked for some time upon Burr, which must now be done if it ever is. Read a little of Ajax not very thoroughly. And in the Afternoon I pursued the business of Mr. Hunt's Article which I finished by evening. This is not so extended nor so thorough as I had designed to make it. But the fact is that time has not enabled me to do it. Evening Gardiner Gorham with us until ten o'clock.

SATURDAY 4TH.

Clear day. Morning Office. Afternoon Quincy. Evening at home.

I kept on working as well as I could this morning although interrupted by one or two persons on business. The labour of this composition of Burr is greater than any thing I have undertaken and it makes me at times a little impatient. I am drawing however towards the end. Home to read Ajax.

After dinner, Mr. Brooks accompanied me to Quincy to see the progress I had made in improvements, and we passed a couple of hours and returned. He has purchased Mr. Webster's house,[1] and today he intimated his wish that my Wife could occupy it with him. Against this I should have no serious objection for the winter months but he desires a person to reside also in Summer at Medford which is not practicable for me. On the whole I prefer my present way of life but I am not so selfish as to make it a sine qua non as it regards my comfort. Mr. Webster is going to Europe and his friends again come forward to pay his debts and set him up. His career is entirely unexampled in our history. And it is much to be desired that it should never be imitated. Evening quietly at home.

[1] At the corner of Summer and High streets (*Boston Directory*, 1838).

SUNDAY. 5TH.

Windy and clouds. Divine service as usual. Evening at home.

I devoted an hour of the morning to the pursuit of my medallic studies for which I have not had much leisure this year, and another to my daughter Louisa as usual. Attended divine service and heard Dr. Frothingham preach from Genesis 7. 16. "And the Lord shut him in." A singular text enough nor did I gather much from the discourse. Afternoon Mr. Bartol from Daniel 5. 6. "Then the king's countenance was changed, and his thoughts troubled him, so that the joints of his loins were loosed and his knees smote one against another." An oratorical style with little at bottom but common place.

Read a Sermon by a Dr. Foster from Proverbs 30. 8.9. "Give me neither poverty nor riches, feed me with food convenient for me: lest I be full and deny thee, and say Who is the Lord? or lest I be poor and steal and take the name of my God in vain." Upon the middling condition in life as productive of virtue and happiness. A sensible discourse. Went on with Tuckers Life of Jefferson.

MONDAY 6TH.

Clear. Morning Office. Afternoon to Quincy.

At the Office working upon Burr which I am now finishing. Nothing else shall take precedence of this because it has been so long upon hand. Home a little late but went on with Ajax. After dinner my Wife accompanied me to Quincy together with my second boy. Found the men at work clearing rocks but having made exceedingly indifferent progress. They blow[1] tomorrow. I was not very well satisfied and manifested my sentiments. They go on tomorrow, but finish in the evening for I shall be exposed to severe expense otherwise in letting these men hang along. Home to tea. Short evening. Continued Tucker.

¹ That is, "blast"; see *OED*, 24, under "blow."

TUESDAY. 7TH.

Clear. Morning Office. Afternoon to Quincy. Evening to Mrs. Frothingham's.

I continued Burr today with so much assiduity as to bring me to the last Sheet which I propose to finish tomorrow. This work must be done and shall be done. Also Accounts and home to read Ajax.

Afternoon to Quincy. The men had made not much better progress in blowing than half what I think will be enough to do the remainder of the wall. But this has been a heavy and expensive business and I have my doubts whether I ought to have undertaken it. I earnestly hope that it will prove the last. Remained to tea and did not get home until after eight o'clock.

My Wife had engaged to go to Mrs. Frothingham's so I went directly there to meet her. Found Mr. and Mrs. J. E. Thayer. People whom I do not greatly fancy.

WEDNESDAY. 8TH.

Cloudy day. Morning Office. Afternoon to Quincy.

I this morning finished my last sketch of Burr. Good, bad or indifferent I am not going to trouble myself more about it. It is not worth the candle to play the game of reviewing. There are passages in this which I know are good but the average is below my usual force. Let it go and I will transfer myself to something else.

At home, finished Ajax, thus completing the plays of Sophocles. I admire them much. Perhaps this last one has single passages of the greatest power, but it is not so skilfully arranged as Œdipus King nor so highly poetical as Œdipus at Coloni, nor so pathetic as Antigone. On the whole, Sophocles is the most remarkable of all the poets of antiquity for the variety of his talent, from the high lyric to the most gentle and simple. I shall return to the study of him hereafter.

After dinner to Quincy. The workmen had completed their labour in blowing and now comes the getting out. I remained until sunset and did not get home until nearly nine. Fatigued and went to bed early.

May 1839

THURSDAY 9TH.

Morning cloudy but it cleared away hot. Afternoon to Quincy.

Morning at the Office engaged in Accounts, but on the whole luxuriating a little in idleness after my preceding labour. At noon with my Wife to see the Allston Gallery of Pictures now exhibiting.[1] A first glance only from which no definite opinions can be formed. I gather from it only that his style has of late degenerated into a bad manner. He is frittering his power into miserable unmeaning pictures of Rosalies and Beatrices, Jessicas and Troubadours, the manual execution of which cannot redeem their insignificance.[2]

After dinner to Quincy where the men were not at work. I sowed a few flower seeds and otherwise wasted my time.

Home by eight and found Sidney Brooks and Mrs. Frothingham there. This did not surprise me but when they went, my Wife communicated to me the account of the accident that had befallen our daughter, Louisa. In crossing the Street below our house, it seems she was run down by a carriage of some kind and taken up for dead, or seriously injured. But upon examination, the Dr. thinks she has escaped with some severe bruises. My God! I think even now of the precipice from which he has saved me, with a feeling of shudder. Trusting as I uniformly do in his protecting mercy, I feel conscious how little I deserve the overflowing measure of his bounty which has been awarded to me. And when I consider what a narrow escape this has been and how constantly we are all of us standing near to danger and destruction, my heart hardly furnishes to my head any distinct manifestation of it's feelings. I felt stunned as if the blow had not passed or as if I was not conscious of it's nature.

[1] Washington Allston had, from 1831 to his death in 1843, a large studio near his home in Cambridgeport to which many visitors came to view his paintings. However, CFA is here referring to the large and important retrospective exhibition of Allston's paintings being shown at the Chester Harding Gallery on School Street in Boston from 1 April to 10 July.

See William H. Gerdts and Theodore E. Stebbins Jr., "A Man of Genius": The Art of Washington Allston (1779–1843), Boston, 1979, p. 135, 173.

[2] Allston's Beatrice is reproduced in the present volume; on it, the other paintings CFA mentions from the exhibition, and on the exhibition itself, see the Descriptive List of Illustrations, above.

FRIDAY 10TH.

Clear day. Division as usual. Evening at Mrs. Frothingham's.

Louisa had a good night and although severely bruised appears not to be materially injured. There was a weight upon my spirit all day as if I hardly knew how to be sufficiently grateful for the mercy that had

4. *Beatrice,* BY WASHINGTON ALLSTON
See pages x–xi

been shown me. My daughter is thoughtless and selfwilled both of which qualities require from her parents a degree of supervision which she may fail of receiving. I must put my trust as I ever do in a superior power, fearing that I may not deserve to be always meeting with mercy rather than with judgment.

Office where I was rather indolent. Attended to accounts and read a little of the North American Review. Afternoon occupied in reading over my Article for Dr. Palfrey the last time. It dissatisfied me utterly. I think it poor and yet I have laboured upon it with pertinacity. Review writing is not my forte. It requires more time and labour than it is worth. I shall send it because I do not think it of any consequence whether it is published or not but I expect no gain to my reputation from it.[1]

Evening to Mrs. Frothingham's. A meeting of the members of the family including Sidney and his Wife who are here. Much as usual.

[1] The letter to the Rev. Palfrey accompanying the review of Matthew L. Davis' *Memoirs of Aaron Burr* and of his *Private Journal*, is in the Adams Papers. The review would appear in the July issue of the *North Amer. Rev.*, 49:155–206. Two drafts in CFA's hand are in the Adams Papers (M/CFA/23.1, Microfilms, Reel No. 317).

SATURDAY 11TH.

Fine day but cool. Time as usual. Evening at home.

Louisa continues to recover. God be praised for all his kindness. I can hardly see a cart without shuddering at the risk she ran.

Office where I had so many interruptions as to be able to do little. Deacon Spear and my father, Mr. N. Curtis and Dr. G. Parkman. My father came in to dine with Governor Winthrop.[1] I also spent about an hour at an auction sale of horses and carriages and succeeded in purchasing a harness, in lieu of the ones stolen last winter.

Afternoon, finished Mr. Tucker's volume upon Banks and currency which is a useful work considering a Virginian composes it.

Evening at home. Mr. Degrand called. Conversation with my father upon sundry matters. He remained at my house for the night. E. C. Adams also.

[1] Thomas Lindall Winthrop had been lieutenant governor of Massachusetts from 1826 to 1832.

SUNDAY 12TH.

Beautiful day. Divine service in Boston and Quincy. Evening at home.

Louisa is improving and appears almost well. I can hardly credit it even when I have every reason to be so grateful. My father and Wife went to hear Dr. Channing in the morning, but I attended as usual at Dr. Frothingham's and heard a very simple youth by name Parker[1] preach from Matthew 22. 37.39. "Jesus said unto him, Thou shalt love the Lord thy God with all thy heart and with all thy soul and with all thy mind, thou shalt love thy neighbor as thyself." Upon this was built a discourse upon the connexion of morality with religion.

Immediately after the service, we went to Quincy. My father, my boy John and myself. Reached there in time for dinner and attended worship in the afternoon. Mr. Lunt preached from Luke 6. 31. "As ye would that men should do to you, do ye also to them likewise." A very good Sermon. He considered first the doctrine of pure selfishness next that of justice, and how superior this was to either. Mr. Lunt is certainly a good preacher but I learn that dissatisfaction with him is creeping into the parish. It is not possible to tell what popularity is. I cannot define it, and do not enjoy it any more than he. There are some men who are not made for it. His talent goes for nothing in the want of it and so does mine.

Returned to Boston and read a discourse of Dr. Holland from Proverbs 22. 6. "Train up a child in the way he should go, and when he is old, he will not depart from it." Upon the necessity of education, sound but commonplace. Evening Mr. and Mrs. Minot called to see us.

[1] Perhaps Theodore Parker who had taken a degree in divinity at Harvard in 1836 (*Harvard Quinquennial Cat.*).

MONDAY 13TH.

Fine day. Morning to Hingham. Afternoon at home. Evening, at Govr. Everett's.

Last year when my Wife and I went to Washington, taking Louisa with us, and leaving John at home, I promised him a trip in a Steamboat somewhere. This promise it has not been convenient to perform until now when I took him with me to Hingham and back in the General Lincoln. The day was fine although rather windy and I enjoyed his first emotions at so remarkable a sight.

We got home to dinner and I felt so much fatigued as to be very glad to sit quiet in my study and read Mr. Quin's Pamphlet, History of the Bank of England.[1] There is much information to be gained from it although somewhat long and dry.

Evening at Governor Everett's. The family and on the whole rather a pleasant party. Home tired.

[1] Perhaps, Michael Joseph Quin, *The Trade of Banking in England*, London, 1833.

TUESDAY 14TH.

Heavy showers all day. Time much as usual. Evening at home.

I had intended to go to Quincy today but the weather made it impossible. At the Office I was engaged in Accounts as usual and in reading the last number of the North American Review. Not much in it of interest. The difficulty with that periodical seems to be that it does not discuss things any body cares about knowing. Continued Mr. Quin in the Afternoon.

I received today a letter from Mr. Hunt informing me of a delay in his proposed publication and also of his desire that my name might be published in connexion with my article.[1] I have no objection and no desire. Evening quiet at home.

[1] Letter missing.

WEDNESDAY 15TH.

Lovely day. Morning to Quincy. Afternoon at home.

I went to Quincy this morning taking with me my boy John whom I proposed to leave with Catherine one of our women who has gone out to open the house. The morning was lovely and the rain of yesterday has had the effect of starting all the vegetation in a surprising manner. For the first time I perceived that my place was really making some advances in appearance. I am now and then encouraged that all my labour will not be positively thrown away. I worked upon the ground in various ways putting in more plants which I have had supplied me in great abundance. Indeed my greatest difficulty is that I have not room enough for them.

Home to dinner. Afternoon, finished Mr. Quin and read Mr. Raguet's papers of the Examiner, published in Philadelphia during the panic.[1] They conflict strongly with my theory. Evening at home. Wrote a little about Mr. Tucker.

[1] Condy Raguet, effective advocate of free trade and authority on currency matters, was the publisher of a series of periodicals in Philadelphia from 1829 to 1839 that included *The Examiner and Journal of Political Economy* (1833–1835) and *Financial Register of the United States* (1837–1838). His *The Principles of Free Trade, Illustrated in a Series of Short and Familiar Essays*, Phila., 1835, was a selection from his editorial articles that had appeared in *The Examiner* (DAB).

THURSDAY 16TH.

The day warm with clouds and showers. Morning Office. Afternoon to Quincy.

I was occupied at the Office in the morning with a variety of Accounts. Settled the business of Mr. Oliver[1] and transacted some for Mr. Johnson. He sends for his Money exactly as if it was all in my hands at six per cent interest and payable on demand too. Luckily his letter came twenty four hours before it would have been too late and I this morning remitted to him his whole balance.[2]

Afternoon to Quincy. It was so showery that I could do nothing and indeed there is not much to do beyond giving orders. I feel now a strong inclination for the quiet of the country and to be once more at my studies and my occupations in writing. Last Summer was the most methodical I ever passed. Home quite late.

[1] Probably Francis J. Oliver, on whom see vol. 6:index.
[2] The letter from T. B. Johnson is missing; the LbC of CFA's response is in the Adams Papers.

FRIDAY 17TH.

Fine day. Morning Office. Afternoon to Quincy. Evening company.

At the Office where I was engaged in Accounts and settling Miss Elizabeth C. Adams affairs. This is one of the trusts about which it is necessary for me to be the most careful. I have got it now in a way which will answer, I hope.

Afternoon to Quincy carrying with me my boy Charles in order to get him out of the bustle and trouble of removal tomorrow. Made my last preparations for the transfer which is a very troublesome business. The place begins to look as if it might pay me for my trouble.

Home late. Edmund Quincy and his Wife and Gardiner Gorham were at the house and spent an hour. Retired being not a little fatigued.

[*Quincy*]

SATURDAY 18TH.

Lovely day. Morning at home. Afternoon to Quincy. Evening at my father's.

My time was wholly taken up today in the preparations for our removal, which have come more heavily this year than usual. I expected my Mother also from Washington and this cost me three journies to the Railway depot before I found her and effected her transfer to

Quincy. The packing and sending out the things at the same time with both families is laborious. Yet at five o'clock in the afternoon, after dining at home, I shut up the town house and moved into the country. Upon no similar occasion have I been so much fatigued. Nevertheless I went down in the evening to see the family who seemed very bright after their journey. Miss Mary Cutts is with them and comes to spend the Summer.[1] To bed early overfatigued.

[1] Mary Elizabeth Estelle Cutts, a close friend of LCA, was a visitor at the Old House for extended periods on several occasions. She was a daughter of Richard Cutts, a representative in Congress from Maine, and Anna Payne, sister of Dolly Madison. JQA wrote the obituary of Richard Cutts published in the *National Intelligencer*, 22 April 1845 (p. 3, col. 6), and later reprinted in *NEHGR*, 2:277–278 (July 1848) as "Notices of the Cutts Family." See also JQA, Diary, 4 Aug., 30 Nov. 1845; 27–28 Aug. 1847; LCA to ABA, 26 April 1848, Adams Papers.

SUNDAY 19TH.

Fine day. Divine service as usual. Evening at my father's.

I occupied myself part of the day in writing a very brief article for Mr. Hunt, also in the usual lesson with Louisa intermitted last Sunday in consequence of her accident.

Attended divine service and heard Mr. Lunt preach from Matthew 3. 11. "I indeed baptize you with water unto repentance: but he that cometh after me is mightier than I, whose shoes I am not worthy to bear, he shall baptize you with the Holy Ghost and with fire." I think I have heard this sermon before and on the whole do not consider it as among the most remarkable of Mr. Lunt. It is with regret that I hear of some little dissatisfaction in the parish with him. I feared it would be so as he is not a man of popular manners, the essential point for a clergyman in these days.

Afternoon Mr. Whitney 1. Corinthians 15. 19. "If in this life only we have hope in Christ, we are of all men most miserable." I could hardly hear him although it is of little consequence as I have often heard the Sermon before.

Read a discourse of Bishop Atterbury. Job 22. 21. "Acquaint now thyself with God, and be at peace." A support under affliction to be found in the knowledge of the attributes of God. Evening at the house of my father.

MONDAY 20TH.

Fine day. Morning reading. Division of time. Evening at the house.

I made arrangements today for the ordinary division of my studies. I propose to begin with an examination of the subject of currency in order to furnish a Review of the work of Mr. Tucker which shall answer. It is a little singular that I should have undertaken to write two Pamphlets upon the subject having done so little in the way of examination of what had been written before. Yet if I had read all I have since I should not probably have expressed my own thoughts so distinctly nor enunciated the propositions which I still believe to be the only safeguards of our Banking system. Read today Mr. Locke's paper upon lowering the value of interest and raising coin[1] and several chapters of Tucker. In the Afternoon, began Lucan's Pharsalia.[2]

My division of time is now designed to be as follows. In the morning, composition and study of Tucker. One hour of German. After dinner, Lucan, and resuming Grimm.[3] But this I do not suppose I shall be able to fall into immediately. Evening at my father's. Walk in the fields with my boys.

[1] "Considerations of the Consequences of Lowering the Interest and Raising the Value of Money," 1691, is in vol. 5 of Locke's *Works* at MQA.

[2] There are three editions in Latin of Lucan's *Pharsalia* at MQA: London, 1751, Zweibrücken, 1783, and London, 1820; the last was CFA's copy.

[3] CFA had read in Baron Frédéric Melchior de Grimm's *Correspondance* several times over the years, finding Grimm satisfying as a critic; see vol. 6:120–121; entry for 9 Nov. 1837, above.

TUESDAY 21ST.

Fine day though cool. To Boston. Afternoon at home. Evening, visit Mr. Lunt.

I went to town today but found myself much wanting in occupation. A few commissions seemed all that I had to do. Nothing new. Returned late having two Tenants in Mr. Ladd and Mr. Apthorp.

After dinner, Lucan book 1, l. 1–250 rather correcting of what I read more carelessly yesterday. There is vigor in the style and an exuberance of imagery with occasional extravagance of language. Read also a little of Grimm.

It is difficult at first to plant oneself regularly to an entirely new train of occupations. Perhaps it is not the best plan but I had become exceedingly tired of my Winter ones and wanted new. Evening walk with my father to see Mr. and Mrs. Lunt.

WEDNESDAY. 22D.

Rainy with cold, raw east wind. At home all day. Evening at the house.

It was a very cold disagreeable day and although wanting fires exceedingly I could not summon resolution enough to order one which made me peevish and uncomfortable. I am very doubtful whether the Stoical system is useful to the temper. I know mine goes on the most easily when I am externally comfortable.

Worked upon Tucker and finished Locke upon raising the value of Money, i.e. depreciating it.[1] A very clear minded man.

After dinner Lucan finishing the first book, but I executed nothing very heartily. Evening at the Mansion house where was nothing new.

[1] CFA's meaning here, badly expressed, would seem to be, "Locke upon lowering the interest rate and increasing the supply of money, i.e. depreciating it." See entry of 20 May, above.

THURSDAY 23D.

Another cold, cloudy day. At home. Evening, the family at my house.

Determined not to suffer so much again from cold I had the furnace heated this morning and enjoyed a very comfortable morning. Finished my review of Tucker's book and began writing upon it, but my vigor flags. I do so much in writing now that I have lost interest in it. Yet I promised and will perform.

Read a part of Lessing, Life of Sophocles or rather notes of what is said about him in the writings of the ancients.[1] Lessing is among the most acute of all the critics I ever read.

Afternoon, Lucan book 2. l. 1–300. And Grimm. But my Mother and the other ladies came in to spend the evening. Nothing at all new.

[1] On the German editions of G. E. Lessing's works at MQA, see entry for 23 July 1837, above.

FRIDAY 24TH.

Cloudy, cold and rainy. At home all day. Evening at the Mansion.

This was my day for going to town but the weather seemed so very unpleasant that I decided to postpone it. Sat down quietly instead to write upon Mr. Tucker, but I must have overtasked myself heretofore or there is some other reason, for the extraordinary indolence which comes over me. I cannot write as I would. Perhaps it will come to me presently.

I read a little of Lessing's Notes of a Memoir of Sophocles which are uncommonly adroit, and show how much may be made by an ingenious man out of very small materials.

Afternoon finished the second book of Lucan's Pharsalia and read

Wellwood's Preface to the translation made by Rowe.[1] Read a little of Grimm.

Evening passed at the house below. There is little or nothing stirring to excite any interest. A season of profound peace is now in the Country, such as we have not enjoyed for a long time, and the people appear to be striving to repair losses as earnestly as possible. Even politics are dull.

[1] Nicholas Rowe's translation of the *Pharsalia*, London, 1720, is at MQA.

SATURDAY. 25TH.

Rain but afterwards cleared up. To Boston. Afternoon out. Evening at the Mansion.

The morning opened with heavy clouds and a thunder shower in the midst of which I went to town accompanied by J. H. Adams. But it cleared afterwards. Time occupied in making calls of various kinds and commissions. I had in fact little to do. I had hurried my work so much before quitting the city that there is nothing left. No doubt in a week or two, it will begin again. To the Athenæum to get some books for my father. Return.

The afternoon was so fine that I was tempted to spend it out in pruning my trees and examining the different things that grow about here. They look promising now, but there are few things more productive of disappointment than arboriculture. Evening at the mansion.

SUNDAY 26TH.

Lovely day. Services as usual. Evening at the Mansion.

I passed the morning, devoting the usual portion of time to Louisa, and reading the two first dialogues of Alciphron, or the Minute Philosopher. This is quite a celebrated work of Berkeley to prove the truth of Religion.[1] As yet I find little that appears to me like serious argument in the Dialogue. Alciphron is made to talk for the purpose of being confuted.

Attended divine service and heard Mr. Morison of New Bedford preach from Acts 17. 23. "For as I passed by, and beheld your devotions, I found an altar with this inscription, To the unknown God," and also from Luke 15. 23. "Let us be merry." One of my uncontrollable fits of abstraction prevented me from deriving as much good from these Sermons as perhaps I ought to have done. I regret them even when I find myself unable to correct myself of them.

Read a discourse of the Reverend John Balguy upon the conduct of the Bereans in being convinced of the truth of Christianity by examination. Acts 17. 11. "These were more noble than those in Thessalonica, in that they received the word with all readiness of mind, and searched the scriptures daily, whether those things were so." This finishes the third volume of the English Preacher. Evening at the Mansion. Mr. Price Greenleaf was there. Dull political conversation.

[1] Bishop George Berkeley, *Alciphron; or the Minute Philosopher, Containing an Apology for the Christian Religion*, 2 vols., London, 1732.

MONDAY 27TH.

Warm but cloudy. Distribution as usual. Evening at the Mansion. Rain.

My morning was not very profitably spent. Yet I managed to put together some materials for the shape of my Review and matured it very considerably in my mind. This process always appears to me a waste of time even when it is in fact the most undoubted improvement of it.

Read a little of Lessing's Contributions to the life of Sophocles but as they appear to me to end only in verbal criticism I shall give it up for Nathan the Wise.

After dinner, occupied in wandering among the fields but read of Lucan book 3. l. 1–300, and a little of Grimm. Evening at the Mansion. It rained a warm rain.

TUESDAY 28TH.

Morning rain but cleared. To town. Afternoon at home. Evening at Mrs. T. B. Adams'.

I went to town this day, but not much of importance to do. Looked over my accounts and found my affairs better than I anticipated. The time for my annual balancing is now coming round. I shall then have occupation enough. A few trifling commissions.

In the Afternoon which was short in consequence of a dinner delayed for the return of my Wife who had gone to Boston, read Lucan 3. 300–535. The same general characteristics throughout. Much sprightly vigor with excess. Also Grimm which is my delassement.[1]

I went up in the evening to see Mrs. T. B. Adams and her family. Mrs. Angier is now there.

[1] That is, relaxation or diversion.

WEDNESDAY 29TH.

Clouds but it afterwards cleared. At home all day. Time as usual.

I devoted my morning to the continuation of Tucker and the review. I am by degrees hammering out the thing into shape but as yet with no great energy. I believe there never was a man who worked so much to so little purpose. Yet courage does not fail me hitherto. As long as I am blessed at home, literary occupation is no more than a healthy amusement.

Read the beginning of Lessing's play of Nathan the Wise. After dinner finished the third book of Lucan's Pharsalia, and continued working upon Grimm who is a kind of standby.

Walk with my father to see Mr. Whitney and from thence to Mrs. T. B. Adams where the family were spending the evening.

THURSDAY. 30TH.

Cleared at last. At home. Time distributed as usual. Evening to see Edmund Quincy.

I continued the work upon Tucker which spreads itself as I go. It now appears to me as if I could make something respectable out of it. But I was interrupted by the man who has this day finished my wall and then by going to the Bank.

I believe I have now got through with all of the serious undertaking about my place. Since I commenced it has involved me in about double the expense originally contemplated and has created a great deal of anxiety. That is now beginning to wear off. I at present look forward with a hope of rest to my labour and of enjoyment of it's result.

Last Summer was perhaps the period of all my life of the most unalloyed pleasure, the greater part of it gained in the quiet of this residence. Ambition here seems to me a dream and the contention and rivalry of social life a vanity fair. Perhaps this is a wrong feeling to nourish inasmuch as we are all of us in duty bound to some individual action. I hope I am conscious of this and will not suffer my indolence to get the better of me.

Lessing, Nathan the Wise. I cannot judge of it well until I finish it. Lucan, Pharsalia. Book 4. 1–235. I spent some time on my ground.

Evening with my father to see Mr. and Mrs. Edmund Quincy who are at the place of his father for the Summer season. He seems to be getting better pretty rapidly. Walk home. Bright starlight.

FRIDAY 31ST.

Fair. Morning to town. Afternoon at home. Evening at the Mansion.

I went to town this morning, accompanied by Miss L. C. Smith. My time almost exclusively taken up in commissions. I had to superintend the getting some boxes from my house, and also some things from Washington. This required going backward and forward so often that it took up much of my time. Home to dine.

Afternoon out among my trees which I try perhaps to take too much care of. Lucan b. 4. 235–470. The fighting is vigorous but there is too much of it.

Evening, visits from J. H. Foster and J. H. Adams. Paid to the latter the legacy which has been in my father's hands,[1] making the last but one of that extensive trust created by the will of my grandfather. I am very glad he is becoming released from it's injunctions which so far as he is concerned he has faithfully fulfilled. After transacting the business we all walked down to the mansion for the evening.

[1] Joseph Harrod Adams had reached the age of 21 in 1838.

SATURDAY JUNE 1.

Cold easterly drizzle. At home all day. Evening at the Mansion.

The weather has been during our stay thus far disagreeable. Clouds and cold and damp have predominated so far as to induce me to regret my removal. I think I will not attempt it hereafter before this date.

I devoted much of my day to writing upon Tucker the first sketch of which I this morning completed. My effort will now be to fill it out, which I hope to set about in earnest next week. Read a part of Mr. Locke's answer to Lowndes proposition to lower the amount of silver in English coin or to raise the value of money.[1]

Afternoon, Lessing, Nathan the wise, the plot of which I do not yet comprehend and finished the fourth book of the Pharsalia. I spent some time out working, digging round some of my trees which might, I feared, be checked by the coldness of the ground. There has not been much rain but the east wind and clouds affect the temperature of the earth which on this hill is not very high at this season. Evening at the Mansion.

[1] "Observations on a Paper entitled 'For Encouraging the Coining of Silver Money in England'" was John Locke's reply in 1695 to the proposal of the secretary of the treasury, William Lowndes (*Works*, 10 vols., London, 1823, vol. 5; *DNB*).

Cold and cloudy. Time divided as usual.

I was occupied with my daughter Louisa for an hour of the morning as usual, in her exercises which are almost too brief to do her good. Yet I would not make them fatiguing.

Read the third and fourth dialogues of Alciphron in the course of the day which are more elaborate and which present strong points. But after all the dialogue style is not a good one unless it is truly carried out. In Cicero, or Plato it is the mere form through which a teacher disserts and not a dispute for victory.

Attended divine service and heard Mr. Lunt from 1. Corinthians 2. 2. "For I determined not to know any thing among you save Jesus Christ and him crucified." A very excellent discourse upon the character of Christianity and it's essential difference between the merely ritual law, and the free thinking philosophy, the one characteristic of the Jews and the other of the Greeks. Mr. Lunt is a thinker and a writer.

Afternoon Mr. J. Angier from Isaiah 3. 10.11. "Say ye to the righteous, that it shall be well with him: for they shall eat the fruit of their doings. Woe unto the wicked! It shall be ill with him: for the reward of his hands shall be given him." A good discourse as I thought upon a future state of rewards and punishment as the result of free action in this world. It might not have been original but it was well put together.

Read a Sermon of Tillotson being the first in the fourth Volume of the English Preacher. Acts 10. 38. "Who went about doing good." The example of Jesus as a benevolent individual. Surely all of us are too much inclined to be selfish.

In the Evening at the Mansion. The weather is cold and cheerless. My boy John complained of feeling unwell. My children's sickness always depresses me. I feel so unworthy of the many blessings which surround me.

Cold and cloudy. Time disposed of at home. Evening at the Mansion.

Much of my morning was given to the beginning of Tucker. I wrote about three pages of review and that was all. But with me the cost of the first step is according to the French proverb.[1]

The Great Western has brought us news from Europe of a very important kind.[2] Every thing within a few years has tended to some great explosion in that quarter, but it is impossible to foresee exactly when it will take place, or how it will affect this country. Perhaps the immediate operation will be beneficial, if it brings over capital to be invested here. On the other hand if simply a creation of debt is the result the effect is more questionable. The Bank of England has raised the rate of interest in consequence of losses of bullion, this puts a stop to our loans and shuts up the remedy which we had against the rise of exchange.

Read a little of Lessing and 300 lines in the fifth book of the Pharsalia. The ladies went to Boston. My boy John still suffering from his cold. Evening at my father's, returning however pretty early.

[1] Probably, "Il n'y a que le premier pas qui coûte," the first step is the difficult one.

[2] The arrival of the speedy *Great Western* in New York brought the most recent reports from England of continued declines in sales and prices of cotton, of advances in interest rates, and of "paralyzed" markets (*Boston Courier*, 3 June, p. 2, col. 5).

TUESDAY 4TH.

Fine day. Morning to town. Afternoon at home. Evening at the Mansion.

This is the first clear day we have had for some time, and this was disfigured by a cold East wind which set in at noon. I went to town where not having much to do but to perform some commissions, I occupied myself with filing up my vouchers for the last three months and arranging my books, in advance for the annual balance.

Home. Afternoon superintendance of work and Lucan B. 5. 300–420. Evening at the Mansion, nothing remarkable to record. Our present life is more quiet even than it is in Boston. Hitherto in the midst of bad weather we have been troubled with exceeding few interruptions. Yet considering this I do not study as much as I ought. Knowledge is the one thing needful.

WEDNESDAY 5TH.

Rain storm. At home all day, distribution as usual.

A very heavy gale from the Eastward brought with it rain and kept me rigidly confined to the house. I worked pretty steadily on my Review of Mr. Tucker which goes on ⟨pretty⟩ well. Continued Lessing's Nathan the Wise and read Lucan finishing all but about ninety lines of the fifth book of the Pharsalia. I continue to think his great fault to be extravagance. Read Grimm whose criticism is just and keen. One of my wonders in the present day is the low standard of it in this country. We are all praise or blame.

Evening at home. The continuance of this very unpleasant weather here has a slight tendency to depress our spirits. Yet we have a fine opportunity for improvement if the disposition was coexistent.

THURSDAY 6TH.

Cloudy. At home all day. Distribution as usual.

The weather promises better. I hope we shall enjoy it for hitherto we have had little of the true pleasure of the country.

I continued my work upon Tucker and made a pretty deep dive into the business. It is a peculiarity of mine to become rapidly tired of any occupation which lasts a great while. This makes it very difficult for me to develope my own thoughts fully enough to be readily understood by others. I am afraid I am falling into this error in the present instance.

Read Lessing, Nathan der Weise and Lucan 5 and 6 books, 100 in each. Dined and took tea at the Mansion. Evening visit to Mr. and Mrs. T. Greenleaf.

FRIDAY 7TH.

Lovely day. To town. Afternoon study. Evening at the Mansion.

I rode to town. Occupied in making up the Quarterly Statements for my father and in expediting Mr. Johnson's affairs as usual.[1] This with commissions, a visit to the house for things &ca. took up the morning. It is my season of leisure at present from Agency business, the rents being all collected.

Home to dine. Afternoon Lucan 6 book 100–300 and attending to out door work, in which I waste much time. Evening at the Mansion. No news.

[1] CFA's letter to T. B. Johnson covering the period is in the Adams Papers (LbC).

SATURDAY 8TH.

Warm day. To town and Medford to dine. Evening home.

I rode to town accompanied by my father. Finished the quarterly Accounts mentioned yesterday, and I now must begin to prepare for the annual balance. Nothing new.

Went with my father to Medford according to invitation. Annual dinner to the trustees of the agricultural Society. Messrs. T. L.

Winthrop, J. C. Gray, H. Codman, E. H. Derby, Josiah Quincy Junr., Phinney, J. Welles, B. Guild, Judge Prescott, Mr. N. Appleton, Mr. Colman, Govr. Everett, Mr. B. Gorham, with Gorham Brooks and ourselves. I have never been much of an admirer of these state occasions but this appeared to me more stupid than usual. The members either had the spirit of dullness or else of caution. They are generally intelligent but few of them are at all brilliant, and the dinner was rather calculated for stuffing with good eatables than for any thing else. They have made a sumptuary law against champagne which is even more stupifying still. We started early for home and got there by eight o'clock. Spent an hour at the Mansion and then home.

SUNDAY. 9TH.

Cloudy but cleared. Exercises as usual, head ach and early to bed.

On first rising I had a light warning of what would come, but hoping that with fasting it would disappear I occupied myself as usual. Attended to the ordinary exercise with my daughter Louisa, and then attended divine service.

Mr. Pierpont preached from that famous text of Genesis 1. 3. "And God said, Let there be light." A poetical discourse drawing a parallel between the value of light in the physical as in the moral world. I was surprised at a quotation of Lord Byron's darkness which sounded to me extravagant in the pulpit. Afternoon from Matthew 4. 4. "It is written, Man shall not live by bread alone, but by every word that proceedeth out of the mouth of God."

Read a discourse from the English Preacher by the Revd. Jeremiah Tidcombe from 2 Samuel 12. 7. "And Nathan said unto David, Thou art the man." Upon the character of Reproof and the state of the receiver of it. I read also nearly the whole of two dialogues of Alciphron, to prove the value of the Christian Religion. But before I had quite finished the last my head grew so much worse that I was obliged to give up all reading and finally to retire to bed. I have not for a long time had such an attack as this.

MONDAY 10TH.

Windy but clear. At home dividing time as usual. Evening, the family with us.

I spent much time this morning upon the review of Tucker and went on as I thought quite vigorously. Two more such mornings will I think finish the business which as usual with me grows tedious as I proceed. Lessing, Nathan der Weise which I must read over once again before I shall succeed in gaining the force of the composition.

After dinner Lucan, book 6. l 300–600 the famous description of Erichtho, forcible but disgusting. Lucan's taste was not equal to his nerve. I worked also for an hour upon my grounds, which at this season begin to require improvement. My head clear but not yet exactly right. The family were all here in the evening and Dr. and Mrs. Woodward.

TUESDAY IITH.

Morning to town. Afternoon at home as usual. Evening at the Mansion.

My morning in the city was very much taken up with accounts so that I did hardly any thing else. I am making my preparations for the usual annual balancing, which is always a process of difficulty.

J. H. Adams went in with me but did not accompany me out. Read of Lucan b. 6 the remainder, and worked upon my place, but I find this fatigues me much.

WEDNESDAY 12TH.

Clear but cool. At home all day. Dine at the mansion and evening.

I pursued my work upon the Review of Tucker so steadily that I finished it before the morning had elapsed. I think it has good points though as usual I want confidence. Finished Nathan der Weise which I do not appreciate and turned to the fables of Lessing in the same volume which are many of them very pleasant.

We dined at my father's. After dinner Lucan book 7. 1–306, and some time spent with my boy John in taking care of my ground which runs away with much of my time. Evening at the Mansion.

THURSDAY 13TH.

Clouds and rain. At home, rather idle. Evening at home.

Looked over the review of Tucker which I have finished and found it on the whole as good as I had any reason to expect. I will send it and take leave of Mr. Hunt for the present who has not as yet made out to publish his first number. Perhaps he will fail in doing so at all. At any rate this makes the last of my positive occupation and in the absence of new I rather idled.

Looked over some of the MS of J.A. at the house and had some conversation with my father about them, who recommended to me to attempt a biography of my grandmother.[1] I do not know that this would be beyond my ability.

Read more of Lessing's Fables and after dinner Lucan 7. 306–616. Also Grimm, but I felt languid all day as from indigestion. Sorry to find these symptoms coming back upon me. My father spent an hour with us in the evening so that as it rained from the North East I concluded not to go down.

[1] On the day before, JQA had been visited by Henry Colman, commissioner of agriculture and former active minister (see entry for 12 March 1837, above) whom he had encountered at the dinner of the Agricultural Society on 8 June. Colman sought from JQA sanction to write a memoir of the life of AA, "whom he said he had almost adored; a proposal which I promised to take into consideration. Mr. Colman is a highly respectable worthy and intelligent man; but the task of writing a memoir of the life of my mother ought to be performed by myself or by my Son" (JQA, Diary, 12 June).

FRIDAY 14TH.

Cool and clear. Morning to town. Afternoon at home. Evening at the Mansion.

I went to town and passed most of my time at the Office engaged in making up my accounts and in copying some papers for my father relative to the affairs of Mr. Boylston. This took most of my time.

Home. Lucan Pharsalia finished the seventh book with the sketch of the battle of Pharsalia. His sketch of Cæsar is below the standard of the historians.

Passed some time in work but felt the coming on of a headach. This is a new state for me which I do not understand or admire and depresses my spirits. I had been so free all the winter. I suspect it is acid and so I took soda which relieved me. Evening at the Mansion where were Mr. Beale and his daughter.

SATURDAY 15TH.

Clear and cool. At home all day. Evening to see D. Greenleaf.

This was the first day that looked much like Summer and I enjoyed it although it was cold. When I remember the hot week of last year, this was a contrast. Busy at home in finishing a long law paper to be copied for my father and in writing over one sheet of my review of Tucker which did not satisfy me. I thought the portion I wrote was an improvement.

Read the remainder of Lessing's fables and part of his dissertation upon fable. Also a part of Texier's sketch of the Constitution of the ancient Roman republic.[1] After dinner Lucan 8, 1–330, and working out upon my grounds. I felt very well all day which encouraged me much. Nothing in this world can be enjoyed without good health.

Evening called to see Daniel Greenleaf. My father accompanied me. Since last Summer Mr. G has lost his Wife and is now a lone person in the world, but he does not appear to mind it much. He showed me this evening the plan of the land called the three corner lot.

[1] A. Adrien de Texier, *Du Gouvernement de la république romaine*, 3 vols., Hamburg, 1796.

SUNDAY 16TH.

Showers and wind. Usual exercises of the day. Evening at the Mansion.

It was quite dark this morning and we were up late. I devoted however my usual portion of time to my daughter Louisa and attended divine service where I heard Mr. Lunt in the morning from Romans 7. 22.23. "For I delight in the law of God after the inward man. But I see another law in my members warring against the law of my mind, and bringing me into captivity to the law of sin which is in my members." A very good sermon upon the contest between duty and inclination which makes all the trial of life.

Afternoon, Mr. Whitney from 1. Corinthians 15. 53. "For this corruptible must put on incorruption and this mortal must put on immortality." This gentleman is decidedly too old to preach. I could not hear him so as to fix any idea.

Read a discourse in the English Preacher. Proverbs 29. 25. "The fear of man bringeth a snare." A good discourse by Dr. James Foster upon that servility to the world's opinion which is rather a prevailing vice of our nation.

Finished Alciphron today, the ten last dialogues contain a close and powerful argument in favour of revealed Religion. On the whole the work is an able one though now probably very little read. In the Evening we went to the Mansion.

MONDAY 17TH.

Windy and cool. At home all the morning. Afternoon, Ride. Evening at the Mansion.

Our season has been by no means an agreeable one. An alternation of rainy and cold and boisterously windy weather make the external pleasures of country life much less than usual. We had a slight frost this morning.

I finished the substitute of the old Sheet for Tucker and then went down to the other house for the purpose of examining old papers. I am now out of occupation and this will not do for me. Indeed I suspect it is already the secret of the reaction that I feel upon my health. My doubt now is whether I will undertake the proposed plan by my father or devote myself to something else. In the meantime I am endeavouring to get rid of a parcel of papers that are embarrassing while left unexamined.

Continued Lessing's Treatise upon Fable. He is too acute a critic, it becomes tiresome. He finds fault with every author for defining fable imperfectly when after all an imperfect definition is not a serious evil for such a thing. A fable is the illustration by anecdote of some moral lesson. That's enough. Nobody fails to understand what a fable is who ever read one. Your acute critics get to be over verbal disputants.

After dinner, Lucan 8. 330–616. This book which gives the fate of Pompey is perhaps the best for vigor and harmony. I took a long ride accompanied by my Wife and we enjoyed the country round Milton much. Evening at the Mansion.

TUESDAY 18TH.

Clouds and latterly rain. To Boston. At home after dinner and evening.

I went to town and was industriously engaged all the morning in business of the Agency, of Mr. Curtis for the Boylston Estate and in my own. This left me little or no time for any thing else. Received a notice that my Tenant in No. 4 Acorn Street vacates which is a vexation.

Return to dinner. Afternoon Lucan finish the 8th book, and read Grimm whose criticism is often extremely amusing. Also Le Comte's description of China about which I am curious.[1] In the evening retained at home by the rain. Mascou, Costume des Anciens Peuples.[2]

---

[1] At MQA is Louis Le Comte, *Nouveaux mémoires sur l'état présent de la Chine*, 2 vols., Amsterdam, 1697.

[2] Perhaps the reference is to a section of Johann Jacob Mascou's *Geschichte der Teutschen*. CFA's copies are at MQA in the original German (Leipzig, 1750) and in English: *The History of the Ancient Germans ... and other Ancient Northern Nations*, transl. T. Lediard, 2 vols., London, 1737–1738. However, CFA's use of the title in French is puzzling.

WEDNESDAY 19TH.

Clear but high wind. At home all day. Evening at the Mansion.

I was at home and wrote over some portion of my Review of Tucker which did not quite please me. Then took a walk to Mrs. Adams to have a few minutes conversation with her son Isaac Hull about his affairs, then to the Mansion where I devoted two hours before dinner to an examination of MS papers of J.A. Found nothing very interesting.

Dined at the same. After dinner Lucan 9. 1–306, and a visit from the Miss Inches. Texier in whom I find much that is useful. Evening after my return from below a little of Mascou.

THURSDAY 20TH.

Clear but windy. At home occupied as usual. Evening family with us.

My time passes with so little variety now that I record its movement rather in compliance with habit than for any other reason. I gave to my Review of Tucker it's final reading and then folded it up for dismissal. This puts me for the moment out of work. I think I shall take up the thread of our history, in connexion with an examination of the MS Papers of J.A. I look over them now without much method.

Lucan 9. 306–540. The march of Cato in Africa, highly extravagant and overwrought. It appears too like the sixth act of a play.

My father was here upon business. He has just received a letter from A. Giusta calling for money.[1] This is not exactly convenient, he having already strained himself to pay off Hull Adams this year. I recommended to him a course which he will in the first place pursue. In the evening the family were with us. Read a little of Mascou.

[1] JQA's indebtedness to his former manservant Anthony (Antoine) Giusta is alluded to in the entry for 8 March 1837, above. The debt, incurred in 1835, would remain unliquidated for another year (JQA, Diary, 28 Nov. 1840). Giusta's career and his relations with the Adamses are recounted in that entry as well as at vol. 6:17, above.

FRIDAY 21ST.

Cloudy but very warm. To Boston with my Wife. Afternoon at home and evening.

My Wife accompanied me to town, and the carriage took Mrs. J. Adams, Miss Cutts and all the children for the purpose of our meeting at the Court house and seeing the Giraffe which is now exhibiting. We found there Mrs. Everett with her children, Mr. Brooks and Mrs. Gorham Brooks with her boy thus with our own tribe making quite a family party. I was curious to see this creature which is so singularly formed and so seldom met with, and my expectations were abundantly gratified. It is said to stand sixteen feet high, out of which the legs make nearly six, the difference in the length of which is much less than I imagined. It is quite tame, fond of apples which it will take from any one and show signs for more. At first sight the neck seems out of all proportion, but I fancy our ideas are merely relative on that subject and adapt themselves to what we see around us.

Office and commissions as usual. Home to dinner. The morning was warm but a sea fog came up by night. Lucan 9. 540–660 and a little work on the grounds. Evening my father sat with us so feeling rather tired I remained entirely at home.

SATURDAY 22D.

Clouds and rain. At home all day. Evening at the Mansion.

My intention had been to accompany my father to town this morning but as I found that the weather did not promise very favorably, I concluded to remain at home. Began this morning, the diplomatic correspondence of the Revolution and read a considerable portion of Silas Deane's correspondence. I also spent about two hours at the lower house reading over the file of Mrs. Adams' letters to my father. They are many of them very good but will not admit of publication just now.

Only a little of Lessing. Afternoon, Lucan. 9. 660–986. The serpents of Africa all enumerated with embellishments. Texier and Grimm. Evening, as it cleared we went to the Mansion.

SUNDAY 23D.

Cloudy but warm. Exercises as usual. Evening at the Mansion.

I devoted my usual time to my daughter Louisa and read some Chapters of Tucker's Light of Nature. This Author has been much admired for his easy familiar way of illustrating metaphysical truths, but it seems to me that he is feeble.

Attended divine service all day and heard Dr. Lamson of Dedham preach from Matthew 20. 22. "Ye know not what ye ask." A poetical discourse upon the unreasonableness of human wishes very much in the allegory of the old school, and also Matthew 25. 21. "Well done, good and faithful servant; thou hast been faithful over a few things, I will make thee ruler over many things: enter thou into the joy of thy lord."

I also read a sensible discourse by the Revd. John Holland upon the duty of attendance at public worship. Hebrews 10. 25. "Not forsaking the assembling of ourselves together, as the manner of some is." Man is so much the creature of habit that he becomes religious as often from the performance of external rites as from internal reflection. And the satisfaction of duty performed grows upon one as time goes on. Read some of Le Comte, Account of China. Evening at the Mansion.

MONDAY 24TH.

Clouds and showers. At home. Visitors. Evening to Mr. Beale's.

My time was not very profitably spent today. I finished Silas Deane's portion of the Diplomatic Correspondence of the Revolution[1] and a file of my grandmother's letters. The rest of the morning was taken up with company. So also in the afternoon I only finished the ninth book of the Pharsalia and about 80 lines of the tenth before Dr. and Mrs. Frothingham came from Boston with three children. He remained but a short time as he was to go to a meeting of the Association of Ministers at Mr. Lunt's. But the ladies came up from the lower house and so there was nothing to be done. They did not go until eight after which I made a hasty visit to Mr. Beale.

[1] On Jared Sparks' *Diplomatic Correspondence of the American Revolution* and the Adamses, see vols. 3:88; 4:xii, 214–215; 5:43.

TUESDAY 25TH.

Day fine. Morning to town. Afternoon work. Evening at the Mansion.

I went to town and passed the greater part of my morning in making up the necessary accounts for the first of next month, but did not succeed in bringing them out right upon a first attempt. This is fatiguing and reminds me of last year.

Home as usual. Lucan 10. 81 – 320, Cæsar and Cleopatra. Much poetical vigour but the poem appears drawing out so far that perhaps it is no great pity it is fragmentary. Work for an hour.

Received from Mr. Freeman Hunt a copy of the Sheets of my Article in his July number.[1] It is very correctly printed. Evening at the Mansion.

[1] "The State of the Currency, by Charles F. Adams" would appear in the July issue of *Hunt's Merchants' Mag.*, 1:44–50.

June 1839

Fine day. Trip to Cohasset. Evening at the Mansion.

This day has been fixed upon for the party to Cohasset which has been in agitation ever since my marriage without ever having before been executed. The Carriage took my Wife, Miss Cutts and three children while I went in the Carryall hired for the occasion, with Mrs. John Adams and two girls. We had a pleasant trip down and met there Elizabeth C. Adams and her brother with Mr. Campbell, and subsequently Dr. and Mrs. Frothingham with three children. Our amusements were much as they usually are at this barren spot.[1] Walking to one beach and riding to Nantasket. The day was lovely. We then dined and had some agreeable singing from the gentlemen, after which we made an arrangement to return home. We arrived before sunset and upon getting there, how I did wonder that people could leave such a spot to seek diversion at Cohasset. In the evening passed an hour at my father's, but my Wife and I had both of us very bad nights.

[1] On the long associations the Adamses had with the Cohasset Rocks, see above, entry for 3 Aug. 1837; also JA, *Diary and Autobiography*, 4:7.

Warm day. At home. Evening at the Mansion.

Mrs. Adams was so unwell that she could not get up this morning, and I felt more exhausted than I have done for many years. I am at a loss for a cause. The day was however passed in a pretty languid way. I began our examination of the Report of the Southern convention which I am satisfied I can show to be unreasonable and absurd.[1] This took most of my active time.

After dinner, finished Lucan. A work which I admire on the whole, particularly when I remember it the work of so young a man. Invention is the attribute of the young but perfecting comes by age, and Lucan was cut off in his prime. Evening at my Mother's.

[1] As is suggested here and amplified in the entry for 3 July, below, CFA had JQA's help in the preparation of the series of articles that would eventuate from an examination of the report of a committee of the Southern Convention held in April in Charleston, S.C. The report, in essence, undertook to demonstrate that national policies had brought about, over a long period, severe decline in the export and import trade in the southern states. Tables from the report in support of this thesis were published in the *Daily Centinel & Gazette*, 18 June, p. 2, col. 3. On CFA's articles in rebuttal, see entry for 4 July, below.

FRIDAY 28TH.

Rain all day. Morning to town. At home rest of the day.

I felt extremely unwell this morning, but determined to go to town notwithstanding. The weather was not propitious but I was on the whole favored by a change of wind so as to have the rain behind me both ways. I did not regret my going as I transacted the business upon which I came and went over much of my accounts. But they do not agree and I am driven to an examination of the difficulty, which is tedious.

Home to dine without any appetite. Afternoon, some of the epigrams of Martial, but I shall never be able to read him connectedly so I propose to go over Tacitus. I have now read at least once nearly all of the Latin classical writers, and I mean to go over them again. Texier, whose book I like much, because it imparts clear ideas.

My father, Mrs. John Adams and Miss Cutts spent the evening with us. My Wife was better.

SATURDAY 29TH.

Fair day. At home. Ride. Evening at the Mansion.

I was better this morning but still far from feeling well. Occupied myself at home pretty steadily in writing upon the Report of the Merchants' Convention of the Southern States. The subject opens up very well, and I hope to make something of it. Yet the labour that it must cost is hardly compensated by evanescent publication of a single newspaper. The Courier gives me a silent admission and no other press allows even that. Such is the spirit of the age.

Read a little of Lessing and Le Comte after dinner. Some exercise working and a ride accompanied by my father round my favorite road by Milton. The weather was fair and the country is now in it's full perfection. The crops are all favorable and the frequent rains have preserved the verdure in it's freshness. The scenery around here in this season is certainly exquisite. I cannot describe the effect it has upon me. Evening at my father's for a short time.

SUNDAY 30TH.

Fine day. Exercises as usual. Evening at home.

I felt better today. Time devoted as usual; partly to my daughter Louisa and partly to reading Tuckers Light of Nature. The Author is a pleasant, good natured, easy tempered writer, but does not appear to me to see so far into a Millstone as he thinks he does. His study is without system which is bad for a metaphysical reasoner.

Attended divine service and heard Mr. Lunt preach in the morning from Ecclesiastes 1. 18. "He that increaseth knowledge increaseth sorrow." This sermon was not exactly in the sentiment of the text but it recommended that moral and religious basis without which learning is but a miserable guide. Afternoon Psalm 139. 7. "Whither shall I go from thy spirit? Or whither shall I flee from thy presence." The omnipresence of the deity.

Read a Sermon of Bishop Atterbury. 2. Corinthians 13. 5. "Examine yourselves, whether ye be in the faith; prove your own selves." Three classes of men the good, the bad and the middling, to the latter of whom this sensible sermon is addressed, presenting certain tests by which their condition may be ascertained by themselves. Read some of Le Comte.

In the evening, my father, Mr. and Mrs. Appleton and Mr. Frederick Whitney spent an hour which prevented my going to meet my Wife at Mrs. Miller's as I had intended.

MONDAY JULY 1.

To town. Afternoon at home. Evening at Mrs. T. B. Adams'.

I went to town today instead of tomorrow which was the day for the usual dinner at Squantum. My father went with me.

I strolled into the bookstore of Little & Brown and casually looking into the new number of the North American Review found my Article in full. This is handsome in Dr. Palfrey to say the least of it. The piece is much longer than I had expected and perhaps than it ought to be. But I felt more gratified at it's being there than at any of my preceding publications without my knowing exactly why, for upon looking over it I felt humble enough at the imperfections of the work which are glaring enough.[1]

Occupied at the Office in my Quarterly Accounts with my father. Return to dine. Afternoon, some exercise out of doors and two or three visitors. A visit to Mrs. T. B. Adams' where were all the family. Miss Cutts goes tomorrow to the Eastward.

[1] For CFA's feelings on sending the article to Palfrey see above, entry for 10 May.

TUESDAY 2D.

Day fine and warm. At home. Dine at Squantum.

I was pretty busy most of my morning in writing upon my new undertaking of the Report of the Southern Convention. The publications of yesterday have given me new courage and I go on with industry. Yet after all what is it this matter of publication that it should change the disposition of a man for a single moment. The world is full of books and many poor ones. It is of very little consequence whether I add or take away one from the number. My compensation is only in my industry which keeps me satisfied that I do not suffer what talent there is in me to lie unemployed.

A visit from Edmund Quincy and his Wife and then with my father to Squantum to the annual dinner of the Neponset Bridge Proprietors. A smaller company than usual and a poorer dinner. Mr. Wales, Dr. Frothingham, Mr. Lunt, Mr. J. Head, Dr. Woodward, Mr. T. Greenleaf and his son Price, D. Greenleaf, J. Bass, E. Miller, Frederick A. Whitney, and Mr. S. Torrey and G. W. Beale with ourselves. I was a little provoked that I. H. Adams and Mr. Campbell were purposely omitted by Mr. Miller. What can have been the feeling? Pretty dull time.

Home where I enjoyed the evening better. My Mother went to Boston to take Miss Mary Cutts.

WEDNESDAY 3D.

Fine day after rain. At home. Dine at the Mansion.

I was busy in pursuing my papers during the morning. There is abundance of subject and I am only afraid of tiring out the patience of readers before I develope it. It is impossible to divine any thing more absurd than the Carolina pretensions. Yet they carry a kind of weight with them from the confidence with which they are pressed. And it seems as if there was nobody here to resist them but ourselves. My father throws in his power of reasoning on the principle of Government whilst I fill up the practical details of common sense.

Dined at my father's as usual. Afternoon work and began the perusal of the Annals of Tacitus. They are familiar to me already.[1] LeComte also. Something might be made out of that if necessary.

Evening, E. C. Adams, with her brother and Mr. Campbell were with us for a little while and we then joined them to go down the hill. A little singing and then home.

[1] On CFA's earlier reading of Tacitus and on the editions in MQA, see vol. 1:102.

THURSDAY 4TH.

Showery but warm. At home. Evening call at the Mansion.

The sunrise was announced by cannon from the City and many of the surrounding towns. I arose and observed the scene with interest from one of the chamber windows. I could hear the ringing of the bells very plain, and see the smoke of the guns. The scene of early morning is always beautiful.

My time mainly taken up in writing. Finished the third of my comments upon the Carolina Report and determined to send them off to the Press.[1] There is in the Post of this morning a complimentary notice of my Article upon Burr. It ascribes the Authorship to the Editor, and hence there is no reason to suspect any motive towards or against me, nor yet is a purchased puff to spread the sale of the work.[2] It is astonishing how much this trifling incident encouraged me. It shows that I can do pretty well in somebody else's opinion but my own. Texier, Tacitus and Le Comte.

Nobody came in the evening as expected. We had a slight thunder shower and the air was so damp that the fireworks did not appear so well as last year. Mr. Beale and his daughter Caroline were here for an hour after our return from the Mansion. On the whole I have rarely passed a more quiet day of our Anniversary.

[1] The articles on "The Southern Commercial Conventions" appeared, unsigned, in the *Boston Courier* on 6 (p. 2, cols. 2–3), 9, 11, and 18 July, p. 2, cols. 1–2. They were written to make New England readers aware of important movements in other sections, especially in South Carolina, that seemed designed "to alienate the southern and southwestern States from the rest of the Union." The thesis of the articles is that the reports of the annual meetings or conventions of southern merchants reveal that present dangers to the Union do exist. Further that the loss of foreign trade by the South, the basis of their discontent, is, contrary to their view, not chargeable to the policies of the federal government but rather to the "developement of the western country," which has made agriculture in the South "an exceedingly difficult and precarious occupation."

[2] The *Boston Morning Post*, in its review article (4 July, p. 1, col. 5) on "The North American Review for July," said, "The review of *Davis's Memoirs and Journal of Burr*, which we believe to be from the pen of the editor [i.e. Palfrey], is the best thing in the number. We find but little in it to condemn, and much to praise. In speaking of Mr. Jefferson there is none of that villainous blackguardism which distinguishes the pages of the orthodox New York Review. On the contrary, there is a very good defence of him against the charge of having used corruption to obtain the Presidency, in 1801. There are many passages of striking beauty in this article, one of which [at p. 200–201] we cannot refrain from copying, on account of the kindly spirit which marks its close, and which does its author infinite honor."

FRIDAY 5TH.

Fogs and mist. To Boston. Company at dinner. Evening at the Mansion.

I went to the City in the morning and was occupied most of my time in Accounts. Finished drawing up those belonging to my father and the rest of my time in trying to get my balance Right but failed, so I brought my books out with me to continue to work upon them.

Found upon my return, I. Hull Adams and Mr. Campbell with Elizabeth C. Adams and my father, who all dined with us. The Afternoon was therefore devoted to them and the Evening too. An hour of which was passed at the house below.

SATURDAY 6TH.

Fog and rain. At home, dine at the Mansion and evening.

I devoted my whole morning to the examination of my books without however succeeding in detecting the error that had taken place. The day was dull and rainy. I dined at my father's by request as the two young men and E. C. Adams were to dine there too. Nothing new of any kind.

A little of the first book of the Annals of Tacitus. The text is as familiar to me as if I had never read any thing else. And yet when I was at College I certainly slighted the study of it much. Perhaps reading Crevier last winter which is in many parts a mere translation may explain it. An hour at the Mansion below.

SUNDAY 7TH.

Showery and warm. Exercises as usual. Evening at the Mansion.

Passed my morning hour in my usual avocations with my daughter and reading a chapter or two of Tucker's Light of Nature. He is not of the class of writers who please me for he dilutes his thoughts too much.

Attended divine service and heard Mr. Kent preach from Matthew 28. 9.17. "And as they went to tell his disciples, behold, Jesus met them saying, All hail. And they came and held him by the feet, and worshipped him. And when they saw him, they worshipped him: but some doubted." Afternoon Genesis 28. 17. "the gate of heaven." Mr. Kent is a very worthy man but he is exactly of that kind of person which I cannot follow. And yet I tried hard enough. My mind has been subdued to do wonders in comparison with what it once did but this as yet is beyond it.

Read a sermon in the English Preacher John 4. 9. "For the Jews have no dealings with the Samaritans." A sensible though not particularly striking discourse upon the injury committed by the indulgence of violent hatred in questions where mere differences of opinion are concerned. The author is John Balguy whose name I have seen quoted in English magazines with more commendation than any work which I have read of his appears to merit. Evening at the Mansion. Nothing new or remarkable.

MONDAY. 8TH.

Showery but warm. At home. Ride after dinner. Evening at E. Quincy's.

I devoted another morning to the examination of my books in the course of which I went through for the second time, the whole of my cash account, and brought out all my balances correctly with the exception of the general balance upon which the same error remains. I therefore gave it up as a bad business. The science of accounts is very well in its way but it must not be pushed to absurdity. I have now spent a week or more about an error of $10, which cannot be in any of the main accounts for they all come right.

After dinner, a little of Tacitus, and a ride accompanied by my father. We went round Weymouth and for the first time within my recollection I went to see the Meeting House and the parsonage which were the places of abode of Mr. Smith, and the birth place of my grandmother. There are very interesting associations connected with this scene in my father's mind, but I have none at all. Yet I was glad to see the spot.

Evening, in the carriage to see Edmund Quincy. Mrs. Quincy the elder there and I. H. Adams and Campbell, with E. C. Adams went with us. She had expressed a wish to hear them sing. We remained until ten and then came home in the rain. E. P. Greenleaf there. Edmund Quincy is a red hot temperance man and indeed rather wild in most things just now.

TUESDAY 9TH.

Showers. To town. Return to dinner. Afternoon at home, head ach.

Since I have come to Quincy this summer, my head has troubled me in an unusual degree, so much as somewhat to depress my spirits. I went to town in fair weather but it threatened showers in one of which I was caught in the Streets and another when returning home. Time taken up in paying and settling accounts and dropped in at Warrens' where I bought a coin or two. Nothing new.

Buckingham publishes my second paper today upon Carolina having already published the first on Saturday. I drew back the third today for correction, but returned it before leaving town.

Afternoon a little of Tacitus, but the doubtful state of my head made me work very languidly. Evening at the Mansion for an hour.

WEDNESDAY 10TH.

Warm. To Cambridge. Examination, home, head ach.

A very unusual thing with me my head ach continued through the night and troubled me all day though not sufficiently so to be positively disqualifying. Arose early and rode to Cambridge through Roxbury, Brookline and part of Brighton. I have never seen the country look more beautifully. The crops are all reaching maturity and these towns by their nearness to the market are becoming perfect gardens. Certainly the prosperity of this part of the country resting as it does so largely upon industry is wonderful.

Attended the examination of the last division of the Sophomore Class in Alcestis of Euripides and Electra of Sophocles. It was very indifferent. The young men were either of the lazy or the stupid and made but a poor figure. There was no other member of the Committee present, but they called in two supernumeraries, Mr. Dixwell the teacher of the Latin School, and Mr. McKean. The dinner afterwards was very stupid, and much smaller than usual. I recollected Dr. Frothingham's remark how stupid they were, and how true it struck me upon this occasion.

Returned home through town. Finished the first volume of the Annals of Tacitus, and worked a little upon my ground. Evening at the Mansion but my head prevented me from taking much pleasure in it.

THURSDAY 11TH.

Fine day but showery. My father 72. To town. Dine at the Mansion. Evening also.

I went to town as I proposed to go to Cambridge again tomorrow. My time much taken up in business, but I made out to reach the Athenæum and to call and see Warren who showed me a new coin or two and a collection of medals, some of which I should like much to have but he wishes to force them all down for the sake of a few. This is always the way in sales of coins, and a bad way it is.

Home. Dine at my father's. His birth day, the seventy second year complete of a life of industry and honour. May it continue to be fruitful of good works. There were present only the family, Mr. Campbell and Hull and Elizabeth.

Began the second book of the Annals of Tacitus. Ten Sections. Evening at the Mansion. Nothing new.

FRIDAY 12TH.

Warm day. To Boston and Cambridge. Examination and return. Evening company.

I went to Boston early this morning but yet did not reach it in season to be taken up by the carriage as proposed so that I followed on in my own vehicle to Cambridge. Reached it in time for the beginning of the examination of the first division of the Junior class in the Prometheus bound of Aeschylus. This is a piece of which I never read more than the first hundred lines or so and it stands by itself somewhat in its character. The recitations were good and correct but none of them extraordinary. Yet on the whole this class with which I have now been through an entire Greek college course of studies has shown the best of any, although it has rather lost than gained since the Freshman year. Much has been done to improve the studies but much remains to do to make it thorough. Judge Merril and Mr. Hillard were there and we met a large Committee at dinner which had come to examine the library. The party was therefore not so dull as usual although it was not lively.

Home again through Boston. Tacitus, 2d book, from section 10 to 30. Evening at the Mansion.

SATURDAY 13TH.

Warm day. At home all day. Evening at the Mansion.

After a week of so much and such unusual movement with me I was glad to seize the occasion of a quiet day. My time was taken up in finishing the fourth paper upon the Southern Convention, which consumed the whole morning. I have ended it as if promising a longer discussion. But I do not feel inclined to waste my ammunition. The whole of my work is just so much labour thrown away. I must feel a strong sense of duty to self impelling me to exertion when it would be so much more easy to take mine ease. I believe I have had enough of composition for the present.

After dinner Tacitus B. 2, s. 31 to 42 inclusive. Then interrupted by visits from Edward Brooks and his Wife, and Sidney's Wife who took tea and remained until sunset. Afterwards a short visit to the other house.

Showery and cool. Exercises in the usual way. Evening at the Mansion.

I passed a portion of my morning as usual in my lessons to my daughter Louisa who is thus receiving the rudiments of religious instruction.

Attended divine worship and heard Mr. Lunt from two texts 16 Judges 28.29.30 and 23 Luke 32.33.34. The verses are too long to transfer, but the idea proposed was a striking one and for aught I know original. A contrast between Samson as the perfect physical man with Jesus Christ as the incarnation of moral excellence; between the complete developement of the natural passions of man under the rudeness of the primitive age and ritual law of the Jews, and the full influence of the spiritual nature as displayed in the doctrine of the new dispensation, between the death of revenge and the death of forgiveness. The view taken was masterly but short as could not be otherwise during the period of a sermon.

Afternoon, Acts 10. 15. "What God hath cleansed, that call not thou common." The opening of Christianity to the Gentiles and the destruction of the exclusiveness of the Jewish system. Mr. Lunt is fond of contrasting these at all times. But his discourses always contain thought.

Read a sermon of Dr. Clarke from John 21. 22. "Jesus saith unto him, if I will that he tarry till I come, what is that to thee? Follow thou me." A sensible discourse upon needless curiosity and the investigation of merely trifling points of doctrine. Read some of Tucker's Light of Nature finishing the first volume. I am not much inclined to metaphysical researches, but do not desire to be wholly unacquainted with them. They improve the capacity of attention which is perhaps the most indispensable quality for effective mental action.

Mr. Campbell and I. H. Adams here for a short time. They leave tomorrow for New York. We passed an hour at the Mansion.

Fine day but not entirely without rain. At home. Dine and evening at the Mansion.

I spent the morning in reading excepting a short time devoted to a modification of my article. It was pleasant to be able to go over the words of others, and not to be always marshalling them for one's self. Read a part of the Diplomatic correspondence of the Revolution, some chapters of Texier on the Roman affairs and a little of Lessing's very ingenious dissertation upon fable. He is certainly an extremely acute critic.

As my Wife took an early dinner to go to Boston, I went down to the Mansion to dine. Afterwards, Tacitus and some work in the garden and on my grounds. Evening again below.

TUESDAY 16TH.

Fine day. Morning to town. Afternoon at home reading. Evening at the Mansion.

I rode to town and was occupied the greater part of my time in various commissions. Walked up to see my house in Acorn Street vacated today but found it shut up, so that I had my walk for nothing.

Nothing new. After dinner finished the second book of the Annals of Tacitus. This review is interesting if not useful. A little work besides, after which Grimm.

Evening at the Mansion which seems to be our regular course.

WEDNESDAY 17TH.

Fine day and warm. At home. Dine at the Mansion and evening.

This season is a fine one although the early part of it has proved so inconvenient. The summer weather is now setting in finely.

Mr. Hunt has sent me another letter with a request for an examination of Alexander Hamilton's Pamphlet.[1] I have felt a little inclined to make some strictures upon it before this and so I sat down today to try my hand at them. But I did not go very far.

Read some of Texier and more of Lessing. Dinner with the family below. After it, the third book of the Annals of Tacitus. The Claudian family do no honor to human nature. Tiberius seems to have been a singular mixture of discordant elements, but a thorough politician of a small scale. Grimm who is always amusing to me. Evening at my father's.

[1] Letter missing.

THURSDAY 18TH.

Warm day. Morning to town. After dinner at home. Evening at the Mansion.

Although not my day, I went to town this morning, partly for the purpose of accommodating my father who wished to go in and partly to attend to my house in Acorn Street which has lost the best tenant I ever had. The weather extremely warm. And as has often happened with me, I had more to do in walking than usual.

Returned as usual. Afternoon Tacitus book 3d of Annals, c. 20 to 40. I find this particular book is one with which I am not so well acquainted. Grimm and Le Comte, finishing the first volume of the latter.

My last paper upon South Carolina was published this morning with which I am inclined to think I shall terminate my labours for the Courier. It is a little observable how tenaciously the press adheres to it's rule of entire silence respecting any thing I write. It carries it so far as in the case of what I write under my name for the New York Magazine, to omit my particular article in the general notice of that publication which has that signature whilst they notice the one I wrote anonymously.[1] There is something rather complimentary in this, but it is uphill work. I believe I am beyond the day of discouragement. Evening at the Mansion.

[1] Notices of the first issue of *Hunt's Merchants' Mag.* had been printed in a number of newspapers since its publication in June. None, apparently, that had come to CFA's attention singled out for mention his signed article that had appeared in the issue (above, entry for 25 June). The irony that impresses him here probably derives from the praise recently given his unsigned and misattributed *North American Review* article (above, entry for 4 July). His second signed article in *Hunt's* (below, entry for 25 July) would be praised as "a lucid, practical, and philosophical exposition" in the *Quincy Patriot* (10 Aug., p. 2, col. 4), but this would receive no mention in the Diary, nor would it assuage the bitterness he felt over his neglect in the Boston press.

FRIDAY 19TH.

To town, not returning until evening.

This was a day of great heat. I went to town accompanied by my Wife. Passed the morning much as usual, various commissions requiring an unusual portion of exercise from me. Walk up to Acorn Street but found the house shut up.

Mrs. A. had agreed to dine with Mr. and Mrs. Edward Brooks today and I joined her there, where we were met by Mr. Brooks the elder. Pleasant time enough, but after it I undertook to walk to the Athenæum to see the Gallery, which was rather uncomfortable, the Gallery itself was over warm so after running over the newspaper files in the reading room to find notices of any thing done lately by me, without success, I went back and immediately after tea returned home.

The evening at home was delicious and I could not help thinking how much better it was not to stir from it. The very first summer evening we have had and in itself perfectly exquisite.

SATURDAY 20TH.

Extreme heat. At home. Bath after dinner. Evening at the Mansion.

The morning was one of the warmest we have in the course of a year, but it brought on a very violent thunder shower which qualified the heat. I occupied myself very quietly in sketching some remarks upon a late Pamphlet of Alexander Hamilton's upon the state of the currency. Mr. Hunt promises to keep me occupied quite as much as I desire.

Texier and Lessing. The storm distracted my attention a little. After dinner, Tacitus, but I took my two boys John and Charles with me to Mount Wollaston where we enjoyed a salt water bath. They appear to have conquered their apprehension of it but have not yet sufficient familiarity to attempt to swim. I did not make out to read more than twelve sections. Evening at the Mansion.

SUNDAY. 21ST.

Rain and clouds. Exercises as usual. Evening at the Mansion.

There was very heavy rain early but it soon ceased and continued cloudy all day. I devoted an hour of the morning as usual to my daughter Louisa. My lessons are short and simple. Two Chapters of the Bible to read, and the portion of the common Prayer book to repeat which contains the commandments, and the analysis of duty. This with a hymn makes the exercise.

Dr. Frothingham came up from Boston and preached. We heard him from Ezekiel 47. 12 "And the fruit thereof shall be for meat, and the leaf thereof for medicine." A discourse upon the Scriptures, considering them as a whole and replying to the objections most commonly presented against them. These objections were stated strongly and answered satisfactorily. There was beauty in the composition, great unity and keeping in the figurative language drawn from the application of the text and unusual warmth in the delivery. I thought I never had heard the Dr. to more advantage.

Afternoon, Deuteronomy 34. 8. "So the days of weeping and mourning for Moses were ended." A singular selection on the subject of mourning drawn from the character of Moses and the regret of the

Jews for his death. I dined at my father's with the Dr. and his son Thomas, who took tea with us and returned to town in the evening. We had a pleasant visit from them.

After a short evening visit at the other house, returned home in time to read a sermon Luke 16. 13. "No servant can serve two masters: for either he will hate the one, and love the other; or else he will hold to the one and despise the other. Ye cannot serve God and Mammon." Bishop Hoadley does nothing but weaken the text in what he says and yet sensible enough.

MONDAY. 22D.

Warm but showery. At home. Evening at the house below.

The day was so sultry that it brought on a heavy shower by night attended with a little thunder. I was at home with the exception of a short time passed at the bath, with my boys.

I revised my remarks upon Hamilton's pamphlet and took them into a new draught. This is rather superfluous labour, I suppose. Texier and a little of Lessing.

After dinner, read the remainder of the third book of the Annals of Tacitus. The merit of this author is in his sketchiness if I may so say. A few words make a picture or qualify a description. Perhaps the best thing of his is the character of Tiberius. A little of Grimm, my progress with whom is very slow. Short visit at the Mansion.

TUESDAY 23D.

Warm morning and showers. To town. Afternoon at home. Evening at the Mansion.

I went to town. Time taken up partly in a visit to the house in Acorn Street where there are a regiment of men doing repairs, and partly in accounts and commissions.

The arrival of news by the Great Western made some sensation inasmuch as it brought accounts of a continued want of money in England and a fall in cotton. The prospect is thick ahead. No chance of any more relief by loans, and exchange consequently rising.

Home to dine. Afternoon, Tacitus, 4 book, 20 sections. And a little of Grimm and Le Comte. Evening at my father's. The sudden changes of the weather and getting my feet wet have given me the ague in my face.

WEDNESDAY 24TH.

Moist weather. At home, dine at the Mansion and evening.

I suffered during the night and all of this day with the affection of my teeth, so that I was not able to enjoy much of any thing. Occupied in finishing the new draught of remarks upon Hamilton's Pamphlet, and afterwards in reading the Diplomatic Correspondence of the Revolution from which I do not gather much. Texier and finish Lessing's remarks upon Fable. I shall not read more of him at present. This German acuteness is dreadfully fatiguing. Began Meissner's Alcibiades, a sort of historical romance.[1]

After dining at my father's, I read of Tacitus to the 41st section of the fourth book. What a marvellous account of the vices and crimes of a wicked generation. But is our's any better? Evening, depressed by pain and glad to go to bed.

[1] August Gottlieb Meissner, *Alcibiades*, 4 vols., Leipzig, 1781. JQA's copy is at MQA.

THURSDAY. 25TH.

Clouds but warm. At home. Mr. Brooks and Sidney and his Wife to dine. Quarries.

My face continued to pain me all night and this morning, but it gave signs of relenting. The weather is exceedingly moist for the season of the year.

I read a little while, walked down and paid a long visit to my mother and found a copy of my Article in Mr. Hunts next magazine.[1] It is full of errors. I sat down to correct it when Sidney Brooks and his Wife came in and after them Mr. Brooks. My father had been invited to join them and came upon his return from Boston. The dinner was pleasant enough but I could not enjoy it.

Directly afterwards, the whole party got into the Carriage and rode to the Quarries to see the columns and other work for the New York Merchants' Exchange.[2] Returning, I had all of my friends to tea. Mr. Brooks spent the night here.

[1] CFA's review of George Tucker, *The Theory of Money and Banks Investigated*, would appear under the title "The Theory of Money and Banks" in *Hunt's Merchants' Mag.* for August, vol. 1, p. [110]–124. A draft is in the Adams Papers, M/CFA/23.1, Microfilms, Reel No. 317.

[2] The construction of the new Merchants Exchange in New York City, 1836–1842, with its great Ionic columns of Quincy granite, was the architectural event of its time. Its designer was Isaiah Rogers, formerly of Boston; see vol. 3:xiv; *DAB*.

FRIDAY 26TH.

Fine day. To town. Afternoon at home. Evening at the Mansion.

I went to town this morning and was much occupied in visiting the House in Acorn Street which is still under repair and what is worse which is not yet asked for. Then at the Office. My pain is leaving me. Mr. Brooks did not stay with me as I expected, but returned to town.

I dispatched to Mr. Hunt my last article upon Hamilton's Pamphlet[1] together with the corrected sheets of the other. I feel now as if I would allow myself a little vacation from the labours of composition which have been pretty incessant for six or eight months.

Afternoon, Tacitus, 20 sections of the fourth book of Annals. A little out of door work also. In the evening at my father's.

Much talk today of a cotton circular issued by Southern men in New York, which is to be sure a curious thing enough.[2] Met Mr. Buckingham who spoke of it as if he thought I might be disposed to notice it. I believe not. The people most interested in this subject have left me to work my material as best I could without ever manifesting the smallest sign of sympathy. I have done it as a matter of duty. If they wish for more, they must bow down to their own wooden idols to get it.

[1] This, his third article for *Hunt's*, would appear in the September issue, vol. 1, p. 214–227, with the title, "Banks and the Currency."

[2] The text of a "Cotton Circular" signed by fourteen prominent southerners who had met in Macon, Ga., in June and again "accidentally" in New York city on 5 July was printed in the *New York Commercial Advertiser* on the 25th and reprinted in the *Daily Centinel and Gazette* on 27 July, p. 1, cols. 4–5. The circular was addressed to the "cotton-planters, merchants, factors, and presidents and directors of the several banks in the Southern states" and appealed for the creation of machinery by which a third of the cotton crop would be withheld from the market with financing by the banks. The object sought was a steady and advantageous market in London or Liverpool for American cotton.

SATURDAY 27TH.

Fine day. At home. Afternoon to visit Mr. and Mrs. S. C. Gray. Evening at the Mansion.

My morning was consumed in a sort of studious idleness. Finished reading the first volume of the Diplomatic Correspondence of the Revolution. Also the second volume of Texier, whose book is a very excellent developement of the Roman polity. I think I have really acquired much information from it. But am I right? or is not my mind a sort of sieve through which all runs but the coarser and less valuable materials of knowledge? Continued Meissner's Alcibiades.

After dinner, finish the fourth book of Annals of Tacitus before going over to see Mr. and Mrs. Gray at Dorchester where we took tea. A pretty antique place which belongs to John Welles. Home and brief visit below.

SUNDAY 28TH.

Fine day. Exercises as usual. Evening to Mrs. Quincy's, and at the Mansion.

After the usual course with my daughter, I read a little of Tucker's Light of Nature and attended divine service. Heard Mr. Lunt preach from Hebrews. 4. 3. "For we which have believed do enter into rest." A curious and paradoxical proposition that rest is the most desired of all things, and yet that it is that rest which results from the faithful performance of active duties. It may be so, but it appears to me that there is some confusion of terms in the whole process. Or if not, that the ideas conveyed are calculated to be rather curious than useful. Afternoon John 6. 38. "For I came down from heaven, not to do mine own will, but the will of him that sent me." This was a much finer discourse upon the selfdenying character of the Saviour.

Matthew 10. 16. "Behold, I send you forth as sheep in the midst of wolves; be ye therefore wise as serpents, and harmless as doves." A sensible discourse of Dr. Smalridge in the English Preacher upon the necessity of Uniting Wisdom and innocence, the one being not alone sufficient to form the Christian character.

We went to pay a visit to Mrs. Edmund Quincy, the ladies to see Mrs. Parker her mother who is staying there. E. Quincy was not there but had gone to town. We returned early and spent a short time at the Mansion.

MONDAY 29TH.

Clear. To town. Afternoon at home. Evening at the Mansion.

I went to town this morning, partly for the sake of accommodating my father who wished to go and partly to superintend the repairs going on in Acorn Street. I was also engaged in other business, particularly in attempting to bring to a close the accounts of the Estate of T. B. Adams. This has been hanging on a great while, and still bids fair to trouble me somewhat.

Returned to dinner. Afternoon, Tacitus, the fragment remaining of the fifth book with nine sections of the sixth. The dark period of the reign of Tiberius developes itself by degrees and shocks one more and more at every step. Evening at my father's. Nothing new.

TUESDAY 30TH.

Warm. To town. Afternoon at home. Evening at the Mansion.

Morning in the city again. Most of my time taken up with the Account of T. B. Adams which I at last brought into order. There is nothing now remaining but to pass it through the Probate Court, which I hope to do in a few days. The town quite alive with the accounts of the arrival of the British Queen, with news from England of a commercial character not very encouraging.[1] There seems every indication of a crisis in money matters of a more serious and durable character than the last was. I know not the end.

Home. Read Tacitus, twenty sections of the sixth book, more obscure and doubtful text than the first three. Le Comte China and a little of Grimm. Took tea at the house below as my Wife had gone out to make a visit to Mrs. Seaver from which she returned at about eight.

[1] The *British Queen* docked in New York on the 28th. It brought further reports of depressed cotton prices and increases in the interest rates (*Boston Courier*, 31 July, p. 2, cols. 1–4).

WEDNESDAY 31ST.

Heavy southerly showers. At home all day, dine and evening at the Mansion.

My day passed very quietly. Most of the morning devoted to reading the second volume of the Correspondence of the Revolution. This contains the letters of Arthur Lee which as being more controversial than the rest are more entertaining. They are also well written. I also made some progress with Texier and a good deal with Meissner's Alcibiades of which I do not form a very high opinion.

After dining at the Mansion, returned and read the remainder of the sixth book of the Annals. I make my study so long that I do not get on very fast with China or Grimm. Evening at my fathers.

Thus pass the months in a quiet and happy way. Nothing to put in a Diary worthy of a single remark and no reason to be otherwise than pleased that it is so.

THURSDAY. AUGUST 1ST.

Fine day. At home.

I was at home all day, reading Arthur Lee's correspondence which is interesting and well written. Texier and Meissner's Alcibiades, which last I got interested in more than was proper. The pictures drawn are rather too sensual. I believe I have had enough of the book and will take up something more useful.

Tacitus, the first twenty sections of the fragment of the eleventh book. The stultification of Claudius and the abominations of Messalina. From the death of Tiberius, this is a jump over the madness of Caligula, which must have afforded fine colours for the pencil of the historian. What is the secret of the power of this writer, that he can put a thought so briefly into bright light? I must try to analyze it for the sake of improving my defects of style.

FRIDAY. AUG. 2.

Fine day. To town. Afternoon at home. Evening visit to Dr. Woodward.

I went to town this morning and my time was taken up for the most part with business at my Office. Read over my Article upon Tucker in which the errors are not corrected so that I feel ashamed of it. An apologetic letter from Hunt.[1] I believe I must stop in that quarter.

Home to dinner. Finish the eleventh book of the Annals. The death of Messalina bad enough but there have been many French women near the throne quite as bad. The Wife of Henry the 4th for instance, as described by Brantome.

My father went today on a fishing party with Hingham gentlemen to Cohasset but I excused myself. A short return visit to Dr. Woodward in the evening.

[1] Freeman Hunt's letter is missing.

SATURDAY. 3D.

Day fine. At home. Evening at the Mansion.

I passed my time quietly but pretty steadily all day. Read and finished Arthur Lee's Correspondence and that of his brother William's with a portion of Mr. Izard's who seems to have been the least valuable of all the Officers we had abroad. A true Carolinian full of all sorts of whimsies. Texier, and being doubtful of what German I would read, took up Plutarch's Life of Alcibiades from which I gather all that Meissner puts into his Romance. After dinner, Twenty sections of the twelfth book of Annals of Tacitus, Le Comte and a good deal of Grimm.

The weather is now settled and delightful and I think the view from my portico in the morning is beautiful. Evening at my father's.

273

SUNDAY 4TH.

Fine day. Customary exercises. Evening at Mrs. T. B. Adams'.

I occupied one hour in going over the usual exercise with my daughter and read besides some of Tucker's book which does not fix my attention. There appears to be very little method in his pursuit, and the difficulty of tracing any connexion between one portion and another of the work discourages one from the whole.

Attended divine service all day and heard Mr. Lunt preach from 1. Corinthians 10. 31. "Whether therefore ye eat or drink or whatsoever ye do, do all to the glory of God," and the same Epistle 12. 6 I think. "There are diversities of operations, but it is the Same God which worketh all in all." The latter sermon pleased me most as designing to prove that religion was the result of the developement of man's nature in every portion of it, whether through the senses, or the reason or the imagination or the passions. Mr. Lunt writes with a great deal of beauty and sometimes his delivery seems to me like a strain of sweet but languid music, on the ear, hardly powerful enough to rouse the attention to great action and yet charming enough to regret its stop.

A sermon by Bishop Butler from the English Preacher, on the Love of God. Matthew 22. 37. "Thou shalt love the Lord thy God, with all thy heart, with all thy soul and with all thy mind." A discourse closely reasoned and characteristic of the Author.

The afternoon was quite perfect. The air clear and not too warm and the landscape refreshing. Read a little of Grimm who fills up my odd moments.

Evening to Mrs. T. B. Adams' to see Mrs. John Angier who was there for the day, and seized the occasion for a short visit to Mr. and Mrs. Miller. Mr. Price Greenleaf was there, and my father came in shortly afterwards.

MONDAY. 5TH.

Fine day. At home. Ride. Evening, visit from E. Quincy and Mr. Parker.

This day was passed very quietly at home. Read the Correspondence of the Revolution, being that of Izard, Laurens and the commencement of Franklin's. Also Texier, but my German does not flourish from the want of a text book. So I went over the Life of Alcibiades in Plutarch. How much in that biography as indeed in all those of that writer.

Read after dinner only ten sections of the twelfth book of the Annals of Tacitus, as I went to ride accompanied by my father round Milton Hill. The Country looks very beautifully. Evening at home. Edmund Quincy and his Wife's brother, Mr. Parker came in and passed an hour. The former appears much better.

TUESDAY 6TH.

Hazy but fine. To town. Afternoon visitors. Evening at the house below.

I went this morning to town and was occupied very much with applications from tenants and with the performance of commissions. I know not why but things seemed to go well with me today. This is a peculiar and unaccountable circumstance in my life that without my knowing why or wherefore, I shall be at some moments a little elated and at others equally depressed. The course of my life has been so smooth that it ought not to be subjected to such alternations, at least without some evident reason for them.

Home. Afternoon, only five sections of Tacitus as I was interrupted by a visit from Mrs. Perkins and Mr. and Mrs. Rogers who spent an hour. At the Mansion in the evening.

WEDNESDAY 7TH.

Warm and dry. At home. Dine at my father's and evening visit.

I spent a large part of my morning in a manner somewhat different from my usual one. My first experiments in budding were made this morning upon a variety of stocks of wild pear and apple trees which are in my vicinity and which at present cannot be said to yield any profit to any one. Whether they will take or not I cannot say, the heat of the day which I did not expect is against it, but at any rate there is not much lost. I had a little time left for Texier.

We dined at the Mansion and spent the evening as usual. I finished the twelfth book of the Annals ending with the death of Claudius. Which is the worst character Messalina or Agrippina? I incline to think the latter. Visit with my father, Mr. and Mrs. John Greenleaf, and Mr. Cranch.[1] J. Carr my father's tenant lost his child this evening, so late obtained.

[1] On the visit to the Adamses' aged relatives, the John Greenleafs, at which Christopher Pearse Cranch and other connections were present, see the entry for the present date in JQA, Diary. On Cranch, see vol. 6:230.

THURSDAY 8TH.

Morning warm but weather changed. At home, bath. Evening at my father's. Mr. Ward.

I spent the greater part of the morning in budding trees, it being a favorable time for it, warm but cloudy and threatening rain. At noon went down to Mount Wollaston with my two boys and took a bath. The water was fine but a change of wind to the eastward made the air cold.

A little of Texier. After dinner Tacitus, book 13 of the Annals twenty sections. The beginning of Nero. No time for any thing else.

Tea at my father's, after which there came a man from New York calling himself Ward, with a letter from Mr. Hunt, and whose object was to procure a Lecture for the Mercantile Library Association during the next winter.[1] Against the whole system of lecturing I have strong and serious objections, and my participation in it is not a matter of much selfcongratulation, whenever I do it. But my duty seems to be to contend against the obstacles which have been raised against my progress in every way that I can, and here is an opportunity presented in a foreign city which has been rather sedulously denied to me at home. Shall I seize it? My only doubt arises from the difficulty of hitting upon a good topic. I did not answer positively tonight, but requested a short time for reflection.

[1] The letter to CFA from Freeman Hunt (29 July), introducing Elija Ward of the Mercantile Library Association, is in the Adams Papers.

FRIDAY 9TH.

Cloudy morning with light showers but it afterwards cleared. To town. Afternoon at home.

Rode to town where my time was very much taken up with visits to tenants and business in general. I was not very successful in my applications, but succeeded in letting my house, and also a part of my Office rather as a favor than otherwise. This relieves my mind a little although I have been at great expense for the first in repairing it. Nothing particularly new.

Home in a cloud of dust. My father dined with me, so that I read only ten sections of Tacitus. Evening at the Mansion. Depression of spirits today.

SATURDAY 10TH.

At home, fine day. Afternoon, visitors and to Weymouth. At my father's.

My morning was not passed altogether profitably, for after a little reading only at home I went down to the Mansion and became engaged in a rather fruitless examination of old MS papers. Found two or three old sermons and other papers of my great-grandfather Smith and one or two other things of some little interest but not much.

Home where I made further progress in Texier and began Menzel's History of German Literature,[1] a book I have borrowed from Dr. Frothingham. His opening is completely characteristic of his nation. But he is a thinker and will pay perusal.

After dinner, seventeen sections of Tacitus, being interrupted by visitors. Mrs. Carter and Mr. and Miss Sigourney from Boston with Mr. Lunt to pilot the way. They made only a call of form and we started after it in the carriage to go to Weymouth and see Mrs. Tufts and her daughters.[2] By we I mean my father, wife, Mrs. John Adams who spent the day with us and myself. Home late after a pleasant ride, and a short visit at the Mansion.

[1] Wolfgang Menzel, *Die deutsche literatur*, 2 vols., Stuttgart, 1828.
[2] On the widowed Mrs. Cotton Tufts Jr. (Mercy Brooks), see vol. 5:82.

SUNDAY. 11TH.

Pleasant day. Usual Exercises. Evening at the Mansion.

I spent an hour in my usual way with my daughter, teaching her some little notion of religion. Read a little of Tucker's Light of Nature which does not grow in my regard as I go on.

Attended divine service and heard Mr. Lunt preach from Jonah 4. 9. "And God said to Jonah, Doest thou well to be angry for the gourd? And he said, I do well to be angry even unto death." An interesting abstract of the book from which the text is taken with some moral applications of the story which never occurred to me before. Also from Matthew 15. 5.6. "But ye say, Whosoever shall say to his father or his mother, It is a gift, by whatsoever thou mightest be profited by me; And honour not his father or his mother, he shall be free. Thus have ye made the commandment of God of none effect by your tradition." I recollect this discourse when it was preached before, a very good one.

Read also another discourse of Bishop Butler on the same subject and text of the one last Sunday, and marking the closeness of thought which distinguishes his writing. The ladies went down to Mrs. Quincy's, but I spent the evening with my mother.

MONDAY 12TH.

Cloudy with showers. At home. Evening, a short ride. At the Mansion.

I devoted three hours of my morning to a copy of a letter of my grandmother's sent to me by the kindness of Mrs. John Greenleaf. It is long and in the nature of a Journal so that I finished only about a quarter part.[1] Finished Texier which is a good book and read a little of Menzel.

After dinner, I went out, deeming it a favorable opportunity and put in a multitude of buds being my second experiment, the first having been but partially successful on account of a mistake in setting the buds too low in the tree. I took a short ride accompanied by my father after tea and returned soon. Rest of the evening at the house.

[1] The journal letter is probably that from AA to Mrs. Greenleaf's mother, Mary Smith Cranch, 6–30 July 1784, describing her voyage to join JA and her first days in London. Now in MWA, the letter in its entirety was included in AA, *Letters*, ed. CFA, 1840, p. 199–241.

TUESDAY. 13TH.

Clear and cool. To town. Afternoon company. Evening at the Mansion.

My daughter Louisa is eight years old this day. As she grows, she becomes the subject of greater hopes and anxieties. I see in her the germ of much that is good and the prospect of weeds that must be skilfully eradicated or they will prevent a crop. Heaven prosper my endeavors.

I went to town and was busily engaged in my affairs which worry me a little at present.

Home. After dinner, only three or four sections of Tacitus before Edward Brooks and his Wife came to take tea. Of course, nothing more. Evening at the Mansion.

WEDNESDAY 14TH.

Cold and foggy. At home, dine and evening at my father's.

I passed some time in the morning in continuation of the work of copying a long letter. I have now seriously commenced the duty of preparing the work which I have been meditating during the Summer, and shall continue it easily as I find it convenient. It will afford me a kind of agreeable occupation for some time to come, and in the mean time I will try to arrange in my mind the elements of a biographical summary.[1]

The materials for the Lecture worry me much more and I must be collecting them.[2] Yet on the whole I like the kind of life I now lead exceedingly, for it seems to furnish me with a hope of earning an honest reputation without putting me into the region of violent passions and overstrained wishes and fears. The life of the politician in this country most particularly is a life of terror and of personal sacrifices which are hardly compensated even by the most brilliant momentary triumphs. And every day the thing grows worse instead of better.

Read an hour in Menzel who thinks justly, and moderately. At my father's there dined with us Mr. and Mrs. Lunt, who also remained until after tea. I therefore did nothing during the afternoon but put in three buds into apple trees.

[1] JQA had suggested to CFA the preparation and publication of a memoir of AA (see the entry for 13 June, above). CFA, stimulated by the idea and by the warmth with which her letters had been received when included in his Massachusetts Historical Society lecture (entry for 23 Jan. 1838, above), thereafter must have thought of combining the memoir with a collection of the letters. Reading the letter lent him two days before by Mrs. Greenleaf seems to have convinced him to proceed.

[2] Doubts about accepting the invitation to address the Mercantile Library Association in New York (entry for 8 Aug., above) seem also to have been resolved.

THURSDAY 15TH.

Cold east wind. At home all day. Evening at my father's.

I continued my work upon the letter without doing quite as much as I have upon any preceding morning. This single letter will have cost me nearly five days. It is however much the longest.

Read an hour in Menzel and was interrupted some time by visits from Mrs. Edmund Quincy, Mrs. Greene and Miss Quincy.

After dinner, finished the thirteenth book of Annals of Tacitus. This will aid me in my medallic studies. And had time for Grimm who has been somewhat neglected this summer. How little of what man wishes to do, does he find himself able to accomplish.

FRIDAY. 16TH.

Cold easterly wind. To town. Afternoon and evening at home.

I went to town this morning accompanied by my father. Called at the Athenæum to procure a book or two upon credit, a subject which I must begin to look up. Storch, Political Economy,[1] I found instructive. The subject will bear working, I think. There were persons at the Office to see my father much of the time so that I had little opportunity for business.

Home as usual. It had been cold all the morning but set in to rain after dinner. I read twenty sections in the fourteenth book of Tacitus, and some of Grimm. In the evening I was at home, and read aloud to my Wife the first act of King Lear.

[1] Heinrich Friedrich Storch, *Cours d'économie politique*, 5 vols., Paris, 1823–1824.

SATURDAY 17TH.

Cold and fog. At home all day. Evening visit to Mr. Appleton's.

My occupation this morning was pretty steady. I finished the long letter which has taken me all the week. Read and reflected upon the material for a Lecture and a little of Menzel. This with a walk with my children into town consumed the whole morning. After dinner Tacitus book 14 of Annals, s 21 to 40, and Grimm, who is a kind of cold scoffer at whose selfsufficiency one is apt to become a little angry.

In the evening, the ladies went up to take tea with Mrs. Adams, and I walked up to pay a visit to Mr. Appleton. He has a large family of grown up children. Not particularly interesting.

SUNDAY 18TH.

Clearing off. Exercises as usual. Evening at the Mansion.

I went through the ordinary routine of exercises for this morning with my little girl and read also some of Tucker, but with slackened interest.

Attended divine service and heard Mr. Russel[1] a gentleman now officiating at Hingham in the room of Charles Brooks preach in the morning from 1 John 4. 20, "For he that loveth not his brother whom he hath seen, how can he love God whom he hath not seen?" and in the afternoon from John 15. 4 "Without me ye can do nothing." A good sensible preacher without making himself very interesting.

Read a discourse in the English Preacher from Titus 2. 10. "That they may adorn the doctrine of God our Saviour in all things." A very excellent one by the Revd. Dr. Rogers upon the use of good practical morals as a support to the Christian profession. There is plain, downright sense and acute reasoning combined.

Le Comte, his Account of the curse of proselytism in China as practised by the Catholic missionaries is curious. A little of Grimm and evening at the house below. Can I let this day pass without remembering that I am thirty two.

¹ CFA has here mistaken the name of the day's preacher, Rev. Oliver Stearns, who is properly named by JQA in his entry for the day. Charles Brooks had resigned his pastorate in the New North Meeting-House in Hingham early in 1839 to become a professor of natural history in the University of the City of New York. He was succeeded in Hingham by Mr. Stearns, Harvard 1826, who would remain until 1856. He was afterwards president of the Meadville (Penna.) Theological School and professor in the Harvard Divinity School ([Thomas T. Bouvé and others], *History of the Town of Hingham*, 3 vols. in 4, Cambridge, 1893, vol. 1, pt. 2, p. 50–54).

MONDAY 19TH.

Fine day and warm. At home. Afternoon ride. Evening at the Mansion.

Upon entering another year of my life, it is usual with me to look back and take a reckoning from the past. Yet I have little or nothing material to record. My life is one uninterrupted series of blessings which I feel I do not deserve by any active merit of mine, but which it is my constant effort to make myself at least less unfit for. This is the motive for my endeavours to attain a respectable position which have not been entirely without success. Although but little seconded by any and very strongly resisted in secret by some, yet I feel encouraged to think that my labours have not proved altogether without use. Today I see the Emancipator, an Abolitionist Newspaper, republishes my Articles upon the commercial convention of the South with a commentary which is complimentary.¹ My vanity must not be led away by these things. But putting a firm trust in divine providence to guide me in the strait path, I will endeavor to walk with fear and hope. In my family I have been favored more even than usual, as my Wife has regained a share of health greater than I could have anticipated after her severe reductions.

I was at work in budding much of my morning and spent the remainder in copying and Menzel. After dinner, seventeen sections of Tacitus book 14th, and a ride taking my boy Charley. I went down to the beach of Mount Wollaston. The sea, the sky, the sun and green earth all combined to make a picture of beauty such as is not often to be enjoyed by us, but when it is, the effect is exquisite. Lovely evening, partly spent at the house below.

[1] With the promise to follow with others of the series, *The Emancipator* (New York) on 8 Aug. reprinted from the *Boston Courier*, "The Southern Commercial Convention, No. 1." The accompanying commentary read: "We are encouraged to find four or five influential papers awaking to the importance of this subject ["Slaveholding Plots and Pretensions"], and already daring to call in question the imprescriptible right of slaveholders to domineer over the free states.... In this work the Cincinnati Gazette, the New York American and the Boston Atlas have rendered a noble service.... The Boston Courier has at times allowed a tolerable discussion of slavery topics. And lately it has given room to a series of well written and sound principled essays.... We do not mean to be understood, however, as endorsing all the sentiments of the writer" (p. 1, col. 1 – 2).

TUESDAY 20TH.

Beautiful day and warm. To town. Afternoon at home. Evening at the Mansion.

I went to town today where the principal matter of interest seems to be the news from England by the Liverpool Steamer. It is singular to observe the difference already existing in the relations between the new and old world from the adoption of Steam Navigation. The commercial world is blending into one and the political state of Europe bears more directly upon our's. The age is one of movement through all of which I see nothing so clearly as the truth of the line of Bishop Berkley, "*Westward* the star of empire takes it's way."[1]

Home. Finished the fourteenth book of the Annals and read twelve sections of the fifteenth. Memorable is the history of Nero, a man naturally of good disposition but corrupted by power and by the appliances of vice, to so great a degree as to leave a name synonimous with wickedness and cruelty. Lovely evening at my father's.

[1] An Adams family misquotation of Bishop George Berkeley's "Westward the course . . ."

WEDNESDAY 21ST.

Warm day. At home. Evening visit to Mr. Lunt.

This was of the hottest of the season. I passed my time very busily in copying and gave only an hour to my study of the subject of credit, and another to Menzel. We dined at my father's but I read twenty sections of Tacitus nevertheless. On the whole a very industrious day.

The copying is the most laborious part and that which perhaps is the most serviceable to me. Yet it is a tribute due to excellence from her own family which she is not likely to receive excepting from me. Could I do any thing of my own that would do me more credit? I doubt. In the evening I went to Mr. Lunt's. Dr. and Mrs. Woodward there. Conversation general and not interesting.

THURSDAY 22D.

Warm day, bath, at home. Evening to Mrs. Adams's.

Another extremely warm day. I went and took a bath at the Wharf this morning alone, the pleasantest of the season. Then at work upon copy which I pursued vigorously until noon. An hour devoted to Storch's Economie politique, another to Menzel, both good and profitable studies. After dinner twenty sections of Tacitus and Grimm.

Mrs. John Adams and E. C. Adams dined with us and my father spent the day in town. In the evening I walked home with the latter of the ladies mentioned and spent an hour in conversation with Mrs. Adams. The men have been engaged yesterday and today in clearing the ditch below my house.

FRIDAY. 23D.

Warm day. To Boston. After dinner at home, and evening.

I went to town this morning and heard of an accident that befel Mrs. Everett yesterday by which she broke her arm. She is however pretty well under it. Elizabeth C. Adams went with me. I was much taken up in the manner common with me, in small commissions and accounts and in drawing up a statement for the heirs of T. B. Adams whose estate it is now my desire finally to settle. I did not however finish it before it was time to return.

Called on Dr. Bigelow as I went home to consult him about the baby who is teething. Then home which felt agreeably in comparison with the heated atmosphere that I left. A city is not for me in summer. Finished the fifteenth book of the Annals of Tacitus which is the last of the perfect books. What a record of the folly and crime of Nero! A little of Grimm. Evening at my father's. A most beautiful moonlight night.

SATURDAY 24TH.

Warm day. At home, bath. Work as usual, evening at the Mansion.

I devoted myself to the usual train of occupations, with the exception of an hour for the bath to which I went with my father. I copied two or three letters and read Storch who is a very clear and sensible writer, but my programme is a pretty extensive one and I must shortly begin to devote more time to it than I do if I expect to fill it up well. This copying too can not be postponed a great while.

Afternoon, twenty sections of the sixteenth book of the Annals, and a little of Grimm. An hour at the Mansion in the evening.

SUNDAY 25TH.

Warm. Exercises as usual. Evening at the Mansion. Mrs. Angier.

I spent an hour with my daughter in her lessons. Read more of Tucker and attended divine service all day. Heard Dr. Francis preach in the morning from Acts 17. 31. "Because he hath appointed a day, in the which he will judge the world in righteousness by that man whom he hath ordained." I could not fix my attention upon this discourse respecting the judgment. That in the afternoon was more interesting from Acts 21. 11 "And when he was come unto us, he took Paul's girdle and bound his own hands and feet and said, Thus saith the Holy Ghost, So Shall the Jews at Jerusalem bind the man that owneth this girdle and shall deliver him into the hands of the Gentiles." Upon the language of action and treated with some variety of illustration as well as original thought. But Dr. Francis is not one of those who seem to find any path into my feelings. His voice is harsh and his delivery formal and cold.

Afterwards read a sermon by Bishop Conybeare from Matthew 25. 5. "While the bridegroom tarried, they all slumbered and slept," upon the infirmity of human nature and it's sources, sensible and moderate. Finished today Mr. Huskisson's Dissertation upon the depreciation of the English currency,[1] the most wonderful part of which seems to be that it was deemed necessary to maintain it. In the evening Mrs. Angier and E. C. Adams were with us to tea and we accompanied them to the house below.

[1] William Huskisson, *Question concerning the Depreciation of our Currency*, London, 1810.

MONDAY 26TH.

Warm day. At home, bath. Usual occupations. Evening visit to Mr. Whitney.

My time was consumed much in the manner that it usually is. I devoted some time to copy which goes on pretty slowly, and to Storch's chapter upon credit and paper money with which I am certainly much edified. I think him next to Smith of all the writers whom I have read.

In consequence of my going to bathe I was obliged to forego reading Menzel whose spirited style amuses me. Reading is on the whole a very great pleasure when the writer puts in action the mind of the reader. Whereas writing as an elaboration of thought is exceedingly tedious and painful. Yet a reasoning mind commonly will succeed in turning over an old train into a new shape and perhaps may draw something out of it worth recording. Menzel however shows us what this impression in a studious age will lead to and that is to the multiplication of worthless books.

After dinner, finished the remainder of the fragment of the sixteenth book of Tacitus whereby we lose the closing scene of the tyranny of Nero. I have refreshed my ideas by this perusal very much.

A ride to Mount Wollaston and Germantown afterwards, accompanied by my father. A visit in the evening to Mr. Whitney's to see his son Frederick who was not at home. Returned early.

TUESDAY. 27TH.

The warmest of the season. To town with my father. Home. Evening below.

I was much exhausted today by the various commissions I had to perform as it was very hot and I hardly sat down before twelve o'clock. It seems to me that it always happens that in the hottest weather I have most running to do. Finished the paper for the heirs of T. B. Adams but did not get through a copy before it was time to return.[1] My father came in and went out with me.

After dinner began the first book of the History of Tacitus and read ten sections but spent some time in overseeing the men who were upon my road today. Evening at the house below.

[1] The estate of Lt. T. B. Adams amounted to approximately $4,600. When divided into 33 parts, his mother received 20 parts, each of his two sisters 5 parts, and each of his three brothers 1 part. Distribution was effected and the estate settled in October (CFA to Legatees, 27 Aug., 9 Oct., LbCs, Adams Papers).

WEDNESDAY 28TH.

Cold change. At home all day. Usual occupation. Evening at the Mansion.

The temperature fell very fast today from the point which it has maintained for a week or ten days past. I remained at home superintending the work doing upon my road and working a little myself until my time came that I devote to copying. Read Storch's Note upon Law's system which begins to give me some idea of it, but I must go more deeply into it.[1] I think I can do something out of it.

Dined at my father's after which read Tacitus History b. 1. S. 10–30. This appears to me much the most elaborate work. Tea and evening at the Mansion. Nothing new.

[1] John Law, a Scotsman, occupied in France, 1715–1720, a succession of fiscal offices leading to that of controller-general of state finances. Through them he applied the tenets of his "System," with extraordinary success at the outset but ending in the unmitigated disaster called the "Mississippi bubble." The "System" provided for a vast increase in credit through the issuance by a state bank of paper currency redeemable at a fixed value and acceptable in payment of taxes. In the resulting expansion of industry and trade, a state company was created and given a monopoly in the handling of trade and banking in and with France's foreign possessions. When the state bank, the mint, and the company were brought under unified control, shares were offered to an eager public, were wildly oversubscribed, and brought sensational profits to the holders. Failure of the "System" came only when the speculators and investors, seeking to convert their new paper fortunes into specie, forced the bank to suspend cash payments. Panic and all but universal bankruptcy marked the end (*DNB*).

THURSDAY 29TH.

Cold and cloudy. At home all day. Evening at the Mansion.

I have not much to record of this day beyond what happens very regularly. I devoted a couple of hours to copying and one to studying out Law's System in Stewart's Political Economy.[1] I am gaining the details by degrees but the measures are so intricate that it will require a great deal of time and patience to evolve them. I think yet that I shall find something which will pay me for it. But I lose my German.

After dinner Tacitus book 1, sections 30–50 of the history, and an hour's work upon my grounds. Evening spent at the house below. My father had been to Cambridge to the Φ B K and returned late.

[1] Dugald Stewart, *Notes of Lectures on Political Economy*, 2 vols., Edinburgh, 1802. These volumes contain the notes, purportedly verbatim, taken by a student at Stewart's lectures in 1800. Stewart's own text was first published in his *Works* in 1854 (*DNB*).

FRIDAY 30TH.

Stormy. To town, return to dine. Afternoon and evening at home.

I arose very early this morning in order to be prepared if my father inclined to accept Mr. Loring's invitation to a fishing excursion at Cohasset. But the wind was East and had been blowing so hard all night that he concluded to remain at home.

I went to Boston. Time taken up in little commissions as usual. Finished my copy of the paper for the heirs which is to be forthwith presented. Just as I was starting to come home Mr. Freeman Hunt came in and kept me some time. He had nothing new to say but seemed

desirous of procuring for me a review of Mr. Felt's book on Currency.[1]
I told him, I had hardly the time, particularly as I was busy about collecting materials for this proposed lecture upon credit which I ought to make good if I make anything.

Reached home late and just as a heavy rain and gale of wind from the Northeastward was setting in, which continued all day and all night blowing with furious violence. Read Tacitus book 1 s 50 to 70, and being at home in the evening went on with Lear. Being situated upon the north corner the noise of the wind prevented my sleeping soundly for several hours.

[1] Joseph Barlow Felt, *Historical Account of Massachusetts Currency*, Boston, 1839.

SATURDAY 31ST.

Clearing up. At home all day. Evening at the Mansion.

The night proved an exceedingly tempestuous one but the wind declined towards morning though it was Sunset before it was entirely calm. I occupied myself very steadily in copying and afterward began a sketch of a Lecture which seemed to me to run very easy. I have reflected upon the subject so much already as to have matured my thoughts. This is fortunate as today I received a letter from Mr. Ward leaving me the alternative of writing a new one or taking the old Revolutionary one of which I am rather tired.[1]

After dinner Tacitus, finishing the first book of the History, the struggles of Galba, Otho and Vitellius, fearful days. A little outdoor work and then in the evening at my father's. The night was brilliantly clear, a singular contrast to last night.

[1] The letter from Elijah Ward is missing. However, LbC of CFA's reply, 3 Sept., is in the Adams Papers.

SUNDAY. SEPTEMBER 1.

Lovely day. Exercises as usual. Evening at the Mansion.

I have no variation to record in my usual course of proceeding this morning. After an hour devoted to my daughter I attended Divine Service and heard young Mr. Cranch preach in the morning from 7 [6] John 63 "The words that I speak unto you they are spirit, and they are life," and after dinner from Job 7. 17.18. "What is man that thou shouldest magnify him? and that thou shouldest set thine heart upon him? And that thou shouldest visit him every morning and try him every moment?" Mr. Cranch does not seem to me to possess the kind of qualifications necessary for a preacher of the present day, but he has mildness and good feelings. His morning Sermon upon the force of the Christian doctrine as a living and breathing existence was well conceived but feebly executed.

Read a sermon of the Revd. John Mason upon the duty of an inoffensive conduct. 1. Corinthians 10. 32. "Give none offence." The reasons for avoiding offence and the occasions when it ought to be hazarded given in a very modest and sensible manner.

Copied a paper for my father and read rather inattentively a chapter or two of Tucker. Evening at my father's.

MONDAY 2D.

Beautiful day. At home. Time passed as usual. Ride. Evening at my father's and Mrs. Adams'.

I cannot give much variety to my present record. My mornings are usually spent in copying or writing or reading Menzel all three of which I did a little of, but I clearly see that if any thing is to be done by me I must bend my whole force to it.

After dinner read twenty sections of the second book of Tacitus History and went out to take a ride accompanied by my son John. I followed the old track round Milton which is beautiful. The storm has done much damage, and is said to be more severe than has been for many years.

On my return home found Miss Harriet Welsh who had come out of town in company with Mr. and Mrs. De Wint. I went to see the latter in the evening at Mrs. T. B. Adams', returning home by way of my father's.

TUESDAY 3D.

Lovely day. Mrs. Adams with me to town. Afternoon at home. Evening at my father's.

Our weather since the storm has been the perfection of the season. I went to town this morning accompanied by Mrs. Adams. Time taken up in commissions and a variety of accounts. I shall have a respite I hope from Boston occupation for this month. Mr. Winch from Weston called upon me about his business which is not yet done. I promised to be ready by the 20th and must bear it in mind. After doing up all I had, returned home.

Afternoon, Tacitus b. 2 s. 20–40, and a little work. Evening at my

Mother's. Miss Harriet Welsh with us all day, no particular news. My wedding day.

WEDNESDAY 4TH.

Fine day. At home. Dine at my father's. Supervisors meeting. Pic Nic.

I cannot pass over yesterday without remembering that it completed ten years of my married life. Ten years which have been happy far beyond what is the ordinary lot of mortals. Perhaps of all my good fortune, a great share of which had unquestionably been mine, the circumstance of my marriage was the greatest incident. For it stimulated me in the right direction and prevented the preponderance of my constitutional shyness and indolence. And moreover it placed me in a connexion with relations which has proved entirely agreeable and satisfactory. Of my Wife I need not speak as the passage of time has only contributed to make me prize her more highly. And my children are healthy and promising. I will not look forward because I have no right to expect of the future as much as I have enjoyed in the past. God be praised for his goodness to me thus far. May no unworthiness of mine hasten its discontinuance hereafter. I trust in his mercy now as I have ever done.

I was at home until noon and worked steadily upon my Lecture, after which I went to my father's to attend a meeting of the Supervisors of the Adams Temple and School fund and dined there with them after it was over. President Quincy, Mr. T. Greenleaf, Mr. Miller and Mr. Beale, Mrs. DeWint and her daughter Julia made the company. Dinner was very well. After it was over, we went to a Pic Nic being the same kind of entertainment which we had in this town one year ago. There was a tent on the green below where the citizens had assembled when we got there and where some of them danced, the sight was pretty and rural.

After returning to take tea at home, my father and Wife and Mary went to the Hotel where was a ball much like last year. The company was not so thoroughly well behaved, there was more noise and disturbance than at that time, but on the whole it was a nice shade only of difference. I was rather pleased than otherwise at the spectacle. It was one which could not be seen in any other country, and is characteristic of our Institutions. We returned home before ten and I felt fatigued from so much standing.

THURSDAY 5TH.

At home all day. Occupation as usual. Evening at the Mansion.

This was a warm day with a damp Southerly wind but it cleared before night without rain. I was steadily occupied in writing and made some progress. This with a little of Menzel was all of my morning's work.

After dinner, Tacitus history book 2. s 40 to 60. "The death of Otho" is perhaps the last specimen of the active principle of the Roman education in Republican days. He was too weak to live virtuously was yet noble enough to die resignedly. The removal from the scene of action was a weakness which shows that his temper was mild. It was the secret of his destruction. Evening at my father's.

FRIDAY 6TH.

Fine day but warm. To Boston. Afternoon company. Evening at the Mansion.

I went to town this morning and pretty steadily occupied at the Office, first in drawing up a Lease to John Winch one part of which I did and next in taking in the Account of T. B. Adams into a new draft. This with a moderate number of commissions passed my time.

Home. Afternoon devoted to Edward Brooks and his Wife and Mrs. Frothingham who came out to take tea. I accompanied the former on a visit to my father for a few minutes. Evening at the Mansion. Mr. and Mrs. DeWint, Mrs. T. B. Adams, Mrs. Angier and Elizabeth there. A little unwell from a head ach.

SATURDAY. 7TH.

Warm morning but change. At home. Bath. Evening at Mrs. T. B. Adams'.

I was pretty steadily occupied in writing upon my Lecture until noon. It goes on quite swimmingly but I doubt whether it will be very fit to deliver. The subject will not admit of that kind of ornament which takes every where but most especially in New York.

Just as I was relaxing by reading Menzel, my boys came in to beg me to go down to the bath with them at Mount Wollaston. I consented and we took a refreshing bath in the face of an East wind which changed the temperature of the air very quickly, and before night brought up a heavy fog from the Sea.

Read Tacitus history b. 2. s 60–80. and Grimm. Evening an hour at my father's and another hour at Mrs. T. B. Adams' where were the younger ladies of our family, to see Mrs. Angier. Miss Miller and her brother were there.

SUNDAY 8TH.

Warm and showery. Exercises as usual. Evening an hour at the Mansion.

I have to record only a repetition of the exercises usual in my Sunday, first with my daughter and then at meeting and at home. The day was rainy so that the attendance was thin. I heard Mr. Lunt preach first from James 5. 11. "Ye have heard of the patience of Job." This was a discourse written as far as I could judge in consequence of a suggestion of my Wife in conversation the other day, that Job did not deserve his character for patience. He went on to consider the character of Job, his trials, the reproaches of his Wife and reasoning of his friends and finally his own submission, the character of his complaint being rather the anguish of suffering nature than repining or murmurs. He cited as a parallel case, the cry of the Saviour on the Cross which he regarded as quite as valuable a historical trait as any in the Testament.

The afternoon sermon was from that remarkable verse in Genesis. 49. 4. "Unstable as water, thou shalt not excel." The dying address of Jacob to his first born whose crime had probably been the result of a fluctuating character. Mr. Lunt made it's application to religion which he affirmed to be unstable when not firmly based upon faith. Both these sermons were very good and deserved a better audience.

I read one by Dr. Chandler from the English Preacher, from Micah 4. 5. "All people will walk, every one in the name of his God." Upon the natural tendency of man to superstition or the worship of idols. The rain was not constant but so frequent that I only went to my father's. My mother was unwell upstairs. Spent an hour with her and returned.

MONDAY 9TH.

Warm and cloudy. At home. Occupied as usual. Evening at the Mansion.

I continued my occupations all the morning and finished a very considerable part of my Lecture. It pleases me well while I write it, but my feeling is never one of much confidence. So much is there in reputation that my late efforts have been attended with twice the success that I had from earlier and much more laboured ones. Read some of Menzel too.

Afternoon, Tacitus, finishing the second book of the history. I like it better than the Annals. A little work and evening, an hour's visit to my father's. Nothing new.

Medford

TUESDAY IOTH.

Fine day. To town, thence to Medford. Mr. Brooks' and Gorham's.

Mr. Brooks has for some time past been urging my Wife and myself to go to Medford. We accepted the invitation and fixed today. Accordingly we started, my Wife in the Carriage and my father to Boston with me. I spent the morning in town in business of various kinds, and at one started with my Wife and I with our boy John.

We got to Mr. Brooks' house to dinner. And passed the afternoon and evening there with the exception of a short visit to Gorham Brooks', where were Mrs. Edward and Sidney Brooks and Edward paying a visit. The sensation to me here was one of loneliness which I have not before felt and know hardly how to account for. The place looks pretty but cold. During our stay at Gorham's there came up Mr. Cushing and Hodgkinson. The former much as I had heard of him, I had never seen before. A coarse looking man. The latter gentlemanly and handsome but very English farmerlike. Retire early from positive want of occupation.

WEDNESDAY. I ITH.

Fine day. To town, back to Medford, dine at Gorham Brooks. Evening at house.

I went to town this morning accompanied by Mr. Brooks. Found upon arriving that the Great Western had arrived and brought news not decisive of any thing. I attended during a great part of the morning a sale of the books of T. Lyman who is going to Europe. I had expected to find a library of much value, but infer from what I saw that he sold only what he considered superfluous. I was under no temptation to buy much, and left the place with a feeling of misspent time.

Mr. Brooks returned with me and we all dined with Gorham and his Wife. He lives in very handsome style with all his luxuries about him.

I left there to take a stroll to the grove which used to be my favorite resort in my young days when I was a lover. And never since the death of Mrs. Brooks did the sense of contrast so forcibly present itself.[1] Then this house was always full and always regarded as the centre of family union. Now it is secondary to all the rest. This is not the fault of Mr. Brooks senior who feels very evidently the deficiency of his own position, but he is in a manner obliged to submit from a dislike to making any difficulties in his family. And in other respects he is made comfortable enough. Nature however has not changed in the interval though man has, and no one more so than myself. How much of my earthly career has passed and how hope has changed into posession! I pray God, I may become wiser and better. The evening was short and dull.

[1] For the feelings entertained by CFA during his courtship and the early months of his marriage toward Mystic Grove, the Peter C. Brooks estate in Medford, see vols. 2:xi; 3:10; and the indexes to those volumes. For the impact of Mrs. Brooks' death upon her family and upon CFA, see vol. 3:168–172.

Quincy

THURSDAY 12TH.

Cool. To town, thence to Quincy. Afternoon at work. Evening at the Mansion.

I left Medford this morning hardly with unwillingness for my want of my usual occupation and my thoughts made me dull. Mr. Brooks accompanied me in my ride round by the Registry Office at East Cambridge where I was desirous of leaving some deeds, then into town.

At the Office where I made occupation enough. Then to Quincy where I returned to dine. Found every thing much as I left it and the children apparently contented and happy. I dined at the house below and spent the afternoon in working out. The house seemed so still and solitary that I did not greatly relish it. Spent the evening at my father's. And retired pretty early.

FRIDAY 13TH.

Cloudy and cold morning. Usual occupations. Evening at the Mansion besides meals.

I spent the day very quietly. Tried to continue my Lecture but found myself deficient in clear ideas so I had to go back to the books to study more fully Law's scheme. This took up most of my morning with a little of Menzel. I dined at my father's and in the afternoon studied Tacitus, B. 3. s 1–30.

The quiet of the house is very great and strange to say it does not seem to promote my studies. Man is such a creature of habit and the things which he dreads at one time become so necessary to his happiness at another. The noise of children is generally cheerful and excites that variety of sensations which make at once the occupation and the pleasure of life. I did not work so well because I felt more lonely. Evening at my father's.

SATURDAY 14TH.

Clear and pleasant. To town, home. Mrs. Adams returns. Evening ladies here.

It was quite a pleasant change from yesterday and I went to town for the purpose of preparing the house for the general cleaning which it is to undergo this autumn. To this end I took one of my women, Catherine, in with me who helped the removal of all the furniture. But I got through barely in time for a very little necessary business at the Office and return to dinner. Mrs. Adams also returned in the carriage from her Medford visit.

After dinner, Tacitus b 3. s 30–50. the history of the civil war after the death of Nero. My mother, Mrs. T. B. Adams, Miss Julia DeWint and Miss Smith took tea and spent the evening with us. Retire early.

SUNDAY 15TH.

Pleasant day. Usual exercises. Evening at the Mansion.

I have not the opportunity for so much miscellaneous reading on this day of the week now as formerly. My time is taken up for an hour with my daughter and then I attend divine service.

Mr. Lunt preached in the morning from Matthew 28. 8. "And they departed quickly from the sepulchre with fear and great joy." I know not why but this discourse did not interest me as much as usual partly I suppose in itself and partly because I had heard it before. Mr. Whitney in the afternoon from John 16. 22.28 "And ye now therefore have sorrow: but I will see you again, and your heart shall rejoice and your joy no man taketh from you," &ca. I could not gather much of the discourse from Mr. Whitney's failing voice.[1] He has now passed service in the pulpit.

Read a discourse being the first one in the collection of Sermons called The English Preacher, the fifth volume, by Tillotson. Joshua 24. 15. "If it seems evil unto you to serve the Lord, chuse you this day whom you will serve." Service of the Lord or a religious life recommended.

I began today Herschel's Treatise on Astronomy[2] which I desire to know something of. But my desire for knowledge is so multifarious it makes me a tiro in all. Evening at my father's.

[1] JQA, in his Diary, reports the text of the afternoon sermon to have been taken from Luke 16. 27.28 and quotes the apposite verses.

[2] London, 1833.

MONDAY 16TH.

Warm day. At home as usual. Afternoon ride to Brookline and evening at Mansion.

I devoted most of my morning to the prosecution of my Lecture upon credit which did not however get on so fast as heretofore. There is a necessity for cautious investigation.

In the Afternoon, I started with my Wife to return the visit of Mr. and Mrs. Rogers at Brookline. The distance is very considerable and when we arrived there we found nobody at home, so we had our labour for our pains. Returning we passed by Jamaica Pond and the beautiful country around it. Evening for an hour at the house below.

TUESDAY 17TH.

Fog but became warm and clear. To town. Afternoon at home. Evening at Edmd. Quincy's.

I went to town this morning, accompanied by Miss Julia DeWint whom I left at Mrs. S. A. Otis'. Then to the Office. Engaged with the Painter all day, showing him what I wanted done at my house. Nothing further of consequence. Return home where I read Tacitus b. 3. 60 to 82, having read ten sections yesterday which I did not minute down. This is now pretty much all I can do in an afternoon as they grow so short.

Evening, walk down to see Edmund Quincy, a visit I have owed for some time. There were Miss Sophia Quincy and Mr. Wright or Dwight, a gentleman whom I did not know. We got into a lively and spirited literary conversation which I enjoyed the more from it's rarity with me. Home by ten.

WEDNESDAY 18TH.

Rain and damp but warm. At home. Evening at home.

My head was not entirely at ease this morning and I was apprehensive of a bad day but it passed off before evening entirely.

I devoted a large part of my morning to my Lecture which I brought to a close at last. But I fear it will not do. At any rate I now mean to lay it away for a month or two, in order to give myself the advantage of cool criticism. This is what I rarely have been able to bestow upon a work, and as this is not designed to be flashy I must try and make it up with substantial merit, although New York is not the precise sphere for that article.

A little but not much of Menzel. Mrs. T. B. Adams dined with us. Afternoon, Tacitus, finish book 3 and read 20 sections of book 4. Evening the family took tea with us and remained until nine o'clock. The children none of them very well, rather suffering under the change of season.

THURSDAY. 19TH.

Fine day. At home all day. Evening at the Mansion, and dine there.

I this morning resumed my labour in copying the letters which I remitted in order to make a draught of my Lecture. This is necessarily slow and tedious, but I hope it will come to something. Read a little of Menzel also, whose work rather hangs heavily with me in the theological part. I know none of the writers of whom he speaks even by name and do not put much faith in his entire theory respecting them. There are however occasionally acute remarks and happy illustrations. Dined at my father's. Read Tacitus b. 4. s 20–40. This is all I can do. The evenings which I do not employ now grow long.

FRIDAY 20TH.

Beautiful day. To town. Afternoon at home. Evening, visit to Mrs. T. B. Adams' and Mansion.

My time in town today was taken up for the most part in attending upon the mechanics who are working at my house. I got them in train today so that the work will I hope steadily go on, but it threatens to be a pretty heavy job. Then to the Athenæum to see about the return of some books which had not yet been made. On my return to Quincy, I was accompanied by Miss Mary B. Hall who is to make us a visit of a few days.

Afternoon, Tacitus b 4. s 40–60. and this was all. I have been upon occasional half hours looking into Herschel's Essay on Astronomy. In the evening I walked up to Mrs. T. B. Adams' on business. Met there with Mr. Greenleaf and Mr. Miller. The evening was uncommonly beautiful. Home at ten by way of my father's.

SATURDAY 21ST.

Fine day. At home. Afternoon ride. Evening at the Mansion.

My work upon the letters went on pretty briskly this morning and I begin to perceive the end of the undertaking. Mrs. Greenleaf has furnished me a valuable stock with which to fill up a long interval.[1] I read also some of Menzel, always a lively and often a just writer.

After dinner, Tacitus b. 4. s 60–70, went out to take a ride accompanied by my father. Went down to the farms and from thence through the cross roads to Milton Hill. The evening was beautiful and I enjoyed it much. Tea at my father's and evening. Nothing material.

[1] During the years 1784–1788 AA was with JA in Europe. Her letters in that period were written mostly to her sisters, Mary Smith Cranch and Elizabeth Smith Shaw, and to her niece Lucy Cranch, later Mrs. John Greenleaf. The letters in Mrs. Greenleaf's possession, to her mother and to herself, were those she allowed CFA to copy for publication in the volume he had in preparation (AA, *Letters*, ed. CFA, 1840; entry for 12 Aug., above). In that volume, p. 199–395 would be given in large part to these letters, supplemented by a lesser number to Mrs. Shaw, lent by her daughter, Abigail Adams Shaw (Mrs. Joseph Barlow Felt). On the later history of the collections of AA's letters, see *Adams Family Correspondence*, 1:xxx.

SUNDAY 22D.

Fine day. Exercises as usual. Evening, family with us. J.Q.A. 6 years.

I devoted my morning to the usual course of occupation with my daughter and only changed the subject for my superfluous time from the study of Tucker which turns out unprofitable to that of Herschel's Astronomy.

Attended divine service and heard Mr. Newel of Cambridge preach from 1 Corinthians 13. 9.10.11. "For we know in part and we prophesy in part; But when that which is perfect is come, then that which is in part shall be done away. When I was a child, I spake as a child, I understood as a child, I thought as a child: but when I became a man, I put away childish things." And in the Afternoon from Genesis 2. 15. "And the Lord God took the man and put him into the garden to dress it and to keep it." Mr. Newell is very sensible but he wants energy. His manner gives to his matter an inertness which appears effeminate. I think Menzel is right in one particular that there must be something wrong in the forms of Protestant worship which turn off so much of the attention from the subject to the Preacher.

Read a Sermon in the English Preacher by Mr. Balguy. Psalm 97. 1, "The Lord reigneth, let the earth rejoice." The active government of God a certain and joyful truth. Menzel wonders at the fact of the ordinary character of all the sermons that have been the result of so many centuries of weekly preaching. The reason is that the text is better than any amplification of it. The sole useful end of a sermon is exhortation and that must be done much within the circle of old truths.

In the evening the family were all with us and Mr. Degrand and E. P. Greenleaf. After they had all gone I read the news by the British Queen which looks badly. We must be rapidly nearing a crisis in the United States.[1]

My boy John this day six years old. How much have I to be thankful for in him and how much cause to pray for his continued progress in mental and moral and physical health!

[1] The *British Queen* docked at New York on the 20th, bringing news of declines in the value of securities, of rising interest rates, and of a state of crisis in the money market (*Boston Courier*, 23 Sept., p. 3, cols. 2–4).

MONDAY 23D.

Continued fine day. At usual occupations. Ride and evening at the Mansion.

My morning passed in pretty steady application to the business of copying which went on pretty smoothly. I also read some of Menzel, beginning his discussion of the department of philosophy which promises to be more interesting to me. After dinner, finish the fourth book of Tacitus and read five sections of the fifth. These are remarkable as introducing some remarks upon the Jewish character and traditions.

Went out and took a ride to Mount Wollaston beach and from thence round to Newcomb's landing with the two boys as my companions. The day was finer and clearer even than it's predecessors, and we enjoyed it much. In the evening, down to the Mansion as usual.

TUESDAY 24TH.

Fine day. To town. Return to dinner. Evening at the Mansion.

It was a lovely day like all the days since Miss Hall's visit who today returned to town with me, to our great regret, who have been pleased to have her with us.[1]

My time much occupied in town with visiting my house where all the workmen are in full operation, and with matters of business, so that I was a little later at home than usual. When I got there, I found our town usually so quiet, in a perfect turmoil with a general muster which was held in the Hancock Lot. As usual, worthless people of all kinds were upon the spot and made one or two rows, the first of which was too near my father's house not to disturb the females. The day however passed off without much difficulty and before sunset the spot was clear.

Evening, we paid our usual visit to the Mansion. Nothing of material consequence. Finished the History of Tacitus.

[1] Mary Brooks Hall, daughter of Peter C. Brooks' sister, Mrs. Nathaniel Hall of Medford, had been a guest for four days or more. A special bond between Mary and ABA had been created by Mary's assuming the household responsibilities at the Brooks home in Medford for a period after the death of Mrs. Brooks. See vols. 2:155; 3:123, 181; 5:122; and JQA, Diary, 20 Sept. 1839.

WEDNESDAY 25TH.

Clear morning. At home. Visitors. Evening at the Mansion, where we dined.

The morning was lovely but it clouded before night in such a manner as to signify the last of the summer weather. I have enjoyed it much. Continued my labour in making copies which will now be soon at an end, so far as this collection is concerned. I also read some of Menzel which makes up the usual course of my mornings.

Dined at the house below, after which I read twenty sections of the Essay of Tacitus De Moribus Germanorum, a very curious relic of antiquity respecting a part of the world not much known at that date. Yet the seed of all the great nations of modern times. Tea and evening below. Thunder storm in the night.

THURSDAY 26TH.

Morning cloudy but cleared with high wind. At home. Evening at the Mansion.

I remained all the morning pretty constantly devoted to the business of copying which I brought very nearly to a conclusion as to the letters to Mrs. Cranch. On the whole the labour has not been so great as was anticipated. But it is only as the beginning of labour with me.

Read Menzel upon Philosophy who in this department is thoroughly German with the best of them. After dinner Tacitus de Moribus Germanorum, section 20 to 40. This was all my work as the evening takes largely of the hours formerly devoted to study. This is usually spent at the house below in not very useful conversation.

FRIDAY 27TH.

Fine morning but heavy wind and rain in the Evening. Boston and Hingham.

I went to town this morning and was much occupied with calls at my house to watch the progress of the painters and thence to see some of the Tenants about repairs. After the period of business was over, I called in to see the Mechanic's fair which was held in Quincy Hall over the market. There were many curious things exhibited, and many useful ones. I was most pleased with the agricultural machinery and the cutlery and some pieces of furniture. But I had not time to examine with minuteness as I had engaged to dine with Mrs. Frothingham at two o'clock prior to meeting my father in order to go down to the Boat.

A certain Mr. Greenough had invited a number of persons to go down into the harbour to see the effect of a certain new kind of Oil which he thinks burns brighter in a light house than whale oil or sperm oil. We being of the number went down and found many persons of the party but a great doubt of the propriety of trying the experiment on so windy a night. After some dispute as to the prospect of it's continuing to blow or of it's becoming calm, it was finally decided to go as far as Hingham and there act according to the event. The boat had a rough time and the evening set in dark and gloomy. I found on board A. H. Everett, O. W. B. Peabody, B. T. Reed, and a few others of my acquaintance with whom I had a pleasant conversation.

When we reached the landing Mr. Greenough invited us to the Old Colony House whither by the officious interference of Captain Sturgis of the Revenue Cutter we were marched up to the music of his band with a form which I thought made us only ridiculous. After taking tea, as the trip out to the Light house proved impracticable, Mr. Greenough proceeded to execute experiments in the hall. He showed two lights, one of which was supplied with his preparation, the other with common oil. And the result of all the different trials was undoubtedly in favor of the former as giving a whiter and better light. But we were not able to judge of the quality of the oil or of his preparation nor of the expense of the different substances. He showed us that his mixture was more inflammable than oil or even Spirits of the ordinary strength.[1]

These experiments lasted until nine when the boat returned with the gentlemen to town, but we preferred hiring a vehicle to take us directly home, so that we reached our houses at about half past ten in a pretty heavy rain.

¹ To this account the journal entry in JQA's Diary adds only the names of those who marched in the procession behind the band and crew and a somewhat more precise description of Benjamin Franklin Greenough's "preparation" or "mixture." JQA named it a "chemical oil" and "chemical compound." The demonstration seems to have evoked no conclusive judgments and to have been without immediate significance.

SATURDAY 28TH.

Clear day but cool. To town, early return and afternoon at home. Evening at the Mansion.

As by the summary proceeding of last evening I had left my horse in town, the next thing seemed to me to be to regain the control of him, so I went to town in the Omnibus and after reading the Morning Newspapers I returned without attending to any business. But as the day seemed fair I thought I should like to ride through Roxbury and Milton over what is called the old road. Modern processes cut short the distances between places but they do not come attended with the beauty of the ancient. This is all along it's whole length a highly improved road and every foot of it's pretty and interesting.

I got home precisely at noon and immediately sat down to work as usual. Finished the copying of Mrs. Cranch's MS of my grandmother. After dinner Tacitus, Life of Agricola. Evening at the Mansion. Miss Cutts returned there this evening.

SUNDAY 29TH.

Clear day though cold. Exercises as usual. Visit to Mrs. Quincy. Evening at the Mansion.

After my regular lesson with Louisa, I attended divine service as usual but upon rather an uncommon occasion. This was selected as the day of Anniversary of the second century since the gathering of the Church, and Mr. Lunt seized the occasion to deliver in his two discourses an interesting account of our church experiences.

His text in the morning was from 8 Deuteronomy 7.9.10. 11.12.14.17. Rather too long to insert. In the Afternoon John 4. 20 "Our fathers worshipped in this mountain." The subject was somewhat dry but he enlivened it by eloquent passages thrown in here and there very neatly and very adroitly. His notice of my grandfather affected me to tears. I am unable to give any satisfactory abstract of the discourses and hope to see them printed in order to keep me in the recollection.[1] The house was full all day and the attention was flattering. Mr. Lunt is one of that class of men who are not appreciated by their generation. He has done more than many who have twice his reputation.

I dined at my father's with I. P. Davis who was there. After service went down with the ladies to see Mrs. Quincy the elder and her daughters who were at her son's for the day. Evening at the Mansion.

[1] Mr. Lunt's sermons were printed as *Two Discourses, delivered September 29, 1839, on Occasion of the Two Hundredth Anniversary of the Gathering of the First Congregational Church, Quincy,* Boston, 1840. The events of 1636–1639, centering upon the theological controversy involving Rev. John Wheelwright at Mount Wollaston, are the subject of the first sermon. The second undertakes the history from 17 Sept. 1639 (O.S.), the date of the gathering of a distinct and independent church at Mount Wollaston under pastors William Tompson and Henry Flynt. The journal entry in JQA's Diary provides a somewhat fuller account of the occasion than does CFA's.

MONDAY 30TH.

Fog and rain. At home. Evening at the house below. Visiters.

I passed all my morning in copying or comparing the copies already made with my Wife who gave me her assistance today. This made me omit German, and I was interrupted also by visiters, Mrs. Quincy with Mrs. Edmund and Miss Susan being here before dinner, Mrs. H. and G. Dawes for a short time and Sidney Brooks with his Wife to tea. I therefore finished only a few sections of the Life of Agricola.

As Mrs. Adams had just gone to ride when her brother came, I was obliged to entertain them alone for some time. Sidney left with me a letter to C. A. Davis from Mr. Horsley Palmer which is a curious manifestation of the course of human affairs.[1] They left us shortly after six and we spent the evening at the Mansion.

[1] The allusion escapes the editors.

TUESDAY 1ST. OCTOBER.

To town. At home Afternoon. Evening at the Mansion.

I have accidentally made a wrong entry of what happened this Afternoon as being of yesterday, instead of recording that I followed up steadily the collation of the manuscripts and passed an hour alone visiting the house below. My morning was spent in town in active occupation, visiting my house twice, and in various duties so that I found myself shortened in time. Home however before three and then the record follows as it ought.

WEDNESDAY 2D.

Fine day. At home, dine and tea at the Mansion. Evening at Mr. Beale's and Mrs. A's.

The morning was so fine that I passed an hour or two of it at work and thus shortened the term of time for my writing. I also went down earlier than usual to the house below in order to make up the record of the Temple and School fund.[1] This with some seeking after letters consumed the hour I usually devote to German.

After dinner, Tacitus, a few more sections of the Life of Agricola, but I cannot now accomplish what I could. A little of Grimm. Evening after tea at my father's, call in to see Mr. Beale and from thence to Mrs. T. B. Adams' where our younger ladies were. Return at ten.

[1] CFA was the clerk of the Adams Temple and School Fund; see vol. 4:x, 386, 391 – 392.

THURSDAY 3D.

Mild day. At home. Visit from Dr. and Mrs. Frothingham. Evening ladies at home.

I spent about an hour in copying this morning, when Dr. Frothingham with his Wife and children drove up in fulfilment of their long promised visit. The day was very favorable and I carried the Dr. quite a walk to see some of our various quarries to which I had myself scarcely ever before been. In the mean time his conversation was pleasant as it generally is with me and instructive. He has a way of thinking quite his own which however seems to me as he grows older to mark itself very forcibly upon the mind and principally by it's clear separation from the fancies of the activity of the age. They did not leave us until sunset.

The ladies from the house below took tea and spent the evening with us. So that on the whole I have made no great progress in reading this day.

FRIDAY 4TH.

Fine day. To town. Mechanic's fair. Home. Evening, two visiters.

I went to town this morning, but the greater part of my time was taken up in accompanying the ladies who went in the carriage, to the

Mechanic's Fair. For my own part I saw little or nothing more than I did before. The crowd was greater and there was the same inability to fix the wandering attention upon any single object. Yet the general effect is undoubtedly indicative of the progress the country makes in industry, and the vigour with which the wits of the New England people push their enterprise. I did not get away until nearly one when I had to pay a visit to my house and do some commissions before I could return home so that it was later than usual.

Afternoon, finished the life of Agricola which after all is rather a tribute of affection than a remarkable history. In the evening, a visit from Mr. F. A. Whitney and Mr. Cranch detained us at home until too late to go to the other house.

SATURDAY. 5TH.

Clear but cool. At home. Evening, visiter. At the Mansion.

I spent the first part of my morning with the boys trying to catch fish but was disappointed. I find this like most of my boyish fancies declining. Then upon my return home, finished copying the letters to Mr. Jefferson, after which I began upon those to my father, a couple of files of which I have been able to find in the chaos of my father's MSS.[1] Read also Menzel finishing the first volume of his work. His sketch of German Philosophy seems to regard Kant as the wonder of the world. Some time or other I must take up Kant.

In the Afternoon, Tacitus, Dialogue of Orators. There is much dispute respecting the authorship of this—and the argument for or against Tacitus appears to me equally strong. The style is certainly not that of the other works, but it is very forcible and now and then betrays glimpses of it. It looks like a youthful effort bearing only certain marks of identity with maturer ones. Perhaps these are fallacious.[2]

Edmund Quincy took tea with us and spent the evening. For the first time he came out with some of his notions to me and made me regret that so amiable a disposition had allowed itself to be loaded with so much of the extravagance of life. I spent only half an hour at the house below.

[1] Eight letters to JQA would appear in AA, *Letters*, ed. CFA, 1840, but none of the letters to Jefferson was included.

[2] Present-day critical opinion supports the view that while the *Dialogus de Oratoribus* is an early, stylistically atypical work of Tacitus, it has a legitimate place in the canon.

SUNDAY 6TH.

Very clear but cool. Usual exercises. Evening at the Mansion.

After the usual time passed with my daughter, I attended divine worship and heard Mr. Lunt preach from 2 Samuel 24. 24. "And the king said unto Araunah, Nay; but I will surely buy it of thee at a price: neither will I offer burnt offerings unto the Lord my God of that which doth cost me nothing." A discourse upon the connexion between religious feeling and self sacrifice. A principle which has it's origin in the action of the mind to explain which would require a philosophical treatise. The discourse was however very good. Afternoon Proverbs 17. 17 "A friend loveth at all times." Upon friendship, it's value and utility.

Read a discourse of the English Preacher by the Revd. Jeremiah Seed decidedly more to my taste than any I have yet seen in the collection. Text Proverbs 15. 17. "Better is a dinner of herbs where love is, than a stalled ox and hatred therewith." It is preceptive but full of good sense and sound judgment, upon the modes of cherishing the domestic affections.

I forgot last Sunday to notice the discourse of Dr. Rogers Psalm 119. 63, upon virtuous connections which I read without recording. Visits from Mr. and Mrs. Harrod, and evening at the Mansion.

MONDAY 7TH.

Fine day. Work as usual. Afternoon ride. Evening visit to Mr. Harrod.

I passed the greater part of my morning in copying some of the letters out of my father's correspondence. These are striking and characteristic. Also Menzel, but my attention taken off by a desire to get through with collating the letters to Mrs. Cranch.

Afternoon, went to ride through Milton taking Miss Cutts with me. Evening, called at Mrs. T. B. Adams to see Mr. Harrod. Found him there with his whole family. Quite a spectacle. He seems an amiable, pleasant man. Return by way of the Mansion home. Nothing particularly new.

TUESDAY 8TH.

Fine day. To town. Afternoon and evening at home, family and visiters.

The weather has been uncommonly fine thus far in the Autumn and the frosts set in quite late. This is much pleasanter for us who found last season very uncomfortable owing to the quantity of rainy weather we experienced during this month.

I went to town and was incessantly occupied with the accounts of the quarter and various duties. I am pressing the settlement of T. B. A's affairs which have already been hanging too long. Home.

Afternoon, Tacitus, Dialogue of Orators. I begin to incline against his being the Author. We had in the evening, the family and Mr. and Mrs. Lunt with her sister Mrs. Robbins. The news is only of some very remarkable and extensive fires in New York. Otherwise, the public is in a state of calm.

WEDNESDAY 9TH.

Fine day. At home. Evening at the Mansion.

I was occupied most of my morning rather idly, in working upon my grounds and in finishing off several letters which I proposed to dispatch. This with Menzel took up my morning time without going at all upon the letters of A. A.

Menzel has now got upon Education and his observations are exceedingly acute and true as well of this country as of Germany. There is some similarity in the mind of the nations. Activity and fondness for novelty, Omne ignotum pro magnifico.[1]

Read a few more sections of Tacitus or rather the Dialogue ascribed to him, but I cannot think he could ever have written so. There is merit in the composition nevertheless. What a fascinating subject Oratory is and how the Ancients handle it. We are feeble in the comparison for the reason that we do not make it a business. Evening at the Mansion.

[1] That is, everything unknown is taken to be great.

THURSDAY 10TH.

Pleasant day. At home. Dine and evening at the Mansion.

I was quietly engaged all the morning in pursuing my usual occupations. Copied several letters and read Menzel. After dinner finished the Dialogue on Oratory and with it all that is supposed to have come down to us of Tacitus. This perusal is the first thorough one I have ever given to this Author and has been exceedingly useful. Tacitus is a thinker and he makes you feel what the value of history is, as a mingled record of good and evil.

We dined and spent an evening at my father's. The ladies brought home from their ride a rumour of the failure of the United States Bank and a general suspension of all the rest. As we could get no definite information about it, we were obliged to rest content and wait until tomorrow. But it is a result which we cannot have avoided to foresee when we reflect upon the immense amount of foreign indebtedness we have run into and the injudicious expansion of the Philadelphia Banks. What the effect upon the future will be, we must wait and see.

FRIDAY. 11TH.

Clear and pleasant. Morning to town. Home. Afternoon. Evening, visit to Mrs. T. B. Adams and below.

I went to town accompanied by Mrs. Adams' maid, Catherine. Time taken up in business and the settlement of the accounts of T. B. A.

The people in State Street in a state of much excitement from the combination of foreign and domestic news which arrived today. It seems that while the United States Bank found itself unable on yesterday to pay a large amount say $300,000 of Post Notes which then came due, the Steamer Liverpool brings intelligence of the protest of its drafts in France by Hottinguer to the amount of a million and a half, which though they were subsequently covered by the interference of Rothschild, had the immediate effect of shaking all American credit in Europe. It seems however that the New York Banks have not yet stopped, and that the Boston Banks will go with New York. But I fear that the causes for pressure lie too deep for easy remedy and the accounts of the state of the crops in England and the condition of the Bank of England are not encouraging. On the whole, things look gloomy enough. The Country is under no guidance worth having, and there is no present appearance that it will procure any or even be disposed to call for it. It is of no use to groan. We must trust in a higher power who brings out his great ends by his own means the uses of which are known only to him.

Afternoon at home reading Herschel's Essay on Astronomy. Evening at the Mansion partly and at Mrs. T. B. Adams' where I was paying away money, which I do not as things now are propose to keep. Rather unwell with a head ach.

SATURDAY. 12TH.

Wet, foggy day. At home all day.

I awoke early this morning at the sound of an alarm bell for fire but found myself suffering far too severely with head ach to go out. This continued when I got up and for two hours was equal in severity to any thing I have experienced but it then went off. I afterwards employed myself, partly in copying and partly in superintending Kirk who was setting trees. This business must be followed up now with some steadiness. It was wet and disagreeable to do it today.

Afternoon, read Herschel's Astronomy which interests me much. Evening I went alone to the house below and spent an hour. Nothing materially new beyond what I heard yesterday. The Baltimore Banks it is said have determined to go on paying specie. If they can sustain themselves, what a position for Philadelphia! But that is next to impossible.

SUNDAY I3TH.

Foggy and damp though warm. Exercises as usual. Dine and evening at the Mansion.

I read Herschel's Astronomy pretty steadily during all the leisure time I had from the usual course of things on this day.

After the period given to my daughter I attended divine service and heard Dr. Parkman preach in the morning from Philippians 2. 3. "In lowliness of mind let each esteem other better than themselves." Upon humility and from 1 Corinthians 15. 33. "Be not deceived: evil communications corrupt good manners." Upon the danger of accidental intercourse with ill principled men. Dr. Parkman has much good sense often wrapped in strange covers. I dined at my fathers with him, although suffering from a cold and hoarseness which I have acquired I scarce know how.

Read another sermon of Seed's from Proverbs 18. 1. "Through desire, a man having separated himself, seeketh and intermeddleth with wisdom." Upon the early pursuit of wisdom, a discourse not merely marked with strong direct sense but also with extraordinary beauty of images and diction. I must be allowed here to express my opinion that these two sermons of Seed's which I have read are far superior to all the rest of those combined in the English Preacher so far as I have yet gone. I wonder I have not heard more of them. Evening, Mr. Beale and his son here for an hour after which we were at the Mansion.

MONDAY I4TH.

Heavy rain. At home all day and evening. Hoarseness and cold.

I found myself somewhat incommoded by my cold, how I caught

308

which is far beyond my comprehension, but as the weather was very bad with a decided prospect of a North Easterly storm of some continuance I felt content to remain in the house and devote myself to my usual train of occupations.

Read a part of an article on the Bank of England in McCulloch's Dictionary,[1] and continued my work on the letters. After dinner I took up Menzel seriously and made great progress in his second volume. He writes well at times but evidently under strong prejudices and has all the national characteristics. Moreover his book makes me estimate the German mind rather below what I had done before. It wants practical basis, the thing which makes the English literature so useful as well as attractive.

Evening with my Wife at home. Read over several numbers in the last North American Review, very sensible. My father made a call to see how we did. We hear today by the Newspapers of the suspension of specie payments by the Baltimore Banks. This was no more than I expected.

[1] John Ramsay McCulloch, *A Dictionary ... of Commerce and Commercial Navigation*, 2 vols., London, 1832. CFA's copy, now in MQA, is of the 1840 edition.

TUESDAY 15TH.

Heavy rain. At home all day.

The rain continued to fall so heavily all day that I felt no inclination to go to town nor to try my cold by any movement out of doors. My time passed rapidly enough at home in reading some of McCulloch's Article commenced yesterday, and in copying some farther articles as usual. I also looked over a file of letters with a view to selection. They are however of a later date and very few of them will bear publication yet. On the whole I have already obtained a pretty good stock of letters to begin with.

Afternoon continued Menzel with some assiduity. His account of history is interesting. Decidedly averse to the literary reputation of Muller whom he appears to me to treat too roughly. He is evidently full of prejudices — and political zeal.

My father came in for a moment in the evening to inquire how I did. My cold is better. Nothing new excepting that the Rhode Island Banks have all decided to suspend specie payments, and those of the District of Columbia.

WEDNESDAY 16TH.

Fine day. To town. Return at noon. Dine and evening at my father's. Afternoon, Penn's hill.

The clearing of the weather gave us a most lovely day today. I went to town and my time entirely taken up in business affairs. Found the money market in great agitation from the progress of a movement in favour of suspension of specie payments which has been made. This is backed by the Manufacturing interest, whose business is hazarded as well as by many of the solid and all of the doubtful Merchants. There is however great resistance and the issue of the struggle is uncertain. I have very little hope of a favorable end in Boston.

Return to dine at the house below. After dinner, my father and I accompanied Deacon Spear to see the Wood on the lot opposite to the Penn's hill houses. It is very pretty wood but the neighbors who live round there cut off so much that the question reduces itself down to this, that they or the owner will get it. Evening at the Mansion.

THURSDAY 17TH.

Lovely day. At home.

This was a most remarkable day for the season. Soft as the month of June. I was occupied most of my morning in superintending the transplanting of trees which I am doing to a great extent in consequence of my father's being about to clear his garden of all his seedlings. I shall fill my border and then have no where else to put them.

Afternoon, Menzel but pursued without much vigour. Evening at the Mansion. I felt a little depressed this evening I know not exactly for what reason. But I have not felt entirely well myself and the children are now and then ailing which at this season makes me anxious.

FRIDAY. 18TH.

Lovely day. To town. Afternoon, planting. Evening at the Mansion.

Another extraordinary day. I rode to town. Found myself much occupied as usual in the details of business.

Had some talk with Harry Cabot however about the present state of pecuniary affairs. He wants me to explain to the public the causes of the difficulties in our paper system. But of what use is it to me when he admitted today he had never heard of my letters to Mr. Biddle? I do not however know that I might not be of service, and so I have sent to Mr. Hunt today a proposal to write an article for his December number.[1] I think also of putting in one or two very brief ones in the Courier.

Home. After dinner out with Kirk to superintend transplanting, in which I have thus far been much favoured. Evening my Wife was so fatigued by going to town that she did not accompany me to the Mansion.

[1] The letter to Freeman Hunt is missing.

SATURDAY 19TH.

Rain and clouds. At home all day. Evening at the Mansion.

The rain fell heavily in the morning with warm weather which cooled off at night with a northeaster. I was pretty steadily engaged all day upon the papers which I proposed to draw up for the Courier in answer to the Philadelphia exposition. They contain a very brief statement which I will expand for Mr. Hunt in case he wants it. But the labour of the thing is not trifling, particularly when taken in connexion with my other work. Evening for an hour at my father's. Nothing new.

SUNDAY 20TH.

Cloudy and cold. Exercises as usual. Evening at the Mansion.

I spent an hour in my usual course of reading with my daughter and spent all of my superfluous time during the day in writing the articles I am projecting.

Attended divine service and heard Mr. Lunt preach from Isaiah 28. 15 "We have made a covenant with death." A serious and perhaps rather gloomy train of thought connected with the subject of Death and occasioned by the decease within a week of two young members of the parish. But I was thinking so much of other matters that I could not very well fix my attention. Afternoon Proverbs 4. 7. "Wisdom is the principal thing, therefore get wisdom." An admirable discourse upon the distinction between wisdom and learning.

I afterwards read a sermon in the English Preacher from Dr. Doddridge upon persecution. Luke 9. 55.56. "But he turned and rebuked them; and said, ye know not what manner of spirit ye are of; for the Son of man is not come to destroy men's lives, but to save them." Very sensible and rational. The Evening was passed at the Mansion. It set in quite cool in the night which was clear.

MONDAY 21ST.

Cold morning. At home writing. Evening at the Mansion.

This was a sharp morning and indeed continued quite cold throughout the day. I devoted myself pretty steadily to writing the articles I
had proposed. In the course of the day I had finished two out of three
of the papers and from a hasty resurvey of them I was better pleased
than usual. But it is not possible to judge of articles of this kind without the intervention of time from the warmth of composition which I
cannot well give. Luckily imperfection is the character of our press, so
that I am only in good company when I make errors in style. I have
not had occasion or rather have not allowed myself time to rewrite.

The men began to work over the field to prepare it for ploughing
and I walked for a short time down to the Bank. This with the exception of our usual trip to the house below for the evening was all the
exercise out of doors which I took. The only news of importance is
that the Banks in New York did actually rub through Saturday and the
departure of the Liverpool.

TUESDAY 22D.

Cold morning. To town with my father. Afternoon writing. Evening
at the Mansion.

A sharp frost this morning reminding us of the rapid approach of
winter, but a clear and pleasant day. My father accompanied me to
town where I was engaged as usual in a great variety of occupations,
all incident to the particular season of the year, when we make our
usual migrations from country to town.

The town as usual in agitation about the currency matter which will
not probably be settled shortly. Sent my two articles to the Courier and
received an answer from Hunt to my letter.[1] Home early. After dinner
continued writing. Evening at the Mansion.

[1] Freeman Hunt in his reply (19 Oct., Adams Papers) assented readily to CFA's proposal for an article and suggested publication in November. The essay, enti-tled "The State of the Currency," would appear over CFA's signature in *Hunt's Merchants' Mag.* for December (vol. 1, p. 505–517). It is an amplified version of the three papers CFA was currently writ-ing for publication in the *Courier*. They appeared in the issues of 24, 26, and 29 Oct., p. 2, cols. 1–2, with the title, "The Philadelphia Manifesto," and were signed "A." In form they were a review of what purported to be "an exposition of the causes which have led to the re-newal of the suspension of specie pay-ments on the part of the banks in Phila-delphia." Denying the validity of the banks' position, as he had in his letters to Biddle, CFA maintained that both the action of the government in refusing to recharter the Bank of the United States and the subsequent policy of Biddle in winding up its affairs resulted in stretch-ing the credit system far beyond its health and brought on extravagant specu-lation.

WEDNESDAY 23D.

Lovely day. At home. Dine at the house below and Evening at Lyceum.

The day was extraordinarily fine. We have been as much favored in the season this year as last year we were otherwise. I was at work most of the day with Kirk in making the necessary preparations for the Winter, protecting my plants and shrubs. We were much favored in having this fine opportunity. But I snatched only the intervals for writing, and made slow progress.

We dined at my father's as usual. In the evening Mr. A. H. Everett and L. Jarvis were there and took tea after which we attended his [Everett's] Lecture at the Lyceum upon the subject of the Literature of the Bible, taking the distribution of philosophy, poetry and History. He very lightly skimmed over each interspersing fine passages of poetry or prose extracted from a great variety of authors. There was no great expenditure of original thought but much address in the selection of good points and taste in the adaptation of his extracts. On the whole he was extremely successful. And this is the secret of Lyceum lectures, flashy and popular. Remainder of the evening at the house below.

THURSDAY 24TH.

Fine day though hazy and warm. To Braintree. Lecture. Evening at the Mansion.

I worked very steadily upon my third paper and finished it. The Courier published the first today, and it reads to suit my taste. At noon I went to the house below to join my father in going to Col. Minot Thayer's at Braintree. This being the day fixed upon for the delivery by him [JQA] of the Lecture promised by him to the Braintree people. Col. Thayer had invited him and through him me to dine with him. When we got there at one o'clock we found a considerable assembly of persons, some from Boston and others from Braintree itself. Among the rest were Mr. John Welles, Edward Brooks, J. P. Bigelow, T. W. Phillips and the Revd. Mr. Blagden. Of the Braintree people I knew none although I was introduced to them all. Our dinner was a plentiful one as our host said entirely the produce of his farm. Nothing but water or lemonade on the high temperance plan. Of course it was a mere satisfaction of hunger,[1] and after it was over we proceeded to the meeting house of Dr. Storrs where after many ceremonies the Lecture was delivered.

It was a Lecture professing to be upon Education but rather without general plan, and the most remarkable position of which was that the

Reformation was a question of Education. This is no doubt true in one sense but it is false in another. Reading and writing no doubt were necessary to the full exercise of private judgment, but it has been generally found that a high state of intellectual education leads to indifference to religious belief in cultivated society if not to positive scepticism. There were passages of great force and brilliancy and owing to a hint of mine the Lecture was shortened so as to be within very tolerable limits of time. It appeared to be highly successful and we returned home before sunset after a short visit to Dr. Storrs. Evening at the Mansion. Little Fanny has been quite sick there for a week.

[1] The dinner is further described in JQA's Diary: "Instead of two or three friends as I had expected there was a company of about 30 persons, and a dinner for at least 60. He said it was all the produce of his own farm; but there was Turkey, Mongrel [Mongol?] Goose, Ducks, Ham, Squab pie, a large variety of vegetables. Apple and cranberry sauce, and lemonade to drink but neither wine nor cyder."

FRIDAY 25TH.

Pleasant day. To town with my Wife. Home to dine. Evening at the Mansion.

I went to town and was pretty constantly engaged in running about upon different errands. The town as usual under much uneasiness as the accounts from New York look rather more discouraging. I do not know how we shall come out but this I think is pretty clear that the storm will be a fearful one before it is over.

Called to see Judge Southard but he was not in. He delivered a Lecture before the Lyceum last night sent for to do so. How this lecturing flourishes. Home. After dinner, reading in McCulloch's Dictionary of Commerce. Evening at the house below.

SATURDAY 26TH.

A lovely day. At home. Transplanting trees. Evening at the Mansion.

This was a very remarkable day. I spent two or three hours of the morning in commencing my promised article for Mr. Hunt, but the beauty of the weather was such that I sallied out to avail of it in setting a few more trees, but I have nearly made up the complement for my piece of ground. The mode of making a plantation is undoubtedly perseverance only, and I have now carried it on very steadily autumn and spring for three years without as yet any very visible result. This would at first seem discouraging but it is the nature of all plantation not to realize soon. Afternoon so tired of writing that I went on with Menzel

314

whose book has dragged for some days. The Courier published my second paper this morning which reads pretty well. Evening at my father's where were Miss Harrod and E. C. Adams.

SUNDAY. 27TH.

Beautiful day. Exercises as usual. Evening at the Mansion.

I devoted the hour before service to my daughter Louisa and then attended the regular exercises. Mr. F. Cunningham preached in the morning from Matthew 22. 12. "And he saith unto him, Friend how camest thou in hither not having a wedding garment?" An idea of Swedenborg that spirits seek after death a situation for which they are suited in order to enjoy happiness seems to have led the preacher into a train of thoughts about fitness which he left exactly as he found them. Afternoon Ecclesiastes 3. 1. "To every thing there is a season." Trite and commonplace in the extreme.

Cunningham dined at my father's where I joined him. Fourteen years have passed since we graduated together at Cambridge. He the prominent and the promising, I, the indolent and the dissipated. Time has been cold to him since and placed him very far below me in the world's estimation. He has moreover been unfortunate in his domestic relations by marrying a woman marked for early but lingering death, and without children, whereas I have been fortunate. There is a moral in this which I hope I may take to heart. I trust I am not ungrateful for all my blessings, and it is not in a spirit of improper pride that I read this lesson of human vicissitude. But the greatest disappointment in Cunningham is in the extreme mediocrity of his performances, which show a want of something more than the gifts of external fortune.[1]

Read a Sermon by the Revd. J. Holland upon charity. 1 Corinthians 13. 1. "Though I speak with the tongues of men and of angels, and have not charity, I am become as sounding brass or a tinkling cymbal." A judicious discourse upon this ancient subject. Mr. Price Greenleaf called for half an hour after which we went to the Mansion.

[1] CFA had, on several earlier occasions, been led to moralize on the course of Rev. Francis Cunningham's career and on his own since their student years at Harvard; see vols. 3:394; 4:421; 6:367.

MONDAY. 28TH.

Fine. To town. Afternoon at home. Evening at the Mansion.

I went to town this morning out of time because I wished to take with me Catherine, who is about to begin to put our house in order, which looks as if it needed it enough. My time was accordingly very much engrossed by the different calls upon me in order to get going.

The public seems to continue in agitation about the suspension of specie payments but the resistance to it appears to gain ground which surprises me. Talked with S. C. Gray today who seems in good courage.

Return to dine, where my father joined me in place of my Wife who had gone with my mother to Boston. Continued Menzel afterwards. Evening visit to the Mansion.

TUESDAY 29TH.

Fine. At home. Nothing material. Evening at the Mansion.

I did not make as much out of the morning as I should have done. Kirk occupied me part of the time in planting trees, and I was engaged in other necessary arrangements in advance of winter about the place, a little more. And to confess the truth in addition to all this I did not take to my work kindly. My thoughts lagged heavily.

This morning completed the publication of my three papers upon the Philadelphia Manifesto. If I can judge at all of my productions, I should say they were about as good as any thing I have done with the exception of an occasional error or two of haste, and one of reasoning. But error is always liable to creep into such judgments.

Afternoon, felt so indolent that I read Menzel lazily. The long evenings now create a great waste of time. Evening at the Mansion. Fanny continues an invalid there.

WEDNESDAY 30TH.

Fine. To town. Return to dine at the Mansion, where also Evening.

I went to town this morning and was taken up as usual with matters pertaining to the removal of my family to town which I now think we will delay until the middle of next week. Mr. Curtis called in about business of Mrs. Boylston's Agency and Mr. W. T. Andrews on behalf of the nominating Committee of the Whig party to notify me of the selection of me as one of their candidates for the House of Representatives this year, and to inquire if I would accept. I was so situated as not to be able to give many minutes to reflection but the possibility of such an event had been in my mind within three or four years past and circumstances have rather conduced to strengthen me in the inclination long existing to decline the nomination.

The place is of little consequence, surrounded as it is with a host of colleagues, the year is one in which a multitude of little harrassing local questions will come up, to take sides about which is unavoidable and yet is throwing away a portion of influence that might be used to better purpose, and above all the Whig party now on it's last legs in the State is endeavouring to enlist me as a soldier after I have fought my own way to reputation of some sort against it's pressure when it was strong. I therefore declined verbally to Mr. Andrews, and as I was so situated as not to be able to explain the reasons I wrote him a short letter before leaving town.[1] This is not done without deliberation. But inasmuch as it may have the effect of putting me out of political life forever I consider it of importance. Political life is not of itself at this time and in this country an object of reasonable desire so far as happiness is concerned. Nothing but a sense of duty to the public can conquer my sense of this truth, and inasmuch as that can be more effectively performed in my belief by my remaining a perfectly independent citizen than by taking such a situation I know of no principle in the way of pursuing my inclination. Thus much for this business but having so decided, it is incumbent upon me not to vacillate nor to fall into temptation. The whisperings of vanity or ambition should not be allowed to overbear the injunctions of wisdom and prudence. But I ought not to conceal my gratification at the nomination, for it very far removes from my mind an impression long entertained that injustice was done me by my fellow citizens in Boston against none of whom have I ever to my knowledge done any hostile act.

Return to dine but at my father's, where I found that little Fanny was not so well. This is a distressing case enough.[2] Evening there also, only reading a little of Menzel in the interval. Mrs. T. B. Adams came down on a business also of a distressing kind,[3] so that my spirits were under something of a weight.

[1] To William T. Andrews, LbC, Adams Papers.
[2] See entry for 2 Nov., below.
[3] She had that day been advised to undergo surgery for cancer (JQA, Diary).

THURSDAY 31ST.

Chilly with clouds. At home. Evening at the Mansion.

I was at home all day but was unable to make the progress in writing which I expected because of some little transplanting left to do. As the season is now nearly over, I thought it as well to finish off with the remaining trees which have been taken up, although I had no place left very favorable to put them in. This over which took nearly all day I had no time left for any thing else so that my article for Hunt's Magazine appears not likely to be ready.

Evening at my father's. He had been to town and dined at Lieutt. Govr. Winthrop's. He had learned there the fact of my refusal of yesterday and as he says of the appointment of a Committee to wait upon me and urge my acceptance. I. P. Davis and R. C. Winthrop had both spoken to him of it with regret and had requested of him to use his influence with me to withdraw it, which he seemed a little inclined to do. I stated my reasons very simply to which he made no reply. This is rather a flattering circumstance to me who have not been heretofore used to any complimentary excesses, and perhaps this little will turn my head. I however see no reason to shake my confidence in the justice of my determination.

FRIDAY NOVEMBER 1ST.

Chilly with clouds. At home. Evening at the Mansion.

As it was on the whole more convenient for me to go into town tomorrow, and as my father was in a way to need my vehicle today I thought I would remain at home, and having no temptation to go out, I really did make better progress than usual in my article, but I have wholly remoulded the former draft so that the progress is rather crablike, and I am not sure that I shall be satisfied with it even in it's present form. The day was cold and cheerless and gave me many symptoms of inclination for my town house.

Evening at the Mansion where my father was, having returned from the dinner at Dr. Parkman's. He mentioned to me that he had seen Mr. Brooks at dinner who had expressed to him his regret at the course I had taken about the representative business, that Governor Everett had written to him about it that he might use his influence with me to procure the withdrawal of my letter, and that I. P. Davis had urged him to withdraw it upon his own responsibility, but this he could not undertake.

Of course all this is quite gratifying to my vanity. But my importance in Governor Everett's eyes springs quite as much from the weakness of the Whig party as from kindness to me. Yet I would not be considered as in so small a matter as this disposed to disregard the wishes or opinion of those who are older and discreet friends too. I hope by this time the matter is settled for me so that there need be neither appearance of retreat nor of slight to those whom I feel every disposition to respect.

SATURDAY 2D.

Weather much the same. To town. Afternoon at home. Evening at the Mansion.

I went to town this morning instead of yesterday. Occupied much of the day in the various little duties which must be performed in order to get transferred to town. Just as I was starting my father stepped out and strongly advised me if my place had not been filled up to retrace my steps. I of course felt very willing to defer to such authority although my own judgment did not second it, and agreed to do so if an opening remained. But as nobody came near me about it while in town, I inferred that the matter was settled and in such a way that I escape all disregard of my friends' wishes. This is as it should be. I believe the matter is settled right. Some talk with Mr. Brooks about it who was brought round to my way of thinking, from his general dislike of political life. I also received from Govr. Everett a kind letter which came too late.[1] He urged the probable strength of the vote for me as a test of public opinion. He knows how to flatter.

After working for Mr. Curtis I returned, and spent the afternoon at home in writing. In the evening to the Mansion where Miss Cutts had arrived from Boston. Poor little Fanny continues suffering from her illness to so great a degree as to render it doubtful whether the family will be able to move for some time to the southward.

[1] Edward Everett to CFA, 31 Oct., Adams Papers.

SUNDAY. 3D.

Weather much the same. Usual exercises. Evening, visitors and to the Mansion. Ride.

After the hour devoted to Louisa, I attended divine Worship as usual and heard Mr. Lunt preach although without paying him so much attention as I should. His text was from 2 Corinthians 7. 1. "Having therefore these promises, let us cleanse ourselves from all filthiness of the flesh and spirit, perfecting holiness in the fear of God." Afternoon from Luke 17. 21 "Behold, the kingdom of God is within you." I recollect hearing this discourse before. But my thoughts were going upon the subject I am writing upon for Mr. Hunt. This is wrong I know but sometimes it is not possible for me to help myself.

Immediately after service was over I went in the Carriage with my Wife to see Mr. and Mrs. S. C. Gray who are still at Dorchester. We were cordially received and made a brief but agreeable visit, returning home to tea.

In the evening we had a visit from Mr. Beale and his son and daughter so long that I could only go a short time to the Mansion. The family are very dull there on account of the long and alarming illness of Fanny, who suffers much.

After returning to my house I read a sermon by the Revd. J. Foster D. D. from Isaiah 40. 6. "All flesh is grass and all the goodliness thereof is as the flower of the field." A sermon upon death.

MONDAY 4TH.

Clear and cold. To town. Afternoon at home. Evening, visitors and to the Mansion.

I went to town to day taking my man Albert with me to work at the house for the day and return in the carriage in the afternoon. My time taken up in performing the endless number of little preparations essential to the commencement of housekeeping.

Met I. P. Davis and conversed with him about the Representative business. The ticket is out today and is neither bad nor good. Happening to go to my grocer's to purchase articles for the house, the first thing he did was to accost me about the opinions I held respecting the license law. He thought I was still on the ticket. He told me that the grocers meant to get the sentiments of each side and to select indiscriminately from among those friendly to their object of a repeal of the law. Of course, here would have been the first rock for me and Governor Everett's great vote would have vanished into thin air. I congratulated myself therefore upon my good fortune in having avoided a great whirlpool of vexation about very small things.

If I am to go into political life at all, which is by no means an object that any man of good sense should desire, it shall be when my services will be wanted and when I can do the country some effective ⟨good⟩ service. That time may indeed never arrive. And my ambition may have no scope for it's exercise. Well, I shall have avoided great trials of my impetuous temper, some exposition of human weakness and perhaps disgrace. My confidence is great that I shall be enabled by the guidance of divine mercy to walk the path which may be allotted me, whether that path be high or low. I have at least jumped over this difficulty, and it has not been a small one.

Home to dine. My father dined with me alone as my Wife instead of going to town as she had arranged went to the other house to stay with Fanny. She, poor child instead of growing better grows worse and my father tells me he despairs of her recovery. I had hoped it is not yet quite so bad as that.

Short afternoon, spent out of doors in the useful business of attempting to burn my corn stalks, in which after much effort I failed. Mr. and Mrs. Lunt called in the evening and sat an hour after which they joined us in a visit to the other house for a short time.

TUESDAY 5TH.

At home. Fine day. Evening at the Mansion.

We are all in a state of great depression of spirits from the declining condition of Little Fanny. Even my Wife who has heretofore retained her cheerfulness about it appears now to despair. This makes our stay here quite melancholy.

I was occupied a greater part of the morning upon my article for Mr. Hunt which I brought well forward to completion. It is not what I intended but the time prevents my doing more. And indeed my disposition also which is a little fatigued by the long service I have now been in. Since the early part of last November my pen has been running almost without cessation.

The afternoon was passed in making all the preparations for removal. The day had been very fine but it clouded towards sunset and appeared very threatening. After a visit from Mr. I. J. Carr[1] I called as usual at the Mansion and sat with the family.

[1] In the MS, Mr. Carr's initials appear to be I or J. However, the likelihood is that the visitor was John G. Carr, an Adams tenant and the only Carr referred to earlier in the Diary.

[*Boston*]

WEDNESDAY 6TH.

Clouds in the morning but it cleared. To town. Evening, Lecture.

The night was a very stormy one and the morning opened so unpromisingly I had great doubt whether we should be able to go. After some wavering, we finally concluded to go and our decision was confirmed by the result for it cleared away.

The morning was very much consumed in the various duties which removal makes necessary, sending off the small stock of luggage and putting the house in order. At last I left about 11 o'clock accompanied by Albert and reached town in time to give the necessary orders before my Wife came in. She remained in order to shut the house up. I went to the Office and devoted some time to business. Home at a little after one, where I found all the family at length arrived and the removal accomplished with far less of trouble than I have ever experienced before. Yet we were necessarily in confusion again replacing clothes &ca.

In the evening I was engaged to deliver to the Franklin Association my Lecture. This is a Society which assemble at a Chapel in Pitts Street the situation of which I had never before been acquainted with.[1] It is a nice place and the assembly was just about respectably full. I knew very few of the faces however and could not help thinking how strange it was that in the same town so many human beings should pass through life without ever being conscious of meeting each other. The Lecture appeared to tell as well as usual. This is the fifth time of it's delivery. Returned home at nine and retired rather earlier than usual.

[1] The Franklin Literary Association was a community self-education effort of the sort that sprang up from time to time, sometimes connected with a church or a fraternal group. In the present instance, support came from wealthy individuals of whom Peter C. Brooks was one (subscription paper, [1840?], C. E. French Papers, MHi). It was not among the formally constituted educational and literary organizations listed in the *Massachusetts Register* or the *Boston Directory*. Apparently it had no connection with the Franklin Lectures, so listed, which conducted a series of public lectures in Masonic Hall, and before which in December CFA would repeat once again the popular lecture on AA (below, entries for 21 and 23 Dec.).

THURSDAY 7TH.

Fine day. Office. Afternoon at home and Evening.

I began today upon my town life. The regular series of occupations not very interesting to record, but sufficiently so to keep me contented and happy.

I forgot to mention that yesterday I found an article in the Courier criticizing my review of the Philadelphia Manifesto. The temper in which it was written betrayed to me for the first time the shape which malevolence will assume towards me. A pretty broad stroke at my situation with some hints about aristocracy in order to destroy the force of my argument.[1] Well, this must be the consequence of distinction. I perceive now for the first time the force of my labours in gaining me reputation. Nevertheless I thought it prudent to turn the edge of this article by a mild reply swallowing the honey and rejecting the gall in the composition.[2] Office, did work and by night I finished the article for Hunt.

[1] The first two papers had elicited comment in a letter signed "Monitor" in the *Boston Courier* on 28 Oct. (p. 3, col. 4). The letter published there on the 6th (p. 2, col. 5), over the signature "Mercator," was somewhat more critical but not unfriendly except in objecting that CFA's statement, "The weak never gain much of the sympathy of the community, nor command their respect ..." sounds like the utterance of "a high-toned aristocrat" and is "uncalled for" and "unkind."

[2] In his reply, signed "A," CFA asserts that "Mercator" had totally misunderstood his meaning, that in speaking of the "weak" he referred to the "morally weak" (*Courier*, 8 Nov., p. 2, col. 3).

FRIDAY 8TH.

Fine day. Office. To Quincy to dine. Return to tea. Evening at work.

I devoted some time to labour in my Office in finishing off various little matters of account that have been troublesome and drafted a Will for Louisa C. Smith agreeably to a wish expressed by herself to me the evening before I left Quincy.

At noon I returned and my Wife accompanied me to Quincy. We found Fanny better and the family much encouraged. I went to see her and found her lively but with a burning spot in her cheek that told of internal disease. Her mother appeared today in a state of extraordinary exultation, which carries it's moral with it. What mere puppets we are, the sport of every touch.

I returned to town alone leaving my Wife to spend the night. Intended to have done much work but found my study cold and cheerless and so I only brought up arrears of Diary.

SATURDAY 9TH.

Cold but clear. Office. Time as usual. Evening at home.

I went to the Office as usual. My time not entirely at my own disposal as my father and Mr. Curtis both came in and spent a little while, but nevertheless I accomplished a draft of my Quarterly account to my father and the giving in of my Account on T. B. Adams' Estate to the Judge. This I shall be glad to get off of my mind.

Home where I found my Wife returned from Quincy and not at all encouraged about Fanny's condition. I fear we are to see grief in this direction. My father and Mother have suffered in abundance of this kind already and they are getting older and less able to bear it. I grieve for all and for myself. A melancholy thing it is to see the young decline. May God have mercy upon us all and upon me who am not worthy of the many blessings he has heaped upon me.

I began to review Storch and the materials for my Lecture which looks flat to me now that I read it over.

SUNDAY 10TH.

Cold and cloudy. Exercises as usual. Evening, Degrand, H. G. Gorham.

I devoted the morning hour to my daughter Louisa as usual. Attended Divine service at Dr. Frothingham's in Chauncy place and heard there Mr. Fox of Newburyport preach in the morning from Philippians 3. 14. "I press toward the mark for the prize of the high calling of God in Christ Jesus," and in the afternoon from Luke 10. 29. "And who is my neighbor." These were both of them good and sensible discourses without attracting my attention as much as they should have done. Indeed I am beginning to fear that I shall never be able to correct this unfortunate tendency of mine to wander in my thoughts during the delivery of any oral discourse.

After a brief visit to Mrs. S. A. Otis' to see the copy which Osgood is making of the Picture of my Grandfather,[1] I read a Sermon on Self-government by the Revd. Benjamin Ibbot, Proverbs 16. 32 "He that is slow to anger, is better than the mighty; and he that ruleth his spirit, than he that taketh a city." Dr. Ibbot did not appear to me remarkable.

At tea time Mr. Degrand came, just from Quincy, giving us a distressing note from my mother about the state of little Fanny.[2] She has had two bad days and Dr. Holbrook is at his wit's end, so that the object of the note was to induce Dr. Bigelow to go to Quincy and see her tomorrow. I immediately went down for the purpose and after a conference with him made an appointment to go to Quincy in the morning.

H. Gardiner Gorham came in afterwards and spent an hour in small conversation of indifferent matters, after which I set about making up arrears in Diary.

[1] Samuel S. Osgood had been commissioned by Andrew Jackson Downing to paint a copy of Stuart's 1823 portrait of JA; see above, entry for 22 January. The copy is unlocated (Oliver, *Portraits of JA and AA*, p. 259).

[2] The note from LCA is missing.

MONDAY 11TH.

Fine day. To Quincy. Return Afternoon. Evening at home.
A cool but clear and bright November day. As soon as practicable

after breakfast I started to go to Quincy accompanied by my Wife. We came round by Milton hill in order to stop at Dr. Holbrook's and notify him to meet Bigelow at the time agreed upon. But he had gone to Boston. We found the family in a state of distress such as may be conceived, which was however relieved by the result of Bigelow's examination so far as that hope which had been almost extinct revived.

I had but a dull and unprofitable day of it as my father was busy and the other members of the family were much taken up of course. It was the day of general election but I lost my vote which would otherwise have been what it never was before, *regularly* Whig. Returned to town by sunset leaving my Wife. Devoted the evening to new modelling a page or two of the article for Hunt which I positively folded up to send.

My boy Charles I sent this day upon a visit to his old Nurse at Portsmouth Mrs. Fields, through her sons who were going. So unused am I to part with my children that I feel a dislike to have them out of my sight. And yet it is not man's vocation to be confined and I ought to repress a weakness which will cost me even more serious pain in advanced life. My trust in all cases is in a higher power.

TUESDAY 12TH.

Lovely day. Day divided as usual. Evening at home.

At the Office where I finished up all the remaining business which I had on hand. Made the draft of my Quarterly Account and sent it. Then to the Athenæum to get books for my proposed Lecture. I want to read myself full upon the subject. For I have some doubt as yet of the issue.

The Election Returns come in badly for the Whigs so that it is exceedingly doubtful whether the Governor is elected again. Under these circumstances it is matter of greater congratulation to me that I have not to take up their battles.

Began today the first drama in the collection by Euripides of Hecuba, which I propose to make my winter's work. Read part of Mr. Gallatin's Pamphlet upon the currency deserving of perpetual study.[1] And in the evening Ganilh, Political Economy.[2] My Wife returned to dinner, accompanied by Miss Cutts who went back in the afternoon. The child remained much in the same state.

[1] Almost an annual occurrence; see above, entries for 28 Dec. 1836, 18 Nov. 1837.
[2] Charles Ganilh, *Des systèmes d'économie politique*, 2 vols., Paris, 1809, or *Le théorie de l'économie politique*, 2 vols., Paris, 1815.

WEDNESDAY 13TH.

Fine day. Office. Time as usual. Evening at home.

I have little or nothing new to record this morning. My town life is now so very regular that a Diary suffers much from the monotony. At the Office I have now finished all that I had to do and today sat down to read the Chapter upon currency in Sismondi's valuable work upon Political Economy. He leans much against credit. Read a hundred and twenty lines of Hecuba during the hour before dinner.

Afternoon, resumed Menzel who does not increase in my esteem as I go on. Evening at home. Mr. Brooks came in and passed a short time. He returns to his town residence today. Finish Gallatin and Ganilh.

THURSDAY 14TH.

Clouds and light rain. Division as usual. Evening, my father's Lecture.

I was at the Office reading No. 105 of the North American Review. The accounts this morning seem to favour the opinion that the State has chosen Morton for Governor and Everett will retire. This is rather new and unexpected but I cannot say surprising. On the whole it is even more of a punishment than I had desired for the threefold combination against my father which originally brought him in.[1] I care but little as between the two parties generally for the one seems to have as little of steady principle as the other.[2]

At home. Hecuba. Menzel. In the evening I accompanied my father to the Masonic Temple where he was to deliver a Lecture upon the Smithsonian fund. The room was full of Mechanic Apprentices and their friends with a very small sprinkling of other persons whom I knew. The Lecture was interesting and more successful in the delivery than usual with him.[3] It bore rather hard upon the Administration and upon Mr. Woodbury.[4] After he had finished what he had for this evening he accompanied me home and after that, I began upon my redraught of the Lecture.

[1] The early returns indicating the defeat of Edward Everett for reelection by the Democrat Marcus Morton were later confirmed (*Boston Courier*, 18 Nov., p. 3, cols. 2, 4). Everett had originally come to the governorship when Gov. John Davis was elected to the U.S. Senate to fill the unexpired term of Nathaniel Silsbee. That result had been brought about by the alliance of Everett with Daniel Webster and Davis in the prolonged and ultimately successful effort by the whigs, masons, and federalists in the Massachusetts legislature in Jan.–Feb. 1835 to deny the senate seat to JQA (vol. 6:63, 68, 74–75, 78–81). CFA had also entertained substantial reservations about Everett over many years despite the familial connection (see entry for 6 Aug. 1836, above, and vol. 3:9–10).

[2] The National Republican and Democratic parties.

[3] The lecture on the Smithson bequest was the first of two that JQA had prepared for delivery before the Mechanic Apprentices' Library Association in Boston. The second would, as it turned out, be read for him by the Rev. Lunt before both the Apprentices' Association and at the Quincy Lyceum. The texts of the two lectures, an account of their composition, delivery, and contemporary publication, are contained in *The Great Design, Two Lectures on the Smithson Bequest by John Quincy Adams*, ed. Wilcomb E. Washburn, Washington, The Smithsonian Institution, 1965.

[4] Levi Woodbury, secretary of the treasury.

FRIDAY 15TH.

Rainy but mild. Division as usual. Evening visit to Governor Everett.

My morning was not very well employed as my Office hours now need some special occupation. Read an article in Hunt's Magazine by Judge Hopkinson which is very sensible[1] and tried another upon Stone's Life of Brant but failed. This is the work which Dr. Palfrey sent to me to review.[2] Hecuba.

My father dined with me and returned to Quincy taking my Wife with him afterwards. After dinner, Menzel. In the evening, I went down to see Governor and Mrs. Everett. Had much conversation with him upon the present condition of affairs and the Election. He seems entirely disgusted with politics and now that it is over rather desirous of having it decided against him, for the present aspect is that the choice must devolve on the House. Continued my Lecture.

[1] Judge Joseph Hopkinson's article on "Commercial Integrity" appeared in *Hunt's Merchants' Mag.*, 1:377–390.
[2] See the entry for 26 Sept. 1838, above. The review article read is probably that by James Handasyd Perkins in the Oct. 1839 issue of *North Amer. Rev.*, 49:277–316.

SATURDAY 16TH.

Mild and pleasant. Office. To Quincy to dine. Evening return, head ach.

I awoke this morning with a dull feeling the precursor of head ach which did not fail to take it's usual course through the day until it sent me helpless to bed. At the Office I was occupied in the usual way. Deacon Spear came from Quincy and I was busy in accounts. The political news is not varied at all by the last returns. Either Morton or nobody is elected.

I went to Quincy at one o'clock and found the family in great distress. Little Fanny had passed a bad night and this day was speechless. The apprehension of course was that she was near her end. But the physician called in, Dr. Woodward, and Dr. Holbrook ascribed it to the effect of a violent anodyne given last evening which had operated otherwise than he had expected. This relieved the present apprehension although as it seemed to me not entirely with reason. I fear the poor child will not survive many days and that her end has been rather hastened than retarded by the mode of treatment adopted by Dr. Holbrook. This is altogether melancholy. I dined at Quincy and in the afternoon early we returned home.

Little Charles returned today from Portsmouth safe and well. I hardly know how much I prize my children until they are absent. My evening was utterly useless to me from my head ach.

SUNDAY 17TH.

Lovely day, clouding however towards night. Usual exercises. Evening to Mr. Brooks'.

This was one of our most charming mornings. After the usual exercises with Louisa I attended as usual divine exercises at Chauncy place and heard Dr. Dewey of New York[1] preach in the morning from Job 23. 1 to 5, too long to quote. He began by a general sketch of the book of Job preparatory to his introduction of the particular purpose of quoting the text which was to show a tendency in man perpetually to look upward from the mere business of this world and seek a higher power freed from the struggles of this life. This aspiration was only to be satisfied by Religion. The afternoon was upon a collateral subject. Matthew 4. 4. "It is written, man shall not live by bread alone but by every word that proceedeth out of the mouth of God." Religion being the desire of man this could only be gratified by the exercise of faith and virtue. Dr. Dewey is a very popular preacher and is to some extent deserving of esteem. But his sermons left me cold as they found me and created rather an idea of excessive pretension than of fulness of wisdom or piety.

I had a very pleasant walk with the children round the Common and after service read a Sermon by Dr. Clark from the English preacher, Proverbs 10. 9. "He that walketh uprightly, walketh surely." It was a new version of the old maxim, "Honesty is the best policy," which after all is not at the summit of all moral excellence. Yet it is a safe practical guide for men who will not refine.

Evening, Thomas and Francis Frothingham came in for an hour after which we went to Mr. Brooks' house but not finding him at home, sat with Mr. and Mrs. P. C. B. Junr. The Account from Quincy today by Thomas who brought in Louisa C. Smith is not favorable. She had not entirely recovered her Speech as predicted. My fear is that there was a combination with the medicine of a more powerful kind to bring about the effect.

¹ On Rev. Orville Dewey, see vol. 6:388–389.

MONDAY 18TH.

Fine day. Distribution as usual. Evening at home and at E. Brooks'.

I went to the Office as usual this morning and was occupied in accounts and a variety of other little duties but the employment of my hours does not entirely satisfy me. Home at noon to read Hecuba.

The accounts we receive from Quincy are very discouraging. Afternoon Menzel. Evening with the children until eight after which we went to Edward Brooks', calling for half an hour to see Sidney and his Wife. On my return home went on with my Lecture.

TUESDAY 19TH.

Fine day. Morning at Office. To Quincy to dine. Return to tea. Evening at home.

I went to the Office this morning but was not occupied very usefully. Something or other I must soon do. My carpenter called and I gave him a commission or two as also my man whom I dismissed so unceremoniously last night as to put me to some present inconvenience.

At noon I went home and rode with Mrs. Adams to Quincy. We found the family much as usual, but Fanny in a state of insensibility. She has not recovered from the shock of Saturday whence it is plainly to be inferred that the medicine was not the cause. The disease on that day appears to have reached the brain. And it was an unlucky coincidence for Dr. Holbrook that his remedy was productive of some effects so similar that he ascribed them all to it rather too hastily. I am afraid the disease has gone on in stages with certainty to it's end.

Home by sunset. Evening with the children and in my study, writing.

WEDNESDAY 20TH.

Cold and clear. Office as usual. Regular division. Evening at home.

I went to the Office this morning as usual and was occupied in my ordinary mode. Nothing new. Home in order to attend to details put out of order by my man's departure. Found my Wife who had returned from Quincy where she spent the night, with Dr. Bigelow. Her account is confirmatory of my worst apprehensions. The Dr. now pronounces the case to be dropsy on the brain very decided. The complaint appears then either to have thoroughly baffled their penetration, or it has very suddenly changed it's character. Mrs. Goods the child's nurse was at my house just from Washington and went to Quincy in the afternoon's stage. Evening quietly at home. Continued my Lecture.

THURSDAY 21ST.

Office. Thence to Quincy. Cold and snowy. Return. Evening at home.

I went to the Office where Mr. Ladd came and talked and paid rent. Received a notice from Quincy that the poor child Georgiana Frances Adams died last night at a few minutes before six. When I look back and think over this rapid decline, it makes me feel what a brief and uncertain light this mortality is.[1] God alone knows the object of our creation and his inscrutable decree recalls in the same manner that he gives. Our province is to live as we may and trust to his mercy not to deal with us according to our deserts.

I hurried home and thence after making some arrangements and notifying the Mechanic Apprentices that my father would not lecture I went to Quincy.[2] The family were of course in much distress but my mother's grief touched me the most deeply. To her who has so few objects of pleasure around her it is grief indeed. The mother is in great distress but she vents it more in words. I dined out there and devoted myself as much as possible to the various members of the household. Came back at sunset in a very cold north wind. Evening at home.

[1] The onset of the illness of Georgeanna Frances Adams, age nine, had apparently manifested itself more than a month earlier. However, she had had a serious illness in infancy affecting mouth and lungs (vol. 4:90) and seems to have been a delicate child in the intervening years.

Although the physicians continued to speak of a "lingering disease and possible recovery" for another fortnight, JQA recorded in his Diary on 4 Nov.: "I have long been afflicted with an apprehension that this poor child was destined to short life. I have watched the symptoms of her disease with a trembling heart and with sinking hope." On the next day he wrote: "I saw her in one of her paroxysms of pain—the case is remediless." His daily notes show that from the 16th she became "speechless but not insensible." On that date the doctors prescribed "strymonium," a narcotic derived from a poisonous plant or weed usually employed in the treatment of asthma or bronchial conditions to reduce coughing and pain (*Pharmacopeia of U.S.*, 1851). The editors have found no further clue to nor name for her final illness, but see below, entry for 13 Jan. 1840.

[2] Unknown to CFA, JQA had asked the Rev. Lunt to deliver the lecture for him (see above, entry for 14 Nov.).

5. GEORGEANNA FRANCES ADAMS AND MARY LOUISA ADAMS IN 1835,
BY ASHER BROWN DURAND

See page xi

FRIDAY. 22D.

Cold. Morning to Quincy. Home to tea and evening.

As my father wished me to be near him so that he might have somebody to call upon in case of need I went out there and was engaged partly in helping on the necessary arrangements for the funeral and partly in copying letters for him. Affliction has a peculiar operation upon him by exciting his nervous sensibilities over much and rendering him alive to many small evils and inconveniences. I strove to do every thing that I could for him but often he will do them for himself.

Called to see Mr. Wolcott on the part of my father and notified him of Mrs. John Adams' wish to have the episcopal service read, which he promised to do. This done and others I returned home having a very cold ride. Evening at home.

SATURDAY 23RD.

Cool. Carriage to Quincy. Funeral. Home. Evening quiet.

After a little business at the Office, I joined my Wife at the house and we went in a Carriage to Quincy with Louisa and John, and Richard G. Greenleaf. Of course little was done there or thought of but the funeral which took place after an early dinner.

There were only the few citizens of our acquaintance. Mr. Wolcott read the Episcopal service in a very hard wooden manner, after which Mr. Lunt made a prayer in a manner peculiarly impressive and of a most affecting character. A short procession followed and we committed the remains of the poor child to the tomb.

Twenty one years ago I followed the same road for the first time after the decease of my grandmother and since then how many changes have taken place. How many of our family have since been gathered in to the same inclosure who were then warm with life and hope in how many cases disappointed. The idea is a melancholy one. This poor little one has no memory to leave behind her but a pleasing one to her friends as she was lovely in her youth and innocence and simplicity beyond most children of her age. May God have mercy upon her and upon the survivors of her race.

We returned home shortly after the ceremony, leaving my Mother ill in her bed from the effects of the exertion she has made.[1] Dull and melancholy evening.

[1] JQA, in his journal entries, has recorded the sad events of this and the preceding days in great detail.

SUNDAY 24TH.

Clouds and rain. To Quincy. Service as usual. Home with Miss Cutts, Mr. Thornton.

I started for Quincy immediately after breakfast and in order to reach there in time for morning service. My father wished a Note to be read according to the customary form of the Congregational service, and I therefore came here to attend the service.

There was present of the family only Miss Cutts and my father and Louisa. Mr. Lunts prayer was very brief and proper. His Sermon from Ezekiel 2. 9 and 3. 1 and 2. "And when I looked, behold, a hand was sent unto me; and lo, a roll of a book was therein. Moreover, he said unto me, Son of man eat that thou findest; eat this roll and go speak unto the house of Israel. So I opened my mouth and he caused me to eat that roll." Mr. Whitney preached in the afternoon but what his text was I could not remember, and his sight and enunciation are so bad that it is painful to listen to him.

Immediately after the afternoon service I returned to town accompanied by Miss Cutts who wished to take leave of her friends. Found at home Mr. Thornton an acquaintance of her's who spent the evening. Read a sermon by Dr. Squire, Matthew 6. 19.20. "Lay not up for yourselves treasures upon earth, where moth and rust doth corrupt and where thieves break through and steal, but lay up for yourselves treasures in heaven, where neither moth nor rust doth corrupt nor do thieves break in and steal." A very ordinary production as it seems to me. Miss Cutts remained at my house tonight.

MONDAY. 25TH.

Heavy rain. At home. Evening visit at Mr. Crowninshield's.

The day opened warm with a strong southerly wind and heavy rain, so that I was not able to go to Quincy as I intended. My time was therefore spent in attempting to do up a little of the arrears which my being taken off so much of late have caused in my Diary. Snatched an hour also for Hecuba which is very easy.

Afternoon Menzel in whom I take very little interest. Indeed the time appears to me so much wasted that I must strike into something else.

As it cleared in the evening, we joined Miss Cutts at her friend's Miss Crowninshields. The old gentleman and his Wife there. He is a singular man but with much ignorance and illiterateness joins a great deal of Yankee acuteness and the economical principle.

TUESDAY 26TH.

Cold and clear. To Quincy. Evening at home. Mr. Brooks.

After devoting an hour to business, I went to Quincy accompanied by my Wife, meeting my father on the road to town. Found the family much as usual but doubting about their departure. This made me anxious, believing as I did both that they ought to go soon and could go soon without inconvenience. Accordingly I made an effort at persuasion which proved to be successful and tomorrow was fixed for the day. My father returned to dinner, after which I transacted business with the Bank and then returned to town. Our ride was very cold. I hope it is the last of the season. Mr. Brooks spent an hour with us in the evening.

WEDNESDAY 27TH.

Weather moderating. To Quincy. Return with the family. Evening at home.

I was much engaged in preparing funds for my father, and securing tickets for the family to New York. This over I went to Quincy and found the preparations actively going on for a general departure. My mother seemed better than I expected to see her.

After an early dinner they got into the Stage and I accompanied them leaving my horse for the Winter. We arrived at the Railroad depot so much earlier than necessary that I walked to my house and brought down the boys John and Charles to see the family off. At last they went and I returned feeling as if a load had been removed from my mind.

Evening spent at home beginning to take some rest from the incessant movement and exertion which has been going on for a week together, following another of great mental distress.

THURSDAY 28TH.

Fine day. Thanksgiving. Service as usual. Evening at Mrs. Frothingham's.

I arose this morning with a sense of relief which I have not had for some time. The State of my father's family had filled me for some time back with a set of gloomy apprehensions which their very indefiniteness tended to make more painful. Quincy and the old house are rather gloomy places for the winter season and I feared they might be confined there by sickness even after little Fanny's decease. Thank heaven, they have at least started for other scenes and although these may contribute but little to amuse or to cheer them, they yet place them upon an active theatre where some diversion may chance to be favorable. I now hope to hear of their safe arrival. In mere weather they must have been highly favored.

Attended divine service and heard Dr. Frothingham preach from Psalms 107. 8.15 &ca. "Oh that men would praise the Lord for his goodness and for his wonderful works to the children of men." A good discourse but I was rather inattentive.

Walk round the South Cove home. Mr. Brooks dined with us, and I felt grateful to the divine being for his continued care and protection of us through the past year. Evening to Mrs. Frothingham's where we had a game of whist among the children and a little supper afterwards.

FRIDAY 29TH.

Continued fine weather. Time as usual. Evening to the Theatre.

We are now commencing again upon the usual routine of winter life. At the Office where I passed my time in accounts and papers as usual. Nothing materially new. Home to read Hecuba, which goes on well whenever I have any time to follow it. At the Athenæum where I procured Mr. Bancroft's book for the purpose of giving it a deliberate examination.[1] After dinner gave up Menzel and began Bancroft.

Evening to the Theatre with my Wife. Charles Kean in The Iron Chest razeed[2] and a new play of Bulwer's, The Lady of Lyons. Claude Melnotte.[3] It is impossible to be more disappointed than I was. When I saw this young man some years ago in The Hunchback I thought him quite promising. Since then he has fallen into the faults of bad recitation and violent rant so that there are hardly any good points left. The play of The Iron Chest is no great favorite with me but it always tells upon an audience.[4] The present version of it is the cream of all it's stage tricks condensed into three acts. Bulwer's play is not bad. A little too much of love sickness about it, but on the whole affecting and agreeable. Home by eleven.

[1] Probably the first two volumes of George Bancroft's *History of the United States* (10 vols., Boston, 1834–1874), published together in 1837 but constituting the 2d edn. of vol. 1 and the first appearance of vol. 2. Both dealt with the period of colonization and reflected a "democratic" or Jacksonian view.

[2] That is, abridged (*OED*).

[3] In Bulwer Lytton's *Lady of Lyons*, first produced in 1838, Claude Melnotte was the central figure (Odell, *Annals N.Y. Stage*, 4:206).

[4] *The Iron Chest*, a play with music, by George Colman the younger had been produced in London in 1796. CFA's earlier view of Charles Kean is at vol. 4:413.

Fine day. Office. Roxbury Probate Court. Evening at home.

The weather at least has been highly favorable to the family, if it is like what we have had here. I went to the Office and transacted business with Deacon Spear from Quincy and others. Then I determined to walk to Roxbury to attend the Probate Court there for the passing of my account as Executor of the Will of T. B. Adams. Met Judge Leland on the way and walked with him talking politics generally. The Account was speedily passed after our arrival at his house and I returned before three o'clock. Thus I hope this business will be off my mind. Continued reading Bancroft. Evening at home, reading Nicholas Nickleby to my Wife, after which I went on with the third and I hope the last draught of my Lecture.

Chilly and clouds. Exercises as usual. Evening, H. G. Gorham.

A change in the weather but I hope by this time the family are clear of it. Lesson as usual with my daughter until Service when I attended at Chauncy Place and heard Dr. Frothingham in the morning from Matthew 21. 5. "Tell ye the daughter of Sion, Behold thy King cometh unto thee, meek." Upon Advent Sunday and commemorative of the event of which it is the Anniversary.

Afternoon, a young Buckingham son of the Printer just beginning. I. Peter 2. 22 "Who did no sin neither was guile found in his mouth." Upon the character of the Saviour whether a divine being, free from all danger of sin, or a mortal agent. He reasoned in favour of the latter, on the ground that he was said to have been tempted which implies the possibility of falling. One phrase struck me as curious. He called Jesus the *last* of the noble army of Martyrs, both in the sermon and the prayer.

Afternoon, a sermon by the Revd. John Balguy "Who for the joy that was set before him, endured the cross, despising the shame." Nothing very extraordinary. In the evening at home. H. G. Gorham came and paid a visit.

Cloudy and cold. Office. Distribution as usual. Evening at home.

The day was cheerless. I was at the Office engaged in making up the arrears of my Diary and in bringing up the small business of the Office which has got behind hand. Nothing new of material consequence. Home to read Hecuba.

After dinner, Bancroft. He certainly has taken a great deal of pains in investigating the truth and although I feel some distrust of his conclusions, yet I cannot help admiring his industry. Evening at home, reading Nicholas Nickleby and afterwards on with the Lecture.

TUESDAY. 3D.

Cloudy and chill. Distribution as usual. Evening at home. Mr. Brooks.

Office as usual. Nothing to record. The days follow each other with great uniformity. I did a little in the way of filling up Leases but rather neglected occupation. The December number of Hunt's Magazine contains my article on the currency which I think pretty good.[1] Home to study Hecuba. After dinner continued Bancroft. I do not like to take the trouble of comparison but it ought to be done by somebody.

Evening, I read a little of Frank[2] to the children and after they had gone to bed, Nicholas Nickleby to my Wife. This is very well written and shows much genius in the Author. But what is fame in these days when this great sum of labour is spent for the mere gratification of a few careless readers of a monthly periodical? Afterwards, working on my Lecture which goes on slowly.

[1] See above, entry for 22 October.
[2] The editors do not know what book is meant.

WEDNESDAY 4TH.

Chilly but cleared before evening. At home as usual.

I had nothing material to record today. My time passes monotonously enough. Made a call upon old Warren the coin collector who has picked up a great parcel of stuff, but some very curious things in his travels in Canada. Strange to tell, he got three ancient Roman coins in common circulation, which I bought of him. They are not rare and are somewhat worn.

Received a letter from my father giving me the agreeable intelligence of the safe arrival of the family.[1] My Wife went to Medford with her father to attend the dedication of the new Meeting house and did not return until evening. Bancroft, and after tea, Frank to the children and Nickleby to my Wife, after which the Lecture.

[1] To CFA, 1 Dec., Adams Papers.

THURSDAY 5TH.

Clear and beautiful day. Office. Division as usual. Evening at home.

My time at the Office is so little improved that I must set about some novel plan of occupation. The accounts from Washington are not very favorable to a plan of general organization. The disputed seats of the Jersey members remain still the great obstacle, aggravated by the refusal of the clerk to move one way or the other. Nothing further. Home to read Hecuba.

Afternoon, Bancroft. I can hardly yet make up my mind as to the merits of this work. I see unquestioned industry and some enthusiasm but no nice discrimination in moral questions, and some self conceit. I should rely upon his facts but distrust his philosophy and his inferences. Evening, Frank to the children, and Nicholas Nickleby to my Wife. After which, working upon my very interminable Lecture.

FRIDAY 6TH.

Fine day. Office. Division as usual.

I pursue my affairs regularly enough, but the season of the year always affects my spirits a little and some circumstances of the time have a tendency to increase it.

The arrival of the Liverpool today is rather productive of encouragement as to business, but the country is in so unsettled a state as to give little reason for confidence in any thing.

Accounts and then home to Hecuba. After dinner, Bancroft. I commonly devote an hour of the evening to hearing my children's lessons in reading. Frank and Nickleby.

SATURDAY. 7TH.

Cloudy. Office. Distribution as usual.

At the Office. The accounts from Washington are in the same strain with that of the preceding days. Deacon Spear was here with bills from Quincy most of which I paid. They are pretty heavy. Hecuba which I read a little too fast. I want a good edition. After dinner Bancroft, and in the evening, Nickleby and Frank and the Lecture. I begin to fear that this will not do. I cannot shorten it and there are passages which I fear must be dry.

SUNDAY 8TH.

Rain and clouds all day. Exercises as usual. Evening at home.

After my usual course of lessons with my daughter Louisa, I attended divine service and heard Dr. Frothingham preach from Isaiah 5. 4. "What could have been done more to my vineyard that I have not done to it." A moral discourse upon self improvement which I did not attend to as I ought. In the Afternoon Romans 8. 9. "Now if any man have not the spirit of Christ, he is none of his." Mr. Dwight a young man who has got as much of the mysticism of the new school as will be sufficient to destroy that practical use which is after all a characteristic of the English race and makes it superior to every other. He is feeble.

Read in the English Preacher a Sermon by one John Adams D.D., a singular name in England whose history I know nothing of. Acts 28. 5.6. "He shook off the beast into the fire and felt no harm. Howbeit they looked when he should have swollen or fallen down dead suddenly; but after they had looked a great while and saw no harm come to him, they changed their minds and said that he was a God." A Sermon upon rash judgment remarkable for that very practical judgment and sound sense of which I was just treating. Evening at home reading Nickleby, and Frank, after which continued my terrible labour upon the Lecture.

MONDAY 9TH.

Heavy rain. Office. Athenæum. Division as usual. Evening at home.

The rain poured very heavily in parts of today. I was at the Office in business. The news from Washington is that the confusion being daily more striking, Mr. Rhett finally took advantage of a speech of my father's which had a great momentary effect to put him in the chair as chairman to organize the House. This is a position which I fear he will be unable to avail himself of. The pith of the whole matter is that the Jersey members decide the majority of the house. And the two parties are rabid. I hope the country will not experience so much of disgrace as I believe they will. At any rate, the part my father has thus far acted will be creditable to him.[1]

Went to the Athenæum to study Numismatics and was kept there until dinner time. Afternoon, study Bancroft. Evening, finish Nickleby and on with the Lecture. This was City Election day. My classmate J. Chapman was chosen, a good selection and I hope will do him honor.[2] Evening, Lecture, which drags.

¹ The House having been unable for three days to complete its membership and thereafter to elect a presiding officer, JQA spoke to the problem and offered a solution on the 5th. R. B. Rhett of South Carolina then moved the election of JQA to preside until organization could be completed. He assumed the chair and continued in it for the next ten days. The events are detailed in JQA's journal entries for those dates.

² On Jonathan Chapman Jr., newly chosen mayor of Boston, see vol. 3:127, 380–381.

TUESDAY. 10TH.

Fine day. Distribution as usual. Evening at home.

It was clear this morning after the heavy blow of last night. Office where I saved half an hour to begin Storch, Economie Politique. I have taken a very great liking to this writer and propose to study his style and thought. Read Hecuba.

Afternoon finish the first volume of Bancroft. I am afraid my dislike of his book springs out of my distrust of the man. Began a number of The London and Westminster Review sent me as particularly good, by Dr. Frothingham. The first article about Carlyle rouses my profound distaste. The style is artificial and the thought is very strained. Modern times do not appear to me to show the results which they pretend.

Evening at home, reading the letters of Horace Walpole,¹ and finish the Lecture, which when I look it over gives me some misgivings.

¹ It is not clear which of the collections of Walpole's correspondence CFA refers to. Before 1840, separate volumes of correspondence with George Montegu, William Cole, and Sir Horace Mann had been published.

WEDNESDAY 11TH.

Lovely day. Distribution as usual. Evening at Mr. Brooks'.

The weather remains extraordinarily pleasant for the season and today was such a one as we have few at any time of the year. At the office where I was so occupied about arrears of Diary and accounts that I could not read further of Storch.

Then home where I finished Hecuba. This is the easiest of all the greek dramas that I have ever yet read. There are many fine points of pathos in it, and many moral reflections of great beauty. But I feel the want of greek and latin notes, and a critical apparatus. Inasmuch as I cannot afford to purchase one new and I cannot elsewhere procure it, I think I shall postpone the Author and go back to a thorough re-examination of Sophocles with the edition I procured last year that is very complete.

After dinner, read The Review without much increase of pleasure.

There is nothing flatter than the aspirings of middling minds to appear great by putting themselves on Stilts. Tried to read my Lecture loud to ascertain its length but was interrupted. Evening, to see Mr. Brooks where were several of the family. Miss L. C. Smith was with us to spend the day.

THURSDAY. 12TH.

Rain, but cleared up in the evening. Distribution as usual. Evening at Mrs. Frothingham's.

The morning looked very dark and threatening but it turned out to be only a very short Southerly rain. Office nevertheless where I read a little of Storch and brought up my arrears of Diary. Home where I began Sophocles with the Œdipus Tyrannus and read forty lines very thoroughly.

In the Afternoon I read through my Lecture in one hour and five minutes which in delivery would take an hour and a half. This is too long. And I find deficiencies to be filled up which would add another half hour. I am now disposed once more and for the last time to re-model the whole, and I began upon it today. After all, if this does not suit I can retreat upon my old performance which I know I can make successful.

Evening, to Mrs. Frothingham's where was a little party of young and old, few of whom I knew. Home at eleven.

FRIDAY 13TH.

Pleasant day. Distribution as usual. Evening at home.

I was at the Office this morning with my time much taken up in writing. Began a letter to my Mother but was interrupted by Winch the Tenant of the farm at Weston who came to pay rent. Then home where I read about forty lines more of the Œdipus.

In the afternoon, reading and writing upon my Lecture. I never was in more doubt in my life. I think what I have written is pretty good but I doubt it's telling well upon an audience. Evening at home, reading.

The accounts from Washington are very bad. The dignity of the country is much implicated in this proceeding. I hope my father will get through with credit in this perhaps the most perillous situation of his life.[1]

---

[1] JQA's ordeal as presiding officer would end on Monday, the 16th, when sufficient votes were mustered to elect a Speaker.

SATURDAY 14TH.

Day pleasant. Distribution as usual. Evening Mr. Brooks.

I was at the Office where I again attempted to finish my letter but was interrupted by Deacon Spear who came from Quincy and settled matters of accounts due. This with the reading of the Newspapers consumed my time. I suppose it is important to keep up with the times but it consumes a great deal of valuable time with little apparent result.

The accounts from Washington appear a little more favorable to a settlement today. But there is no knowing. Afternoon, reading a volume on Banking by Mr. Raguet of Philadelphia which Mr. Hunt has sent to me with a pamphlet by Mr. Sullivan.[1] Evening, Mr. Brooks came in and passed a couple of hours, after which I went on with my Lecture.

[1] Condy Raguet's *Treatise on Currency and Banking*, Phila., 1839, is at MQA. Freeman Hunt's letter of 9 Dec. is in Adams Papers.

SUNDAY. 15TH.

Cloudy with snow, rain and a very heavy gale. Exercises as usual. At home.

This was the first day of real winter and it brought with it all the worst accompaniments of the season. Snow, then heavy rain and finally the severest winds we have had for a great while.

I attended divine service all day notwithstanding and heard Dr. Frothingham preach from Acts 18. 17. "And Gallio cared for none of those things." A sermon upon the tendency of the day to contentious disputations about trifles, I suppose having reference to the controversies now going on between many of the Unitarian clergy. In the afternoon a very brief discussion of the text in Ecclesiastes 1. 2. "Vanity of vanities all is vanity."

The wind was so furious as to twist my umbrella in a moment, and to bring down signs so that it was hardly safe to walk in the Streets. Read a sermon in the English preacher from Titus 3. 1. "Put them in mind to be subject to principalities and powers to obey magistrates." A sensible and judicious discourse by a Mr. Osborne upon obedience to the laws and authority of Rulers. Went on with my Lecture. The Storm lulled for a time but recommenced at about eleven o'clock in such a manner that I feared to go to bed, thinking some of the windows might be blown in. I have not within my experience any knowledge of such a tornado.

MONDAY 16TH.

Snow all day with high wind. Office for an hour, day at home.

The Storm lulled at about one o'clock this morning but the snow continued falling all day and evening and the wind though moderated was still high.

I remained at home engaged in my usual occupation for an hour after breakfast, that is, making a thorough classification of my collection of coins and medals. This is of far greater value than I had imagined, and I am constantly occupied in improving it without incurring too heavy expense. My time at the Office is my least profitable time.

Read Sophocles, I find I have still much to do to master the whole force of the text, but it grows easier to me at every trial. Afternoon Mr. Raguet's book on Banking, and Evening at home reading Walpole's letters which are very amusing. Lecture.

TUESDAY 17TH.

Fine, distribution as usual. Company at dinner and in the evening.

A beautiful winter's day. Office where I had but little leisure. My letter to my Mother has now remained in statu quo so long that I must give it up and try again. The accounts from Washington show the same state of disorganization that has existed all along. One thing seems to me very certain that the Administration have not a clear manageable majority of the House, and they must make terms. Read a difficult chorus in the Œdipus tyrannus.

Afternoon I had Mr. Brooks, Edward and Mr. and Mrs. Frothingham to dinner, and expected Mrs. Gray and Mrs. Hall from Medford who however disappointed us. It was as well that they did for just as dinner was served my man was taken ill and we had to get on as well as we could. We did get through better than I expected. Elizabeth C. Adams with us in the evening. After which I was still busy with my Lecture.

WEDNESDAY. 18TH.

Clear and fine weather. Time as usual. Evening at E. Brooks'.

The Storm appears to have cleared the air and given us fine winter's weather. I was at the Office but had no opportunity to go on with my letter which must be abandoned. Two Tenants, came and overpowered me with words. Walk to the Athenæum and thence round home, but I neglect my exercise a great deal too much. Read about seventy lines of Œdipus Tyrannus.

After dinner looked over Pinkerton on medals and the first volume of the Memoirs of the Academy of Inscriptions.[1] Read with my boy John as usual. Evening paid a visit to Edward Brooks and his Wife. Nothing very new. Then went on with the Lecture.

[1] At MQA is CFA's copy of John Pinkerton, *Essay on Medals*, 2 vols., London, 1789; also 4 vols. (Amsterdam, 1719–1736) of the Académie Royale des Inscriptions et Belles Lettres, *Histoire, avec les mémoires de littérature*, which was ultimately published as 50 vols., Paris, 1701–1793.

THURSDAY 19TH.

Cold and clear. Time divided as usual. Evening at home.

The account from Washington is that a Speaker has been at last chosen, Mr. Hunter of Virginia, a young man never spoken of at the commencement of the Session. This has been done by the union of the Nullifying interest of Mr. Calhoun, dissatisfied with the hostility to them of Mr. Benton by which Mr. Pickens and Mr. Lewis were successively rejected as candidates for the situation, with the Whig party which threw it's whole force with remarkable energy and precision. What the result of this movement may be, it is not possible to foretell, but the blow is a severe one against the Administration and may lead to it's downfall. I do not know what to think of it in other respects, for Harrison is a poor creature as a leader enough.

At work at Office. Short walk. Œdipus Tyrannus which as usual furnishes me with my pleasantest reading. How much pleasanter than the excitement of political contest.

After dinner finished the articles upon medals in the first volume of the Memoirs of the Academy of Inscriptions as well as something of Pinkerton. My Wife was quite sick with a bad head ach all day so as to be obliged to go to bed, and I wrote all the evening upon my Lecture.

FRIDAY. 20TH.

Cold but clear. Division as usual. Evening at home.

I do not know whether I have said that my occupation for one hour after breakfast every morning is in making a catalogue of my Cabinet of coins and medals. This is interesting as connected with the fine set of Roman Silver which I have acquired.

Then to the Office where I received some letters from my mother and felt bound to do my best to answer them. So I sat down and devoted my remaining time and continued at home in the Afternoon until it was a very poor letter finished.[1] An hour of Greek as usual. Read some of Pinkerton. Evening Walpole and the Lecture which goes on increasing when too long already.

[1] The letters of LCA were of the 13th and 15th; these, with CFA's to LCA of the 20th, are in the Adams Papers.

SATURDAY 21ST.

Moderating. Distribution as usual. Dine with Mr. Brooks. Evening at home.

I devoted my time to the usual course of morning proceedings. At the Office. Deacon Spear came in, and I had an application to repeat my old Lecture from the Managers of the Franklin Lectures, on Monday Evening at the Masonic Temple. These are now mere common place matters, that excite about as much attention as a Sunday Sermon.

Took a brisk walk round the Common and felt better for it. Then home reading Œdipus. Dined with Mr. Brooks. Nobody there but the family. That is Edward and Chardon and the three sons in law. Pleasant enough. The first dinner in the new house.[1] Home to tea and quiet evening. Walpole, after which, on with the Lecture.

[1] Peter C. Brooks had purchased the residence of Daniel Webster (above, entry for 4 May), along with the furnishings. Brooks' former home on Pearl Street would become the residence of his son Gorham. Although Brooks took possession following purchase, he did not begin his occupancy of the house until his return to the city in November from his Medford residence (Brooks, Waste Book, 6, 14 June, 26 Nov., 31 Dec. 1839; above, entry for 13 Nov.).

SUNDAY 22D.

Cloudy and wind. The usual exercises. Evening to Mrs. S. C. Gray's.

A very dark day for a short one making it still shorter. I had a brief lesson with my children, for I am now bringing my eldest boy John into train. Then attended divine service.

Heard Dr. Frothingham in the morning from Luke 2. 40. "And the child grew." A sort of Christmas sermon which did not seize upon my attention as much as I wish. Afternoon, Mr. Ware from the same book 17. 21. "Behold, the Kingdom of God is within you." Perhaps it would be a good plan to analyze the grounds for inattention to moral discourses. I cannot command myself at all. Read a sermon in the English preacher being the last of the fifth volume, and by a certain Dr.

Mackewen from 2 Timothy 4. 7.8. "I have fought a good fight, I have kept the faith," &ca. too long to quote but indicative of a termination of a career of usefulness and piety. Took a good walk between services.

Evening Edmund Quincy came in and took tea. He is so curious that I do not care to have much intimacy with him. So many topics upon which we cannot venture to talk with him, and so few in which we can agree. He talked much about T. K. Davis from whose account of him I rather infer he is insane. We afterwards went over to see Mr. and Mrs. S. C. Gray. Several persons there who settled down to Mr. and Mrs. Pratt and F. Gray. Pleasant evening and then home to continue Lecture.

MONDAY 23RD.

Clouds and light snow. Office as usual. Evening Lecture.

The weather was dull and gloomy all day. I occupied myself much as usual, in drawing up old Leases and so forth. There is some little news from Europe which does not however very much alter the state of the case in this country. We shall have hard times next year.

I went home and read eighty five lines of Œdipus. I am on the whole well satisfied with the review for it gives me a much more full conception of the force of the play. Afternoon, Pinkerton. I propose now to turn my attention to the MS again which I have remitted for so long.

Evening, Mr. Brigham called at my House and accompanied me to the Masonic Temple where was a middling collection of persons among whom I recognized but few acquaintances. I was favorably received, and delivered my Lecture as successfully as ever. I thought the readings were more effective than I had known them. This is the sixth time I have delivered it, always very successfully and yet with little apparent increase of audiences. Returned home before nine, and went on with my Lecture on credit.

TUESDAY. 24TH.

Mild and cloudy. Office. Evening at Dr. Frothingham's.

After my usual course of occupation in medals I went to the Office and spent my time in making up Arrears of Diary and finishing the drawing out of some Leases which I have had some time on my hands. The streets were wet and I did not walk. Home where I read the Œdipus. I find I can read about eighty lines in an hour so as fully to understand them.

346

Afternoon I began upon the work of the MS again but the time is so short as to make my progress not very rapid. I did not even get through a single letter. Read a little of Pinkerton who has some learning but a little Scotch captiousness.

Evening, went down to see Dr. and Mrs. Frothingham found there Mr. Brooks, and W. G. Brooks, and Mr. Foster. Pleasant conversation and then home. Continued the Lecture which is now drawing to a conclusion for the fourth time and is again much varied from what it was.

WEDNESDAY 25TH.

Clear, lovely day. Office. Museum with the boys. Evening, children at the house.

This is Christmas Day. A day of great festivity in many parts of the world but one which is not much celebrated here. I went to the Office and passed an hour, but returned home early in order to take my boys with me to the New England Museum, a place which hardly deserves it's character. Yet it is much better than it used to be when I went there many years ago. There is not so much that is positively offensive. The boys were much delighted but I noticed with pleasure that they rather sought the exhibitions of stuffed animals than the wax figures and trash. The whole thing is however very much dilapidated.[1] We returned home and I read a hundred lines of Œdipus. Received today from my mother a present of a tea set of old china which will I hope gratify my Wife. Wrote on my Manuscripts and finished Pinkerton's first volume. Evening, the children of Mrs. Frothingham and Mrs. Everett had a little Christmas party at our house. Dr. and Mrs. F. with us. Lecture nearly done.

[1] The New England Museum, located on Court Street between Brattle Street and Cornhill, had been established in 1825 as successor to the Columbian Museum, which had been founded in 1795 and had been at Tremont and Bromfield streets since 1806. In 1839 the Museum was acquired by a new owner, Moses Kimball, and this perhaps occasioned the present visit (Samuel G. Drake, *History and Antiquities of Boston*, Boston, 1856, p. 806, 814). An account of the wax figures in the museum as they were in an earlier day is in Winsor, *Memorial History of Boston*, 4:10.

THURSDAY 26TH.

A lovely day. Division of time as usual. Evening at home.

After my usual time passed in coins, about four or six of which I succeed in investigating daily, I go to the Office, and what little spare time I get from the Newspapers and business I devote to Storch whose book I am trying to read. At the Athenæum and from thence home where I go on with Œdipus. Miss Smith dined and spent the evening with us. On with the MS and with the Notes on Storch. Nothing very new. Evening, Walpole and the Lecture. Time monotonous enough.

Cloudy. Time distributed as usual. Evening at home.

This season of the year commonly passes with much uniformity, but I think there is more this year even than usual. I work upon coins, then go to the Office and upon my return read Greek with great regularity.

The President's Message arrived today to enliven us but unluckily it contains nothing but a long and unsatisfactory argument upon credit and banking which results in nothing. I am more and more impressed with the nothingness of his policy.

Afternoon, copying and Pinkerton. Evening, Walpole and Lecture. We had another severe gale all night.

Clear and cloudy. Time as usual. Evening at home. H. G. Gorham.

I went to the Office as usual. Time passed in ordinary way. The storm of last night is thought even more severe than that a fortnight since. It certainly had more effect upon my house as it unloosed all the lead on the ridge causing it to leak badly. The damage in the harbour and bay is very great. Home to read Œdipus. Afternoon as usual. H. G. Gorham came in for an hour in the evening. I finished my Lecture again.

Windy and cold. Exercises as usual. Evening, visitors. Call to see Mr. Brooks.

The weather is very tempestuous this season. After my usual exercise with my daughter, I attended divine service and heard Dr. Frothingham from Revelation 4. 1. "And I heard a voice which said come up hither." Very good but I liked the Afternoon sermon better from 2 Peter 5[3]. 6.7 and 8, too long to extract but bearing upon the notion of a Millenium which has lately been revived by one or two preachers who hold forth among the illiterate about here.[1] The notion of a deluge as a fact of early occurrence is universally impressed upon mankind by the concurrence of all races of men, that of a termination of the world by fire at some future time is also an impression which has been general. The thing has been predicted to happen extremely often but has always failed and there is no more reason for believing any special moment than there ever was. The millenium too has been a favorite idea with many great minds, but in this as in all other things the true course is to trust to divine providence.

Read a sermon by Tillotson from Philip[pians] 3. 20. "For our conversation is in heaven." The preparation for a future state is one of the points most essential for the regulation of this life. I am rather surprised at the reputation which Tillotson has earned for his discourses appear to me in the highest degree common. Thomas and Francis Frothingham came up to tea, after which we made a short visit to see Mr. Brooks.

[1] That is, the adventist followers of William Miller, or Millerites, who were currently preaching a second coming in 1843. Among the followers of Miller in Boston, Joshua Vaughan Hines was the most prominent (*DAB*). The subject is renewed in the entry of 23 Feb., below.

MONDAY 30TH.

Clear and very cold. Office as usual. Nothing new. Evening, W. C. Gorham.

I devoted my time much as usual. Nothing very material of any novelty. Mr. Gilpin sent me an early copy of the President's Message, which is civil. I feel half inclined to review it which would be much otherwise. Home to read Œdipus which goes on pretty swimmingly. Letter from my Mother in not very good spirits.[1]

Afternoon, reading Storch in fifth volume of Notes. I find a striking coincidence with my views. Looking over Bank Abstract also. Much change for the better since 1836 but property is all down now and incomes are exceedingly shortened.[2]

Evening, W. C. Gorham made us a visit which he has not before done for a long while. He is pleasant but much thrown away. Evening, writing MS.

[1] 23 Dec., Adams Papers.
[2] By Massachusetts law, the governor annually issued a circular requiring returns from each bank in the state showing its condition in some detail. The returns were processed by the secretary of the commonwealth and an abstract printed, primarily for the use of the legislature. Title and format varied somewhat from year to year. That for 1839 read "Abstract Exhibiting the Condition of the Banks in Massachusetts, on the first Saturday of November, 1839; prepared from official returns." Because the economy had been severely depressed in 1837 and 1838, CFA's thought was that comparison with 1836 would provide a truer picture of the current situation.

Clear and continues very cold. Office and Auction. Evening to Edward Brooks'.

The weather seems to be now setting in for winter. After my usual time devoted to coins, I went to the Office but did not remain there long as I was attracted to an auction where were to be sold a great many things suitable for the New Year. Nothing could satisfy one more of the difficulty of the times than the rate at which things go at Auction. If a person happens to have ready money, this is the high season for it. But I am not one of those, though I was much tempted and actually did succumb in many cases. Nothing otherwise remarkable.

Home to read Œdipus. After dinner, Storch with whom I do not much get on. Studying out the President's Message. I am afraid I cannot give the time to it which it deserves. Evening to see Edward Brooks and his Wife where we had a pleasant hour of conversation. Then home after which I wrote.

Thus finishes the year 1839 and another decimal figure will appear upon the roll of time. When I look back upon it, it presents to me the same gratifying return which has marked its predecessors. I have been happy and fortunate if under divine providence such a term may be used. I have had occasion to remember how suddenly we may be plunged in this life from one condition to another, as well in the wonderful escape from a horrible accident of my own child in May last, as in the melancholy end of my niece Fanny. My family has been unusually blessed with health and my labours such as they have been met with their full deserts. On the whole, I have only to submit myself to God in humble adoration, and in supplication that he will not deal with me according to my Offences, but will accept the tribute of a grateful heart in lieu of my unworthiness.

JANUARY 1840.

WEDNESDAY 1ST.

The New Year opened with cold. I look upon it and upon myself and when I reflect upon the future, and what it may bring, I recoil as if it could not continue what has been hitherto so bountifully given me. This is not the right feeling for a Christian, but in truth there is danger of my being spoiled by prosperity. I strive to remember that life is a path of trouble, vicissitude and danger, and that the most cautious steps in the progress are the safest and yet in them there is no certainty without the guidance of a higher power. To this I trust far more than to myself or the world.

After a little time devoted to coins, I went out and was engaged pretty busily most of my morning in money affairs. I accomplished the payment of my Mortgage to the Mass. Life Ins. Co. although at a moment of all others, perhaps the most inconvenient to myself. In order to effect I was obliged to borrow of Mr. Brooks a portion of the sum he was kind enough to lend on my own terms. Indeed when I called for it today he offered to make me a gift of it, but I declined upon the ground that I might appear to beg it and asked him to treat me exactly upon the footing of an ordinary debtor. This he at last agreed to do. He is very generous to his children, and as I am not one excepting indirectly by marriage I feel myself much bound to take no advantage of my situation.

The morning thus passed off. I returned home and continued reading Œdipus tyrannus. After dinner Storch's fifth volume, but I do not turn my time to best account. Evening at home very quietly. Nothing further.

THURSDAY 2D.

Cold quite severe. Time distributed as usual. Evening at home.

I was so much taken up all the morning with the important task of paying bills that I hardly had a moment for any other kind of occupation. They come in so thick and heavy that it is very difficult for me to find the wherewith to meet them, especially as my father's resources do not yet for some time come in.

Home where I read Œdipus. The rest of the day passed as usual. It is impossible to be more monotonous than we are this year. Not the slightest variety. I read to the children at home in books suitable to them and then read to my Wife from Walpole's Letters, which are quite amusing and lastly write something or other upon the President's Message. But whether to publish or not I have as yet great scruples.

FRIDAY 3D.

Cold. Time as usual. Evening at Governor Everett's.

My record has nothing to vary it from preceding days. I went to the

Office and although not at all incommoded with duns as I was yesterday yet had so much to do in bringing up accounts that I found it impossible to bring up my Diary which is falling into arrears.

Home after a sharp walk. Finished the Œdipus Tyrannus which has given me much gratification to read. I think it a masterpiece of dramatic construction. Afternoon Storch.

Evening to see Governor and Mrs. Everett. Nobody there but the family, Dr. and Mrs. Palfrey, and Mrs. Hunt a lady known to them with her children, Mrs. Hale and her children and Mr. H. Chapman who plastered me with flattery and talked as fast and as superficially as ever. Return home at ten, pleasant enough.

SATURDAY 4TH.

Cold. The winter appears to be set in. Time as usual. Evening at home.

After my usual time in coins I went to Market and Office. Plenty of calls for money which I answered as fast as I was able. Home after a walk. Began Œdipus Coloneus, a play which I thought the most poetical of those of Sophocles when I read it before. The remainder of the day as usual.

My record will soon decline to a single line. I ought however to have mentioned that I received another application to repeat my Lecture, by the Lyceum through their Secretary Mr. George T. Bigelow. This I consider as somewhat a victory, for two years ago when Mr. Everett, Mr. Bancroft and myself were in succession before the Historical Society and not unequally successful, the former two were immediately called to repeat at the Lyceum and I was left out. I have overcome scruples since. Evening at home. Sent one paper on the Message.

SUNDAY. 5TH.

Moderating. Services as usual. Evening at home.

The day was dark and I was up so late as to be quite unable to finish my usual lesson with my daughter before service. Attended as usual and heard Dr. Frothingham all day from Psalms 90. 5. "As with a flood" and from Acts 26. 27. "I know that thou believest." Very good both of them but my mind has fallen into so unsettled a state that I do not attend quite as well as I used to do. The passage of time and the new year seemed to me to be described in the former sermon, first by regarding the flood from antiquity and then from the future. In endeavoring to analyze the causes of the defects of interest in most of Dr.

Frothingham's discourses, I know none more striking than that his laboured attempt at *novelty* of thought removes him too much from the reach of most men whose mental path is commonly a very beaten track. The motto from Terence, Homo Sum, is one which no speaker should keep out of his mind.[1]

Afternoon, read in the English Preacher, a discourse by the Revd. Mr. Leechman upon Prayer, its uses and advantages and the duty of praying, Matthew 26. 41. "Pray that ye enter not into temptation." A very sensible and judicious discourse. Evening at home. Continued Walpole's Letters which are extremely amusing. After which I went on with my comments upon the President's Message.

[1] For the motto, see above, entry of 13 Aug. 1838.

MONDAY 6TH.

Clear and cold. To Cambridge — Examination, return. Afternoon at home. Evening writing.

We arose much earlier than usual in order that I might be ready to start for Cambridge upon the usual examination. Judge Merril and Mr. Cleaveland in the Carriage with me. The examination was of the Junior Class in the Clouds of Aristophanes and was far better than I had expected. So formidable an idea had I entertained of the difficulty of the text that I had feared to go out, but upon reading the piece following the class, I was not only agreeably disappointed as to the difficulty but moreover very much amused by the piece itself. It has a comic humor in it which I did not fully appreciate in the translation published by Mitchell and made by Cumberland.[1] The Class appeared exceedingly well. At dinner we were stupid and I missed the old company on the Committee.[2] Home. The remainder of the day and evening passed as usual.

[1] A copy of Richard Cumberland's translation published by Thomas Mitchell (2 vols., Phila., 1822) is at MQA.

[2] Judge James Cushing Merrill and George Stillman Hillard had been on the examining committee most frequently with CFA. Others who had served included Rev. Francis Cunningham, CFA's classmate, and John Chipman Gray.

TUESDAY. 7TH.

Clear. Office and usual distribution. Evening at Mrs. Frothingham's.

My paper of criticism upon the Message appeared in The Courier of this morning.[1] "Le jeu ne vaut pas la chandelle."

Office where I am engaged and distressed with accounts. My affairs look more discouragingly than I have ever known them since I was a responsible person. This will not do. I must turn over a new leaf respecting them. Circumstances have contributed to bring a great pressure of accounts upon the present Quarter with small means to meet them, and I fear there is not much prospect of their improvement. But on the other hand the necessary expenses of life are much diminished. I think I will rid myself by a positive effort of the amount of debt which presses upon me.

Reading Œdipus Coloneus. Afternoon at home. Evening to Dr. Frothingham's where were the family. Conversation much as usual.

[1] On p. 2, cols. 1–2, and continued in the same space in the issue of the 9th; both unsigned.

WEDNESDAY 8TH.

Clear and fine. Office. Time as usual. Evening at home.

After the time usually devoted to the study of coins, I was at the Office and had little time beyond what was necessary for the disposition of accounts. They harrass me considerably and will compel me to sacrifice some stock. The loss of income from Manufacturing property and from one of my small houses is also very inconvenient. But I suppose in these times I must have my share of inconveniences and put up with them.

Home where I read Œdipus Coloneus. My antiquities give me my most agreeable occupations. After dinner continue Storch. Evening at home. Writing without success.

THURSDAY 9TH.

Fine day. To Cambridge. Home. Afternoon reading. Evening, Lecture. Mr. Brooks'.

Early rising to go to Cambridge in company with Judge Merril, for an examination of the Sophomore class in the Iliad of Homer. The result was as bad as that on Monday was satisfactory. I think it a little singular that the recitations in Homer have been uniformly so indifferent. It rather argues a neglect of easy books. I find Parker of whom much was expected appeared badly.[1] The College Government have granted the Committees leave to take books from the library which is a great thing and I immediately availed myself of it. Returned home at three. Afternoon, reading.

In the evening I went down to the Odeon and according to my agreement again delivered the Lecture which I have already been through so often. The place is a very different one from any which I have heretofore tried. It has more of the appearance of a popular assembly and the Lecturer, of a theatrical performer. I had some doubts about my voice, which excited me to make an unusual effort. I think I succeeded well although the audience was not so quickly moved as it had been at previous times. There was here as on the former occasion at the Masonic Temple one single manifestation of disapprobation, I know not for what. The house was very full and the applause quite considerable. From here I went to Mr. Brooks' where were Edward and his Wife, and my Wife. Pleasant hour and then return home.

[1] Apparently the reference is to Henry Tuke Parker, Harvard 1842, whose later career was distinguished (*Harvard Quinquennial Cat.*).

FRIDAY 10TH.

Fine day. Time distributed as usual. Evening at home.

We arose early in case of being called to go to Cambridge as I had agreed to fill a vacant place but the contingency did not happen so I devoted the time to medals.

Office as usual. Nothing very new. As the period approaches for going to New York I feel more and more disinclined to go. After all what is popular applause in this country but an *ignis fatuus* which will mislead us forever from the true point of selfcontent.

Home to read Œdipus Coloneus which I find I did not read very thoroughly before. It is however a fine play and if to be considered as the production of extreme old age is wonderful. For my afternoons I have taken a lazy fit and indulge in miscellanies. I cannot even screw myself up to finishing the commentaries of the Message. Evening Walpole.

SATURDAY 11TH.

Cloudy. Office. Division as usual. Evening at home.

I went through the usual course of occupation today. Wrote two letters, one to Mr. Johnson requesting of him to draw upon me,[1] and one to Mr. Ward to know exactly what the terms are upon which I am to go to New York.[2] I do not care for this going out to warfare at my own charges. Nothing new excepting that as I was returning home I stopped in for a moment to see Warren the virtuoso and he told me that he had just arrived from Washington and that Louisa was sick when he left.

Home to read Œdipus Coloneus. The rest of the day passed in luxurious desultory reading. Evening as Louisa had two or three of her School friends, I took the opportunity to continue my copying of MS which goes on rather sluggishly. Charles rather unwell.

[1] CFA to T. B. Johnson, LbC, Adams Papers.
[2] CFA to Elijah Ward, LbC, Adams Papers.

SUNDAY 12TH.

Clouds and snow. Exercises as usual. Evening at home.

My regular lesson with my children, for John is now coming in to read the Bible with his sister. After which attended divine service and heard in the morning Dr. Frothingham from Psalms 100. 5. "And not we ourselves." I am ashamed to say what a slight impression it made upon me. Afternoon Mr. Bartol from 1. Thessalonians 5. 16.17. "Rejoice evermore. Pray without ceasing." The union of the two as forming cheerful religion was the theme of his discourse. It had good and bad points in it.

The day was so uncomfortable that I did not walk. Miss Welsh brought in quite an alarming account of the condition of Louisa at Washington, which was procured through Mrs. Lawrence. I am deeply concerned for it. For I know not what the result would be to my father, and mother, whose relaxation is all now in that child. My own children were all more or less ailing today. This with the state of my private concerns makes me gloomy. Yet my trust is ever in the Deity that he will not deal with us entirely according to our sins.

Read another discourse by Mr. Leechman upon prayer in continuation of the last. Job 21. 15. "What profit would we have if we pray unto him." Upon the advantages of prayer and a general answer to the common objections. We spent the evening at home dull enough. Read some imaginary conversations by Walter S. Landor, conceited dogmatical and unsound.[1]

[1] CFA's earlier reading of *Imaginary Conversations* produced a similar reaction (vol. 6:131).

MONDAY 13TH.

Snow and clouds. Distribution as usual. Evening to Edward Brooks.

The day was dark and gloomy and I felt somewhat with the weather. After my usual time in coins I went to the Office and devoted my time to filling up the arrears of Diary which last week had created. Received a letter from my mother giving encouraging accounts. Her letter is short but it gives me reason to believe that Louisa's illness has been exceedingly serious.[1] Thence to the Athenæum.

Home to read Œdipus Coloneus, but what with my own children, my affairs and the accounts from Washington I was very much depressed. After dinner, The Townley Gallery in the publications of the Society for diffusing knowledge.[2]

Evening, went to Edward Brooks'. Mr. and Mrs. Dutton Russel there but nothing new. Talk of T. K. Davis who from all accounts is I am afraid decidedly deranged. Home and read Landor.

[1] To the family in Washington, still distraught over the death of Georgeanna Frances, the illness of her sister Louisa had overwhelmed them by the "apparent similarity of the cases." Louisa had suffered from "inflamation of the bowels and bladder," severe pain, and high fever. However, "the doctor says the two cases differ and that at the present time all is favorable" (LCA to ABA, 9 Jan., Adams Papers). Later letters report convalescence and recovery (same to CFA, 21 Jan.; to ABA, 26 Jan., 20 Feb., all in Adams Papers).

[2] The volumes on the Townley Gallery in the British Museum are in the *Library of Entertaining Knowledge* of the Society for the Diffusion of Useful Knowledge.

TUESDAY 14TH.

Clear. Division as usual. Evening at home.

There is nothing new. Even politics do not appear to furnish any variety. The world wags quietly. Office engaged in accounts and from thence to the Athenæum where I rather wasted my time. Desultory, miscellaneous reading in a library is among the most fascinating of all pleasures to me although it creates rather superficial knowledge.

Home to read Œdipus Coloneus. I do not get on very fast with it. Afternoon the Townley Gallery, and Law's Essay on Money and trade.[1] My Wife went with Mrs. Story to Medford to spend the evening with Mrs. Gray, and I devoted the time to a thorough revision of my Lecture on credit which I find long. Began Prescott's Ferdinand and Isabella.[2]

[1] John Law's *Money and Trade Considered, with a Proposal for Supplying the Nation with Money*, first published in Edinburgh, 1709, is in vol. 13 of John Somers, *Collection of Tracts*, London, 1815.

[2] A copy of the 3-vol., Boston, 1840, edn. of William Hickling Prescott's *History of the Reign of Ferdinand and Isabella* is in MQA.

WEDNESDAY 15TH.

Clear. Distribution as usual. Evening at Mrs. Frothingham's.

Time passes fast and brings on with it my projected journey to New York which I face with more and more ill will. Office. Nothing done.

I forgot to say yesterday that I attended a meeting of The Suffolk Insurance Co. yesterday in which I found that we were called upon to sacrifice above a quarter part of the Stock. This was the very measure which was last year resisted. And a whole year has done little or nothing for the Stock. Well, this is bad like every thing else at present.

Nothing material. Home to read Œdipus after a visit to the Athenæum. Afternoon, Law upon Money and trade, and the Townley Gallery. Evening, we went down to see Dr. and Mrs. Frothingham. Pleasant conversation. And return, growing very cold. Prescott's Ferdinand and Isabella.

THURSDAY 16TH.

Severely cold. Distribution as usual. Evening at home. Dr. Palfrey.

The morning was the sharpest we have had. I went to the Office. Distressing intelligence came of the loss of the Steamer Lexington by fire with every one on board but three. As there were many passengers belonging to Boston it came on this cold morning like a chilling blast. There has never been in this vicinity any accident at all to compare with this and the sensation made upon the public was quite equal to it.[1] It comes peculiarly to me now at this moment when I am about to make the passage myself. But my trust is in the Deity who if it is his will, is likely to call for my life just as certainly on shore as at sea.

Home after making a call upon Mr. Webster a day after the fair.[2] Reading Œdipus which I go through with slowly. After dinner the Townley Gallery and Law. Evening at home, reading a new home [book?]. Dr. Palfrey made us a short but pleasant visit. He wishes me to write again for the Review. I should like to but know not what to take. Continued Prescott.

[1] Accounts of the burning of the *Lexington* on 13 Jan. in Long Island Sound appeared in the *Boston Courier*, 17 Jan., p. 2, col. 2; 18 Jan., p. 2, cols. 1–2.

[2] The editors can throw no light on "the fair" nor on Daniel Webster's suggested connection with it.

FRIDAY 17TH.

Extremely cold. Distribution as usual. Evening at Mr. Lothrop's.

I this morning finished my catalogue of the collection of silver of ancient Rome which I possess and in making it, my opinion of it's value has much risen.

Office. Received more details of the extraordinary disaster of the Lexington. It turns out that there were not quite so many on board but of these several of Boston, well known and much respected. Dr. Follen, Mr. Abraham Howard, Mrs. Russel Jarvis and others. The incident is among the most distressing.

Received a letter from New York and wrote in answer that I would try to get on.[1] But the boats are all deranged and I hardly know how to manage it. Œdipus Coloneus making great progress.

After dinner, the Townley Gallery and finishing John Law. Evening at Mr. S. K. Lothrop's. Nobody but the family and Dr. and Mrs. Palfrey. Rather dull.

[1] The lecture on "Credit" planned for delivery in New York before the Mercantile Library Association had presented problems to CFA almost from its inception (entries for 7, 18 Sept. 1839, above). He had completed in the intervening months no fewer than four versions, none of which entirely satisfied him (above, entries for 30 Nov., 10, 24 Dec.). By the time he had completed a revision of the fourth draft (entry for 14 Jan., above), he had already written to Elijah Ward (11 Jan., LbC, Adams Papers) again expressing his doubts as to the appropriateness of the lecture for the occasion and his concerns about its length. He offered Ward a choice once more. He would, if desired, reserve the paper for publication and deliver the lecture on AA, a proven success. Ward replied on the 15th (Adams Papers) expressing a preference for the lecture on AA. CFA's present response of the 17th has not been found, but it is clear that he acceded to Ward's view (below, entry for 23 Jan.). The undelivered lecture, "The Principles of Credit by Charles Francis Adams," was printed in the March issue of *Hunt's Merchants' Mag.*, 2:185–210, with a headnote: "The following lecture was originally prepared for the Mercantile Library Association, but as when finished it appeared too long, and in some portions too abstract, for delivery as a lecture, the author substituted another in its place, reserving it, however, in its original form, for publication in our Magazine."

SATURDAY 18TH.

Cold. Distribution as usual. Evening at home.

My morning was very much taken up in making the necessary arrangements prior to leaving town. After the best information I could get upon the subject I find it will be necessary for me to go to New York over land. Accounts &ca.

The affair of the Lexington appears to be making a very deep sensation here. The cold weather which set in immediately after the accident deprives most of the passengers of the little chance they might otherwise have had.

Home where I read Œdipus. Afternoon as Dr. Palfrey sent me the number of the New York Review in which is contained an article which he desired me to notice I took it up and read it. The subject will need some investigation but will I think, do.[1] Evening at home.

[1] John Gorham Palfrey, editor of the *North Amer. Rev.*, had brought to CFA's attention the article in the *New York Rev.* for Jan. 1840 entitled "The Politics of the Puritans." From his investigation of the subject would come an article; see entries of 28 and 30 Jan., 9 Feb., below.

Moderating. Exercises as usual. Evening H. G. Gorham.

The weather looked a little moderating today though still severe enough. After my exercises with my daughter, I attended divine service and heard Dr. Frothingham preach from 1. Samuel 20. 3. "There is but a step between me and death." A very beautiful and touching discourse upon the late conflagration of the Lexington which drew tears from most of the audience. There were several persons on board who had been much connected with this congregation, Mrs. Jarvis and children and Mr. Finn the actor as well as Dr. Follen. I know of nothing which has lately happened here that has brought to the soul of every body such a harrowing sensation. At the Post Office today there were accounts of two more saved.

Afternoon, sermon from Isaiah 44. 16. "I am warm, I have seen the fire." Upon the cold from a text too remarkable not to recall the fact of it's being a repetition. Read a sermon by Mr. Tidcombe in the English Preacher from Psalms 73. 3. "For I was envious at the foolish when I saw the prosperity of the wicked." Upon the unequal distribution of good and evil as we see it in this life. A fruitful topic for commonplace.

Evening H. G. Gorham spent an hour with us, and I went to bed early as it seemed from the accounts very clear that I must get to New York tomorrow overland.

[*Hartford*]

Mild. Ride to Springfield and thence to Hartford.

Before day break I arose and prepared myself for my Journey. Took breakfast and rode to the depot of the Worcester Railroad, from thence at 7 o'clock I started in one of the cars. The day was cloudy but mild and it cleared before night.

There was nobody there whom I knew excepting Mr. Lemist a person who formerly kept a shop in Washington Street, and who is going to New York to find some traces of the body of his brother, who was one of the sufferers in the Lexington. We arrived at Worcester at about ten and went immediately forward to Springfield. The interior is heavily covered with snow and presents a very wintry appearance. But this is an easy way of travelling such a long distance.

We arrived at Springfield a little after one o'clock and having taken a very hasty dinner at a poor house we took stages or rather sleighs to go to Hartford. The road is through a series of pretty turns along the bank of the river and even at this season of the year is a pleasant ride. There were in the sleigh, Mr. N. Thayer, Broker of Boston, brother of J. E. Thayer and the Revd. L. Everett a Universalist minister formerly settled in Charlestown but now in Middletown, Connecticut. They made the ride amusing. We reached Hartford after dark and found very comfortable accommodations at the City Hotel.

New York

TUESDAY. 21ST.

Cold and clear. Ride to New Haven and thence to New York.

We were roused at four o'clock which to me was no inconvenience as for some reason or other I had heard the clock strike two, three and four without getting to sleep. After dressing we were carried down to the Depot or rather to the terminus of the Railroad to New Haven and got into the cars as they stood in the open air. There was no fire in them and it was in all respects cheerless and uncomfortable enough. We however had the consolation of finding what used to be a tedious journey quite a short process and of arriving at New Haven to break-fast.

But here our troubles began, for we found that the Steamboat did not go nor was it likely to go so we had to make up our minds to go overland. This road is one which for many years I have not passed over, but when I did, it left indelible traces in my memory of discomfort so that I was prepared to expect the same today. I was not disappointed. The sleighs were poor, the delays vexatious and the stops uncomfortable so that it was two o'clock in the morning when we were turned into the street at No. 21 Bowery with not a single soul to look to nor any accommodation to get to a hotel.

After some delay we picked up a black fellow who was straggling about and followed him and our trunks to the Astor House which we reached at ten minutes before two o'clock. In passing along I could not help being struck with the lonely character of the streets. I did not imagine that New York ever was so quiet. And the only sign of life was at Tammany Hall where there was a brilliant illumination and ball. The contrast was striking enough.[1]

[1] The Astor House, five stories of Quincy granite, occupied the block fronting Broadway from Barclay to Vesey street. Begun in 1834, the hotel was opened in 1836 and continued in operation at that site until 1913 (Stokes, *Ico-*

nography of Manhattan Island, 5:1727, 1741). Tammany Hall had been built during 1811–1812 on the southeast corner of Nassau and Frankfort streets and would remain as the "Great Wigwam" until 1867 (same, p. 1533–1534, 1543).

WEDNESDAY 22D.

Rain hail and snow. Walking. Evening at Clinton Hall.

The sleep of a few hours was not refreshing to me inasmuch as waking brought with it the consciousness of a sharp head ach. The weather was bad being snowy and on the whole the aspect of things cheerless enough. After a light breakfast I walked out, to see if Sidney Brooks had started, and upon calling at his store found that he left town yesterday.

The snow began to turn into rain and I found no acquaintances and no sign of an inquiry on the part of the Mercantile Library Association if I was there. I do not remember in my life that I ever felt more dolefully. My fear that I should be utterly unable to execute my engagement at all aggravated my uneasiness very much. I starved myself and this probably prevented my being obliged to give up entirely. But finding things so out of joint and myself so poorly I set about inquiring the readiest means of getting away, and finally engaged a seat in the stage going out tomorrow morning.

This done I called to see Hunt the publisher of The Merchants' Magazine and set him in quest of Mr. Ward who finally called to see me at five o'clock. He notified me of his abdication and that the new President would call with himself at 7 o'clock to take me to Clinton Hall. Accordingly we went at the specified hour, the rain pouring in torrents.

Clinton Hall is a neat building erected for the accommodation of this Society and contains a Lecture Room, Library and Reading Room, besides a small room for the Directors into which I was introduced.[1] But I soon found by various whisperings among the young men that there was no audience. They charged this to the weather and finally requested of me to postpone the delivery of my Lecture until tomorrow evening. My own inclination was to go on that I might get away in the morning. But I answered that I had come to please them and not myself and if it was their desire that I should wait I would. This they finally determined upon. So the matter was announced to the few who had the energy to come.

The Directors then carried me round their Library and showed me many new books as well as old ones. They pride themselves as all young men do more upon the number than the selection, but this is on the whole creditable. I was not however in good order to think about it so I was glad when the time came for me to be transferred to the Astor House and thence to bed, tired and dull.

[1] Clinton Hall, erected for the Society in 1829–1830, was located at the southwest corner of Beekman and Nassau streets (Stokes, *Iconography of Manhattan Island*, 5:1681, 1686).

THURSDAY 23D.

Clear day. Much exercise. Evening, Lecture.

The weather cleared very mild and for some hours there was a general thaw which however lasted but a few hours and gave way to a very sharp northwester. My head ach was gone and after breakfast having dismissed my Stageman who called for me I sat down to write letters to my Wife and Mother.[1] This done I went out to perform some little commissions which I was too much discouraged to execute yesterday and made a visit to Mrs. Davis. Thus the whole morning vanished fast enough.

After dinner I met with a companion in a young Mexican named Cuesta who was a fellow traveller from Boston and a very gentlemanly man. After dinner I passed some time in trying to find if the Steamboat to New Haven would go tomorrow but without success. My walk however and other occupations took up the time so that I was not ennuié.

At seven the gentlemen came again in a Carriage and transported me to Clinton Hall where I found a tolerable but by no means very large collection of people. They apologized and seemed very uneasy for what was a very simple thing. Their second course of which this was the beginning has not taken very well. The Lecturing system is already overdone here and the courses marked out are abandoned. I regretted only my having accepted their invitation as well on my own account as theirs. But it being now too late to change I went on with my Lecture which I delivered now for the eighth time as it appeared to very general acceptation. Then home to bed.

[1] Neither letter has been located.

FRIDAY 24TH.

Cool. Left by the Stage. Morning out. Dine and evening at Mr. Davis'.

I arose early this morning and put every thing in order to start by the Stage which had agreed to call for me as I thought, but after waiting two hours in vain I walked to the Office and found it had left me. This was vexatious as it threatened to make me a delay of Sunday. I tried to persuade the Agent to change me into the Mail but he would not. Throughout the whole business it is impossible to describe the extent to which the unaccommodating spirit is carried on that road. I left in disgust extracting nothing more than a promise that if a passenger in the Mail could be found voluntarily to exchange with me he would let me know by half past three o'clock.

On my return home I found Mr. C. A. Davis who called and asked me to accompany him to his counting room where he kept me some time in conversation upon currency and politics. After this I went down to inquire if the boat would go to New Haven tomorrow, which being answered in the affirmative gave me satisfaction enough to reconcile me to the delay. The remainder of the morning passed rapidly in executing little commissions and in reading at the Reading Room in Clinton Hall. A very pleasant place to resort to.

Mr. Davis called at dinner time to take me to dine with him which I was glad to do having given up my Stage Agent. Nobody at table but Mrs. Howell, Mr. Dekay, Mrs. Davis's brother, and Miss Julia her daughter who is a pretty girl enough. The dinner was tres mince, but plenty of wine and good conversation so that I remained until late in the evening and thereby failed to make the visit I had intended to the Coldens.

Much talk with Mr. D. about Biddle respecting whose course of policy I expected he would entertain opinions very different from mine, but I found he rather confirmed by positive facts within his experience the truth of the inferences which I had drawn from more general reasoning. Home and to bed but for some reason or other I could not sleep for some hours although perfectly tranquil.

New Haven

SATURDAY 25TH.

Cold and clear. Steamer New Haven to New Haven.

I was up betimes and marched down to the Slip where the Steamer was and went on board. Found plenty of passengers and an abundance of freight. We started at seven and with a hearty goodwill I bid good bye to the City of New York, a place where I find very little disposition to remain for any length of time. But upon this visit, it has seemed to me more repulsive than ever for its motley and ragged population and it's money seeking spirit.

The boat made very good headway for an hour and a half when it got into the ice. The prospect for ten miles a head was all dreary and in the midst of it we got aground. This was not a very good incident and I began to think we were likely to be frozen in. But the tide was coming in and after two hours and a half the boat again moved. The prospect was then better and the boat went bravely to work grinding up the packed ice for many miles until it became very clear that we should get through.

This was the only cheerful intelligence of the day, for as we were going the same track with the unfortunate Lexington, with all the details before us of that disaster and conscious that their bodies were somewhere under our path, I could not resist the feeling of gloom which these ideas created. And when we passed the very spot and I looked round to see what our chance would be under similar circumstances with cotton and spirits on board as full as we could hold and a hundred and fifty passengers with but a single boat, I could not wonder that the mortality turned out so great. The incidents as they are told are too affecting. They harrow the soul.

We reached New Haven safely at eight o'clock and it being too late to send out a train tonight to Hartford we lodged at The Pavilion. Much too crowded for comfort, but thankful to have got so far.

Worcester

SUNDAY 26TH.

Railroad to Hartford and thence to Worcester.

The impatience of some of our company which does not appear to be quite of the best class, caused our getting up nearly two hours before it was necessary or expedient. For the train of cars which the agent had engaged to send through at five o'clock did not start until half past six. The morning was very cold and I suffered much inconvenience from it in my feet. We however went through to Hartford which we reached before ten and stopped to take breakfast at the United States Hotel.

We found conveyances ready to take us on and at eleven the whole company exceeding thirty in number started in three sleighs. The day was cold and I suffered a good deal from it as my India rubber shoes rather stop than promote the circulation. The only pleasant fellow passenger we had was Mr. J. W. Otis with whom I made acquaintance.

Our route was slow from the deep snow and for two stages not very safe as the track was narrow and leaving it for a moment hazarded an upset. One of these we experienced which hurt nobody excepting one imprudent man who was looking out of the window and who got his face flayed by the crust of ice in the snow. It did not detain us however from our journey which we persevered in to the loss of dinner that we might get to Worcester by night.

We did arrive in fact at a little before twelve o'clock at the Temperance House where after getting something to eat we were ushered into a shocking cold room and got to bed thankful to God that the labours and dangers of this Journey were at an end.

Boston

MONDAY 27TH.

To Boston. At home all day. Evening small party at Miss Jones'.

We were roused at six this morning and after partaking of a *good* breakfast the first thing of the kind I have seen since Friday afternoon we went to the Depot of the Worcester Railroad and entered a car to Boston. The trip was made briefly and before eleven o'clock I had the happiness and satisfaction of again embracing my Wife and children and sitting by my own fireside. God be praised for the same and the next time I start upon such a wildgoose chase may I be set down for an ass.

The peculiar circumstances attending the outset of the journey, the severity of the season and the inconveniences in travelling all contributed to make me more nervous and gloomy than I should have been. It is over now and I have learnt one lesson by it, not to go from home in the winter season without good reason moving me thereto. A Lecture to a parcel of boys is not such by any means.

I remained at home all the day dressing and refitting myself to my study, as I am determined now to make up for my lost time. In the evening went with my Wife to a small party at Miss Jones'. Her own family and a few of her friends. Pleasant enough but not material.

TUESDAY 28TH.

Snow. At home, distribution as usual. Evening, small party at Mrs. Ritchie's.

I went down to the Office and employed myself much in matters of account. Since my departure various companies have made Dividends and these I immediately set about collecting and with the proceeds paying off a great number of the accounts that have been hanging on since New Year. My Journey has not even paid it's way and my affairs scarcely look more encouragingly than they did. Mr. Johnson has not however drawn upon me.

Home to read Œdipus Coloneus. Afternoon commencing work upon my projected article. I find it will require much investigation. I must look up all the authorities and refresh my recollection with the history. If I make an antagonist, it will be necessary to be well armed.[1]

Evening to Mrs. Ritchie's by invitation. A small party of about a hundred, one third of whom I knew. Tolerably pleasant. Home at eleven.

[1] The author of the *New York Review* article had advanced the view that the contest in England in the 17th century "between Churchmen and Puritans was merely a political one, and *not*, as is usually represented, a religious one." CFA's article, undertaken to refute this position, would hold that it was mainly a religious conflict, made political only because religion at the time was a matter of political regulation.

WEDNESDAY 29TH.

Bad weather, rain and ice. Dine at Mr. Brooks'. Evening at home.

Office making a call upon Mrs. Sidney Brooks on the way. The streets dangerously slippery. Still occupied in travelling through the Accounts which had been laid over. It is a gratification to pay them.

Home where I go on with Œdipus Coloneus. I find this was rather superficially read before. And it is in itself among the most difficult of the plays.

Went to dine with Mr. Brooks. The first dinner of the family I have seen for a long while. Every member in town present and a very pleasant time. We did not stay, but returned home where we had a very quiet evening.

THURSDAY 30TH.

Clear. Usual routine. At home.

I resumed the medals this morning and thus fell exactly into my old habits as if there had never been any change. At the Office making up the arrears of my Diary from where I went down to the Athenæum to look up the works necessary for my proposed undertaking. Picked up Sharon Turner and Hallam, and more than all, the little tract called the Planter's Plea[1] which makes the basis for the whole edifice of The

New York Review. With these and with what I can procure elsewhere I shall be able to get along. Home to read Œdipus.

Afternoon, went to work reading and endeavoring to methodise. But this is a very difficult process. I ordinarily do not commence it until I begin to write but this is far too laborious. I must habituate myself to closer mental exercise as a principle of economy. Evening at home.

[1] Of the works of Sharon Turner, the *History of the Reigns of Edward VI, Mary, and Elizabeth* (London, 1829) seems most apposite for use in the article on the "Politics of the Puritans" CFA was preparing. *The Constitutional History of Eng-* *land, from ... Henry VII to ... George II* (2 vols., London, 1827) seems likeliest of the works of Henry Hallam. John White was the author of *Planter's Plea, or, The Grounds of Plantations Examined*, London, 1630.

FRIDAY 31ST.

Clouds and snow. Division as usual.

I have very little to remark. My days pass monotonously enough. I am writing up my arrears of Diary, and arranging my accounts which I have nearly accomplished. There is a satisfaction in thinking that one owes nothing although tomorrow the thing may again occur.

Continue my review of Œdipus Coloneus. I wonder much at the writers who so often say of the Greeks that they knew nothing of the higher female affections. It appears to me that the character of Antigone is from first to last an impersonation of the very highest kind of female excellence and one which I do not know to be surpassed in any language.

Afternoon, a chaos of authorities against every thing advanced by the New York Review. The getting clear light out of it will be troublesome. In the evening at home. Walpole. Suffering from a cold.

SATURDAY 1ST FEBRUARY.

Dull weather. Distribution as usual.

After market, Office. Writing up arrears. Nothing new. The newspapers are dry and dull enough. Home reading Œdipus. After which, reading and reflecting upon my subject. There are several points to be taken care of, first, that I shall not involve myself with the Church by attacking one of it's champions; second, that I shall not expend my strength upon the defence of commonplace or hackneyed points of controversy. With these exceptions I do not see that I have any other precautions to take. Evening at home. Reading Walpole. After which I tried to make a beginning but only spoiled sheets of paper.

SUNDAY. 2D.

Clear and cool. Divine service as usual. Evening to Mr. Brooks'.

After the usual hearing of my children for an hour, having now regularly joined my second child John in the reading of the Scriptures, I attended divine service and heard Dr. Frothingham preach from Joshua 4. 6. "That this may be a sign among you." A communion sermon discussing the peculiar characteristics of that service. I shall soon reach an age now when it will be advisable for me to reflect more seriously upon the propriety of my partaking of it.

Afternoon Dr. Henry Ware Jr. from Luke 10. 40.41.42. the well known verses addressed to Martha and Mary. Upon the attention to worldly matters, a very beautiful discourse much affected in the delivery by the defect of enunciation caused by the loss of his teeth.

Read a Sermon by the Reverend John Balguy Proverbs 12. 15. "The way of a fool is right in his own eyes: but he that hearkeneth unto counsel is wise." Mr. Balguy has had some reputation in the English reviews without much deserving it. Evening, we paid a visit at Mr. Brooks'. Nobody there but C. Brooks. Home shortly after ten.

MONDAY 3D.

Wet and damp clearing off cold. Division as usual. Evening at Mr. B. Gorham's.

My time at the Office is taken up principally in the arrangement of my Diary which continues in Arrears. I have little to place upon it of interest and the mere keeping of so monotonous a record is tiresome. My Greek for one hour is also rather vexatious as I have already read it over and want the stimulus of novelty in the pursuit.

Afternoon examining authorities and attempting to methodize but as yet without success. It is a little curious to notice how many sheets of paper I spoil before I begin.

Went to a small party at Mrs. B. Gorham's. Talk with Miss Jones about coins, and with Dr. Palfrey about my Article. I sounded him today about the severity necessary in the Review. I told him that I feared it would not suit him, but he rather to my surprise professed a preference for that tone. So I shall go on boldly.

TUESDAY 4TH.

Excessive cold. Usual division. Evening at home.

After the time spent in coins, I went to the Office and occupied myself in Diary and accounts.

I propose to give up my Politico-Economical Studies as dry things in which but a very limited number of the Community take an interest and go into more general literature. It is pretty plain to me that the present state of political affairs is such as to forbid me all hope of making any headway in that line. I am too squeamish for the very low standard of morals that is adopted on all sides at present. If circumstances should change, perhaps my principles might be useful.

Œdipus and studying Hazard, and Hallam, and Sharon Turner and The Planter's Plea. Evening at home. Still groping about after a beginning.

WEDNESDAY 5TH.

Very cold morning, but moderated. Division as usual. E. C. Adams.

These two last mornings are severe enough. I went to the Office as usual. An hour of coins and an hour of newspaper reading at the Insurance Office leaves but very little time for the Diary at the Office. Œdipus Coloneus which Schaeffer thinks the finest of all the plays of Sophocles. I balance between the other and Electra as well as this.

Elizabeth C. Adams came to our house today to spend some time. I studied the New York Review and sat down directly after tea so that I had a good long session before me and thus effected my entrance into the subject.

THURSDAY 6TH.

Weather moderating. Time as usual. Mrs. R. D. Tucker's.

Nothing very material to stir up the attention. At the Office where I continue very slowly making up. News not material excepting the symptoms of a struggle in Pennsylvania against the overwhelming effect of their State debt. I received today a proof sheet from Mr. Hunt of my Lecture upon credit. It reads tolerably well. Afternoon after Œdipus, I make it my practice to read authorities and reflect upon the passages I dissect in the evening.

To R. D. Tucker's with my Wife. A small party apparently to the Grattans. I found it rather dull. A supper also. Met there Mrs. J. W. Paige for the first time since she came from Europe. Her extravagance in the midst of her husband's embarrassments makes much talk in private circles. Home early.

FRIDAY 7TH.

Rain. Time as usual. Evening at home.

Office where I received another sheet of proof from Mr. Hunt. I should think the Lecture would make twenty five or six pages of his close text. What with one thing and another I bid fair to keep presses enough going at present. But this only pushes back the great work which I have on hand.[1] I must go on with that and bring it to a creditable conclusion.

Home. Œdipus. Continue examination of authorities and as Elizabeth is with my Wife, I write all the evening. This advances things so much that I think I shall find my work easier than I expected. It will consist a good deal of extracts.

[1] That is, his edition of AA's letters.

SATURDAY. 8TH.

Wet and thawing. Time divided as usual. Evening at home.

My market day which consumes the time I ordinarily devote to Medals. Office where I worked a little upon my Quarterly Account. Nothing however that was effective. I soon left to go home where I read Œdipus Coloneus. It comes easier to me now and I have a much more full conception of the beauty of the piece. Afternoon, reading and continuing my work to which I devoted my whole evening in such a manner as to see land.

SUNDAY 9TH.

Mild but pleasant. Divine service as usual. Evening at home. Edmund Quincy.

I read two chapters in the Old Testament with my two children Louisa and John, and then heard the former go through her other exercises. Attended divine service and heard Dr. Frothingham preach from Psalms 4. 6. "There be many that say Who will show us any good," a very beautiful discourse upon this text which I also heard Mr. Greenwood treat once with much effect. But the rest of the verse makes the answer. Afternoon Luke 14. 24. "For I say unto you that none of those men which were bidden shall taste of my supper." The meaning of this to be a reproof of negligence, inattention to and rejection of the value of the Gospel.

A walk with my children round the Park. Evening, sermon by Mr.

Orr in the English Preacher. Matthew 23. 23. "Wo unto you, Scribes and pharisees, hypocrites, for ye pay tithe &ca." Text too long to quote but the subject the importance of morality above form.

I was at work finishing my review when Edmund Quincy came in who was pleasanter than usual, talking of general literature and indifferent matters. I was glad to get rid of disputed points. He went at eight and we intended to have gone out but it rained. So I finished my Article.[1]

[1] CFA's essay-review, "The Politics of the Puritans," would appear in the April issue of the *North Amer. Rev.*, 50:432–461.

MONDAY 10TH.

Foggy. Division as usual. Evening, Mr. Brooks.

After coins, I went to the Office. Received the last proof sheet of my Lecture in Hunt. I read it over with satisfaction. The close is eloquent, if I may be permitted to judge. But it is not at all possible for any one to make any just estimate of one's self. I never yet read any thing of mine over twice with any thing like the same impression.

Accounts, then Home to read Œdipus. Afternoon, rather indulging after my stretch of the previous week. Read over the Review too to see if I had omitted any thing. Evening, Mr. Brooks called for an hour very pleasantly.

TUESDAY 11TH.

Clear and mild. Distribution as usual. Evening at Edward Brooks'.

After coins I went to the Office. Mr. Warren the antiquary called to offer me some coins which he had lately purchased and I was irresistibly tempted to buy up some of them. I find upon looking over my accounts too much goes into coins. Diary.

Walk round the common. Home where I went on with Œdipus. Afternoon reading Sharon Turner's History of Henry, Edward and Elizabeth. He adopts a rather new method of writing which gives a better general view but his notes though containing a vast deal of information are like all notes serious deductions from the effect of a narrative.

Evening, we went to Edward Brooks' to spend an hour. Nothing materially new. We have not heard from Washington for some time.

WEDNESDAY 12TH.

Mild day. Distribution as usual. Evening at Mrs. Frothingham's.

The regular course of things. I tried to do a little at my accounts but was prevented. But I did Something towards bringing up my Diary. Then home. Finished Œdipus Coloneus which I find Potter agrees in opinion with Schaeffer about. It certainly is a beautiful play and I am very glad that I have been over it again pretty thoroughly. Afternoon, Sharon Turner's Account of the rise of the reformation, and resuming the old MS work which I find rather fatiguing. Evening, a small party at Mrs. Frothingham's. About forty or fifty, some singing by Mrs. Habicht. Nothing new.

THURSDAY 13TH.

Mild. Office. After dinner Proprietors of South Cove. Evening Mr. J. C. Gray's.

After coins, went to the Office. Time devoted to making up Diary which I am at last getting through with. Nothing new. Home after walk. Began Antigone and read with great facility a hundred and forty lines.

Afternoon attended a meeting at the Market Bank of the principal Stockholders of the South Cove Company preparatory to the Annual Meeting to be held tomorrow. Mr. B. R. Nichols who seemed the principal manager reported a plan for the ultimate division of the whole filled up property and satisfaction of all the shares. The details were not digested but I was inclined to favour the scheme if I could be sure that there were not individual interests at work against the general interest. There were a few particulars to which I objected, but the movement seemed to be the other way and I was much in the minority.

Home. Evening to Mrs. J. C. Gray's to a very small party of her family. It was pleasant enough.

FRIDAY 14TH.

Cloudy and east wind. Office. Proprietors of South Cove. Evening at home.

After coins, to the Office. Bringing up Diary bravely. Nothing however that is new. The political world at Washington is dull, the commercial world is dull and we are all dull. Home to read Antigone but got caught in the parlour with company so that I barely finished the most difficult chorus in Sophocles, the song of rejoicing over the discomfiture of the Argian host led on by Polynices.

After dinner, to the United States Hotel to the Proprietors meeting of the South Cove. Mr. Nichols' plan was adopted, nem. con.[1] and the board of Directors elected to match. I was much provoked at the leaving off of Mr. Nathl. Curtis, whose good judgment I would trust more than almost any body's whom I know. At any rate the present plan will give us separate property and the control of all our rights.

Home. Evening, read to my Wife my new Article upon the New York Review with which she seemed satisfied. I am nevertheless writing over a part.

¹ *Nemine contradicente*, without opposition.

SATURDAY 15TH.

Chilly but mild. Office. Division as usual. Evening at home.

After going to Market I went to the Office and at last succeeded in bringing up the long Arrears of Diary occasioned by my week's absence to New York. Deacon Spear came in from Quincy, and I settled my account with him. Mr. Fuller also spent an hour examining Mr. Boylston's Accounts.

Home to read Antigone. After dinner, Sharon Turner, and in the evening reading Walpole to my Wife. Then writing over one sheet of my Article which I shall spread one half in the process. This is very fatiguing.

SUNDAY 16TH.

Pleasant day. Divine Service. Evening at Mr. Brooks'.

After an hour devoted to the instruction of my children I attended divine service and heard Dr. Parkman preach from Ecclesiastes 7. 10. "Say not thou, What is the cause that the former days were better than these? for thou dost not inquire wisely concerning this." Upon the comparative value of ancient and modern habits and morals, and the prevailing tendency to see in the past, merits which are not in the present. The fault of our age is rather in the opposite extreme.

Afternoon 1. Corinthians 9. 22. "I am made all things to all men that I might by all means save some." A very sensible discourse by Dr. Frothingham upon that phrase which taken from Saint Paul's application to himself is now usually made a word of reproach. There is discrimination to be exercised here as every where. The adaptation of one's self to others is to be judged of by the impelling motives which are at the bottom of all conduct.

Read a Sermon by Dr. Foster in the English Preacher 1. Peter 2. 21

"Leaving us an example that ye should follow his steps." The example of Christ as a moral and practical lesson to mankind. Walk with the children.

Evening, we went to Mr. Brooks' and spent an hour very pleasantly. Nobody there but H. G. Gorham. Home where I finished my new sheet and read over the whole being much dissatisfied, feel tempted to write over or throw off.

MONDAY 17TH.

Charming day. Office, division as usual. Evening at Mrs. Everetts.

After my hour in coins, I went to the Office. Occupied in Accounts. Letter from the Salem Lyceum requesting me to deliver my Lecture Wednesday. I wrote back that I never delivered it excepting upon particular request.[1] Home. Read Antigone. Afternoon, Sharon Turner. Reading my Article over very critically.

Evening we went to Mr. Everett's for the purpose of hearing him read his Lecture on the opening of the Lowell Institute.[2] But he had accidentally been unable to recover it from a person who had borrowed it. He read however several letters and part of the Diary of Mr. Lowell. There were several ladies present. Mrs. Henshaw and her daughter, Mrs. Frothingham and Thomas, Miss Welsh and ourselves. Evening pleasant enough and home at ten.

[1] Both letters are missing.
[2] For an account of the event on 31 Dec. 1839, see Ferris Greenslet, *The Lowells and their Seven Worlds*, Boston, 1946, p. 210–211, 233–234.

TUESDAY 18TH.

Lovely day. Division as usual. Evening company at home.

After coins, at the Office. Received another application from Salem for the delivery of the Lecture tomorrow night, to which I consented. So I must even go. My inducement is only to get some money. Finished drafting account for the Quarter.

Home where I read Antigone, which I find I studied pretty thoroughly before. Afternoon, revised my Article for the last time. Too lazy to write any thing better and yet much dissatisfied with this. Never mind. Do better next time.[1] Evening, Sidney Brooks and his Wife to tea and Dr. and Mrs. Frothingham in the evening. Pleasant hour.

[1] The article, with a covering letter, was dispatched (CFA to John Gorham Palfrey, 18 Feb., Adams Papers).

[*Salem*]

WEDNESDAY 19TH.

Cloudy but very mild. Division as usual. Evening to Salem. Lecture.

After coins, I went to the Office and was occupied in accounts as usual. Nothing very material. The Country seems to be staggering under the present disorders of the currency. I see no prospect upon any side which can be considered as the least encouraging. We must brace ourselves down by reducing our expenses, and incurring no extravagance. Home to read Antigone.

After dinner I went down to the Depot of the Eastern Railroad and crossing the Ferry started in one of the cars for Salem. There were in the cars Mr. C. W. Upham and his Wife and Sister, who discovering that I was bound there to deliver my Lecture were civil enough to ask me to tea and in the evening.

The audience was a very large one and very attentive although not disposed to applaud. I thought the effect of it was quite as good as I had known it at any time. Great civilities from Mr. Silsbee, Judge White, Mr. Sprague and others. Pleasant conversation afterwards at Mr. Upham's until ten when I went to the Mansion House to bed.

Boston

THURSDAY 20TH.

Mild, spring day. To Boston. Division as usual. Evening at home. Mr. Brooks.

I arose early and after a rapid breakfast, made the best of my way to town again in the Railroad train which left at half past eight o'clock. The weather was summerlike and the frost appears to be coming out of the ground in all directions. As I was returning, the facility with which we were borne this distance set me thinking upon the effect which all these various roads converging on Boston must have upon the increase of the place. So that notwithstanding the disadvantages attending the present unsettled condition of the currency and the credit system I incline to think this city will get along. This is encouraging to those who like myself are property holders in these parts. Home by ten and then went on with my usual avocations.

Office where a serious application for my house comforted my doubts much. This winter has been about as discouraging one as I know. I have lost half a years rent and all Dividends upon Factory property besides diminished income upon Insurance Stock. This with the increase of cost from the thoughtless expense of last year has made me for the first time in my married life run behind hand in a quarter.

Home to read Antigone. After dinner Sharon Turner. And copying MS. Evening Mr. Brooks at our house.

FRIDAY 21ST.

Clear and mild. Distribution as usual. Evening at Mr. Story's.

Very extraordinary weather for this season of the year. I went out today without any overcoat, a thing unexampled in this climate. After coins, went to the Office. Time wasted there but I succeeded in renting my house. Did not get home in time to read Antigone. No fire in my study and perfectly comfortable.

Afternoon, Sharon Turner and Manuscripts. I am now going to work in earnest to advance that biography. Evening a small party of the family at Mrs. Story's. Not very pleasant but I did very well. Home by a clear moon.

SATURDAY 22D.

Mild weather. Division as usual. Evening at home. H. G. Gorham.

This is my usual day for going to Market and omitting coins. Office as usual where there was nothing new. Finished my Quarterly Account for the year 1839 to send to my father and received a check from Mr. T. B. Johnson which concludes his business. I am glad nowadays to reduce my liabilities as much as possible.

The late failure of C. R. Lowell makes some noise and furnishes another lesson of the danger of unlimited trust of sons in money affairs.[1]

Home to read Antigone. Afternoon, Sharon Turner. Evening, a visit from H. G. Gorham. Nothing new. Read the Elgin and Phigaleian Marbles in The Library of Entertaining Knowledge.[2]

[1] On Charles Russell Lowell and his business failure, see Ferris Greenslet, *The Lowells and their Seven Worlds*, Boston, 1946, p. 239.

[2] Sir Henry Ellis, *Elgin and Phigaleian Marbles* in *Library of Entertaining Knowledge*, vols. 26, 27, London, 1833.

SUNDAY 23D.

Lovely day, but warm. Divine service and duties as usual. Evening to E. Brooks'.

A very uncommon day for this season of the year being very warm, so that I found a surtout oppressive. After my usual lesson with my children I attended divine service and heard Dr. Frothingham from Ezekiel 12. 27 "The vision that he seeth is for many days to come, and he prophesieth of the times that are far off." Another sermon directed against the doctrines of the Millenium which are now pushed by Miller. The Dr. appeared anxious to press his points farther than he did on the preceding occasion and to discriminate between the sorts of prophecy which are to be found in the Bible, those relating to events then approaching and now long since passed, and those referring to a long distant period which are not likely to have any termination that it is in the power of man to define.

Afternoon a certain Mr. Bakewell from England who has come to this country with a view of settling. Sermon from John 19. 30.33. Too long to quote. But it related to miracles and went over the usual arguments upon the subject with clearness and force. His reading in the Scriptures and the Hymns was remarkably good. A rare excellence.

Walk with the children. Read another sermon in the English Preacher upon the example of Christ in continuation of last Sunday, and from the same text. Evening, my Wife and I went to Edward Brooks' and spent the evening. Pleasant enough.

MONDAY 24TH.

Mild. Office. Division as usual. Evening at home.

After coins I went to the Office and finished up the rest of the work I had in arrears so that my further time is at leisure I hope for the remainder of the Quarter. Sent an account and advertised my property.

Home to read Antigone. Afternoon, Sharon Turner and Manuscripts. Evening, the Antiquities in the British Museum. On the whole we were very quiet today, and I was glad to get through so much work. Letter from Washington with favorable accounts.[1]

[1] LCA to ABA, 20 Feb., Adams Papers.

TUESDAY 25TH.

Cloudy and chilly. Division as usual. Evening at Mrs. Armstrong's.

After coins I went to the Office. Nothing there very material, so I determined to go over to East Cambridge and get some deeds which I left six months ago to be recorded. The walk was pleasant enough, and I took the opportunity to look at the Depot of the Lowell Railroad which I never saw before. Found there a Mortgage deed which I had sent over many years ago to be cancelled which has never been executed by my father to this day.

Home in time to read Antigone. Afternoon MS and Sharon Turner. Evening, a large party at Mr. Armstrong's. Many old people and a greater number than I have before seen out this winter. Nothing particularly new. Home late.

WEDNESDAY. 26TH.

Cool and cloudy. Distribution as usual. Evening at Mrs. Crownin-shield's.

After coins I went to the Office where I did not find any thing very material to do. My actual occupation in business lasts about half the quarter. Read today in Hunt's Merchant's Magazine a Lecture by Professor Vethake upon the distinctive provinces of the philosopher and the statesman, containing very good sense.[1]

Intended to have taken a walk but delayed it too long and so returned home and read Antigone. After dinner, MS and Sharon Turner. One Chapter a day which is taking it very easy. My copying does not go on at a much faster rate. On the whole I lead a very lazy life.

Evening I accompanied my Wife to a ball given by Mrs. Crownin-shield to her newly married son Edward. There were present much of fashionable society here, and the entertainment was lavish as usual. I enjoyed myself tolerably well. Home late.

[1] Henry Vethake, "The Distinctive Provinces of the Political Philosopher and the Statesman," *Hunt's Merchants' Mag.*, 2:100–119.

THURSDAY 27TH.

Cloudy and cool. Distribution as usual. Evening to Mrs. Henshaw's.

There is not much deserving of particular notice in the record of my day. The Office hours are a little wasted and the remainder of my time taken up in the ordinary routine. Received a letter from my mother which is tolerably cheerful.[1]

Home where I read Antigone. This play surpasses all the rest of the set in pathos. And the moral seems a high one that the laws of God are to be adhered to in opposition to the threats of man or his prohibition. There is nothing superior to this in modern philosophy or religion. The character of Antigone is a model throughout all the plays.

Afternoon, Sharon Turner and copying manuscripts. Evening, we went to Mrs. Henshaw's to a small party given by her daughter to her young friends. Home late. I am getting tired.

[1] 24 Feb., Adams Papers. The letter is devoted entirely to political developments rather than family matters.

FRIDAY 28TH.

Cloudy with slight rain. Distribution as usual. Evening Mr. Beale. Unwell.

After coins I went to the Office and there almost completed an answer to my mother. I then thought as I felt unwell I would take a walk round the South Cove and look at the condition of the lands. I had some conversation with Mr. Brooks about them who very kindly offered to me the use of any money if I was embarrassed, which I declined but wished to avail myself of his judgment in the location of the lots for my share at the division which is about to take place.

Home where I finished Antigone. Afternoon, the usual occupation. Writing and one chapter of Sharon Turner. Evening at home. Mr. G. W. Beale Jr. called in for a short time. For a day or two past I have felt a very singular pain or rather stiffness in my chest which has gone on increasing until this evening it was rather inconvenient. Went to bed early.

SATURDAY 29TH.

Fine day. Distribution as usual. Evening, T. B. Frothingham.

After my usual market visit I went to the Office and was occupied there as customary in Accounts and conference with Deacon Spear upon sundry matters. Nothing remarkable. To the Athenæum to return a book, home rather late. Began the Trachinians of Sophocles. Nothing new.

My pain which in the morning was acutely distressing continued all day in such a way as to alarm me a little, so unused am I to be sick. Yet I pursued Sharon Turner and copying. Evening, T. B. Frothingham came up and we played whist. Bed early.

Chronology

Chronology

CHARLES FRANCIS ADAMS, 1836–1840

1836

Resides in Boston with wife and three children at 3 Hancock Avenue and maintains an office at 23 Court Street.

June 15 – July 22: Travels to Niagara with wife ABA, via the Hudson River and Erie Canal, then to Montreal and Quebec, and returns via Saratoga and Lebanon Springs.

24, 25: His article "The Slavery Question Truly Stated," completed before his departure, is published in the *Boston Daily Advocate*.

July 11: President Jackson orders the Treasury to issue the Specie Circular, which made gold and silver the "sole acceptable payment for public lands" and led to hoarding and weakened confidence in the state banks.

Aug. 2 – Nov. 1: His annual summer residence at the Old House in Quincy with JQA and LCA continues while construction proceeds on his new house, nearby, for the growing family.

Sept. 1–24: His series in five numbers supporting the election of Van Buren, entitled "To the Unpledged Voters" and signed "One of the People," is published in the *Advocate*.

3: JQA presents to him the "Pine Tree, Deer, and Fish" seal crafted in London in 1816 by JA's order to emblemize JA's contributions to the definitive treaty of peace with Great Britain in 1783 and JQA's success in reasserting the same rights in the Treaty of Ghent in 1814.

Nov. 2: His article supporting the candidacy for Congress of A. H. Everett, entitled "A Word for the Wise" and signed "A Friend to Mr. Everett," is published in the *Norfolk Advertiser*.

14: JQA is reelected to the House of Representatives from the 12th Massachusetts District with scattered opposition.

Dec. 7: Martin Van Buren is elected president.

1837

Jan. 25 – Feb. 8: His series in six numbers, with the title "Mr. Webster and the Currency and signed "A," is published in the *Boston Daily Advocate*.

Feb.: His pamphlet *Reflections Upon the Present State of the Currency*, Boston, 1837, 34 p., a reworking of "Mr. Webster and the Currency" and including additional papers not printed in that series, is published.

Efforts to expel or censure JQA for his persistent effort in the House of Representatives to introduce petitions from women and slaves in defiance of the "gag rules" adopted in May 1836 fail after bitter debate.

March 13: His article on the collectorship of the port of Boston is printed as an editorial in the *Advocate*.

May 10: The New York banks suspend specie payments and are followed by banks at Baltimore, Philadelphia, and Boston.

20: Resumes summer residence at the Old House in Quincy, pending completion of his new house in October.

June 17–20: His article "Calm Thoughts Upon Our Money Affairs," signed "A," is published in the *Quincy Patriot*.

21: In England, Victoria becomes queen.

Aug. 18: Breaks relations with the *Advocate* over the paper's editorial support of the Van Buren Administration's policy on money and banks with which CFA was in profound disagreement.

Sept. 2 – Oct. 7: His series in four numbers, "The Annexation of Texas" signed "One of the People," the first of his many efforts to prevent admission, is published in the *Quincy Patriot*.

Oct. 25, Nov. 1: Delivers two lectures in Quincy on the Northern Discoveries, twice repeated for other audiences on later occasions.

Nov. – Feb.: Prepares biographical notice of LCA, which would appear with her portrait in vol. 4 of Longacre and Herring, *National Portrait Gallery of Distinguished Americans*, Phila., 1839.

Dec. 4: Publishes an article signed "One of the Many" in the *Boston Morning Post* expressing outrage at the murder of abolitionist editor Elijah Lovejoy in Illinois and opposition to the action of Boston officials in denying use of Faneuil Hall for a public meeting of protest.

14: Lt. Thomas Boylston Adams Jr., oldest son of JQA's brother TBA, dies of a fever in Florida while serving in the Second Seminole War.

26: Publishes under his own name a pamphlet, *Further Reflections Upon the State of the Currency in the United States*, Boston, 1837, 41 p., a sequel to his earlier pamphlet but containing no material earlier published.

1838

Jan. 23: Delivers a lecture entitled "Materials for History" upon invitation of the Massachusetts Historical Society at the Masonic Temple, Boston, on the spirit of the American Revolution as seen in the correspondence of AA and JA. During the next two years the lecture would be repeated for eight other audiences. The occasion marks the first time any substantial number of letters from the Adams family archives were communicated to the public.

Feb. 16: Henry Brooks Adams (HA), his fourth child, is born in Boston and later christened in Quincy.

April 17–20: His four "Letters to Nicholas Biddle, President of the Bank of the United States," signed "A Citizen," are published in the *Boston Courier*. They undertake to justify his shift from support to opposition of Biddle's policies, particularly Biddle's stand against the resumption of specie payments.

25 – May 31: Visits Washington, D.C., with ABA and his friend Thomas K. Davis.

May 3: His "Letters to Biddle" are reprinted in the *New York Journal of Commerce*.

11: The *Courier* publishes his letter signed "A Citizen" restating the independence of his views and clarifying further his position, under attack.

14: A disagreement with his friend Davis leads to a complete break in November over whether it is possible to seek political office without thereby sacrificing one's personal principles to the demands of party.

May 21: The Specie Circular is suspended.

June 13 – Nov. 6: Spends his first complete summer at his new house in Quincy.

Aug. 2–8: His article in the *Courier* in four parts, "The Democratic Address" signed "A Conservative," is an unfavorable review of a paper circulated by a committee of Administration supporters in the Congress on currency questions and their bearing upon the slavery issue.

17: Publishes in the *Courier* a rejoinder, signed "A Conservative," to a Washington *Globe* attack on his recent four-part article.

Nov. 13: JQA, though opposed, is reelected to the House of Representatives from the 12th Massachusetts District.

15 – Dec. 1: His unsigned series in seven numbers directed against Van Buren and Calhoun and titled "Political Speculations Upon the Carolina Policy" is published in the *Courier*.

Dec. 14: Replies in the *Courier* to a renewed attack in the Washington *Globe* on "The Democratic Address."

Winter: To counter ABA's prolonged malaise, the Adamses participate more actively than in earlier years in Boston's social season.

1839

Jan. 31: Dispatches to the trustees the 120-page "Catalogue of Brass Coins of the Roman Empire belonging to the Boston Athenæum" he has had in preparation since Feb. 1838.

March 14–23: His series in four numbers, unsigned, with the title "The Prospect for the Currency," taking issue with the secretary of the treasury's report, is published in the *Courier*.

May 9: His daughter, LCA2, is seriously injured when hit by a wagon.

18 – Nov. 6: Renews residence in Quincy.

July: His essay-review of Matthew L. Davis' *Memoirs of Aaron Burr* and of Burr's *Private Journal* is published in the *North American Review*, and "The State of the Currency, by Charles F. Adams" is published in *Hunt's Merchants' Magazine*.

6–18: His unsigned series in four numbers, "The Southern Commercial Conventions," directed at the anti-Union activities rife in the South, is published in the *Courier*.

Aug.: "The Theory of Money and Banks," his review of George Tucker's *The Theory of Money and Banks Investigated*, is published in *Hunt's*. The author's name is attached to this and to subsequent articles in *Hunt's*.

Begins preparing a volume of AA's letters which would be published in 1840, the first fruits of his work on the family papers.

Sept.: His "Banks and the Currency" is published in *Hunt's*.

Oct. 24–29: His article "The Philadelphia Manifesto," signed "A," is published in the *Courier* in three parts.

30: Is offered and declines nomination by the whigs for the Massachusetts legislature.

Nov. 20: Georgeanna Frances, the younger child of his dead brother JA2, dies in Quincy.

Dec.: His "The State of the Currency," an amplified version of "The Philadelphia Manifesto," is published in *Hunt's*.

1840

Jan. 7, 9: His letter, unsigned, criticizing the President's Message, is published in the *Courier*.

20–27: Journeys to New York City to address the Mercantile Library Association in Clinton Hall.

Jan.–Feb.: Two essays, "The Principles of Credit" and "The Politics of the Puritans," are completed. The first would be published in the March issue of *Hunt's*, the second in the April issue of the *North American Review*.

Index

NOTE ON THE INDEX

This Index covers volumes 7 and 8 of the *Diary of Charles Francis Adams* in accordance with Adams Papers practice of providing an index at the end of each published unit.

Every index is designed in some measure to supplement the annotation. The compilers have tried to furnish the correct spellings of proper names, to supply forenames for persons who appear in the text only with surnames, to indicate places of residence and occupations of persons whose forenames are either unknown or not known with certainty, and finally to distinguish by dates persons with identical or nearly identical names. Markedly variant spellings of proper names have been cross-referenced to what are believed to be their most nearly standard forms, and the variant forms found in the MSS are parenthetically recorded following the standard spellings. Undoubtedly the Index contains mistakes and incomplete identifications; the editors would warmly welcome corrections of mistakes of this kind, and indeed of every kind, from users who can put them straight.

Wives' names, with a few exceptions for special reasons, follow their husbands' names. *See*-references under maiden names are used for members of the Adams and collateral families and for women mentioned in the text who married subsequently but before 29 Feb. 1840.

Under major place names (e.g. Boston, Washington) there are appended separate gatherings of "Buildings, landmarks, streets, &c.," the items in which are arranged alphabetically rather than in order of their appearance (as other subentries are throughout the Index).

The Index was compiled in the Adams Papers editorial office.

Index

ADAMS, CHARLES FRANCIS (*cont.*) 253, 360, 361; 8:15, 27, 353–54, 367, 376–77; taxes, 7:334; 8:148; on account balancing, 7:382; 8:261; children's financial future, 8:143, 150, 220; on managing affairs of others, 8:166

OPINIONS AND COMMENTS

General: effects of improved transportation, 7:xxi, 33; 8:89, 282, 376; travel, 7:9, 51, 55; 8:30, 55; modes of transportation, 7:17, 19, 51; acute Yankees, 7:20; 8:154; Niagara Falls, 7:30; Independence Day celebrations, 7:32; 8:258–59; Canadian temperament, 7:33; French and English Canadians, 7:36, 46; uniform of Highlander Corps, 7:40; using dogs for draft, 7:43; U.S. and Canada contrasted, 7:44; effect of commercial interests on a town, 7:45; quarrels about money, 7:58; changing attitude of Bostonians toward JQA, 7:101; attending large lectures, 7:102; untimely deaths, 7:135; Washington's birthday observances, 7:189; fast-day observances, 7:218; 8:18, 209; agitation in the population, 7:259; North Shore towns, 7:271; compares JA and JQA, 7:272; animal magnetism, 7:302; equality of laborers and thinkers, 7:320; arboriculture, 7:328; 8:240; "what is knowledge among us but to be the least ignorant," 7:360; walking around Boston Common, 7:379; precise knowledge in newspapers, 7:396; dueling, 7:406; reason as a guide to life, 8:42; effects upon men when ability is added to ambition, 8:49; value of organizing Mass. state records, 8:85; grandeur of universe, 8:112; contrast between boyhood and manhood, 8:160; American self-complacency, 8:207–208; indifference to human life in America, 8:216; New York and New Yorkers, 8:227; "Invention is the attribute of the young but perfecting comes by age," 8:255; Quincy compared to Cohasset, 8:255; Harvard College dinners, 8:263; New England enterprise, 8:304; human mortality, 8:330; Christmas observance, 8:347; burning of the *Lexington*, 8:365

Arts: women's stage roles, 7:201; love of music, 7:230; theater, 7:310; "comédie Larmoyante," 7:352; Handel's *Messiah*, 7:371; art works, 7:403; study of art over politics, 8:94; art vs. nature,

8:149; Italians as musical people, 8:156; Greek drama, 8:161, 185; conviviality in music, 8:222

Economy: differences between Canada and U.S., 7:34–35; low stock values, 7:74; local conditions, 7:78, 252, 268; 8:262; bank failures, 7:209, 388; 8:4; economic crisis, 7:232, 239–40, 241, 242; currency and banking, 7:256–57, 348, 351, 380, 381, 383; 8:24, 49; stock speculators, 7:328, 352; a national bank, 7:345, 376; 8:12; associated banks, 7:379, 380, 382; current financial situations, 7:386–87; 8:21; bank fraud, 7:399; production and consumption cycles, 7:405; science of political economy, 8:5, 64; sub-Treasury bill, 8:8, 11, 14, 15, 70; payments of specie, 8:21–22, 25; his own theories, 8:62; cotton price control, 8:151; insurance investments, 8:172; joint stock company investments, 8:187; Biddle's resignation, 8:211; European financial crisis, 8:244–45, 298, 307; Southern loss of trade, 8:259; predicts another money crisis, 8:272; 1839 fiscal crisis, 8:307, 310, 312; auctions indicate financial distress, 8:350

Education: Harvard bicentennial, 7:89; "fashion of Apathy which distinguishes every thing at [Harvard]," 7:277; his Harvard studies, 7:291, 391, 398, 399, 400; 8:115, 158; Harvard commencement, 7:305; studying classics, 8:183; learning from past generations, 8:195–96; difficulties in the pursuit of knowledge, 8:212; study of oratory, 8:306; the German mind, 8:306, 309; pleasure of miscellaneous reading, 8:357

History: "Canadian frontier furnishes no great occasion for national pride on our part," 7:31; Punic War, 7:76; character of Romans, 7:81, 82; study of ancient history, 7:182; Amer. Indian civilization, 8:39; power of Parliament over Amer. colonies, 8:98

Literature: his own writings, 7:xvii, 176, 178, 256, 308, 371; 8:36, 80, 90, 111, 117, 127, 191, 205, 215, 242, 258, 263, 287, 321; British periodicals, 7:150; 8:179–80, 337; "My time is better employed digging the earth" than writing, 7:314; his lecturing, 7:319; 8:2, 363, 366; French literature, 7:369, 376; distaste for contemporary literature, 7:388; Southern and Northern oratory,

ADAMS, JOHN QUINCY (*cont.*)
Fund, 7:78–79; 8:289; and Dutee J. Pearce, 7:176; and P. P. F. Degrand, 7:255, 303; attends ordination, 7:265; calls on Van Buren, 8:33; visits art exhibits, 8:39, 144; attends christening, 8:119; attends theater, 8:138; receives visitors, 8:153, 280, 308; and H. G. Otis, 8:174; hears W. E. Channing, 8:234; attends demonstration of a new illuminating oil, 8:300–301

Personal: salt-water bathing, 7:79, 93, 281; 8:85, 86, 283; health problems, 7:88, 100, 119; 8:225; and Harvard, 7:89; 8:101; inspects quarry and nursery, 7:93; books and papers kept in disorder, 7:103, 305, 318; weakness for buying Adams family land, 7:104; trees and gardening, 7:120, 315; 8:124, 134, 310; gift of house lot to First Church minister, 7:167, 177–78; busts of, 7:249; 8:144; visits wine merchant, 7:258; exhausted, 7:269; 8:71; goes fishing, 7:269, 289–90; 8:86, 273, 286; birthdays, 7:277; 8:77, 262; 40th wedding anniversary, 7:285, 286; goes to Boston, 7:286; chests moved to "the Office," 7:288; portraits of, 8:vii, xi, 123, 142; comments on art works, 8:x, 39; uscs telescope, 8:85–86, 95; dislike of adulation, 8:105; public estimation of, 8:195; Sunday service, 8:281, 295; "busy," 8:325

Residences and Travel: journeys to Washington, 7:127, 128, 304, 305; 8:146, 149, 334, 337; returns to Quincy, 7:236, 243; 8:79, 80, 228; birthplace, 8:123; stays with CFA in Boston, 8:137–46, 233; in N.Y. City, 8:225–28
See also Old House

LANDS, INVESTMENTS, ACCOUNTS

Boston rental properties: 7:236, 237; 8:378
Columbian Mills (D.C.): 8:37, 38
Quincy properties: salt marsh, 7:76; quarries, 7:78; extent of, 7:92, 96; woodlot, 7:104, 110; 8:310; farmland, 7:121; property taxes, 7:370; new road through, 8:89; Mt. Wollaston, 8:144
Weston Farm: 8:202, 208
Fiscal situation: 7:199–200, 205, 206, 219, 220, 235, 237; 8:219
Securities owned: 7:65, 72, 217

Trustee of estates: JA, 7:63, 65, 73, 243; W. N. Boylston, 7:80, 167; 8:249
Accounts: 7:119, 127, 228, 278, 377, 379, 382; 8:10, 12, 122, 126, 127, 195, 196, 246, 257, 259, 323, 377; debt to A. Giusta, 8:252
See also CFA—Agent &c. for JQA

OPINIONS AND INTELLECTUAL INTERESTS

Books: plan to build library, 7:4; 8:viii; as resource to CFA, 7:240, 247, 261, 262, 303, 321; 8:66, 67, 89, 131, 175, 215; presentation copy from S. Grimké, 8:121
CFA's estimate: compares to JA, 7:xxiii, 272; speeches, writings, and lectures, 7:xxiii, 101, 272–73, 292; 8:103, 226, 314, 326; tariff policy, 7:18–19; changes in political views, 7:80; battle against Gag Rule, 7:180; Tocqueville's evaluation of presidency, 7:250; member of diplomatic mission, 8:201; contribution to CFA's "Southern Conventions" articles, 8:258
Exposition and Exchange of views with CFA: impending election (1836), 7:106; CFA's writing in support of A. H. Everett, 7:109; Pennsylvania election returns, 7:114; CFA's political views and prospects, 7:148, 160, 161; proposed newspaper, 7:210; politics and finances, 7:214, 254, 266, 282, 293; 8:38, 64; *Reflections Upon the Currency*, 7:233; fiscal crisis, 7:243, 245; "rather warm" on the currency, 7:295; provides pamphlets on Texas annexation and abstract of bank returns, 7:317; 8:16; *Further Reflections*, 7:368, 389–90; slavery, 7:390; Mass. legislative course on banks, 8:4; duel between House members, 8:7, 8, 13, 14; Biddle and the Bank, 8:32; CFA's "Letters to Biddle," 8:36; Calhoun and Clay, 8:50; guesses CFA's authorship of "The Democratic Address," 8:88; influence of college education, 8:107; CFA's "Speculations Upon the Carolina Policy," 8:117, 132; character of Lafayette, 8:133; CFA's lecture on AA, 8:140; CFA's "Southern Commercial Conventions," 8:256; CFA's rejection of Mass. House nomination, 8:318, 319
Public Men and Issues: equates anti-Bankism with support of slavery, 7:389–90; opposed by J. T. Bucking-

433

443

❧ The *Diary of Charles Francis Adams* was composed by Progressive Typographers. Rudolph Ruzicka's *Fairfield Medium*, with several variant characters designed expressly for *The Adams Papers*, is used throughout. The text is set in the eleven-point size, and the lines are spaced one and one-half points. The printing and binding are by the Halliday Lithograph Corporation. The paper, made by the Mohawk Paper Company, is a grade named *Superfine*. The books were originally designed by P. J. Conkwright and Burton L. Stratton.